# PERSONALITY CHANGE AND DEVELOPMENT

## as Measured by the

## Projective Techniques

# PERSONALITY CHANGE AND DEVELOPMENT

## as Measured by the

## Projective Techniques

### By MOLLY HARROWER, Ph.D.

*Clinical Psychologist, New York City; Chairman, State Advisory Council in Psychology, New York State; Associate Research Professor of Clinical Psychology, Department of Psychiatry, Temple University Medical Center, Philadelphia*

GRUNE & STRATTON    New York and London    1958

*To Mortimer Lahm*
*with love and gratitude*

## Acknowledgment

The material presented in this book has necessitated the collaboration of many colleagues in the field of psychotherapy, and under usual circumstances, the names of these colleagues would be incorporated in the text or listed individually in this Acknowledgment. However, in order to take every insurance to safeguard the anonymity of the patients whose records appear herein, the therapists in this instance have requested that their names not appear in connection with the cases they have treated, nor even in a Foreword. This statement must therefore serve to convey my thanks to all who have cooperated so helpfully in this study. My thanks can go specifically, however, to my psychological assistant, Mathilda Steiner, for her helpful checking of the scoring and tabulations, and to my secretary, Esther Perlin, for her thoughtful typing of the manuscript.

# Contents

# Introduction: The scope of the study and the questions raised by the availability of retest data.

The essential conditions for the writing of this book have been the passage of time and the accumulation, over a fifteen-year period, of the test responses of some four thousand individuals to a standard battery of projective techniques.

This number of test records alone, without the dimension of time, cannot be considered a rarity at this stage in the development of clinical psychology. It is safe to estimate that several thousand psychologists are busily accumulating ever-growing files of interesting cases. In fact, the areas in which the psychologist can break new ground with personality evaluations of previously undescribed conditions are rare.

But the inexorable passage of time now sets the stage for the accumulation of material of a different sort. Any test record taken from the files, when used as a base line for comparison with subsequent performances, assumes a different significance. We pass to the stage of acquiring longitudinal studies where we were previously confined to the cross-sectional approach.

Throughout the course of the fifteen years during which these records were accumulated, some fifty or sixty individuals were, for one reason or another, referred specifically for retesting by a physician, therapist, school authorities or parents. The comparisons afforded by these cases formed an important nucleus for our study. To add to these cases, the systematic recall of individuals selected according to various criteria, who were willing to be retested and concerning whom information from various outside sources was obtainable, was undertaken.

We have been interested, in these studies, in several general questions. First, to what extent does projective material actually mirror reported change in behavioral adjustment and change in subjective experience? Specifically, if in the case of Patient A, after several years of therapy, therapist, colleagues and relatives all concur in reporting evidence of better adjustment, and if the patient himself reports greater satisfaction in living, will comparison of the two sets of test data show a comparable increase in the more constructive aspects of personality? Further, if positive changes are found, do they result from a dropping out of pathologic responses in the second test record, from an increase in positive indices of adjustment, or from a combination of both? Conversely, if Patient B, after a comparable period of therapy, finds no lessening in distressing symptoms, no increase in psychological satisfaction, and if his therapist reports his clinical condition as unchanged, do the test findings remain unchanged also, or may they even show deterioration?

A second general area of interest relates to the question of how an individual changes during periods of normal growth and the passage of five, ten and fifteen years. Is there such a thing, we ask, as a "core personality" which remains relatively unchanged? What in the test picture drops out and what is added? All of us as psychologists have many cross-sectional photographs, so to speak, shot by our projective cameras of John Does at specific moments in their lives. We have many composite pictures of age groups showing certain psychological—or test—characteristics as occurring more frequently at one stage than another. But we have very few, if any, longitudinal studies of specific Jane and John Does over the years. It is these patterns of growth with which this study is concerned.

A third question, and one having a direct bearing on the first, concerns the similarities or differences in changes brought about through growth, maturation and life circumstances, on the one hand, and the various forms of successful psychotherapy on the other. Are there different types of change introduced by psychotherapeutic techniques, changes not found as a consequence of other experience?

It is clear that much depends on what we consider *"change"* in test findings, in behavioral adjustment, and in life situations. Not all differences in the raw material of the test findings can be considered to reflect change in the individual in the real sense of the word. We must, therefore, carefully distinguish between fluctuations which may occur from day to day if the tests are repeated and those more basic changes which reflect different ways of perceiving the world and reacting to it.

Similarly, the task of deciding what shall constitute *"change"* as reported by the therapist, parents, relatives or the patient himself is not easy. As we shall discuss later, there are many who believe that the lack of any objective criteria for what constitutes genuine change in behavior must result in the inevitable failure of a study of this kind at the present time. However, we feel that a defeatist attitude of this sort is not warranted and that, while we do lack genuine quantitative measurements in this area, we are shutting our eyes to facts if we refuse to admit that individuals *do* achieve new levels of adjustment, *do* find new satisfactions in work and interpersonal relationships, and *do* pass out of psychological doldrums into times of relatively clear sailing.

When these changes in direction are well documented and have continued for several years we feel that they constitute sufficiently reliable material to make this kind of parallel study worthwhile. As Kubie[18] has so aptly stated: "It is an old and basically sound principle of scientific methodology that no two methods will have precisely the same errors, and that consequently any observation which is made independently by two different methods has a higher degree of accuracy than is the same observation made repeatedly by the same method. Furthermore, the more uncontrollable variables enter into the observation or into the experimental situation, the more diverse methods are required to assure the validity of the observation. These obvious principles make it important to develop diverse methods of psychological observation to bring to bear on the same subject. This is the basic methodological reason why the use of multiple projective tests paralleling psychoanalytic observations are essential for objective evaluation of the observations of both."

The individuals who have been retested in this study may be grouped and contrasted in several ways. There are, first of all, the records of nearly one hundred subjects who were retested within one week's time. We have hoped to glean from a study of this material something about the fluctuations which occur as a result of mere repetition and which cannot be in any way ascribed to change in life situations or changes brought about through therapeutic agents.

Another major category is the distinction to be made between those retested individuals who have sought professional psychotherapeutic help for their difficulties and those individuals who have not received any form of psychotherapy in the interval between tests.

Within the group of persons who have undergone therapeutic treatment we have considered long-term and short-term therapy and individuals who have been followed up for a period of ten years subsequent to relatively short-term therapy. We have material on subjects who have undergone orthodox analysis, and on subjects who have been treated by psychotherapy. We have patients who were considered by their therapists to have been successfully treated and patients who were considered unimproved, in both instances following either short-term or long-term treatment. In addition, we have illustrative cases of special conditions over long periods of time, for example, manic productivity followed by a profound depression, followed by several years of stabilized activity.

Turning to the group of individuals for whom time alone or time and environmental manipulation have been the positive factors, we have cases in which alteration of environmental influences has brought about marked behavioral and test changes. We have illustrations of acutely distressful situations (such as living in a concentration camp) followed by years of flowering in a friendly environment. We have cases of sudden cessation of a peculiarly devastating stress situation with a consequent alteration of the individual's outlook and actual mode of living. We have examples of growth under "average" conditions.

Our aim in presenting this material has been in all cases to provide the raw data where possible so that the reader may make his own judgments and decisions. We have attempted a rough quantitative measure of change, which will be discussed in detail, and have developed Summary Charts to enable a comparison between the therapist's and the test findings to be made at a glance. Throughout we have remained essentially at the documentary level, feeling that until we have sufficient evidence of what actually occurs, extensive theorizing is out of place.

## I. The need for follow-up studies. Collaborating colleagues. Selection of subjects. Presentation of material. Pitfalls inherent in the retesting situation. The test battery.

It is not possible to engage in extensive psychodiagnostic work without repeatedly asking oneself such questions as: How accurate are these descriptions of personality dynamics? What use is being made of them in the planning of treatment? What opportunity will there be for follow-up studies so that tentative hypotheses derived from the tests may subsequently be checked?

It is true that for a small number of cases seen for psychodiagnostic evaluation, information as to the patient's progress does find its way back to the psychologist. This may occur in an informal setting, prompted by a chance meeting between the therapist and the psychodiagnostician, or on rare occasions, the therapist may write a memo confirming some insight from the psychological report or pointing to an apparent discrepancy which has come to light. But by and large, struggle as he may to get a better awareness of the value of his test instruments and of how the information derived from them is being used, the psychologist loses track of the majority of individuals he has tested and must let any research desires lapse in the face of the more pressing service demands that are constantly made on him.

There comes a point, however, when merely being part of a health team and contributing a reasonably valuable item to the sum total of information being gathered on a given patient becomes unsatisfactory, when some over-all, long-range appraisal as to the value of the test instruments themselves, and the capacity of any psychodiagnostician to provide relevant and reliable information and material, become essential questions to be answered.

In this volume and a subsequent one, an attempt is being made to utilize the formidable mass of raw test material available after fifteen years of testing with an extensive battery. The present study deals essentially with a comparison of the difference between first and second test performances, this difference, or lack of it, being compared with other available assessments of the patient. In nonclinical cases, the frame of reference has been the statements of parents, relatives and friends, employers, school authorities, and factual material obtainable from job records and the like. In clinical cases, the therapist's evaluation of the patient's condition at the start and at the termination of therapy has been used. No attempt has been made in this volume to differentiate between, or evaluate the effectiveness of, different kinds of psychotherapy for patients presenting different psychodiagnostic test patterns. In the companion volume to this study, however, with the further active collaboration of some thirty therapists, a more extensive follow-up of several hundred patients will be presented. The material in this second volume, to be published at a later date, will contrast the final clinical assessment of the patient with the raw material from the tests obtained during the pre-treatment psychodiagnostic interview; in other words, the outcome of treatment as estimated by the therapist will be compared with the psychodiagnostic *prediction* prior to initiation of therapy. The larger number of cases to be included in the subsequent volume may permit some assessment of the relative effectiveness of different therapeutic approaches as they relate to levels of disturbance reflected in the initial psychological test. In the present study, on the other hand, the findings document growth and development occurring in the absence of therapeutic intervention, following long-term analysis, long-term psychotherapy, and briefer periods of psychotherapeutic treatment.

We have available much more test and retest data, many more tested and retested subjects, than are included in this volume, but we have deliberately chosen to present a relatively small sample in detail rather than generalize concerning group characteristics of growth and development. In the selection of subjects, two conditions adhered to tended to disqualify some interesting cases which might otherwise have been included. The choice of patients for retesting, where clinical cases were concerned, was contingent on the therapist's ability and willingness to make a detailed, comparative evaluation between the psychological status at the start and termination of therapy as well as an over-all assessment. Moreover, we required that the therapist have available to him follow-up material over a period of several years subsequent to the termination of therapy, thus ruling out cases in which the therapist had not remained in touch with the patient.

For example, fifty patients were retested for one therapist over a three-year period. From these, sixteen have been chosen for full presentation (in Chapters XII and XIII). In each case, more than four years have elapsed since the time the second clinical evaluation was made. These sixteen patients also represent the most clear-cut instances of clinical success and clinical failure on this particular therapist's graded scale of 0 to 4, and since we were concerned with the extent to which there was a parallelism between the psychological and clinical findings, we sought out those cases which were as clear-cut clinically as possible to determine whether the test instruments made an equally sharp distinction.

A different method of selection was adopted for the cases which appear in Chapters X and XI. Here the choice of subject for retesting lay with the therapist, who picked his case from a list of his patients who had received a psychodiagnostic examination some time during the preceding ten years. At the time of this referral, the therapist *gave no indication as to whether or not he had selected a patient who represented clinical improvement or lack of it*. The retesting was done on a completely blind basis. The retest evaluation was made completely independently; improvement, change, or lack of it was reported from the test findings alone. The results were referred back to the therapist, who had, in the meantime, recorded his detailed findings on the Evaluation Sheet (see Chapter III) but did not submit this until after the psychological test evaluation had been received.

The individuals selected for retesting can be divided into three groups: first, those chosen for retesting because it was assumed that relatively little had occurred, either environmentally or psychologically, during the intervening period, namely, those retested within a few days (Chapter IV) and after thirty days (Chapter V); secondly, individuals selected for retesting because certain dramatic events were known to have occurred externally and consequently, in all probability, psychologically during the time interval between testings (Chapters VIII and IX); third, individuals whose therapists considered them as representing either *increased adjustment* or *lack of behavioral and symptomatic improvement* following psychotherapy in one of its various forms.

Since reading about change is much less satisfactory than is the opportunity to compare test findings, the Work Sheets given for each case reproduce the Bellevue-Wechsler scattergram, the Szondi profile, an example of graphic material, and the Rorschach scoring. Rorschach records in their entirety being often quite cumbersome, in many instances only characteristic responses, or a set of responses to a single card, have been given. Where the record as a whole has been reproduced, as in Chapter IV, it is because the scoring alone would not have carried the full impact of the point being made.

Although the presenting of raw material is, scientifically, the method of choice, it carries with it certain difficulties. Frequently, the psychologist is on the horns of a painful dilemma: that which can best illustrate his point—an original response or graphic material, for example—may, because of its very poignancy, identify the patient, if not to others at least to himself. Although it may be assumed that the chance of an individual coming across himself in a scientific publication is slight, nonetheless it cannot be disregarded. If, however, one is too careful in this direction and speaks only in generalities, including reports rather than the test data or reproducing structural aspects of test findings which are unrecognizable, there is the great risk of becoming unconvincing to the reader.

Having struggled with this problem for many years, we have attempted a compromise of the following kind. We have omitted from all Therapist's Summary Sheets (see page 34) and from the majority of clinical reports any mention of a specific diagnosis. Not only might the impact of such diagnostic material be distressing to the patient but therapists and psychologists alike are aware that isolated and unamplified psychiatric labels are often unsatisfactory and arbitrary. Further, at the request of the therapists who have collaborated so wholeheartedly in this study, their names have nowhere been given so that the possibility of their patients being identified through them is excluded. Finally, in approaching each patient concerning retesting the decision was left to the therapist as to whether the research-oriented reason for the retesting would be indicated to the patient.

It should also be understood, in regard to the presentation of this material, that we have deliberately refrained from comment on certain specific difficulties, conflicts, anxieties or preoccupations *which may be still inherent in the "improved" record.* This is documentary material and not a teaching text; thus, no attempt has been made to demonstrate to the student in the field what could be deduced from this raw material were a full psychodiagnostic appraisal required. As far as the cases presented here are concerned, the writer, in the role of psychodiagnostician, has given a detailed report to the referring therapist.

The majority of persons examined and re-examined were given a standard battery of seven projective tests. The earliest cases, those examined some fifteen years ago, were tested only with the Rorschach. Thus, in a few special instances, comparison has been made between the original Rorschach record of the first testing, and the full battery given at the time of retesting.

This battery has included the verbal Bellevue-Wechsler (with attention given to its projective possibilities), the Rorschach, the Szondi, the Figure Drawings, the Holsopple-Miale Sentence Completion Test, the Most Unpleasant Concept Test, and, in the majority of instances, a short form of, or one or two pictures from, the Thematic Apperception Test. Where specially pertinent, but by no means universally, tests of concept formation, such as the Vigotsky, were employed. Additional graphic procedures were introduced on some occasions.

There are probably no two examiners whose manner of working is exactly alike, and it is equally likely that no one examiner at all times approximates the hypothetical paragon of a completely objective administrator of his tests. Nevertheless, we have the feeling that there has been at least internal consistency in the manner of administration of the tests over the ten years or so involved in this study. The only consistent variation from standard procedure which we know of has been the fact that at no time has the testing of the limits in the Rorschach been employed. This was deliberately abandoned in 1940 by this investigator when retesting patients at the Montreal Neurological Institute. Retesting at that time was being done in an attempt to trace restoration of function with its personality concomitants following brain surgery, and it was soon indicated that the testing of the limits was not a desirable procedure under these circumstances since repeat tests too often were confused by the introduction of responses suggested at a previous interview. Although the retesting program described in this volume was not envisaged ten years ago, it has transpired that this omission of the testing of the limits in the Rorschach has actually added to the validity of the retest findings now under consideration. The material would have been subject to the very legitimate criticism that "improvement" on a second record might have incorporated material suggested previously. We feel we have avoided this possible source of contamination, and that what is new in a second record is genuinely so.

## II. Current thinking and research on the problems inherent in retesting.

There is little in the literature at the present time which bears directly on the problem of retesting with a battery of projective techniques. There are writings in several areas, however, which are relevant to the present study. As has been pointed out by other investigators, it is necessary to be aware of some of the pitfalls inherent in such a study as has been attempted here; particularly is it necessary to guard against over-simplification. It may also be of interest, in reference to this study, to consider those reports which deal with repetition of a single test, namely, the Rorschach, following psychoanalytic treatment, psychotherapy and client-centered therapy, as well as those studies which describe changes in the raw material of the tests under experimentally induced conditions. And finally, as background to an understanding of the changes which occur in the retest record, those authors who have furthered understanding of the ideas of psychological growth, ego strength and self-actualization can profitably be referred to. It is not intended to deal exhaustively even with this limited literature, however, but rather mainly to alert readers to the many complexities that exist.

The dangers of over-simplification are thoughtfully handled in a recent article by Schafer[26] in which a question is raised which must be uppermost in the mind of any psychologist who attempts such an experimental study as reported here, namely, to what extent do there now exist concrete criteria by which the depth of personality change may be judged? Schafer feels that the psychoanalytic literature is characterized by relative neglect of this problem, and he is also critical of the criteria that have been used by psychologists in attempts to assess change:

> "Some of the research designs and presentations of data seem to assume naively that all change for the better should proceed in the same direction and should culminate in the same general personality pattern. Many of these studies tend to take for granted the effectiveness of psychotherapy; they do not endeavor to draw distinctions between apparent improvement based on transference and genuine, self-sustaining improvement; they do not attempt to distinguish between insight that is highly intellectualized and insight that has a definite and enduring effect on emotional experience and patterns of interpersonal relationship; they do not explicitly recognize that there are various pathological starting points in the therapeutic situation and that the direction of change may differ considerably from one case to the next, moving, for example, from pathological impulsiveness to some capacity for control in one case and from pathological over-control to some tolerance for impulsiveness in the next."

Having uttered such dire warnings, Schafer neverthless points out four major advantages of psychological test data in the problem of evaluating changes that occur during psychotherapy. He speaks first of the indirect approach which "tends to facilitate the clear emergence of both the self-expressive and the defensive aspects of the patient's functioning." Secondly, he comments on the standardized nature of the tests as contrasted with the therapeutic interview. Thirdly, he feels that the fact that a battery of tests can be employed is important since each test can pose different problems for the patient: "A broad even though spotty survey may thus be made of total ego-functioning in a series of standardized, relatively indirect, unstructured, and impersonal reality situations." The fourth aspect of the test data which Schafer feels is important is that the tests lend themselves to several types of analysis, allowing four avenues of interpretative approach to the tester, namely: the formal scores and their patterns, the content of the responses, the type and degree of organization of thought, perception, and verbalization, and the patient's behavior in the examination situation. Ideally, Schafer feels, "implications drawn from all four sources of information should *converge* in the test analysis or else should complement each other in the sense of bringing out basic conflicts or antitheses in the personality." This formulation of Schafer's has been of great value in assessing the material presented here, and any over-all evaluation has always included consideration of these points.

The material that perhaps comes closest to our own investigation is that of Mintz, Schmeidler and Bristol.[22] In this study, two of the writers served as judges comparing the Rorschach records of twenty individuals treated by the same therapist over a six-year period during the course of clinical practice. The first set of Rorschach records, taken by the therapist herself, was obtained without thought of subsequent comparison with a retest record. The time between the first and second Rorschach testing ranged from four to forty-two months.

The results and conclusions of these authors may be briefly stated as follows: In 17 of the 20 cases, the judges were accurate in distinguishing the records obtained later in treatment from those obtained at the start, from which they conclude: "Personality changes take place during psychoanalysis, and can be recognized through Rorschach records at a frequency far beyond chance expectation (P = .003)." They also state:

"Personality changes during psychoanalysis, insofar as they are reflected in the Rorschach, do not appear to follow a steady and consistent progress toward certain goals sometimes considered as included in a 'good' adjustment, such as emotional control, lack of more than a mild degree of conscious anxiety, consideration of others, and ability to adjust reasonably well to social expectations. In some cases, Rorschachs taken later in treatment do appear to represent movement toward these goals. In other cases, Rorschachs taken later in treatment suggest that the psychoanalytic process is resulting in the breakthrough to consciousness of hitherto unacceptable impulses, with a consequent increase of conscious anxiety and perhaps an increase of discomfort along with greater emotional aliveness."

Another interesting finding was that the five patients who appeared to respond especially well to treatment were not less disturbed than other cases, according to the Rorschach records. From this the authors conclude that despite an accepted belief to the contrary, prognosis is not necessarily more favorable in cases in which pathology is less severe.

Apart from the fact that we can find in our studies much to support what has been said here, certain differences in method between the two studies should be noted. In the first place, the majority of patients studied by Mintz, Schmeidler and Bristol were still under treatment at the time of retesting; our patients were not in treatment when the second test was taken. Another difference lies in the fact that our assessment involved a seven-test battery as opposed to the assessment being made in terms of the Rorschach record alone. While this variety sometimes adds greater complexity and confusion to the findings, it is nonetheless true that the different tests pick up and record different facets of the personality and allow for a more complete picture to be given. In some instances, the very discrepancies found between the tests give further insight into an individual's progress or lack of it. Fromm and Elonen,[7] in their article on the progress of a female homosexual patient, also point out how different degrees of ego strength may be portrayed in the Rorschach, the Szondi, and the TAT.

A third important difference between the present investigation and that of Mintz, Schmeidler and Bristol is that it has been possible for us to carry out follow-up procedures after the termination of treatment. Information on some of our patients is available for as long as five, and even ten, years after the termination of treatment and the second testing. It may be stated here parenthetically that, despite these differences between the two investigations, our experience with patients retested during psychotherapy* allows us to concur heartily with the findings of these authors, namely, that records taken during therapy may at times show a more disturbed picture than those taken prior to treatment.

Piotrowski and Schreiber[24] were among the first to recognize the importance of the projective techniques as a tool for assessing change, or lack of it, following treatment. In their retest study of a group of patients who had received psychoanalysis and a group who had received

---

* These findings not included in the present volume.

psychotherapy, these authors felt that by retesting with the Rorschach an objectivity was given to the comparison of the progress of these two groups which would not have been obtainable without this projective yardstick. They state:

> "Since symptom improvement, or symptom change (whether noted and reported by the patient, by relatives, by the family physician, or by the therapist himself) is, perforce, heavily weighted with subjectivity, and since symptomatic changes have, in the past, constituted the major common criterion for evaluating psychotherapeutic results, a more objective and more accurately verifiable criterion was sought. It was felt that the comparative, or serial, Rorschach method might furnish the sought-after means for validating clinical impressions of basic and deep characterological changes resulting from psychotherapy."

We cannot feel that in our studies the therapists' estimates of improvement were subjectively colored, as these authors feared. Nor do we feel that the Rorschach criteria selected by Piotrowski and Schreiber are in all cases sufficient to differentiate marked improvement in certain cases as opposed to little improvement in others. Particularly in connection with the changes in human movement responses, to which Piotrowski attaches considerable importance, our control studies force us to recognize that Rorschachs given on a day-to-day basis may result in surprisingly different human movement responses which can in no way be attributed to deep characterological change. An example is given later.

Our findings also do not confirm those of these authors with respect to an essential difference between patients considered successfully treated analytically and those responding to briefer or less orthodox forms of treatment. They indicate, instead, that there are individuals who fail to respond and those who respond singularly well to either form of treatment. A detailed study of which personality types may be more likely to improve with one type of therapy than another awaits empirical evidence from material which will be presented in a subsequent volume.

Several investigators have used an objective or "sign" approach to the Rorschach test in order to estimate personality changes following psychotherapy. Among the first to do this was Muench,[23] who combined signs from the Rorschach, Kent Rosanoff Word Association Test and Bell Adjustment Inventory, using these with patients treated by client-centered therapy who were reported to have improved clinically. While Muench was of the opinion that valid results could be obtained with this approach, namely, that improvement could register through objective signs, others who have repeated his work (Carr;[5] Hamlin, Berger and Cummings[10]) have not found the sign method sufficient to differentiate satisfactorily between the first and second test records of patients judged clinically improved.

Other users of discrete items to assess change following psycho-therapy have been Lord,[18] who employed Charlotta Buhler's Basic Ror-schach scores,[4] and Hamlin and Albee,[9] who repeated Muench's original investigation. Hamlin, Berger and Cummings[10] in a further investigation tested patients prior to and following six months of psychoanalytically oriented therapy. In this latter report, the authors paid considerable attention to changes in the type of human movement response given be-fore and after therapy, as has Piotrowski.

In this connection it may be of interest to record here the M responses obtained from the same subject tested on two successive days:

| First record | Second record |
|---|---|
| Dancing | Standing |
| Bowing | Alighting |
| Dancing | Doing a dance |
| Dancing | Bowing |
| | Screaming for help |
| | Persons lying against another person |
| | Mummies lying in a coffin |
| | People ready to strike each other |
| | People standing back to back |
| | Ladies bowing |
| | Clowns tossing |
| | People laughing, poised to dive |

It would be all too tempting, if a period of treatment had intervened between the two tests rather than just one day, to develop hypotheses in terms of the greater number of M's quantitatively and the more varied types of identification which the patient was now able to make!

An extensive investigation by Haimowitz and Haimowitz[8] concerned 56 patients treated by the Rogerian method. Here, again, the Rorschach was used exclusively and was assessed in terms of the presence or ab-sence of the Harrower neurotic signs, on the one hand, while, on the other, ten facets of personality felt by the therapist as particularly likely to reflect improvement were used as a frame of reference against which the specific characteristics of the Rorschach records were compared.

The conclusion reached by Haimowitz and Haimowitz was that by both methods of analyzing the data (Rorschach signs and therapist's evaluation) there was positive indication of improvement subsequent to therapy. They found small but consistent changes in the direction of better adjustment revealed by both methods. There further appeared to be little difference in the over-all effectiveness of individual therapy, group therapy, or a combination of group and individual therapy which had also been a subject of investigation. However, a control group, "de-spite a number of important life changes," showed "no statistically significant difference between pre- and post-tests."

While we would agree with these authors that there is little difference in the over-all effectiveness of various types of therapy, we have not found, among those individuals whose life situations had altered markedly in the interval between tests, the lack of evidence of change that is spoken of here (see Chapters VIII and IX).

Henry and Rotter[14] have studied the effect of immediate influences on projective test productions. They feel, as do many other workers in the field, that: "The results also tend to support the now growing body of literature which emphasizes the need to interpret psychological test results in light of a host of situational variables, no matter how indirect the test, rather than limiting analysis to the test protocols or profiles obtained from several tests or subtests." These authors found that a knowledge of the subject's belief regarding the purpose of the test was an important aspect to be considered in the interpretation of the test results and that a commonsense analysis of the subject's approach to the whole testing situation was a fruitful part of test interpretation. Situational determinants significantly influence test responses in their opinion; elsewhere, they state: "The real significance of this study does not lie in its demonstration of the effect of a different type of instructions but rather in the implication that subjective hypotheses about what the test is testing will have a significant effect on the subject's responses."

It may well be questioned to what degree the knowledge our subjects had that they were being retested affected their productions. Assuming all patients to be spurred by an inner need to "do better" on the second test situation, one can only say that such a uniform need resulted in anything but uniform accomplishment. All subjects knew that some comparison would be made between the first and second test performances and that this comparison was of interest to the examiner, as well as, in the case of those who had received psychotherapy, to the patient's therapist. Most patients also were themselves interested in whether or not, and in what way, the test findings would reflect experiences which they had had. Thus, in one sense at least, relatively constant situational factors may be said to have been operative.

The studies of Kaplan and Berger[16] are also important in this connection, particularly in the light of the large-scale retesting which we undertook on an experimental basis (see Chapter IV). These authors retested 28 students four times with the Rorschach test. In the second, third and fourth administrations the subjects were told to give only new and different responses. Sample answers to various cards were listed, showing a complete change in content. These authors found that the changes were great enough so that in many cases the basic shape of the psychogram showed relatively little stability. On the basis of these findings, they justly cautioned the appropriateness of interpreting a single

Rorschach performance as if it were the be-all and end-all, reiterating that "the responses obtained are only part of the story" and that "the single Rorschach performance cannot be regarded as an adequate, stable or complete representation of the personality characteristics which the Rorschach is able to describe."

We agree heartily with these findings since we have found that mere repetition on two successive days, even without a change in instructions, may result in a wide variation between responses if content alone is considered.[12]

In characterizing individuals whose retest records have shown change in the direction of a fuller, richer and more reality-oriented test protocol, it has been helpful to see their performance in the light of certain published statements by Schafer,[26] Maslow,[20] Klopfer,[17] Holt,[15] Anderson,[2] and others.

For example, Schafer[26] writes of ego mastery as being reflected in: "(1) An adequately rich but not overwhelming representation in the projective test content of the imagery of impulse, affect, anxiety, and conflict; (2) no severe impairment of the formal aspects of the responses; (3) appropriately co-operative behavior in the test relationship and situation." Concerning *richness of content*, Schafer states that this

"richness should be evident if psychotherapeutic discussions have been at all meaningful and tolerable to the patient, except when, as in borderline cases, the content was pathologically rich to begin with. This increased wealth of self-awareness and self-expression should not, however, invade the patient's functioning in impersonal, relatively well-structured problem situations such as those presented by an intelligence test. The absence of such invasion indicates that the regressive, creative self-expressions in the projective tests—as in therapy—are in the service of the ego, appearing temporarily and in appropriate situations and are not based on failure of the ego and invasion of all functioning by conflict. Also, the increased directness and forcefulness of content should be characterized by *variety* and *balance* of themes; some variety and balance should, for example, be evident in statements of mood (happy, neutral, sad), psychological emphasis ('deep' and conflictful, innocuous and conventional), operation of basic drives in interpersonal relationships (sex, dependency, hostility), and socialized inclinations (fun, responsibility, creativeness)."

In elaborating his ideas of the *formal adequacy of a response*, Schafer states that the

"liberated ideas and feelings, however raw, archaic, or dreamlike they may be in content, should not appear frequently in forms that are perceptually arbitrary, logically indefensible, or verbally distorted. For example, in the Rorschach test inaccurately seen sex organs, poorly controlled color responses with hostile connotations, emotionally optimistic scenes which are confabulated, and 'insightful' verbalizations which are peculiarly stilted, precocious, or cryptic are all negative rather than positive signs of change; they suggest failure of the ego in coping with the expanded self-awareness. Similarly, in the Thematic

Apperception Test the content of the stories may be highly charged emotionally but the stories should not be filled with perceptual distortions of the stimuli, obscurely rationalized elaborations of emotional reactions and relationships, arbitrary inferences from fragmentary details of the pictures, emotional and logical non sequiturs, fluidity of characterization, and disruption of verbalization. This distinction between formal adequacy and relative richness—even primitiveness—of content is the rock on which retest analysis is based. It enables the tester to differentiate genuine improvement from the effects of suggestion, imitation, compliance, acting-out of autistic fantasies concerning the therapeutic relationship, and strengthening of resistances due to incomplete or inexact interpretation of the patient's problems."

Phrased in a slightly different way but equally valid is a statement by Klopfer:[17]

"At the adult level, self-realization expresses itself in the ability to form and sustain personalized, differentiated, and reciprocal emotional ties, the ability to put oneself into one's work (Freud's 'Leistung'), and finally in the ability to utilize the archaic forces of the unconscious for creative purposes. In these ways, self-realization leads to a further deepening and broadening of the function of emotional integration."

One of the basic findings in the improved records in the present study—as will become apparent later—has been the decrease in the number of F− responses and the dropping out of personalized or unrealistic answers in the Similarities of the Bellevue-Wechsler. Both Maslow and Klopfer have made observations which make these findings understandable within the general framework of self-realization. Maslow[20] states, for example: A neurotic person "does not perceive the real world so accurately or so efficiently as does the healthy person. The neurotic is not only emotionally sick—he is cognitively *wrong*. . . . The self-actualized person sees reality more clearly: he sees human nature as it is and not as he would prefer it to be." Or again, Klopfer[16] makes an equally pertinent statement: "The primary role of reality testing is to establish a safe balance between the individual's internal need structure (drive impulses) and the external stimulus conditions, within the process of perception. In order that the individual may survive, it is imperative that the projective element (the influence of the internal need structure) in perception be limited to a safe level, thus permitting the development of long-range reactions and secondary thought processes." It appears to be exactly this which has happened when the F− responses are eliminated from the second test record. Their elimination corresponds to better adjustment following more realistic appraisal of life situations.

Another of the basic findings in this study in patients assessed as clearly improved clinically is the appearance of good FC responses in retest records, such responses having been either nonexistent before or else completely overshadowed by the more turbulent CF and C responses. Maslow[20] makes many references to the self-actualizing individual's capacity to receive and utilize love. Self-actualizing persons are defined, for example, as having "experienced gratification, past or present, of the basic emotional needs for safety, belongingness, love, respect, and self-respect, and of the cognitive needs for knowledge and for understanding, or in a few cases, conquest of these needs. This is to say that all subjects felt safe and unanxious, accepted, loved and loving, respectworthy and respected, and that they had worked out their philosophical, religious, or axiological bearings."

Some of Klopfer's statements concerning emotional integration are very significant for understanding the changes which occurred in certain patients in our study. Klopfer[17] states:

> "Emotional integration represents the necessary counterbalance for the process of differentiation of an originally undifferentiated primitive organization through endless steps of 'de-integration' and re-integration to the complicated structure of the personality organization of the adult human being in our culture. At any one of these steps, the current state of integration, of wholeness, has to be modified to make room for new development. It seems understandable that a considerable amount of basic security is necessary to facilitate the canalization of the available life energies into this repetitive process of overcoming a temporary state of 'de-integration' and to re-establish the wholeness of the personality organization on a new level.
>
> "Thus, provided there is an adequate amount of basic security, the available life energy can flow into the construction of a strongly unified, highly differentiated, and hierarchically ordered system of personality organization. An individual who is organized in this manner is able to gratify his needs appropriately, to relate all spheres of living to one another in a meaningful manner, and to profit maximally from his experiences because he is able to establish connections between them. . . . Our concept of emotional integration is thus organismic. *Appropriateness of feeling in the fullest sense of the word is probably the most outstanding behavioral representation of emotional integration, while compartmentalization or division of feelings is the most conspicuous expression of its impairment, even within the limits of normal adjustment.*" (Italics, this author.)

It has appeared to us that in the cases discussed in Chapters VIII and IX, where life stresses have been removed or modified, that these individuals have achieved a new basic security, with the result that available energy is free to flow into the more "strongly unified, highly differentiated" systems spoken of by Klopfer. The greater appropriateness of feeling indicated by the startling rise in FC responses in this group was corroborated by the subjects' own spontaneous comments and in discussion with those in close contact with them. In the same way, those who achieved an increased measure of security by working through their problems in the therapeutic setting spoke of the rewards of newly achieved interpersonal relations which bring emotional satisfaction.

### III. What constitutes "change" on the test battery? The Test Summary Chart. Qualitative and quantitative measures of "change." The Work Sheet. What constitutes "change" in behavioral adjustment? The Therapist's Summary Chart. The Therapist's Evaluation.

How can meaningful change be differentiated from temporary or insignificant fluctuations in the test performance? Every test used in this battery, if the test is repeated within a short period of time, results, in an occasional individual, in a performance which is, at least superficially, strikingly different from the original one. It is our contention, however, that the *level* of the total performance does not change from day to day when the tests are readministered even though isolated variables in any one test may vary considerably. Since the individual is much more than the sum total of all he is able to show of himself in any single test performance, it stands to reason, particularly in the case of mature and rich personalities, that many new facets will find expression through the plastic test material as repeated opportunities present themselves. In fact, we may go so far as to say *some* change always occurs in immediate, repeat situations unless the individual is an unusually restricted and impoverished person. Tests repeated on a day-to-day basis also suggest, however, that there is what may be described as a "core" type of performance.

Each individual tested registers a unique imprint on the interrelated battery of tests, a total performance which allows him to be recognized as himself. The story is told of the throat specialist who could never remember his patients when he saw their faces but when he looked at their tonsils, he could promptly greet them by name. This is not an inappropriate analogy to the experience of a psychologist in the retesting situation; a total test performance may leave an impression as a "test personality" which is recognized as familiar if met up with again after many years.

By use of the Summary of Test Findings (see page 20), we have attempted to establish a form in which minor variations will be lost but meaningful change will register. The first category, the subject's MANNER DURING TEST, is frankly descriptive. Many years of testing, however, make the appraisal of test behavior relatively uniform for any given examiner, and probably there would not be too great a discrepancy between the choices of the majority of those who work in this field. The divisions of this category hardly need to be spelled out, except to say that

# SUMMARY OF TEST FINDINGS

## MANNER DURING TEST

| (1) Overly distressed | (2) Tense | (3) Indifferent | (4) Appropriate | (5) Relaxed and actively interested |
|---|---|---|---|---|
| (1) Hostile | (2) Uneasy | | | |

## I.Q. (Bellevue-Wechsler)

| (1) Below average | (2) Average | (3) High average | (4) Superior | (5) Very superior |
|---|---|---|---|---|

## PRODUCTIVITY (Rorschach)

| (1) Impoverished | (2) Reduced output | (3) Adequate | (4) Better than average | (5) Rich and well-ordered |
|---|---|---|---|---|
| | (2) Compulsive productivity | | | |

## RELATION TO REALITY (Rorschach, Bellevue-Wechsler, Drawings)

| (1) Loose | (2) Lapses—together with good form | (3) Not noticeably disturbed | (4) Essentially firm | (5) Firm and good |
|---|---|---|---|---|

## USUAL-UNUSUAL THOUGHT CONTENT (Rorschach, Unpleasant Concept)

| (1) Bizarre | (2) Tendency toward the bizarre | (3) Adequate | (4) Original trends | (5) Outstandingly original |
|---|---|---|---|---|
| (1) Stereotyped | (2) Tendency toward stereotypy | | | |

## CONSTRUCTIVE FANTASY (Rorschach)

| (1) Absent | (2) Barely accessible | (3) Accessible | (4) Readily accessible | (5) Active but not hampering |
|---|---|---|---|---|
| (1) Withdrawal into fantasy | | | | |

## DRIVE (Rorschach, Szondi, Unpleasant Concept)

| (1) Overpowering aggression | (2) Over-aggressive | (3) Adequate | (4) Clearly sufficient | (5) Sufficient—exceptionally well-directed |
|---|---|---|---|---|
| (1) Hampering passivity | (2) Insufficient drive | | | |

## EMOTIONAL TONE (Rorschach, Szondi)

| (1) Explosive emotions | (2) Getting out of hand | (3) Trend toward emotional expression | (4) Warmth available | (5) Warm, readily available |
|---|---|---|---|---|
| (1) Lacking | (2) Indicated but repressed emotions | | | |

## SOCIAL ATTITUDE (T. A. T.)

| (1) Uncontrolled | (2) Constricted or neglected | (3) Adequate | (4) Well-regulated | (5) Free and flexible |
|---|---|---|---|---|

## ANXIETY

| (1) Disintegrating | (2) Marked | (3) Moderate | (4) Not marked | (5) Lack of evidence of anxiety |
|---|---|---|---|---|

## OVER-ALL EVALUATION

| (1) Markedly disturbed personality | (2) Less than adequate personality with some psychological problems | (3) Adequate personality | (4) Better than average functioning personality | (5) Exceptionally well-integrated personality with excellent potential |
|---|---|---|---|---|

the distinction between *Appropriate* and *Relaxed and actively interested* (scores 4 and 5 respectively) rests on a type of spontaneous comment which may indicate an unusually objective interest in, and awareness of, some of the implications of the tests. Some patients are able to transcend the examiner-testee relationship and be sufficiently free to enter into a general discussion in a way which is not an intellectual front or bluff to cover uneasiness.

In our psychodiagnostic reports considerable space has always been given to a description of the patient's manner, since the value of recording any discrepancy between overt behavior and the over-all test findings has proved to be great. The brief phrases in the Summary Chart cannot hope to carry the weight of a full description but they are, nonetheless, valuable indices which allow differences in manner between the first and second testings to be recorded, as well as being a means of calling attention to discrepancies which may exist between behavior and test findings at a single test session.

The second category, INTELLIGENCE QUOTIENT, employs Wechsler's divisions in terms of the score achieved on the verbal Bellevue-Wechsler. Individuals who fall into the *Below average* group have verbal I.Q.'s of 90 or below, those in the *Average* group, from 91 to 110, those in the *High average,* from 111 to 119, those in the *Superior,* from 120 to 127, and those in the *Very superior,* 128 and over.

The five divisions of PRODUCTIVITY are concerned with the number of answers either to the Rorschach blots or to the alternative series used in some instances as additional material, the Harrower blots. Under 10 responses is considered *Impoverished, Reduced output* would be from 10 to 19, *Adequate* runs from 20 to 39, while *Better than average* describes those records with more than 40 responses. In the divisions *Rich and well-ordered* and *Compulsive productivity* another criterion has been introduced. The record is scored 5 rather than 4 if it shows unusual organizing ability and possesses those characteristics of spontaneous amplification and liveliness which, for want of a better word, we have called *Rich. Compulsive productivity,* on the other hand, describes those records in which responses have been shot out monosyllabically and in enormous numbers, a torrent of material for the sake of quantity rather than quality, records, for example, with as many as 100 responses, with perhaps as high as 50 per cent d and dr, or records in which the total number of R has piled up through vague and empty, repetitious W responses. In terms of general level of production (although quantitatively greater than those in the *Adequate* or *Better than average* group), the quality of the production has appeared to us to warrant a score which is lower on the quantitative scale. We have also taken into account, in terms of PRODUCTIVITY, the richness and amplification of TAT stories, although these alone are not sufficient to change a rating if the Rorschach scores are at variance with the TAT.

Into *Loose,* in the category of RELATION TO REALITY, go those records with high F– per cent in the Rorschach, frankly grotesque or bizarre drawings (see Level 1, page 23), and answers to the Similarities on the Bellevue-Wechsler that indicate highly personalized and unrealistic thinking.

*Lapses—together with good form* serves to classify those Rorschach records in which, for example, striking F– responses are offset by good F+, or those records in which one test may show sharp deviation from the generally satisfactory level of the others.

Into *Not noticeably disturbed* go all the run-of-the-mill records which do not show sufficient pathology to warrant a more unfavorable classification, but which do not reach the level of excellence required to receive a classification of *Essentially firm* or *Firm and good.* A classification of *Firm and good,* for instance, would require not only no areas in which reality testing is inadequate but also the material should possess positive proof of some unusual achievement, as, for example, unusually accurate perception.

Before leaving the discussion of this category, it may be well to give examples of drawings which we have graded in levels from 1 to 4 under RELATION TO REALITY (see Figs. 1–4). There are, of course, problems both in establishing these levels and in placing any one drawing at a particular level with complete certainty. Many times, drawings fall between the classifications even when an extended scale of five or six levels is attempted. As a general frame of reference, however, we have found this concept of "levels" important both in demonstrating that mere repetition results in drawings which, though superficially different, still remain at the same level and, even more important, in demonstrating that in the instance of some of the patients who have received therapy, drawings unquestionably do change from level to level, on rare occasions even skipping a level on the second test performance.

In the assessment of USUAL-UNUSUAL THOUGHT CONTENT, records in which *Bizarre* answers occur or in which there is a perseverative-like stereotypedness receive a rating of 1. When there is a tendency toward the bizarre or stereotyped sufficient to color the record, the thought content is assessed with a rating of 2. Records which fall under *Adequate* are those which show neither psychopathology in the bizarre or stereotype direction nor, on the other hand, answers which can be

FIG. 1.   EXAMPLES OF FIGURE DRAWINGS CLASSIFIED AS LEVEL 1.

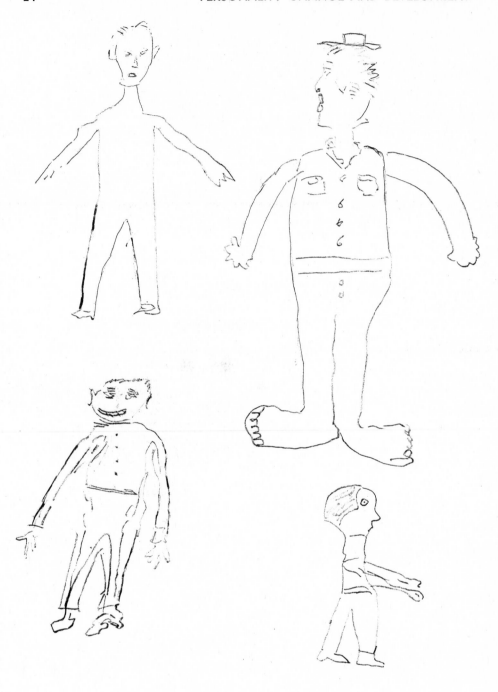

FIG. 2.   EXAMPLES OF FIGURE DRAWINGS CLASSIFIED AS LEVEL 2.

FIG. 3.  EXAMPLES OF FIGURE DRAWINGS CLASSIFIED AS LEVEL 3.

FIG. 4.   EXAMPLES OF FIGURE DRAWINGS CLASSIFIED AS LEVEL 4.

considered original or in any way outstanding. This would hold, also, for the TAT stories and for the content of the Sentence Completion. Also, it is possible to classify the Most Unpleasant Concept Test on this 5-point scale. Records which rate a 4 or 5 classification in this category are those in which the *Original trends* are of good quality and give a distinguished flavor to the test performance as a whole, in greater or lesser degree.

In reference to CONSTRUCTIVE FANTASY, included in category 1 are Rorschach records which are both without any M response at all and those which contain such an overabundance of M and disregard for all other types of response as to suggest complete withdrawal. Constructive fantasy is considered *Barely accessible* when from one to two M responses are present in the record, whereas three through five M responses gives a rating under *Accessible.* M scores of six and seven are considered an indication of fantasy being *Readily accessible,* whereas eight or over is *Active but not hampering* provided the psychogram as a whole is a rich one and there is no finding elsewhere that suggests withdrawal symptoms.

*Overpowering aggression,* in the category of DRIVE, designates those records in which there is evidence in at least two of the tests of a disruptive type of aggression, for example, a +5 or +6 s on the Szondi combined with TAT stories having marked aggressive overtones, a combination of strong FM and explosive color on the Rorschach, or a "blood-thirsty" Most Unpleasant Concept. The reverse of this, *Hampering passivity,* would be a –5 or –6 s on the Szondi, lack of all animal movement on the Rorschach, utilization of only extremely passive types of movement in the human figure, or a Most Unpleasant Concept such as "being aroused from sleep." To be given a rating of 2, the record must show a tendency toward either the *Over-aggressive* or *Hampering passivity* pictures just described. Also included here are records in which some of these traits are present in some tests but not in others.

It is difficult to make significant distinctions between the subdivisions 3, 4, and 5 in the classification of DRIVE since indications of excellence in this area are much harder to determine than are pathologic aspects. A decision to place the test findings of any given individual in something better than the *Adequate* category rests, to some extent, on the general liveliness and directedness of the record as a whole. It is interesting that while the evaluator of the test findings has used these classifications of DRIVE with some hesitation, therapists estimating clinical changes in behavior have made considerable use of them and have found them helpful in indicating the presence and degree of change in this area.

Under *Explosive emotions* in the category EMOTIONAL TONE, we have classified those records in which C and CF with much "explosive content" predominate in the Rorschach responses. Conversely, it is easy to classify as *Lacking* in emotional tone a Rorschach record which gives no indication of color response whatsoever, or which may have at most one single FC response. The Szondi counterpart of the former would be an open or loaded −e, a loaded +s, and, as indicative of explosive anxiety, a loaded +m.

A rating of 2 in the category of EMOTIONAL TONE is given to those records which deviate from the normal in either of the two directions just mentioned but do not show such marked psychopathology: for example, high CF and a low F per cent, moderated, perhaps, by one good FC or other indication of the fact that control is still available. On the other hand, a Sum C of one or two on the Rorschach justifies a rating of *Indicated but repressed emotions.*

We have considered the score of Sum C 2.5 to 3.5 as characterizing *Trend toward emotional expression,* whereas a Sum C 4, including at least three FC, has been considered *Warmth available.* The classification of *Warm, readily available* has been assigned to those records with a Sum C greater than four, if FC predominates.

Although the TAT stories, Sentence Completion, the Most Unpleasant Concept, and graphologic findings do not lend themselves to numerical scoring, all give information on the subject's social orientation and contribute to the assessment made under the category SOCIAL ATTITUDE. Samples of TAT responses that would lead to the rating of *Uncontrolled, Adequate,* or *Free and flexible* social orientation are recorded here. For comparative purposes, all stories are to TAT card 13 MF:

> *Uncontrolled:* "It looks as if the man has beaten up the girl and will now have intercourse with her."
> "This is a nymphomaniac and the young man will now possess her again."
> "The man has killed her. He strangled her."
>
> *Adequate:* "This man is in love. He leaves home to study. The girl he loves follows him and finds his room but has become ill on the journey."
> "A tragic climax of a romance. Two basically unstable people. The girl visited him in his apartment. They had a quarrel and in a blind rage he strangled her. He is now beginning to realize the full import of what he has done and is feeling very disturbed."

Examples of fuller or more constructive types of stories are the following:

> (1) "This young man has in the past attempted to go to school and receive a good education. His experiences in life have been limited and his affairs with

members of the opposite sex few. This is one of his early experiences and he is showing signs of guilt and frustration. However, he will recover, make an adjustment, continue his studies and forget about his guilt."

(2) "This young man comes into his room and discovers a nude lady lying on his bed. After his initial surprise, he realized he was staring and then turned and shielded his eyes. He went out of the room and proceeded to knock on the door as if he were looking for someone. This awakened the young lady and she was able to put on her robe and allow him to enter the room. Thus, there was no embarrassing moment and the young man diplomatically did not mention the incident and the lady was able to explain the circumstances surrounding her presence."

(3) "It is morning and the young man has just awakened and is still fairly sleepy. He has been up late the night before and gotten up quite early to study for a quiz and does not want to awaken his wife. He will soon pick up those books on the table and begin studying and then go out and take his quiz and do well."

There are many ways in which various forms of ANXIETY can make their appearance through projective material. In order that anxiety be rated as *Disintegrating*, the total test performance must show its effects, i.e., failure on many of the Rorschach cards, numerous k responses, drawings that are virtually falling apart, and a Most Unpleasant Concept that involves one of the various types of paralyzing panic.

Anxiety may be rated as *Marked* rather than *Disintegrating* if the Rorschach record shows abnormally high dd per cent, high k, high F per cent, and other evidences of rigid constriction and if various devices are adopted in the drawing of the human figure which reflect the anxiousness of the individual but do not suggest total disintegration. TAT stories with repetitive themes suggesting concern in specific areas, Sentence Completion responses which show that panic may be precipitated, and Most Unpleasant Concepts epitomizing unique fears and phobias, all such reflect *Marked* anxiety.

*Moderate* anxiety is used to classify those records in which the controlling factors are sufficiently in ascendance to suggest that some spontaneity of function is present even though fears and inhibitions due to anxiety are also apparent.

The subdivision *Not marked* serves to classify those records given by individuals who seem to function with sufficient freedom from anxiety in all areas tapped by the test battery. The classification *Lack of evidence of anxiety* is used sparingly and is reserved for those records which are exceptional in their creativeness and indicate genuine enjoyment of living.

The category OVER-ALL EVALUATION is self-explanatory. Some qualitative appraisal is necessary here as to which are the most typical scores for the record as a whole. For example, even with one or two excursions into the columns assigned the value 4, an individual may still end with an over-all evaluation of 3, the *Adequate personality*, or even 2, *Less than adequate*. The OVER-ALL EVALUATION score is not added into the part scores when the degree of change is estimated, but remains separate.

The quantitative score for the record as a whole is obtained by adding the figures in each "box," with the exclusion of the scores for the MANNER DURING TEST and the OVER-ALL EVALUATION. An initial score of 12, for instance, with a second score of 14 would show poor performance each time and no significant improvement. A total first test score of 18 and a retest score of 26 would reflect movement in the direction of greater test-richness. Conversely, scores which are lower in the second testing would suggest a retrenchment or a falling off from a previously attained level of adjustment.

Before turning to the therapist's assessment of change, the Work Sheet used to record the raw material in the cases here discussed may be briefly considered. This device is used for the sake of uniformity and to make available to the reader at a glance the I.Q., the scattergram, the Szondi profile, some evidence of the patient's graphic productions, and the formal Rorschach scores. These Work Sheets were originally designed to carry the quantitative summary and over-all evaluation for the test findings in those cases in which detailed clinical assessments were not expected to be forthcoming from the therapist, i.e., in cases in which a direct comparison could not be made between the Summary of Test Findings and Summary of Therapist's Findings. However, the full collaboration of so many therapists has enabled us in almost all cases to use the more detailed Summary Sheet. These Summary Sheets make the numerical assessment on the Work Sheet redundant, and occasionally we have used this space for additional drawings, or parts of additional drawings, where this seemed particularly appropriate.

The drawings usually included on the left-hand side of the Work Sheet have been reproduced from the originals in their entirety. All have, of necessity, been reduced in size, most a standard forty per cent but in some instances more. When additional drawings are given, they may be only part of the figure if reduction of the total figure into this smaller space would have resulted in the loss of significant detail.

What constitutes change in behavioral adjustment? This is a difficult question, and there are those who feel that studies of the kind under-

# WORK SHEET

## VERBAL I. Q.

| EWS | Info. | Comp. | Digit | Arith. | Sim. |
|-----|-------|-------|-------|--------|------|
| 18 | 25 | 20 | | 14 | 23-24 |
| 17 | 24 | 19 | 17 | 13 | 21-22 |
| 16 | 23 | 18 | 16 | 12 | 20 |
| 15 | 21-22 | 17 | | 11 | 19 |
| 14 | 20 | 16 | 15 | | 17-18 |
| 13 | 18-19 | 15 | 14 | 10 | 16 |
| 12 | 17 | 14 | | 9 | 15 |
| | | | | | |
| 11 | 15-16 | 12-13 | 13 | | 13-14 |
| 10 | 13-14 | 11 | 12 | 8 | 12 |
| 9 | 12 | 10 | 11 | 7 | 11 |
| 8 | 10-11 | 9 | | | 9-10 |
| 7 | 9 | 8 | 10 | 6 | 8 |
| 6 | 7-8 | 7 | 9 | 5 | 7 |
| | | | | | |
| 5 | 6 | 5-6 | | | 5-6 |
| 4 | 4-5 | 4 | 8 | 4 | 4 |
| 3 | 2-3 | 3 | 7 | 3 | 3 |
| 2 | 1 | 2 | 6 | | 1-2 |
| 1 | 0 | 1 | | 2 | 0 |
| 0 | | 0 | 5 | 1 | |

## SZONDI

| SEXUAL | | PAROXYSMAL | | EGO | | CONTACT | |
|--------|--|------------|--|-----|--|---------|--|
| h | s | e | hy | k | p | d | m |
| | | | | | | | |
| | | | | | | | |

## OVER-ALL EVALUATION

| | | | | | |
|---|---|---|---|---|---|
| OVER-ALL RATING | 1 | 2 | 3 | 4 | 5 |
| PRODUCTIVITY | 1 | 2 | 3 | 4 | 5 |
| RELATION TO REALITY | 1 | 2 | 3 | 4 | 5 |
| THOUGHT CONTENT | 1 | 2 | 3 | 4 | 5 |
| CONSTRUCTIVE FANTASY | 1 | 2 | 3 | 4 | 5 |
| DRIVE | 1 | 2 | 3 | 4 | 5 |
| EMOTIONAL TONE | 1 | 2 | 3 | 4 | 5 |
| SOCIAL ATTITUDE | 1 | 2 | 3 | 4 | 5 |
| ANXIETY | 1 | 2 | 3 | 4 | 5 |
| I. Q. RATING | 1 | 2 | 3 | 4 | 5 |

## RORSCHACH

| | | | |
|---|---|---|---|
| R | M | | Fc |
| | FM | F | c |
| W% | m | F- | C' |
| D% | k | F% | FC |
| d% | K | | CF |
| Dd% | FK | | C |
| S | | | |

taken here are doomed to failure since it is claimed no therapist is an in-
fallible judge of his patient's improvement. Others raise the objection
that when many therapists are involved, they will give such different
interpretations to the concept of improvement or lack of it that no uniformity can be obtained. Still others express the fear that patients will
be unwilling to report honestly on their experiences and that relatives
and friends will be biased due to personal prejudices.

As previously stated, we believe such an outlook is unnecessarily
defeatist. We have found ourselves taking a position closely akin to that
of Watkins,[27] who stated: "Criteria for the measurement of therapeutic
success can be validated only indirectly. Recovery may be best deter-
mined by: (1) Agreement among a large number of independent in-
dicators; and (2) Evidences of adjustment maintained over a considerable
period of time. . . . The clinician's evaluation should be checked by independent observations of other clinicians, psychiatrists, physicians,
relatives and associates of the patient." For better or for worse, this
study has been conducted on this basis.

At the start of this study, questionnaires were sent out to all therapists who had referred more than four patients for psychodiagnostic
testing at any time during the ten-year period preceding this study. The
total number of patients involved was more than one thousand. The
information requested from the therapist was that he state concerning
each individual (1) the length of time the patient had been with him,
(2) the type of therapy the patient had received and (3) that he give
an evaluation on a four-point scale as to the degree of improvement, or
lack of it, that had resulted from the treatment.

The questionnaire suggested that the following categories be used:
No Improvement, Slight Improvement, Moderate Improvement, Marked
Improvement—a scale not dissimilar to that described by Miles, Barrabee
and Finesinger.[21] Several therapists independently added an additional
category: "The patient got worse." Others altered the wording of this
four-point scale to come closer to their own assessment of individual
patients. For example, Slight Improvement may have been crossed out
and "Minor Changes" inserted in its place. Or, "Unusually Good Improvement and Adjustment" was recorded in the place of Marked Improvement. We note these alterations simply to show that it is our feeling
that the therapists assessed each case with considerable care. Detailed
findings of this follow-up study belong in the subsequent volume. It is
pertinent here to state only that despite minor changes of wording, all
therapists utilized the four grades or stages of improvement. Too, almost
all were careful to note patients of whom they had lost track and did not

feel justified in commenting on. The task for some therapists involved assessing as many as 200 patients; for others, as few as 4; yet essentially the same categories were required and used.

Discussion with therapists who participated in this study as to what was involved in their concept of improvement resulted in the following five criteria which, it was felt, must be satisfied before "maximum" improvement was stated to have occurred:

1. That the patient should have lost the symptoms with which he came to analysis or psychotherapy.

2. That he should have established warm interpersonal relations.

3. That his psychosexual development should have reached a level permitting him to form a close emotional bond.

4. That in terms of his occupation, he should be holding down a rewarding and satisfying job.

5. That he should have a positive and constructive orientation to life which could be considered something more than the mere loss of disturbing symptoms.

Most therapists, in addition to enumerating such conditions as these, made important distinctions in terms of improvement relative to the patient's initial condition. In almost all cases, therefore, a statement was obtained as to "how far" the patient had traveled. It was pointed out by many therapists that an OVER-ALL EVALUATION rating of 4 at the end of therapy (see Therapist's Chart), i.e., *Better than average functioning personality*, which had been achieved from a starting point of 3 (*Adequate personality*) was felt to indicate something different, therapeutically, than the same OVER-ALL EVALUATION achieved over a previous status of 0 or 1 (*Markedly disturbed personality*).

For the patients who were retested, utilization of the chart, Summary of Therapist's Findings, led to further differentiation and description of the type of improvement that had occurred. Although some therapists penciled in minor changes in terminology or suggested a few additions which could be made, by and large, this Summary Chart was handled not only without difficulty but with the feeling that a differentiated estimate of the patient was possible with its use. Although the Summary of Test Findings has been available for several years, the Therapist's Summary has been used by only one other investigator, namely, by Roman who reports on its use in a recent publication.[25] Roman indicates that the reliability between three therapists' judgment was 90.5 per cent.

Throughout these chapters a circle indicates the first assessment both in the Summary of Test Findings and the Summary of Therapist's Findings. The arrowhead indicates the position on the chart achieved

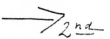

# SUMMARY OF THERAPIST'S FINDINGS

### ESTIMATED INTELLIGENCE LEVEL

| (1) Below average | (2) Average | (3) High average | (4) Superior | (5) Very superior |
|---|---|---|---|---|

### FLOW OF ASSOCIATIVE MATERIAL

| (1) Impoverished | (2) Reduced output | (3) Adequate | (4) Better than average | (5) Rich and well-ordered |
|---|---|---|---|---|
| | (2) Compulsive productivity | | | |

### RELATION TO REALITY

| (1) Loose | (2) Lapses—together with good form | (3) Not noticeably disturbed | (4) Essentially firm | (5) Firm and good |
|---|---|---|---|---|

### USUAL-UNUSUAL THOUGHT CONTENT

| (1) Bizarre | (2) Tendency toward the bizarre | (3) Adequate | (4) Original trends | (5) Outstandingly original |
|---|---|---|---|---|
| (1) Stereotyped | (2) Tendency toward stereotypy | | | |

### CONSTRUCTIVE FANTASY

| (1) Absent | (2) Barely accessible | (3) Accessible | (4) Readily accessible | (5) Active but not hampering |
|---|---|---|---|---|
| (1) Withdrawal into fantasy | | | | |

### DRIVE

| (1) Overpowering aggression | (2) Over-aggressive | (3) Adequate | (4) Clearly sufficient | (5) Sufficient—exceptionally well-directed |
|---|---|---|---|---|
| (1) Hampering passivity | (2) Insufficient drive | | | |

### EMOTIONAL TONE

| (1) Explosive emotions | (2) Getting out of hand | (3) Trend toward emotional expression | (4) Warmth available | (5) Warm, readily available |
|---|---|---|---|---|
| (1) Lacking | (2) Indicated but repressed emotions | | | |

### SOCIAL ATTITUDE

| (1) Uncontrolled | (2) Constricted or neglected | (3) Adequate | (4) Well-regulated | (5) Free and flexible |
|---|---|---|---|---|

### ANXIETY

| (1) Disintegrating | (2) Marked | (3) Moderate | (4) Not marked | (5) Lack of evidence of anxiety |
|---|---|---|---|---|

### OVER-ALL EVALUATION

| (1) Markedly disturbed personality | (2) Less than adequate personality with some psychological problems | (3) Adequate personality | (4) Better than average functioning personality | (5) Exceptionally well-integrated personality with excellent potential |
|---|---|---|---|---|

at the time of the second testing or second clinical evaluation. In most instances, it will be found that the arrowhead has reached a more "favorable" position since we have been concerned here primarily with growth and development and since the majority of our cases were retested when, due to one circumstance or another, the clinical picture had ameliorated. However, there are instances where the arrowhead occupies a less favorable position than the initial circle. In the case of assessments with no arrowheads whatsoever, this means that the first and second assessments are identical, and the joint position is carried by the circle alone.

Occasionally, specific scores have been written into a "box" in addition to the circles and the arrows. This has been done when change has not been sufficient to justify a new category but has occurred within the given category from the lower to the upper limits of what is scorable in this way.

Quantitative scores for the Therapist's Findings are assessed in the same way as for the Summary of Test Findings, i.e., without the inclusion of a numerical score for the OVER-ALL EVALUATION. Needless to say, the Therapist's Findings do not include the category entitled MANNER DURING TEST. There are, therefore, nine digits to be totaled on each chart, with a possible minimum of 9 and a maximum of 45.

## IV. Retesting after minimal time intervals. The "core" personality. Fluctuation as opposed to more basic change.

Unless systematic retest experiments involving a minimal time interval between tests are made, it can easily be assumed that all differences in scores, all changes in the material elicited by the projectives following psychotherapy or dramatic changes in life situations are equally significant and meaningful. Ironically enough, however, when such an investigation *is* undertaken, there is often, superficially, such a startling dissimilarity between an individual's first and second performance that there is a temptation to swing to the other extreme and be skeptical of all changes, to be afraid to give credence even to those differences in test material which do corroborate and parallel demonstrable changes in behavior, attitude and experiences. The solution to this dilemma, which faces every conscientious investigator, must lie in a middle ground and be based on the realization that every individual who is tested possesses many facets which do not find expression in one single testing session.

Parenthetically, it might be added here that there is a trend in our profession to pronounce irrevocable decrees on a patient's liabilities from a single testing as if these liabilities would persist ad infinitum. As a group, psychologists have been much more alerted to pathology than to health, to liabilities rather than to assets, and we tend to assume, sometimes with alarming dogmatism, that the test productions are an absolute reflection of the personality. Only recently has it become scientifically acceptable once more to be concerned with the normal person and to be interested in emotional assets and ego strengths.

All the test instruments used in this battery have been repeated when no time interval, or virtually no time interval, was involved. Let us consider, first, Rorschach records taken less than one week apart. These experiments have been reported elsewhere,[12,13] but the material has never been published in detail. What is important for our purpose here is to realize that at a superficial level, in terms of many aspects of scoring and certainly in terms of content, a very different test protocol may be obtained on two successive days. For this phenomenon to take place, not even the additional instructions of Hamlin, Berger and Cummings[10] that the subject give new responses is needed.

Table I illustrates the findings on 93 subjects who took the Rorschach test on two occasions less than one week apart. This Table shows what we have called "core responses,"* i.e., those that appear in both Record

* The concept of core responses will be developed further in another publication, but it may be of interest to note here that psychograms derived from the core responses alone may

TABLE I. "Core" Responses and Responses Unique to Rorschach Records 1 and 2; 93 Subjects; Time Interval 1 to 3 Days.

| Code # | "Core" Responses | Responses Unique to Record 1 | Responses Unique to Record 2 | Code # | "Core" Responses | Responses Unique to Record 1 | Responses Unique to Record 2 |
|---|---|---|---|---|---|---|---|
| 1 | 4 | 18 | 67 | 48 | 17 | 1 | 9 |
| 2 | 4 | 3 | 17 | 49 | 17 | 19 | 20 |
| 3 | 5 | 8 | 10 | 50 | 18 | 14 | 10 |
| 4 | 5 | 16 | 33 | 51 | 18 | 8 | 6 |
| 5 | 6 | 20 | 20 | 52 | 18 | 20 | 22 |
| 6 | 6 | 2 | 10 | 53 | 18 | 10 | 8 |
| 7 | 6 | 11 | 10 | 54 | 19 | 11 | 9 |
| 8 | 7 | 5 | 41 | 55 | 19 | 6 | 13 |
| 9 | 8 | 2 | 51 | 56 | 19 | 4 | 5 |
| 10 | 9 | 15 | 15 | 57 | 19 | 14 | 18 |
| 11 | 9 | 27 | 50 | 58 | 19 | 3 | 2 |
| 12 | 10 | 2 | 1 | 59 | 19 | 6 | 5 |
| 13 | 10 | 1 | 12 | 60 | 20 | 3 | 10 |
| 14 | 10 | 77 | 76 | 61 | 20 | 3 | 3 |
| 15 | 10 | 0 | 0 | 62 | 20 | 5 | 5 |
| 16 | 10 | 5 | 7 | 63 | 20 | 9 | 12 |
| 17 | 10 | 0 | 20 | 64 | 20 | 6 | 19 |
| 18 | 11 | 4 | 4 | 65 | 21 | 9 | 4 |
| 19 | 11 | 15 | 13 | 66 | 21 | 6 | 5 |
| 20 | 12 | 6 | 4 | 67 | 21 | 0 | 14 |
| 21 | 12 | 6 | 17 | 68 | 22 | 2 | 17 |
| 22 | 12 | 2 | 5 | 69 | 22 | 3 | 28 |
| 23 | 12 | 0 | 6 | 70 | 23 | 10 | 2 |
| 24 | 12 | 42 | 42 | 71 | 23 | 5 | 4 |
| 25 | 13 | 6 | 11 | 72 | 23 | 0 | 22 |
| 26 | 13 | 5 | 7 | 73 | 24 | 4 | 8 |
| 27 | 13 | 6 | 17 | 74 | 24 | 7 | 14 |
| 28 | 13 | 3 | 3 | 75 | 24 | 6 | 7 |
| 29 | 13 | 3 | 17 | 76 | 25 | 8 | 7 |
| 30 | 13 | 21 | 18 | 77 | 25 | 0 | 14 |
| 31 | 14 | 1 | 1 | 78 | 25 | 10 | 16 |
| 32 | 14 | 2 | 16 | 79 | 26 | 19 | 19 |
| 33 | 14 | 1 | 3 | 80 | 26 | 4 | 9 |
| 34 | 14 | 0 | 13 | 81 | 26 | 13 | 13 |
| 35 | 14 | 4 | 2 | 82 | 27 | 14 | 23 |
| 36 | 14 | 6 | 19 | 83 | 27 | 11 | 17 |
| 37 | 14 | 4 | 9 | 84 | 27 | 33 | 32 |
| 38 | 15 | 12 | 26 | 85 | 28 | 25 | 57 |
| 39 | 15 | 5 | 7 | 86 | 30 | 16 | 24 |
| 40 | 15 | 0 | 22 | 87 | 30 | 3 | 7 |
| 41 | 15 | 1 | 1 | 88 | 31 | 20 | 20 |
| 42 | 16 | 6 | 9 | 89 | 36 | 13 | 16 |
| 43 | 16 | 7 | 8 | 90 | 38 | 25 | 23 |
| 44 | 16 | 4 | 4 | 91 | 38 | 24 | 11 |
| 45 | 17 | 1 | 0 | 92 | 39 | 7 | 16 |
| 46 | 17 | 3 | 16 | 93 | 50 | 31 | 13 |
| 47 | 17 | 5 | 22 | Total | 1669 | 861 | 1420 |

1 and Record 2 as opposed to those responses unique to Record 1 and those unique to Record 2.

Table II makes possible a detailed comparison of locations and determinants for 20 of these 93 subjects.

advantageously be compared with psychograms including the total responses given to the first and second Rorschach records. An article by Robert M. Allen,[1] published as this book goes to press, indicates his interest in another aspect of what we have called core responses: "A Note on Persistent Responses in Longitudinal Rorschach Protocols." Journal of Projective Techniques, December, 1957.

TABLE II.  DETAILED RORSCHACH SCORING FOR 20 SUBJECTS (RANDOM SELECTION) RETESTED AFTER 1 TO 3 DAYS' INTERVAL.

| Code # | R (1) | R (2) | W% (1) | W% (2) | D% (1) | D% (2) | d% (1) | d% (2) | DdS% (1) | DdS% (2) | M (1) | M (2) | FM (1) | FM (2) | m (1) | m (2) | k (1) | k (2) | K (1) | K (2) | FK (1) | FK (2) | F (1) | F (2) | F− (1) | F− (2) | F% (1) | F% (2) | Fc (1) | Fc (2) | c (1) | c (2) | C' (1) | C' (2) | FC (1) | FC (2) | CF (1) | CF (2) | C (1) | C (2) |
|---|---|---|---|---|---|---|---|---|---|---|---|---|---|---|---|---|---|---|---|---|---|---|---|---|---|---|---|---|---|---|---|---|---|---|---|---|---|---|---|---|
| 28 | 16 | 16 | 50 | 50 | 50 | 50 | 18 | 18 | 15 | 23 | 4 | 3 | 5 | 5 | — | — | — | — | — | — | — | — | 3 | 4 | — | — | 19 | 25 | 1 | 1 | 1 | — | — | — | 2 | 2 | — | 1 | — | — |
| 88 | 51 | 51 | 8 | 8 | 59 | 51 | 18 | 13 | 15 | — | 3 | 3 | 6 | 8 | — | — | 1 | 1 | — | — | — | — | 30 | 31 | — | — | 71 | 61 | 5 | 4 | 1 | 1 | 1 | 1 | 3 | 3 | 1 | — | — | — |
| 17 | 10 | 30 | 80 | 30 | 20 | 53 | — | — | — | — | 1 | 2 | 3 | 6 | — | — | 1 | 1 | — | 1 | — | — | 2 | 10 | — | — | 20 | 33 | 1 | 2 | 1 | 1 | — | — | — | — | 2 | 5 | — | — |
| 1 | 22 | 71 | 82 | 15 | 18 | 55 | — | 8 | — | 4 | 5 | 18 | 2 | 10 | 1 | — | — | 1 | — | — | 1 | — | 5 | 18 | — | — | 23 | 25 | 3 | 5 | 2 | 2 | 1 | 2 | — | 7 | 5 | 7 | 1 | — |
| 89 | 49 | 52 | 10 | 12 | 49 | 52 | 23 | 13 | 18 | 22 | 5 | 4 | 7 | 7 | 1 | — | — | — | 1 | — | 2 | — | 22 | 24 | — | — | 45 | 46 | 3 | 3 | — | — | — | 3 | 4 | 2 | 4 | 2 | — | — |
| 86 | 54 | 46 | 17 | 15 | 54 | 54 | 9 | 13 | 20 | 23 | 11 | 4 | 11 | 12 | 1 | 1 | 2 | 1 | 1 | 1 | 1 | 1 | 21 | 14 | — | — | 39 | 30 | 5 | 5 | — | — | 2 | — | 2 | 2 | 4 | 3 | — | — |
| 93 | 63 | 81 | 8 | 6 | 51 | 54 | 16 | 21 | 25 | 18 | 6 | 9 | 9 | 8 | — | 2 | 1 | 1 | 1 | 2 | 2 | 1 | 22 | 30 | — | — | 35 | 37 | 2 | 5 | 3 | 3 | 5 | 9 | 5 | 6 | 3 | 6 | 1 | 1 |
| 83 | 37 | 44 | 41 | 25 | 51 | 45 | 3 | 12 | 5 | 18 | 2 | 7 | 7 | 9 | 1 | 1 | 2 | — | 2 | — | 1 | — | 16 | 24 | — | — | 43 | 55 | 4 | 2 | — | — | 1 | 1 | 1 | 1 | 1 | 1 | 1 | 1 |
| 6 | 8 | 16 | 63 | 38 | 25 | 56 | 12 | — | — | 6 | 1 | 3 | 4 | 1 | — | 1 | — | — | — | 2 | — | — | 4 | 5 | — | — | 50 | 31 | 1 | 1 | 1 | — | 5 | 7 | — | 2 | 2 | 2 | — | — |
| 15 | 10 | 10 | 100 | — | — | — | — | — | — | — | 2 | 2 | — | 4 | — | — | 1 | — | 1 | — | — | — | 5 | 4 | — | — | 50 | 40 | — | — | 1 | — | 1 | 1 | — | — | 3 | 3 | — | — |
| 71 | 29 | 28 | 21 | 17 | 72 | 75 | 7 | 4 | — | — | 3 | 6 | 6 | 6 | — | — | 2 | 1 | 1 | 1 | — | — | 5 | 9 | — | — | 31 | 32 | 1 | 1 | — | 2 | 3 | 3 | 6 | 5 | 3 | 1 | — | 1 |
| 53 | 28 | 26 | 32 | 35 | 57 | 58 | 4 | — | 7 | 7 | 2 | 6 | 5 | 9 | — | — | 1 | 1 | — | — | — | — | 10 | 6 | — | — | 36 | 23 | 1 | 1 | 1 | 1 | 2 | 1 | 1 | 3 | 3 | 3 | — | — |
| 68 | 24 | 39 | 38 | 23 | 58 | 64 | — | — | 4 | 13 | 2 | 2 | 6 | 9 | — | — | 1 | 1 | — | — | — | — | 9 | 12 | — | — | 38 | 31 | 2 | 1 | — | 2 | 1 | 1 | 3 | 3 | 2 | 2 | — | — |
| 78 | 36 | 42 | 31 | 21 | 50 | 57 | 11 | 10 | 8 | 12 | 5 | 5 | 6 | 6 | — | — | 1 | — | — | 2 | — | — | 14 | 13 | — | — | 39 | 31 | 4 | 4 | 2 | 4 | 2 | 2 | 1 | 2 | 2 | 5 | — | — |
| 22 | 14 | 17 | 36 | 29 | 57 | 65 | — | — | 7 | 6 | 1 | 4 | 6 | 8 | — | — | — | 1 | — | — | — | — | 3 | 3 | — | — | 21 | 18 | — | 1 | — | 1 | — | 1 | — | 1 | — | — | — | — |
| 36 | 20 | 33 | 50 | 30 | 50 | 64 | — | 3 | — | — | 3 | 5 | 5 | 7 | — | — | 1 | 1 | — | — | — | — | 7 | 10 | — | — | 35 | 30 | 2 | 2 | 2 | 3 | 1 | — | 1 | 3 | 2 | 2 | — | — |
| 29 | 16 | 30 | 44 | 33 | 56 | 67 | — | — | — | 15 | 1 | 10 | 5 | 5 | — | — | 1 | 1 | — | — | — | — | 5 | 8 | — | — | 31 | 27 | 2 | 2 | 2 | 1 | 1 | 1 | 3 | — | 3 | 8 | — | — |
| 8 | 12 | 49 | 100 | 18 | — | 59 | — | 8 | 15 | 24 | 3 | 2 | 2 | 9 | 1 | — | — | 1 | — | 1 | — | — | 2 | 11 | — | — | 20 | 22 | 3 | 3 | 1 | 2 | 1 | 8 | 3 | 3 | 3 | 8 | — | 3 |
| 9 | 10 | 59 | 100 | — | — | 46 | — | 13 | 24 | 3 | 2 | 1 | 1 | 2 | — | — | 1 | 3 | — | — | — | — | 2 | 31 | — | — | 20 | 53 | 2 | 3 | — | 1 | — | 4 | 1 | 1 | 2 | 8 | — | 5 |
| 47 | 22 | 38 | 23 | 16 | 77 | 71 | — | 10 | 3 | 3 | 2 | 4 | 1 | 4 | — | — | 1 | — | 1 | — | — | — | 11 | 17 | — | — | 50 | 45 | 3 | 4 | — | — | — | — | 4 | 3 | 6 | 1 | — | — |

As can be seen in Table I, the subjects in this experiment have been listed and given a code number in an order reflecting the number of core responses. Subject 1 has the fewest responses similar to both records, while Subject 93 has the most. It is interesting to see that for the group as a whole the number of core responses and those responses unique to Record 2 are approximately of the same magnitude: in the first case a total of 1669 and in the second 1420; while those unique to Record 1 are fewer, namely, 861. Thus, virtually all second records following a very short time interval have more total responses, a fact which has been confirmed by several investigators since our initial large-scale study was reported.[12]

Detailed scrutiny of these 93 records reveals that they fall into five basic categories. Let us take Subject 14 who has 77 different responses in the first record and 76 in the second, with only 10 core responses, i.e., those that are similar. Interestingly enough, these two highly dissimilar records, dissimilar if one considers individual answers, bear a personal signature both in terms of the formal scoring and the highly idosyncratic mental approach. They could under no circumstances be confused with other records in this group. This is an excellent example of *many specific differences, yet of a Gestalt similarity*, the first of the five basic categories. The complete record of Subject 14 follows (pages 40-45).

CODE #14

*Card I*

| | | | |
|---|---|---|---|
| 1. Skeleton of a hipbone. | D | F | At |
| 2. Lobster's claws. | d | F | Ad |
| 3. A face. | dr | F | Hd |
| 4. Landscape of trees. | de | FK | N obj. |
| 5. A profile. | de | F | Hd |
| 6. View from an airplane. | de | FK | Vista |
| 7. A polar bear's head. | dr | F | Ad |
| 8. A profile. | de | F | Hd |
| 9. A profile. | de | F | Hd |

*Card II*

| | | | |
|---|---|---|---|
| 1. A butterfly. | D | FC | A |
| 2. Profile of a face. | de | F | Hd |
| 3. Another profile. | de | F | Hd |
| 4. Another profile. | de | F | Hd |
| 5. Cloud. | de | K | Cl. |
| 6. Pieces of meat. | D | CF | Food |
| 7. Like a foot. | D | F | Hd |

*Card III*

| | | | |
|---|---|---|---|
| 1. Like two koala bears. | D | Fc, FC′ | A |
| 2. Map of Italy. | D | F | Geo. |
| 3. A dog. | D | FM | A |
| 4. A bird. | ddS | FM | A |
| 5. Hanging things like inside of cave. | D | F,m | N obj. |

*Card IV*

| | | | |
|---|---|---|---|
| 1. A bat. | W | FM | A |
| 2. Skin of an animal. | W | cF | A obj. |
| 3. A squirrel's head. | d | Fc | Ad |
| 4. A French poodle. | d | FM,Fc | A |
| 5. Petal of a flower. | d | Fc | Pe. |

*Card V*

| | | | |
|---|---|---|---|
| 1. A butterfly. | W | FM | A |
| 2. Profile of Satan. | de | F | Hd |
| 3. Profile of a queen. | de | F | Hd |
| 4. Two ladies looking at each other. | d | M,Fc | Hd |
| 5. Scissors. | d | F | Obj. |
| 6. A profile. | de | F | Hd |
| 7. A glacier. | de | FC′ | N obj. |

RORSCHACH 2

*Card I*

| | | | |
|---|---|---|---|
| 1. A bear. | d | FC′ | A |
| 2. A bat. | W | FC′,FM | A |
| 3. A skull. | DS | FC′ | At |
| 4. Crab's claws. | d | F | Ad |
| 5. A tree. | dr | F | Pl. |
| 6. A man's face. | di | F | Hd |
| 7. A profile. | de | F | Hd |
| 8. A profile. | de | F | Hd |

*Card II*

| | | | |
|---|---|---|---|
| 1. A man's profile. | d | F | Hd |
| 2. A butterfly. | D | FC | A |
| 3. Indian with feathered headdress. | dd | F | Hd |
| 4. Man's profile. | dr | F | Hd |
| 5. Two dogs sitting up. | W | FM | A |
| 6. A seal. | D | FM | A |

*Card III*

| | | | |
|---|---|---|---|
| 1. Two men in dinner dress. | W | M,FC′ | H |
| 2. Map of England. | D | F− | Geo. |
| 3. Bears. | D | Fc,FC′ | A |
| 4. Water horses. | D | FC | A |
| 5. Lady's boots. | dd | F | Obj. |
| 6. Sponge. | dr | c | A obj. |

*Card IV*

| | | | |
|---|---|---|---|
| 1. A bat. | W | FM | A |
| 2. A beaver. | dr | F | A |
| 3. An animal's skin. | W | cF | A obj. |
| 4. A man's profile. | de | F | Hd |
| 5. A man's profile. | de | F | Hd |
| 6. Spine with vertebrae. | di | Fk | At |
| 7. Clouds. | de | K | Cl. |
| 8. Fungus. | de | c | Pl. |
| 9. A snake. | d | FM | A |
| 10. A Chinese pagoda. | D | FC′ | Arch. |

*Card V*

| | | | |
|---|---|---|---|
| 1. A butterfly. | W | FM | A |
| 2. A horse's head. | d | F | Ad |
| 3. Sugar tongs. | d | F | Obj. |
| 4. A woman's profile. | de | F | Hd |
| 5. A cliff with dead rotted tree standing out from it. | dr | F | N obj. |
| 6. A devil with horns. | d | F | Hd |
| 7. A man's profile. | de | F | Hd |

RORSCHACH 1

| | | | |
|---|---|---|---|
| 8. Leg of a chair. | D | F | Obj. |
| 9. Part of a pencil. | d | F | Obj. |
| 10. A profile with a beard. | dr | F | Hd |
| 11. An Indian's head. | de | F | Hd |
| 12. An ant's leg. | dd | F | Ad |

*Card VI*

| | | | |
|---|---|---|---|
| 1. <u>An animal skin.</u> | W | cF | A obj. |
| 2. A butterfly. | D | FM | A |
| 3. A shoreline. | de | FC′ | N obj. |
| 4. Head of a porpoise. | d | F | Ad |
| 5. Head of Pluto. | d | F | Ad |
| 6. A shoe. | dd | F | Obj. |
| 7. A mountain. | de | F | N obj. |
| 8. Another shoe. | dd | F | Obj. |
| 9. Hoof of a horse. | dd | F | Ad |
| 10. A stocking. | dd | F | Obj. |

*Card VII*

| | | | |
|---|---|---|---|
| 1. Clouds. | W | K | Cl. |
| 2. A face. | d | F | Hd |
| 3. A sheep's head. | dd | F | Ad |
| 4. A face. | D | F | Hd |
| 5. A bird's head. | d | F | Ad |
| 6. A boat going through locks. | d | FK,m | Vista |

*Card VIII*

| | | | |
|---|---|---|---|
| 1. A polar bear's head. | D | F | Ad |
| 2. A polar bear. | D | FM | A |
| 3. A map of Italy. | d | F | Geo. |
| 4. A stocking. | d | F | Obj. |
| 5. A rock formation—a sphinx. | D | Fc | N obj. |
| 6. Rocks reflected in water. | D | c,k | N obj. |
| 7. A dog's head. | ddS | F | Ad |
| 8. An eagle. | ddd | F | A |
| 9. A camel's head. | S | F | Ad |
| 10. The body of a caterpillar. | S | F | A |

*Card IX*

| | | | |
|---|---|---|---|
| 1. <u>Head.</u> | D | F | Hd |
| 2. Face. | D | F | Hd |
| 3. Moose. | D | F | Ad |
| 4. Gnome with tall hat. | D | M | H |
| 5. A mask. | d | Fm | Obj. |
| 6. Butterfly. | D | CF | A |
| 7. Face of bear. | D | F | Ad |
| 8. Another head. | ddd | F | Hd |
| 9. Dog's head. | D | F | Ad |
| 10. Alligator. | D | F | A |

RORSCHACH 2

| | | | |
|---|---|---|---|
| 8. A bird. | dd | F | A |
| 9. An old lady's profile. | de | F | Hd |
| 10. A microphone. | dd | F | Obj. |
| 11. A bear. | dd | F | A |

*Card VI*

| | | | |
|---|---|---|---|
| 1. <u>An animal pelt.</u> | W | cF | A obj. |
| 2. A cat with whiskers. | d | F | Ad |
| 3. Leaves of a palm tree. | D | Fc | Pl. |
| 4. Foot with a heavy boot. | d | F | Clo. |
| 5. A canal with locks. | di | FK | Vista |
| 6. A rabbit. | d | FM | A |
| 7. A man's profile. | de | F | Hd |
| 8. A profile resembling Egyptian sculpturing. | de | F | Hd |

*Card VII*

| | | | |
|---|---|---|---|
| 1. Two women doing the "Susie-Q." | D | M | H |
| 2. An African woman's profile. | d | F | Hd |
| 3. A dog. | dr | F | A |
| 4. Clouds. | d | K | Cl. |
| 5. A twig. | d | F | Pl. |
| 6. Swinging doors. | dd | Fm | Obj. |

*Card VIII*

| | | | |
|---|---|---|---|
| 1. Two animals. | D | FM | A |
| 2. Patchwork quilt. | D | F/C | Obj. |
| 3. A frog. | D | F | Ad |
| 4. A wolf. | d | FM | A |
| 5. Backbone of a fish. | dS | F | A At |
| 6. Two birds. | dr | F | A |
| 7. Face of a man sneering. | dr | F | Hd |
| 8. Dog barking. | dr | FM | A |
| 9. A ghost. | ddS | FC' | (H) |
| 10. A duck swimming. | dd | FM | A |

*Card IX*

| | | | |
|---|---|---|---|
| 1. <u>Head of man with pointed hat.</u> | D | F | Hd |
| 2. Cup upside down. | S | F | Obj. |
| 3. Dragon. | d | FM | A |
| 4. Clouds at sunset. | D | K,CF | Cl. |
| 5. Old peasant woman. | dd | M | H |
| 6. Digestive tract. | di | CF | At. |
| 7. Hand with fist clenched. | dr | F,m | Hd |
| 8. A harp. | D | F | Obj. |
| 9. Stockinged leg and boot. | d | FC | Clo. |
| 10. Bear. | D | F | A |
| 11. Mole. | d | F | A |

RORSCHACH 1

*Card X*

| | | | |
|---|---|---|---|
| 1. <u>A crab.</u> | D | FM | A |
| 2. Leaves of dandelion. | D | F | Pl. |
| 3. X-ray of chest. | D | k | X-ray |
| 4. Head of a seahorse. | D | FC | A |
| 5. A beaver. | D | Fc | A |
| 6. Head like a bull's. | dr | F | Ad |
| 7. Sheep. | D | FM | A |
| 8. Two animals with horns. | D | FM | A |
| 9. Vase. | dr | F | Obj. |
| 10. A rabbit's head. | dr | F | Ad |
| 11. A French poodle. | D | FM | A |
| 12. A crab. | D | F | A |
| 13. An animal's head. | dr | FM | Ad |

RORSCHACH 1

$$R = 87$$
$$W = 5 = 6\%$$
$$D = 32 = 37\%$$
$$d = 15 = 17\%$$
$$de = 16$$
$$dr = 7$$
$$dd = 8$$
$$ddd = 2$$
$$S = 2 + 2$$
$$\left. \begin{array}{c} de = 16 \\ dr = 7 \\ dd = 8 \\ ddd = 2 \\ S = 2 + 2 \end{array} \right\} 35 = 40\%$$

$$M = 2$$
$$FM = 12$$
$$m = 1 + 2$$
$$k = 1 + 1$$
$$K = 2$$
$$FK = 3$$
$$F = 52 = 60\%$$
$$Fc = 5 + 2$$
$$c = 3$$
$$C' = 2 + 1$$
$$FC = 2$$
$$CF = 2$$

$$M:C = 2:3$$

RORSCHACH 2

$$R = 86$$
$$W = 7 = 8\%$$
$$D = 23 = 27\%$$
$$d = 18 = 21\%$$
$$\left. \begin{array}{c} de = 11 \\ dr = 13 \\ dd = 9 \\ di = 4 \\ S = 1 + 3 \end{array} \right\} 38 = 44\%$$

$$M = 3$$
$$FM = 15$$
$$m = 1 + 1$$
$$k = 1$$
$$K = 3$$
$$FK = 1$$
$$F = 44 = 51\%$$
$$Fc = 2$$
$$c = 4$$
$$C' = 5 + 2$$
$$FC = 4$$
$$F/C = 2$$
$$CF = 1 + 1$$

$$M:C = 3:4$$

RORSCHACH 2

*Card X*

| | | | |
|---|---|---|---|
| 1. A crab. | D | FM | A |
| 2. A wishbone. | D | F/C | A obj. |
| 3. Mosquito. | D | F | Ad |
| 4. Two potatoes glaring at each other. | D | FM | A |
| 5. An Indian with two feathers. | dr | F | Hd |
| 6. A ruler. | dr | F | Obj. |
| 7. Lion lying down. | D | FC | A |
| 8. Woman's profile. | dr | F | Hd |
| 9. A wild goose flying. | D | FM | A |
| 10. Two dogs. | D | FM | A |

Let us now consider a second pair of records which may be described as bearing a relation, one to the other, of a *"core" which expands.* Otherwise expressed, the initial pattern in Record 1 is contained in, and amplified in, Record 2. Such records, which make up the second of the five basic types, are characterized by a marked rise in the total number of R, by the retention of virtually all of the initial responses to any card, with what might be described as variations on the original theme being played at the second opportunity. There is, in Record 1, an indication of all things which are to come in Record 2. In such records there is a characteristic change in mental approach due to the fact that, while the number of W responses remains unchanged absolutely, their percentage or relative strength alters markedly in the light of the additional material. We have chosen the record of Subject 8 to exemplify this category.

CODE #8

RORSCHACH 1

*Card I*

| | | | |
|---|---|---|---|
| 1. A butterfly. | W | F | A |

*Card II*

| | | | |
|---|---|---|---|
| 1. A mask. | WS | F/C | Mask |

*Card III*

| | | | |
|---|---|---|---|
| 1. <u>Two cannibals with pots over a fire.</u> | W | M,C′ | H |

*Card IV*

| | | | |
|---|---|---|---|
| 1. <u>Rear view of an elephant running away.</u> | W | FM | A |
| 2. Fox terrier's head. | W | Fc | Ad |
| 3. <u>Mask.</u> | Dr | FC′ | Mask |

*Card V*

| | | | |
|---|---|---|---|
| 1. <u>Looks like a bat.</u> | W | F | A |

*Card VI*

| | | | |
|---|---|---|---|
| 1. <u>A dried animal skin.</u> | W | cF | A obj. |

*Card VII*

| | | | |
|---|---|---|---|
| 1. Two girl twins doing a dance. | W | M | H |

RORSCHACH 2

*Card I*

| | | | |
|---|---|---|---|
| 1. Mask with eyes, nose, mouth and ears. | WS | F,m | Mask |
| 2. Two little women kneeling. | d | M | H |
| 3. Two penguins with backs to each other. | D | FM | A |
| 4. Two seahorse heads facing away from center. | D | F | Ad |

*Card II*

| | | | |
|---|---|---|---|
| 1. Two witches dancing. | W | M | H |
| 2. Two firemen with red fire hats stamping out a fire. | W | M,FC,C | H |
| 3. Two black figures facing each other. | D | FM,FC' | A |
| 4. A spearhead in center, gray steel. | d | FC' | Obj. |
| 5. Mask, gray and black with pointed helmet. | d | FC' | Mask |
| 6. Red butterfly. | D | FC | A |

*Card III*

| | | | |
|---|---|---|---|
| 1. Two cannibals bending over a pot or holding two chickens. | W | M,C' | H |
| 2. Two red stomachs. | D | FC | At |
| 3. A red butterfly. | D | FC | A |
| 4. Two kidneys. | D | F | At |
| 5. A mask. | D | FC' | Mask |

*Card IV*

| | | | |
|---|---|---|---|
| 1. Elephant running away. | W | FM | A |
| 2. Two queens with backs together, each wearing a crown, holding hand up near mouth. | Sd | M | H |
| 3. A gray and black mask. | Dr | FC' | Mask |
| 4. Gray and black mask at bottom, too. | Dr | FC' | Mask |
| 5. A shark's tail. | D | F | Ad |

*Card V*

| | | | |
|---|---|---|---|
| 1. A bat soaring. | W | FM | A |
| 2. Bunny rabbit standing up on hind legs. | D | FM | A |
| 3. Two old men's faces with back of heads together. | D | F | Hd |
| 4. A caterpillar peeping over two leaves. | W | FM,F | A + Pl. |

*Card VI*

| | | | |
|---|---|---|---|
| 1. An animal skin—tiger skin. | W | cF | A obj. |
| 2. A totem pole. | D | Fc | Obj. |
| 3. Two old ragged shoes, sole to sole. | D | Fc,FC' | Clo. |
| 4. A snake with head, eyes, and one-third of body lying in a crevice. | D | F | A |
| 5. Butterfly wings. | D | F | Ad |

*Card VII*

| | | | |
|---|---|---|---|
| 1. Two native women with long skirts dancing and looking at each other. | W | M,FC' | H |

RORSCHACH 1

*Card VIII*
1. A coat of arms.                                    W        F/C          Emb.

*Card IX*
1. Two witches dancing.                               D        M,FC         H

*Card X*
1. Looks like two aviators falling in a parachute.    D        M,m          H

|  | RORSCHACH 1 |  |  |  | RORSCHACH 2 |  |  |
|---|---|---|---|---|---|---|---|
| R | = | 12 |  | R | = | 48 |  |
| W | = | 9 = 75% |  | W | = | 9 | = 19% |
| D | = | 2 = 17% |  | D | = | 30 | = 63% |
| dr | = | 1 = 8% |  | d | = | 3 + 1 | = 6% |
|  |  |  |  | dr | = | 3 |  |
|  |  |  |  | S | = | 3 + 1 | = 12% |
| M | = | 4 |  | M | = | 11 |  |
| FM | = | 1 |  | FM | = | 8 + 1 |  |
| F | = | 2 = 17% |  | m | = | + 3 |  |
| Fc | = | 1 |  | F | = | 11 + 1 = 23% |  |
| c | = | 1 |  | Fc | = | 2 + 1 |  |
| C' | = | 1 + 1 |  | c | = | 1 |  |
| F/C | = | 2 |  | C' | = | 7 + 5 |  |
| FC | = | + 1 |  | FC | = | 8 + 4 |  |
|  |  |  |  | C | = | + 1 |  |
|  | M:C = 4:1 |  |  |  | M:C = 11:4 |  |  |

Subject #8 may be considered to have told us his initial story of his personality pattern in the first Rorschach record, and then to have expanded and amplified it in Record 2.

RORSCHACH 2

| | | | |
|---|---|---|---|
| 2. Two native masks. | D | F,m | Mask |
| 3. A stone arrowhead. | S | F | Obj. |
| 4. Two squirrels with tails in air. | Dr | FM | A |

*Card VIII*

| | | | |
|---|---|---|---|
| 1. Two pink mice crawling. | D | FM,FC | A |
| 2. Two horses standing, facing each other and covered with horse blankets. | D | FM,Fc | At, obj. |
| 3. Steep mountain with old castle at peak. | D | FC | N obj. |
| 4. White mask in center. | SD | FC' | Mask |
| 5. Pink and orange butterfly. | D | FC | A |

*Card IX*

| | | | |
|---|---|---|---|
| 1. Two K.K.K. dueling with swords. | D | M | H |
| 2. Two Indians riding horses. | D | M,FM | H + A |
| 3. An orange, partially sliced. | D | FC | Food |
| 4. Gray spinal cord. | D | F | At |
| 5. Two orange and pink witches facing each other. | D | M,FC | H |

*Card X*

| | | | |
|---|---|---|---|
| 1. Two blue-green crabs. | D | FC | A |
| 2. Two pilots drifting from plane suspended by parachutes. Pilots have on gray helmets and pink suits. | D | M,FC, FC',m | H |
| 3. A rabbit's head. | D | F | Ad |
| 4. Two gray sand fiddlers. | D | FC' | A |
| 5. Three balls—gold pawnshop sign. | D | FC | Obj. |

There is a somewhat different relationship between the two records of Subject 24. In this instance the core responses are a relatively small part of both the first and the second record, so that essentially the *same personality theme is played twice over with different content.* In both records, for example, the total number of responses is 54, and the ratio of W to D to d is not noticeably different. What is added in the second record are dr, de, di, dd and S responses. The absolute scores and the ratios of the determinants remain remarkably similar, this in spite of the fact that 42 responses are different in the second record.

CODE #24

RORSCHACH 1

*Card I*

| | | | |
|---|---|---|---|
| 1. Like a butterfly, burned, with holes. | W | Fc,FC′ | A |
| 2. Like a map of Australia. | W | F | Geo. |

*Card II*

| | | | |
|---|---|---|---|
| 1. Like two dwarfs in "Snow White" doing a clap dance. | W | M,FC | H |
| 2. Like the two feet and bit of a tail of a bird. | D | F | Ad |
| 3. Section of central nervous system. | WS | F | At |

*Card III*

| | | | |
|---|---|---|---|
| 1. Like two chaps in dress clothes saluting each other. | W | M | H |
| 2. Pelvis and ureter of kidney. | D | F | At |
| 3. Gray matter of spinal column | D | F | At |
| 4. Head of Roman emperor. | D | F | Hd |

*Card IV*

| | | | |
|---|---|---|---|
| 1. Skin of an animal—probably bear. | W | cF | A obj. |
| 2. Inside of a flower. | d | Fc | Pl. |
| 3. Sacrum. | D | F | At |
| 4. Map of Germany. | W | FC′− | Geo. |
| 5. Sting-ray fish. | W | FM | A |
| 6. A duck quacking. | d | FM | Ad |

*Card V*

| | | | |
|---|---|---|---|
| 1. A butterfly appearance. | W | F | A |

*Card VI*

| | | | |
|---|---|---|---|
| 1. An animal that's been skinned. | W | Fc | A obj. |
| 2. Center of flower. | d | F | Pl. |
| 3. Gray matter of brain. | d | C′ | At |
| 4. Part of a cactus leaf. | d | F | Pl. |

*Card VII*

| | | | |
|---|---|---|---|
| 1. Like the brain all shot to pieces. | WS | F− | At |
| 2. Orkney Islands. | D | F | Geo. |
| 3. Like chops—chicken meat and pastry. | D | Fc | Food |
| 4. Australia. | D | F | Geo. |
| 5. Section through pons. | D | F | At |
| 6. Coast of France. | D | F | Geo. |

RORSCHACH 2

*Card I*

| | | | |
|---|---|---|---|
| 1. A charred butterfly. | W | Fc,FC' | A |
| 2. Two bears dancing. | D | FM | A |
| 3. Two boxing gloves. | d | F | Obj. |
| 4. Two cut-outs like paper patterns for night shirts. | S | F | Obj. |
| 5. Triangles. | S | F | Obj. |
| 6. "The Lions Mountain" in Vancouver. | d | F | N obj. |
| 7. Sacrum of some animal. | D | F | A At |

*Card II*

| | | | |
|---|---|---|---|
| 1. Two clowns doing a clap dance. | W | M,FC | H |
| 2. Cross-section of the central nervous system. | WS | F | At |
| 3. Two black lambs butting and snorting a cloud of red steam. | WS | FM,FC', CF,K | A |
| 4. Mirrored image of a fresh chop. | D | CF | Food |
| 5. Little monkey's head inverted. | de | F | Ad |

*Card III*

| | | | |
|---|---|---|---|
| 1. Two chaps in dress suits being overly polite to each other. They had just hit their heads together and were a little stunned. | W | M | H |
| 2. Sabot or Dutch clog. | D | F | Obj. |
| 3. Pelvis and ureter of kidney inverted. | D | F | At |
| 4. Horns of gray matter in spinal column. | D | F | At |
| 5. Chicken claws. | dd | F | Ad |

*Card IV*

| | | | |
|---|---|---|---|
| 1. Bear skin hung out to dry. Some rips in it. | W | cF | A obj. |
| 2. Flower. | d | Fc | Pl. |
| 3. Little animal's feet at bottom. | dd | F | Ad |
| 4. Pretty, rich fur. | di | c | A obj. |
| 5. Ducks' heads. | d | F | Ad |
| 6. A snowman's profile. | dr | cF | Obj. |

*Card V*

| | | | |
|---|---|---|---|
| 1. A butterfly, very beautiful. | W | F | A |
| 2. Map of northwest corner of Spain. | D | F | Geo. |
| 3. A little like Cornwall. | D | F | Geo. |

*Card VI*

| | | | |
|---|---|---|---|
| 1. Animal skin—mountain lion's deep and rich fur. | W | Fc | A obj. |
| 2. Part of a flower. | D | Fc | Pl. |
| 3. Like the head of 48-72 hour chicken embryo. | D | F | A |
| 4. Lot of crab feet, look as if they are moving. | D | F,m | Ad |

*Card VII*

| | | | |
|---|---|---|---|
| 1. Geographical. | W | F | Geo. |
| 2. Cross-section of 3rd ventricle. | S | F | At |
| 3. Two mutton chops making faces at each other. | D | F,m | Food |
| 4. Death masks. | D | F,m | Mask |
| 5. Like an x-ray tube. | d | F | Obj. |
| 6. Two white figures clasping hands. | S | M | H |

RORSCHACH 1

*Card VIII*

| | | | |
|---|---|---|---|
| 1. Skeleton of animal. | D | F | A At |
| 2. X-ray. | D | k | At |
| 3. Husky dog. | D | FM | A |
| 4. Section through brain. | D | F | At |
| 5. Map of U. S. | D | C/F | Geo. |

*Card IX*

| | | | |
|---|---|---|---|
| 1. Heads of two chaps. | D | F | Hd |
| 2. Chinese head with whiskers. | D | F | Hd |
| 3. Map of North America. | D | F | Geo. |
| 4. Witches blowing trumpets. | D | M | H |
| 5. Little birds lighting on wires. | d | FM | A |
| 6. Head of mountain sheep. | D | Fc | Ad |

*Card X*

| | | | |
|---|---|---|---|
| 1. <u>Big spiders.</u> | D | FM | A |
| 2. Portuguese man-of-war. | D | FC | A |
| 3. A bug. | D | FM | A |
| 4. Locusts. | D | FM | A |
| 5. Fossil of a sea-horse. | D | F | A |
| 6. A flower—inside of a lily. | D | Fc | Pl. |
| 7. Wind-measuring machines. | D | F | Obj. |
| 8. Cherry stones. | D | FC | Pl. |
| 9. Fish in goldfish pond. | D | CF | A |
| 10. <u>Two dogs on haunches.</u> | D | FC,FM | A |
| 11. Trained seal. | D | FM | A |
| 12. <u>Heads of unicorns.</u> | D | F | Ad |
| 13. A fox sitting up. | D | FM | A |
| 14. An octopus. | D | F | A |
| 15. An anteater. | D | F | A |
| 16. Stomach, inflamed. | D | CF | At |
| 17. A turtle. | D | FM | A |

RORSCHACH 2

*Card VIII*

| | | | |
|---|---|---|---|
| 1. Pink bears climbing up sides. | D | FM,F/C | A |
| 2. Two green flags. | D | FC | Obj. |
| 3. Green tree branches. | D | FC | Pl. |
| 4. Two frogs having a competition in croaking. | D | FM | A |

*Card IX*

| | | | |
|---|---|---|---|
| 1. Two pink faces. | D | FC | Hd |
| 2. Two fat boys' faces. | D | F | Hd |
| 3. Bunch of fingers. | dr | F | Hd |
| 4. Two sea creatures fighting. | D | FM,FC | A |
| 5. Two eyes. | d | F,m | Hd |
| 6. A tree. | D | F | Pl. |
| 7. Two bedsores on buttocks. | di | CF,c | At |

*Card X*

| | | | |
|---|---|---|---|
| 1. Two green spiders. | D | FM,F/C | A |
| 2. Two green monkeys. | D | FM,F/C | A |
| 3. Two unicorns. | D | F | A |
| 4. Two gray flying things. | D | FM,FC' | A |
| 5. Two orange dogs. | D | FC,FM, Fc | A |
| 6. Two chick embryos looking into periscope. | D | FM | A |
| 7. Two fierce Arabs. | D | M,m | H |

RORSCHACH 1

R = 54
W = 11 = 20%
D = 37 = 69%
d = 6 = 11%
S =    + 2

RORSCHACH 2

R = 54
W = 9 = 17%
D = 28 = 52%
d = 6 = 11%
dr = 2
de = 1
di = 2    } 11 = 20%
dd = 2
S = 4 + 2

M = 3
FM = 10 + 1
k = 1
F = 25 = 46%
Fc = 6
c = 1
C' = 2 + 1
FC = 3 + 1
CF = 2
C/F = 1

M:C = 3:4.5

M = 4
FM = 9 + 1
m =    + 5
K =    + 1
F = 28 = 52%
Fc = 4 + 1
c = 3 + 1
C' =    + 3
FC = 4 + 2
F/C =    + 3
CF = 2

M:C = 4:4

A fourth type of record is epitomized by those of Subjects 12 and 15 where *no new material,* or virtually no new material, *is added and nothing is lost.* This type of second record seems to occur only with very few total R, and it is now our opinion that inability to change at all in Record 2 is an indication of disturbance rather than stability. Certain types of impoverished personalities cannot profit, one might say, from the second exposure or second opportunity. It transpired that both of these students were doing poor work at the time of testing, and one failed to return to college. The record of Subject 12 is given here.

CODE #12

RORSCHACH 1

*Card I*

| | | | |
|---|---|---|---|
| 1. Like an insect. | W | FM | A |
| 2. Shape of an airplane. | W | F | Obj. |

*Card II*

| | | | |
|---|---|---|---|
| 1. Large mansion, terrace. | W'S | FK | Vista |

*Card III*

| | | | |
|---|---|---|---|
| 1. Two men meeting, talking, hats off. | W' | M | H |

*Card IV*

| | | | |
|---|---|---|---|
| 1. Like a fur rug. | W | cF | A obj. |

*Card V*

| | | | |
|---|---|---|---|
| 1. An insect. | W | F | A |

*Card VI*

| | | | |
|---|---|---|---|
| 1. Fur rug. | D | Fc | A obj. |
| 2. A sword. | D | F | Obj. |

*Card VII*

| | | | |
|---|---|---|---|
| 1. Two women talking—could be statues. | W | F | (H) |

*Card VIII*

| | | | |
|---|---|---|---|
| 1. Frogs. | D | FM | A |

*Card IX*

| | | | |
|---|---|---|---|
| 1. Like a fire, coals, smoke, flames. | W | CF,K,m | Fire |

*Card X*

| | | | |
|---|---|---|---|
| 1. Two men, two knights carrying something. Building, trees, alongside. | D | M,FK | H+Vista |

RORSCHACH 2

*Card I*
1. An insect.                                              W       FM        A

*Card II*
1. Approaching a mansion, terrace, trees.                 W'S     FK        Vista

*Card III*
1. Two men greeting each other. Each having their hats    W'      M         H
   off.

*Card IV*
1. The pelt of some animal.                               W       cF        A obj.

*Card V*
1. A moth.                                                W       F         A

*Card VI*
1. A fur rug.                                             D       Fc        A obj.
2. A sword.                                               D       F         Obj.

*Card VII*
1. Two heads of women in India. Are statues.              W       F         (H)

*Card VIII*
1. Frogs along the bottom of a lake. Grass and weeds      W       FM,CF     A+Nat.
   growing on the bottom.

*Card IX*
1. A great fire, the coals being the red. The green and   W       CF,K,m    Fire
   blue are smoke and the yellowish red, the flames.

*Card X*
1. Two men dressed as knights carrying something to the   D       M,FK      H+Vista
   castle.

| RORSCHACH 1 | | | | RORSCHACH 2 | | |
|---|---|---|---|---|---|---|
| R = | 12 | | | R = | 11 | |
| W = | 8 | = 67% | | W = | 8 | = 73% |
| D = | 4 | = 33% | | D = | 3 | = 27% |
| S = | | + 1 | | S = | | + 1 |
| | | | | | | |
| M = | 2 | | | M = | 2 | |
| FM = | 2 | | | FM = | 2 | |
| m = | | + 1 | | m = | | + 1 |
| K = | | + 1 | | K = | | + 1 |
| FK = | 1 | + 1 | | FK = | 1 | + 1 |
| F = | 4 | = 33% | | F = | 3 | = 27% |
| Fc = | 1 | | | Fc = | 1 | |
| c = | 1 | | | c = | 1 | |
| CF = | 1 | | | CF = | 1 | + 1 |
| | M:C | = 2:1 | | | M:C | = 2:1 |

A fifth type of relationship between first and second Rorschach records is illustrated by those of subjects 80, 87, 92, and many others. These are records in which the core responses far outweigh any additions or subtractions. Yet, this repetition is not one of impoverishment. The characteristic is not that new material has not been added or old responses dropped but that essentially these are *rich records,* basically the same yet *enlivened by sufficient new material* so that they do not appear as stereotyped repetitions.

We could go on expanding and refining these five types of interrelated records indefinitely, but the point to be made stands out from these examples. Change, superficial but often extremely striking, may occur in Rorschach records of the same individual with nothing other than a short time interval between the two testings to account for the change. Nonetheless, the vast majority of second records can be shown to have Gestalt properties in common with the first despite variations in details. Many analogies could be used to drive home this point. One is the well-known melody played in two keys. Another might be derived from the field of architecture in that essentially the same floor plan is laid down in the two tests but the houses may be built larger or smaller or with different building materials the second time. The individual who can only repeat his original floor plan, both in type of building and in material (our category 4), is actually a rarity.

The importance which Szondi attached to fluctuations obtained on a day-to-day basis in the Szondi test is attested to by his writings, and it has frequently seemed to this writer that had the Rorschach test not been so time-consuming, Rorschach too might well have required that an individual project himself several times onto the inkblots before any attempt was made to define his personality structure. In the light of our pairs of Rorschach records, it is quite clear that additional information can be gathered that is not obtainable on a single test. It is toward this end, of course, that the full inquiry and the testing of limits, which have become a part of standard Rorschach procedure, were devised.

Returning to fluctuation in the Szondi, as any one who has worked consistently with this test is aware, recurrent themes in the manner of handling tensions run through the six to ten presentations, so that again the concept of the "core" and "halo" personality is useful. The very realization of the fluidity and flexibility of drive, tensions and needs is, of course, an important part of Szondi's theory.

The fact that the Szondi test is administered only once in our battery makes the intepretation of the Szondi findings, before and after various forms of therapy, a somewhat dubious procedure. Nevertheless, there have been occasions when we have felt that clearly disturbed and un-balanced Szondi records have changed in a positive direction or, con-versely, disturbances not previously characterized by the profile have become dominant. To control our own observations on the Szondi, we have frequently submitted Szondi profiles to independent experts, asking for their opinion on which was the "better" or "worse" picture. Such pairs were presented without identification as to the order in which they had been obtained or the time interval between them.

We have experimented considerably with retesting in Figure Draw-ing. One such experiment, as part of an extensive psychological and physiological study of premenstrual tension, required subjects to draw the male and female figure daily. Over 40 subjects drew the two figures each evening over a six-week period. Our interest at that time related to changes in a self-administered battery occurring at times correlating with premenstrual tension. However, the material allows us to draw certain conclusions, which are somewhat at variance with current ideas.

Well-trained psychological observers were often unable to match the drawings submitted by the same individual drawn on the basis of the same instructions a day or two apart. The figures varied enormously from day to day, not only in what was portrayed but often in the manner of its portrayal (see figs. 5 and 6). In this instance we came up with only one common denominator, which may be said to be roughly com-parable to the "form level" of the old graphologists. Individuals seldom, if ever, crossed the boundary line of the "level" of their performance on a day-to-day basis. Figures 5 and 6 show typical fluctuations on a day-to-day basis.

FIG. 5. DAY-TO-DAY FLUCTUATIONS IN DRAWINGS.

FIG. 6. DAY-TO-DAY FLUCTUATIONS IN DRAWINGS.

To facilitate understanding of this concept of form level, we presented in Chapter III figures which represented four different levels of achievement. Following extended time intervals in successful psychotherapy, we have found that a drawing *may change* from one level of achievement to another. Very rarely, however, did our experimental subjects demonstrate even what could be taken as a possible shift following a short time interval.

Repeating the verbal Bellevue-Wechsler test on a day-to-day basis gave rise to only minimal changes in the test results. Slight fluctuations were found in Digit Memory and Arithmetic. One or two points at most are involved in the changes in the other three subtests.

The Most Unpleasant Concept, on a day-by-day basis or repeated weekly, yielded what can again be described as personal signatures revolving around central themes. In Figure 7, the two drawings on the left are from a series made by an individual tested daily. These are entitled "Monotony" and "Waiting." On the right in Figure 7 are "Loneliness" and "Immobility," the products of a different subject on a week-to-week basis. Although somewhat comparable themes, these have been handled in quite different ways by the two subjects and by each in a consistent manner.

Experimental repetition of the TAT has been discussed by others,[28] but we have found no mention of such a study in connection with the Holsopple-Miale Sentence Completion Test. Our findings with these two tests again revolve around the concept of *changes in level*. At no time in our experimental studies do TAT stories "jump" from poor to good, from *Uncontrolled* to *Free and flexible* social orientation. At most, we have had what might be called a half-point problem in the decision as to whether or not a poor record has changed in the direction of an average production or an average production has changed in the direction of better achievement.

Generalizing from all our findings, we can say that in terms of isolated variables, there can be wide variation on a day-by-day basis in almost any of our test instruments. When the individual's level of achievement is taken into account, however, or when the Gestalt qualities of the total production are considered, a recognizable similarity exists from day-to-day, to the extent that two subjects rarely, if ever, can be confused. In some tests, such as the Szondi, the single profile cannot stand on its own for comparative purposes. However, when embedded within and utilized as part of a battery of tests, it may give meaningful information reinforcing or corroborating trends in evidence elsewhere.

FIG. 7. FLUCTUATIONS IN "MOST UNPLEASANT CONCEPT" DRAWINGS.

As an over-all description of the Rorschach records reproduced in this Chapter, we may say that the initial record of Subject 12 indicates an impoverished and constricted individual; that of Subject 14, a compulsively pedantic, overly cautious and driven individual; while the records of Subjects 8 and 24 fall within normal limits. In no instance has mere repetition altered the over-all characteristic or descriptive label given to these test performances despite the fact that much superficial change is present in the second test.

Surprising as it may seem, repetition of the full battery of tests after thirty days reveals less change than that shown on isolated tests when retesting is carried out after an interval of only one or two days. This is illustrated by the material on twenty subjects presented in the next Chapter.

## V. Retesting with a full battery after thirty days.

Retesting after a month's interval with a full battery of the projectives results in two test protocols which retain common characteristics to a greater degree than do those obtained when the battery is repeated following an extremely short time interval. Perhaps one explanation of this may be the fact that when the second testing follows within a day, or at most a few days after the first, it appears essentially as a second attempt, a second chance to do better, to produce more or to do differently. On the other hand, with an interval of thirty days, the individual perhaps tackles the situation anew but with the added advantage of a reduction in tension since the element of the unknown is now absent. Regardless of the explanation, however, the fact remains that a thirty-day time interval resulted in test productions that, almost without exception, varied less than those discussed in the previous Chapter.

Six examples of the findings obtained when the test battery is read-ministered after a thirty-day interval are presented in detail on the following pages, together with charts summarizing the Rorschach findings for the total group of twenty subjects. In the evaluation of six individual cases, we have utilized the abbreviated, quantitative Summary Sheet entitled OVER-ALL EVALUATION which appears on the Work Sheet proper. This is identical with the Summary Sheet discussed in detail on page with the exception that the verbal descriptions have been omitted. Because of this omission, it is not possible in this abbreviated scale to distinguish between the two opposing descriptions having the same numerical rating which occur in the categories entitled PRODUCTIVITY, THOUGHT CONTENT AND EMOTIONAL TONE. Which of these two descriptions is intended, however, can easily be seen from the recorded raw material. Whether the rating 1 in EMOTIONAL TONE refers to absence of emotional responsiveness or to the most blatant, explosive display of feelings can obviously be decided from the accompanying Rorschach scores.

In the first case presented, Subject 307, we find virtually identical drawings following the thirty day interval, a Rorschach record characterized by an unusually high F per cent, an identical distribution of W, D, d, DdS percentages, and a quantitative OVER-ALL EVALUATION score of 25 in the first instance and 24 in the second.

The Szondi scores suggest rather marked mood variations overlaid on the core personality. The loaded +s in Work Sheet 1 accompanies the aggressive, claw-like digits on the male figure in the Figure Drawings, whereas in Record 2 the hands are clenched and the strong −m suggests a more defeatist, frustrated attitude.

The next case, Subject 306, again exemplifies similarity between the two performances, the quantitative OVER-ALL EVALUATION score being 21 in the first and 19 in the second. The Drawings are recognizably the work of the same individual. The Rorschach is characterized in both instances by marked constriction and absence of emotional responsiveness. The passivity and inertness of this individual is suggested by the virtual lack of FM responses and the open h and s scores on the Szondi. There is a shift in the direction of greater concern with minutiae in the Mental Approach, as reflected in the Rorschach scores, a shift which may be considered a recognized characteristic of retesting per se.

Although in the two protocols of Subject 303 the female figures in the Figure Drawings face in the opposite direction and such minor differences as the treatment of the hair occur between Records 1 and 2, sufficient similarity exists so that both sets of drawings fall into the same level of achievement (we have rated both these as 3+ on a 5-point scale). Specific points of likeness can be detected, for example, the strange, geometrically shaped hand, the bust emphasis, the size and placement of the drawings. The Rorschach record, apart from the expected shift in the direction of larger details in the second testing, is identical in structure and closely similar even in content. The F per cent level remains the same in both instances. The quantitative OVER-ALL EVALUATION results in a difference of only 2 points, the initial assessment being 27, the second 25.

Turning to Subject 302, one finds a more disturbed individual as reflected by each of the test instruments. The Drawings have a bizarre quality and rate lower than all others in this series on both occasions. The Rorschach also reflects pathology both in the poverty of output and the qualitative aspects of the responses. In this instance the Szondi remains surprisingly constant; the marked repression in the ego vector, the primitive handling of sexual impulses, the ambivalence in regard to object relationships are found in both profiles. The quantitative OVER-ALL EVALUATION is 19, as assessed from the first record sheet, and 17 in the second.

The record of Subject 301 is an example of a type of change which suggests that the first testing situation constitutes more of a threat than do subsequent ones. The broken lines in the first Drawings are more marked than in the second, and while both the male and female figures are recognizably the product of one individual, the second attempt shows somewhat more poise. Greater control appears to be exerted throughout the second testing situation, as reflected by the increase in F+ per cent and by the decrease in CF and C scores. This additional control, however, results in inhibition of that small excursion into fantasy life which this individual originally expressed in two human movement responses. In the second testing, one good human movement response drops out. The quantitative OVER-ALL EVALUATION score remains identical, being 25 in both tests.

Subject 305 illustrates a different trend, a trend found in four of the twenty cases, which might be formulated in this way: Concomitant with the greater safety felt during the second test, for certain gifted individuals the second test seems to provide less of a challenge. In the case in question, if this hypothesis is correct, the lack of challenge reduces the output markedly (from 57 R to 34), brings down the M responses (from 16 to 8), and results in a decrease in the good form-color responses (from 4+2 in the first to 2 in the second record). Interestingly enough, as will be seen in Table III, all three individuals having lively M responses showed a marked decrease in good human movement answers on the second testing. Two of these cases also show a decrease in FM from 8 to 1 and 7 to 3. Subject 305, in the Drawings of the human figure, seems to show the reverse tendency from that discussed previously in Case 301. Here, the second attempt could be described as a loose and careless version of the original one although still retaining many identifiable characteristics.

Comparison of the Rorschach records obtained following a thirty-day interval with those obtained following a short interval reveals greater similarities in the records as a whole in the thirty-day group. By and large, Figure Drawings, too, vary less than those obtained on a day-to-day basis. The scores obtained from the abbreviated Bellevue-Wechsler are virtually identical in all but one case, that of 301 whose answers gained sufficient precision and clarification to justify higher scoring on the Comprehension and Similarities.

The following records illustrating test productions when retesting is carried out after a thirty-day interval are all of males between the ages of twenty and thirty.

## = WORK SHEET = # 307

1

### SZONDI

| SEXUAL | | PAROXYSMAL | | EGO | | CONTACT | |
|---|---|---|---|---|---|---|---|
| h | s | e | hy | k | p | d | m |
|  | X |  |  |  |  |  |  |
|  | X |  |  |  |  |  |  |
| X | X |  |  | X | X |  |  |
| X | X |  | X | X | X |  | X |
| X | X | X | X | X | X | X |  |
|  |  |  |  |  | X | X |  |
|  |  |  |  |  |  | X |  |

### OVER-ALL EVALUATION = 25

|  | 1 | 2 | 3 | 4 | 5 |
|---|---|---|---|---|---|
| OVER-ALL RATING | 1 | 2 | 3 | 4 | 5 |
| PRODUCTIVITY | 1 | 2 | ③ | 4 | 5 |
| RELATION TO REALITY | 1 | 2 | ③ | 4 | 5 |
| THOUGHT CONTENT | 1 | 2 | ③ | 4 | 5 |
| CONSTRUCTIVE FANTASY | 1 | ② | 3 | 4 | 5 |
| DRIVE | 1 | ② | 3 | 4 | 5 |
| EMOTIONAL TONE | 1 | ② | 3 | 4 | 5 |
| SOCIAL ATTITUDE | 1 | 2 | ③ | 4 | 5 |
| ANXIETY | 1 | 2 | ③ | 4 | 5 |
| I. Q. RATING | 1 | 2 | 3 | ④ | 5 |

### RORSCHACH

| R | 33 | M | 2 | | | Fc | 1 |
|---|---|---|---|---|---|---|---|
|  |  | FM | 1 | F | 27 | c | |
| W% | 30 | m | | F– | 1 | C' | |
| D% | 61 | k | | F% | 85 | FC | |
| d% | 3 | K | | | | CF | 1 |
| Dd% | 6 | FK | | | | C | |
| S | | | | | | | |

## = WORK SHEET = # 307
### 2

### SZONDI

| SEXUAL | | PAROXYSMAL | | EGO | | CONTACT | |
|---|---|---|---|---|---|---|---|
| h | s | e | hy | k | p | d | m |

### OVER-ALL EVALUATION = 24

| | 1 | 2 | 3 | 4 | 5 |
|---|---|---|---|---|---|
| OVER-ALL RATING | 1 | 2 | 3 | 4 | 5 |
| PRODUCTIVITY | 1 | 2 | ③ | 4 | 5 |
| RELATION TO REALITY | 1 | 2 | ③ | 4 | 5 |
| THOUGHT CONTENT | 1 | 2 | ③ | 4 | 5 |
| CONSTRUCTIVE FANTASY | 1 | ② | 3 | 4 | 5 |
| DRIVE | 1 | ② | 3 | 4 | 5 |
| EMOTIONAL TONE | ① | 2 | 3 | 4 | 5 |
| SOCIAL ATTITUDE | 1 | 2 | ③ | 4 | 5 |
| ANXIETY | 1 | 2 | ③ | 4 | 5 |
| I. Q. RATING | 1 | 2 | 3 | ④ | 5 |

### RORSCHACH

| R | 25 | M | 2 | | | Fc | l |
|---|---|---|---|---|---|---|---|
| | | FM | | F | 22 | c | |
| W% | 24 | m | | F– | | C' | |
| D% | 64 | k | | F% | 88 | FC | |
| d% | 4 | K | | | | CF | |
| Dd% | 8 | FK | | | | C | |
| S | | | | | | | |

## WORK SHEET  # 306

### SZONDI

| SEXUAL | | PAROXYSMAL | | EGO | | CONTACT | |
|---|---|---|---|---|---|---|---|
| h | s | e | hy | k | p | d | m |
|  |  |  |  |  | X | | X |
| X |  | X |  |  | X | | X |
| X |  | X |  | X | X | X | X |
| X | X | X | X | X | X | X | X |
|  |  | X | X | X |  | X |  |

### OVER-ALL EVALUATION = 21

| | 1 | 2 | 3 | 4 | 5 |
|---|---|---|---|---|---|
| OVER-ALL RATING | 1 | 2 | 3 | 4 | 5 |
| PRODUCTIVITY | 1 | 2 | ③ | 4 | 5 |
| RELATION TO REALITY | 1 | 2 | ③ | 4 | 5 |
| THOUGHT CONTENT | 1 | ② | 3 | 4 | 5 |
| CONSTRUCTIVE FANTASY | 1 | 2 | ③ | 4 | 5 |
| DRIVE | 1 | ② | 3 | 4 | 5 |
| EMOTIONAL TONE | ① | 2 | 3 | 4 | 5 |
| SOCIAL ATTITUDE | 1 | ② | 3 | 4 | 5 |
| ANXIETY | 1 | ② | 3 | 4 | 5 |
| I. Q. RATING | 1 | 2 | ③ | 4 | 5 |

### RORSCHACH

| R | 25 | M | 3 | | | Fc | 1 |
|---|---|---|---|---|---|---|---|
| | | FM | 1 | F | 18 | c | |
| W% | 36 | m | 1+1 | F− | 1 | C' | |
| D% | 48 | k | | F% | 76 | FC | |
| d% | 4 | K | | | | CF | |
| Dd% S | 12 | FK | | | | c | +1 |

# WORK SHEET

## 2

# #306

## SZONDI

| SEXUAL | | PAROXYSMAL | | EGO | | CONTACT | |
|---|---|---|---|---|---|---|---|
| h | s | e | hy | k | p | d | m |
| | | X X | X X | X | X X X X X | | X X X |
| | X | X X X | X X | X X X X | X X | | |

## OVER-ALL EVALUATION = 19

| | | | | | |
|---|---|---|---|---|---|
| OVER-ALL RATING | 1 | 2 | 3 | 4 | 5 |
| PRODUCTIVITY | 1 | 2 | ③ | 4 | 5 |
| RELATION TO REALITY | 1 | 2 | ③ | 4 | 5 |
| THOUGHT CONTENT | 1 | ② | 3 | 4 | 5 |
| CONSTRUCTIVE FANTASY | 1 | ② | 3 | 4 | 5 |
| DRIVE | ① | 2 | 3 | 4 | 5 |
| EMOTIONAL TONE | ① | 2 | 3 | 4 | 5 |
| SOCIAL ATTITUDE | 1 | ② | 3 | 4 | 5 |
| ANXIETY | 1 | ② | 3 | 4 | 5 |
| I. Q. RATING | 1 | 2 | ③ | 4 | 5 |

## RORSCHACH

| | | | | | |
|---|---|---|---|---|---|
| R 30 | M 2 | | | Fc 1 |
| | FM | | F 25 | c |
| W% 17 | m 1 | | F- 1 | C' |
| D% 33 | k | | F% 87 | FC |
| d% 27 | K | | | CF |
| Dd% 23 | FK | | | C |
| S | | | | |

=== WORK SHEET ===

## SZONDI

| SEXUAL | | PAROXYSMAL | | EGO | | CONTACT | |
| h | s | e | hy | k | p | d | m |
| X X X | X X X X | X | | X | X | X | X |
| | X | X X X | X | X X X X | X | X X | X |

### OVER-ALL EVALUATION = 27

| | 1 | 2 | 3 | 4 | 5 |
|---|---|---|---|---|---|
| OVER-ALL RATING | 1 | 2 | 3 | 4 | 5 |
| PRODUCTIVITY | 1 | 2 | ③ | 4 | 5 |
| RELATION TO REALITY | 1 | 2 | 3 | ④ | 5 |
| THOUGHT CONTENT | 1 | 2 | ③ | 4 | 5 |
| CONSTRUCTIVE FANTASY | 1 | ② | 3 | 4 | 5 |
| DRIVE | 1 | 2 | ③ | 4 | 5 |
| EMOTIONAL TONE | 1 | ② | 3 | 4 | 5 |
| SOCIAL ATTITUDE | 1 | 2 | ③ | 4 | 5 |
| ANXIETY | 1 | 2 | ③ | 4 | 5 |
| I. Q. RATING | 1 | 2 | 3 | ④ | 5 |

### RORSCHACH

| R 21 | M 1 | | Fc 1 |
|---|---|---|---|
| | FM 1 | F 11 | c +2 |
| W% 57 | m 1 | F− | C' +2 |
| D% 29 | k | F% 52 | FC |
| d% | K 2 | | CF 3 |
| Dd% 14 S | FK 1 | | c |

# WORK SHEET

#303

2

## SZONDI

| SEXUAL | | PAROXYSMAL | | EGO | | CONTACT | |
|---|---|---|---|---|---|---|---|
| h | s | e | hy | k | p | d | m |
| X X | X X | X | X | X | X | X | X X X |
| | | X | X X X X | X X | X | X X | X X |

## OVER-ALL EVALUATION ≈ 25

| | | | | | |
|---|---|---|---|---|---|
| OVER-ALL RATING | I | 2 | 3 | 4 | 5 |
| PRODUCTIVITY | I | ②| 3 | 4 | 5 |
| RELATION TO REALITY | I | 2 | 3 | ④ | 5 |
| THOUGHT CONTENT | I | 2 | ③ | 4 | 5 |
| CONSTRUCTIVE FANTASY | I | ② | 3 | 4 | 5 |
| DRIVE | I | ② | 3 | 4 | 5 |
| EMOTIONAL TONE | I | ② | 3 | 4 | 5 |
| SOCIAL ATTITUDE | I | 2 | ③ | 4 | 5 |
| ANXIETY | I | 2 | ③ | 4 | 5 |
| I. Q. RATING | I | 2 | 3 | ④ | 5 |

## RORSCHACH

| R 20 | M I | | Fc 2 |
|---|---|---|---|
| | FM | F 11 | c +1 |
| W% 25 | m I | F— | C' +1 |
| D% 45 | k | F% 55 | FC |
| d% 10 | K +1 | | CF 4 |
| Dd% 20 S | FK I | | c +1 |

## WORK SHEET   #302

1

### SZONDI

| SEXUAL | | PAROXYSMAL | | EGO | | CONTACT | |
|---|---|---|---|---|---|---|---|
| h | s | e | hy | k | p | d | m |
| X | | X | | | X | | |
| X | | X | | | X | | X |
| X | X | X | | | X | | X |
| | X | X | X | X | | | X |
| | | X | X | X | | | X |
| | | | | X | | | |
| | | | | X | | | |
| | | | | X | | | |

### OVER-ALL EVALUATION = 19

| | 1 | 2 | 3 | 4 | 5 |
|---|---|---|---|---|---|
| OVER-ALL RATING | 1 | 2 | 3 | 4 | 5 |
| PRODUCTIVITY | 1 | ② | 3 | 4 | 5 |
| RELATION TO REALITY | ① | 2 | 3 | 4 | 5 |
| THOUGHT CONTENT | 1 | ② | 3 | 4 | 5 |
| CONSTRUCTIVE FANTASY | 1 | 2 | ③ | 4 | 5 |
| DRIVE | 1 | 2 | ③ | 4 | 5 |
| EMOTIONAL TONE | ① | 2 | 3 | 4 | 5 |
| SOCIAL ATTITUDE | 1 | ② | 3 | 4 | 5 |
| ANXIETY | 1 | ② | 3 | 4 | 5 |
| I. Q. RATING | 1 | 2 | ③ | 4 | 5 |

### RORSCHACH

| R 13 | M 3 | | Fc 2 |
|---|---|---|---|
| | FM 3 | F 4 | c |
| W% 85 | m | F- 1 | C' |
| D% 15 | k | F% 39 | FC |
| d% | K | | CF |
| Dd% | FK | | C |
| S | | | |

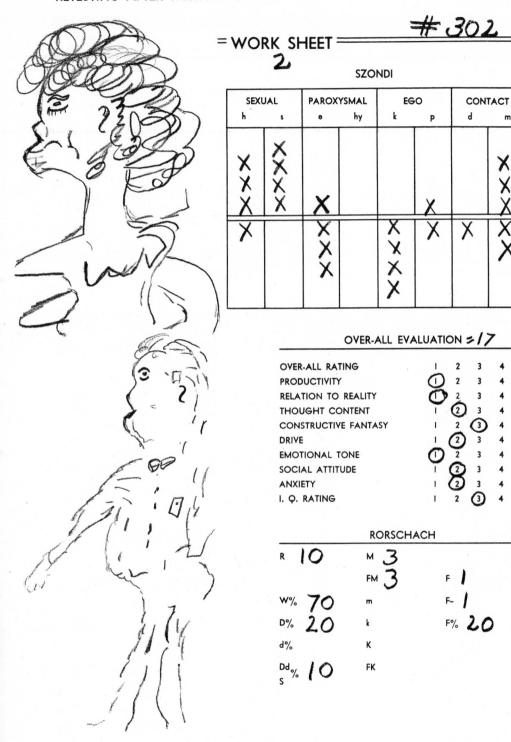

= WORK SHEET =  # 302

2

## SZONDI

| SEXUAL | | PAROXYSMAL | | EGO | | CONTACT | |
|---|---|---|---|---|---|---|---|
| h | s | e | hy | k | p | d | m |
| X X X X | X X X | X | | | X | | X X X |
| | X X X | X X X | | X X X | X | X | X X |

## OVER-ALL EVALUATION = 17

| | | | | | |
|---|---|---|---|---|---|
| OVER-ALL RATING | 1 | 2 | 3 | 4 | 5 |
| PRODUCTIVITY | ①| 2 | 3 | 4 | 5 |
| RELATION TO REALITY | ① | 2 | 3 | 4 | 5 |
| THOUGHT CONTENT | 1 | ② | 3 | 4 | 5 |
| CONSTRUCTIVE FANTASY | 1 | 2 | ③ | 4 | 5 |
| DRIVE | 1 | ② | 3 | 4 | 5 |
| EMOTIONAL TONE | ① | 2 | 3 | 4 | 5 |
| SOCIAL ATTITUDE | 1 | ② | 3 | 4 | 5 |
| ANXIETY | 1 | ② | 3 | 4 | 5 |
| I. Q. RATING | 1 | 2 | ③ | 4 | 5 |

## RORSCHACH

| | | | |
|---|---|---|---|
| R 10 | M 3 | | Fc 2 |
| | FM 3 | F 1 | c +1 |
| W% 70 | m | F- 1 | C' |
| D% 20 | k | F% 20 | FC |
| d% | K | | CF |
| Dd% 10 | FK | | C |
| S | | | |

**=WORK SHEET=**    **#301**

**1**

### SZONDI

| SEXUAL | | PAROXYSMAL | | EGO | | CONTACT | |
|---|---|---|---|---|---|---|---|
| h | s | e | hy | k | p | d | m |
| X | X | | | | | | |
| X | X | | | | | X | X |
| X | X | X | X | | | X | X |
| X | X | X | X | X | X | X | X |
| X | | X | | | X | | X |

---

### OVER-ALL EVALUATION = **25**

| | | | | | |
|---|---|---|---|---|---|
| OVER-ALL RATING | 1 | 2 | 3 | 4 | 5 |
| PRODUCTIVITY | 1 | 2 | ③ | 4 | 5 |
| RELATION TO REALITY | 1 | 2 | ③ | 4 | 5 |
| THOUGHT CONTENT | 1 | 2 | ③ | 4 | 5 |
| CONSTRUCTIVE FANTASY | 1 | ② | 3 | 4 | 5 |
| DRIVE | 1 | 2 | ③ | 4 | 5 |
| EMOTIONAL TONE | 1 | 2 | ③ | 4 | 5 |
| SOCIAL ATTITUDE | 1 | 2 | ③ | 4 | 5 |
| ANXIETY | 1 | 2 | ③ | 4 | 5 |
| I. Q. RATING | 1 | ② | 3 | 4 | 5 |

---

### RORSCHACH

| | | | | | | |
|---|---|---|---|---|---|---|
| R **32** | M **2** | | | | Fc **l** | |
| | FM **4+1** | F **18** | | c | | |
| W% **22** | m **1+1** | F- **l** | | C' | | |
| D% **47** | k | F% **59** | | FC **l** | | |
| d% **9** | K | | | CF **2+** | | |
| Dd% S **22** | FK **l** | | | c **l** | | |

# = WORK SHEET =
### 2
**# 301**

## SZONDI

| SEXUAL | | PAROXYSMAL | | EGO | | CONTACT | |
|---|---|---|---|---|---|---|---|
| h | s | e | hy | k | p | d | m |
| X X X | X | X X X | X X | | | X X X | X |
| | | X X X | X X X | X X X X | | X | X |

## OVER-ALL EVALUATION = **2.5**

| | | | | | |
|---|---|---|---|---|---|
| OVER-ALL RATING | 1 | 2 | 3 | 4 | 5 |
| PRODUCTIVITY | 1 | 2 | ③ | 4 | 5 |
| RELATION TO REALITY | 1 | 2 | ③ | 4 | 5 |
| THOUGHT CONTENT | 1 | 2 | ③ | 4 | 5 |
| CONSTRUCTIVE FANTASY | 1 | ② | 3 | 4 | 5 |
| DRIVE | 1 | 2 | ③ | 4 | 5 |
| EMOTIONAL TONE | 1 | ② | 3 | 4 | 5 |
| SOCIAL ATTITUDE | 1 | 2 | ③ | 4 | 5 |
| ANXIETY | 1 | 2 | ③ | 4 | 5 |
| I. Q. RATING | 1 | 2 | ③ | 4 | 5 |

## RORSCHACH

| | | | | | |
|---|---|---|---|---|---|
| R 35 | M 1 | | | | Fc 2 |
| | FM 4 | | F 24 | | c |
| W% 20 | m +1 | | F- 1 | | C' |
| D% 63 | k | | F% 71 | | FC 1 |
| d% 11 | K | | | | CF |
| Dd% 6 | FK 2 | | | | C |
| S | | | | | |

===== WORK SHEET ===== # 305 =====

1

## SZONDI

| SEXUAL | | PAROXYSMAL | | EGO | | CONTACT | |
|---|---|---|---|---|---|---|---|
| h | s | e | hy | k | p | d | m |
| X | | | | | | | |
| X | X | | | | | | |
| X | X | | | | | | |
| X | X | X | | X | X | X | X |
| | X | X | X | X | X | X | X |
| | X | X | X | | X | X | |

### OVER-ALL EVALUATION = 37

| | | | | | |
|---|---|---|---|---|---|
| OVER-ALL RATING | 1 | 2 | 3 | 4 | ⑤ |
| PRODUCTIVITY | 1 | 2 | 3 | 4 | ⑤ |
| RELATION TO REALITY | 1 | 2 | 3 | ④ | 5 |
| THOUGHT CONTENT | 1 | 2 | 3 | ④ | 5 |
| CONSTRUCTIVE FANTASY | 1 | 2 | 3 | 4 | ⑤ |
| DRIVE | 1 | 2 | ③ | 4 | 5 |
| EMOTIONAL TONE | 1 | 2 | 3 | ④ | 5 |
| SOCIAL ATTITUDE | 1 | 2 | 3 | ④ | 5 |
| ANXIETY | 1 | 2 | 3 | ④ | 5 |
| I. Q. RATING | 1 | 2 | 3 | ④ | 5 |

### RORSCHACH

| | | | |
|---|---|---|---|
| R 57 | M 16 | | Fc 5 |
| | FM 7 | F 14 | c 1 |
| W% 67 | m 4+2 | F- | C' 1+1 |
| D% 27 | k | F% 25 | FC 4+2 |
| d% 2 | K 1+2 | | CF 1+1 |
| Dd% 4 | FK 3+1 | | c |
| S | | | |

# = WORK SHEET = # 305

## 2

### SZONDI

| SEXUAL | | PAROXYSMAL | | EGO | | CONTACT | |
|---|---|---|---|---|---|---|---|
| h | s | e | hy | k | p | d | m |
| X | X | | | | | | |
| X | X | | | | | | |
| X | X | X | X | X | X | | X |
| | X | X | X | X | X | X | X |
| | | X | X X | | | | X X |
| | | | X | | | | X X |

OVER-ALL EVALUATION = 33

| | | | | | |
|---|---|---|---|---|---|
| OVER-ALL RATING | I | 2 | 3 | 4 | 5 |
| PRODUCTIVITY | I | 2 | ③ | 4 | 5 |
| RELATION TO REALITY | I | 2 | 3 | ④ | 5 |
| THOUGHT CONTENT | I | 2 | 3 | ④ | 5 |
| CONSTRUCTIVE FANTASY | I | 2 | 3 | 4 | ⑤ |
| DRIVE | I | ② | 3 | 4 | 5 |
| EMOTIONAL TONE | I | 2 | ③ | 4 | 5 |
| SOCIAL ATTITUDE | I | 2 | 3 | ④ | 5 |
| ANXIETY | I | 2 | 3 | ④ | 5 |
| I. Q. RATING | I | 2 | 3 | ④ | 5 |

### RORSCHACH

| R | 34 | M | 8 | | | Fc | 4 |
|---|---|---|---|---|---|---|---|
| | | FM | 3 | F | 11 | c | |
| W% | 47 | m | 2+1 | F- | | C' | 1 |
| D% | 44 | k | | F% | 32 | FC | 2 |
| d% | 6 | K | | | | CF | 1+1 |
| Dd% | 3 | FK | 2+1 | | | C | |
| S | | | | | | | |

Tables 3 and 4 list the detailed Rorschach scores of the twenty subjects retested after thirty days. A few general comments may be made to highlight the most characteristic findings and to contrast them in particular with the Rorschach scores of the 93 individuals retested after an extremely short time interval.

TABLE III.   "CORE" RESPONSES AND RESPONSES UNIQUE TO RORSCHACH RECORDS 1 AND 2; 20 SUBJECTS; TIME INTERVAL 30 DAYS.

| Code # | Core Responses | Responses Unique to Record 1 | Responses Unique to Record 2 |
|---|---|---|---|
| 3017 | 7 | 11 | 16 |
| 3010 | 8 | 0 | 11 |
| 3016 | 9 | 9 | 14 |
| 302 | 10 | 3 | 0 |
| 304 | 10 | 24 | 14 |
| 303 | 11 | 10 | 9 |
| 3011 | 12 | 5 | 6 |
| 3015 | 13 | 6 | 5 |
| 3019 | 14 | 9 | 20 |
| 3014 | 15 | 2 | 2 |
| 3012 | 17 | 24 | 2 |
| 306 | 17 | 8 | 13 |
| 301 | 17 | 15 | 18 |
| 307 | 18 | 15 | 10 |
| 3013 | 23 | 2 | 6 |
| 309 | 23 | 12 | 7 |
| 3020 | 24 | 17 | 6 |
| 305 | 26 | 31 | 8 |
| 3018 | 27 | 11 | 8 |
| 308 | 31 | 52 | 6 |
| Total | 332 | 266 | 181 |

Concerning R, one finds that the characteristic shift toward more responses in the second record is not nearly so marked here as in the group retested after a short time interval. Eleven individuals, or 55 per cent of the total group, have virtually the same number of responses in the second record; they fall within the same range of productivity when assessed by the criteria set up in Chapter III. Six individuals produced fewer responses on the second testing, while only three produced more. This is in contrast to the more than 70 per cent of short-time-interval cases having an increase in number of responses in the second record.

The group retested after thirty days shows a slightly higher percentage of individuals who retained the same type of mental approach during the second testing, while characteristic of the short-time-interval group was the shift away from W responses to a higher D, d, and dds per cent. However, it is true that insofar as there is a shift in this group, it is also in this same direction, from the general to the concrete. Thirteen cases, or 65 per cent, retained an identical mental approach, with seven showing the shift to greater specificity.

TABLE IV. DETAILED RORSCHACH SCORING FOR 20 SUBJECTS RETESTED AFTER 30 DAY INTERVAL.

| Code # | R (1) | R (2) | W% (1) | W% (2) | D% (1) | D% (2) | d% (1) | d% (2) | DdS% (1) | DdS% (2) | M (1) | M (2) | FM (1) | FM (2) | m (1) | m (2) | k (1) | k (2) | K (1) | K (2) | FK (1) | FK (2) | F (1) | F (2) | F- (1) | F- (2) | F% (1) | F% (2) | Fc (1) | Fc (2) | c (1) | c (2) | C' (1) | C' (2) | FC (1) | FC (2) | CF (1) | CF (2) | C (1) | C (2) |
|---|---|---|---|---|---|---|---|---|---|---|---|---|---|---|---|---|---|---|---|---|---|---|---|---|---|---|---|---|---|---|---|---|---|---|---|---|---|---|---|---|
| 309 | 35 | 30 | 29 | 23 | 51 | 53 |  |  | 20 | 3 | 3 | 4 | 1 | 1 |  |  |  |  |  | 1 |  |  | 21 | 18 |  |  | 60 | 60 | 1 | 1 |  |  |  |  | 1 | 1 | 3 | 3 | 2 |  |
| 3010 | 8 | 19 | 63 | 37 | 37 | 63 |  |  |  |  | 2 | 2 | 2 | 2 |  |  |  |  |  |  |  |  | 4 | 13 |  | 1 | 50 | 68 | 2 | 3 |  |  |  |  | 1 | 1 | 1 | 1 |  |  |
| 3011 | 17 | 18 | 64 | 61 | 22 | 24 |  | 4 | 17 | 18 | 4 | 2 |  | 2 |  |  |  |  |  |  |  |  | 5 | 7 |  | 1 | 35 | 44 | 5 | 2 |  |  |  |  | 1 | 1 | 4 | 2 |  |  |
| 3012 | 41 | 19 | 37 | 21 | 51 | 74 |  | 17 | 12 | 10 | 5 | 4 | 2 | 2 | 1 | 1 |  |  |  |  |  |  | 14 | 15 |  | 1 | 37 | 58 | 3 | 2 |  |  |  |  | 1 | 1 | 2 | 3 |  |  |
| 3013 | 25 | 29 | 24 | 17 | 52 | 63 |  | 3 | 17 | 10 | 10 | 5 | 4 | 2 | 1 | 2 |  | 1 |  |  |  | 1 | 13 | 9 | 1 | 1 | 52 | 52 | 5 | 2 |  |  |  |  | 1 | 1 | 1 | 1 |  |  |
| 3014 | 17 | 17 | 76 | 65 | 24 | 29 |  |  |  |  | 6 | 4 | 3 |  |  |  |  |  | 1 |  |  |  | 14 | 13 |  |  | 53 | 52 | 3 |  |  |  |  |  |  |  | 1 |  |  |  |
| 3015 | 19 | 18 | 63 | 33 | 37 | 61 |  |  | 5 | 6 | 5 | 5 | 3 | 2 |  |  |  |  | 2 |  |  |  | 5 | 10 |  |  | 47 | 61 |  |  |  |  |  |  | 1 | 1 | 2 | 1 |  |  |
| 3016 | 18 | 23 | 61 | 26 | 26 | 52 |  |  | 13 | 14 | 6 | 5 | 2 | 4 | 1 |  |  |  |  |  |  |  | 6 | 11 |  |  | 24 | 28 | 2 | 2 |  |  |  |  |  |  | 4 | 5 |  |  |
| 3017 | 18 | 23 | 94 | 33 | 6 | 52 |  |  |  |  | 3 | 4 | 2 | 3 |  |  |  |  |  |  |  |  | 9 | 10 |  |  | 47 | 33 |  |  |  |  |  |  |  |  | 4 | 8 |  |  |
| 3018 | 38 | 35 | 37 | 29 | 29 | 61 | 9 | 3 | 14 | 13 | 6 | 5 | 3 | 4 |  |  |  |  |  |  |  | 3 | 13 | 13 |  |  | 35 | 57 | 3 | 3 | 3 |  | 1 |  | 1 | 2 | 5 | 5 | 1 |  |
| 3019 | 23 | 23 | 61 | 33 | 13 | 52 | 11 |  | 9 | 6 | 13 | 4 | 4 | 2 |  |  |  |  |  |  |  |  | 31 | 23 |  |  | 63 | 66 |  |  |  |  |  |  |  |  | 2 |  |  |  |
| 3020 | 41 | 30 | 20 | 59 | 6 | 33 |  |  | 10 | 4 | 9 | 4 | 4 | 3 | 1 | 1 |  |  |  |  |  |  | 14 | 20 | 2 |  | 30 | 67 | 3 | 2 |  |  |  |  | 1 |  | 2 |  |  |  |
| 304 | 34 | 24 | 56 | 38 | 26 | 47 | 7 | 5 | 4 | 6 | 4 | 4 | 4 | 3 | 1 | 1 |  |  |  | 1 |  | 3 | 20 | 14 | 2 | 2 | 47 | 58 | 3 | 4 |  |  |  |  |  |  | 4 |  |  |  |
| 301 | 32 | 35 | 22 | 70 | 33 | 15 |  |  | 9 | 6 | 2 | 4 | 4 | 4 |  |  |  |  |  | 1 |  | 1 | 14 | 24 | 1 |  | 44 | 71 | 2 |  | 2 |  |  |  | 1 |  | 2 | 2 |  |  |
| 3022 | 13 | 10 | 85 | 70 | 7 | 15 |  |  | 2 | 11 | 4 | 8 | 1 |  |  |  |  |  |  |  |  | 1 | 4 | 1 | 1 |  | 30 | 39 |  |  |  |  |  |  | 1 | 1 | 1 |  |  |  |
| 303 | 21 | 30 | 36 | 17 | 15 | 47 |  |  | 3 | 3 | 9 | 9 | 3 | 3 | 1 | 1 |  |  |  |  |  |  | 11 | 1 | 1 | 2 | 52 | 59 |  |  |  |  |  |  | 1 | 1 | 4 | 3 |  |  |
| 306 | 25 | 20 | 57 | 25 | 48 | 29 |  |  | 10 | 23 | 6 | 2 |  |  | 1 | 1 |  |  | 1 | 1 |  |  | 27 | 1 |  |  | 76 | 52 | 1 | 2 |  |  |  |  | 1 | 1 | 2 | 4 |  |  |
| 307 | 33 | 25 | 30 | 24 | 61 | 48 | 4 | 8 | 20 | 10 | 2 | 2 |  |  |  |  | 2 |  |  |  |  |  | 18 | 25 | 1 |  | 85 | 55 | 1 | 2 |  |  | 1 | 1 |  |  | 2 |  |  |  |
| 305 | 57 | 34 | 67 | 47 | 27 | 44 | 2 | 6 | 8 | 6 | 2 | 2 |  |  | 1 |  |  |  |  |  |  | 2 | 14 | 22 | 1 | 1 | 25 | 88 | 5 | 5 | 1 |  | 1 |  | 3 | 5 | 1 |  |  |  |
| 308 | 83 | 37 | 11 | 14 | 64 | 64 | 7 | 5 | 16 | 18 | 1 | 1 |  |  | 4 | 2 |  |  | 1 | 3 |  | 2 | 68 | 27 | 2 | 1 | 76 |  | 5 | 1 | 1 |  | 1 | 1 | 3 | 1 | 2 |  |  | 1 |

We have already spoken about the surprising loss of M responses in the second record in those instances in which human movement answers were unusually frequent and lively, but a glance down the M column reveals that with the exception of these outstanding cases, the number of M responses remains remarkably constant. FM responses in the first and second records do not differ markedly, except in the few cases previously mentioned.

In considering the F per cent, we have taken a 5-point scale, grouping together those below 30%, 30-44%, 45-59%, 60-74%, and 75% and over. With this as a frame of reference, it will be found that 11 of the 20 subjects retain the same level throughout the testing, 6 show a shift toward greater constriction, while 3 move in the opposite direction. It should be noted, however, that the shifts are not large, and in only one instance is the transition more than from one classification to the next.

Shading responses will not be found to vary greatly except in a few instances. Number 308, for instance, loses four of the five original Fc's in the general trend toward a less rich and varied production which he shows in the second testing. When a response of this kind is absent in the first record, it is not apt to appear in the second.

Considering all the color responses together, we find that out of a total of 60 possible items, 39 or 65 per cent are identical in the second record. Where color is adequately represented in the first record, it will appear again in the second. Absence of a specific type of color response in the first record almost invariably finds the individual showing the same lack in the second testing.

An over-all estimate of this chart, both for individuals and the group as a whole, shows a striking similarity between the first and second performance in the Rorschach test when the test is repeated at the end of a thirty-day interval.

## VI. Retesting with a full battery after one year.

The passage of one year's time between testing sessions reduces the importance of mere repetition as a factor in the retest results and makes more influential the time interval itself. For purposes of comparison, it is useful to see how much change may be expected under ordinary life circumstances. Subjects Y1, Y2, Y3, Y4, Y5, and Y6 are the same age and were exposed, as freshmen, to the same external college environment in the year intervening between tests. While all claim to have been subjected to no untoward or unusually stressful experiences during the year, nonetheless we cannot consider this time interval as a void. Some opportunities for growth and some anxiety-producing experiences can be assumed to have occurred.

The statistical studies which we shall later present for large numbers of subjects retested after one-year, two-year and three-year intervals are not available at this time, but the six samples presented here give an indication of the variations which may be found. All subjects are males in their early twenties.

A comparison of the Work Sheets of Y1 (pages 84-85), retested following a year's interval, reveals a rather marked rise in I.Q., from 115 to 130. The pattern of the scattergram, however, remains the same; the relative positions of the tests have in no way changed. The Information test and memory for Digits remain the lowest, Comprehension stays in a medium position, while the Arithmetic and the Similarities are performed best of all.

The Szondi shows the same distribution in five of the eight factors, the hy and k being reversed in terms of tension and discharge.

The Figure Drawings on each occasion were rated as approximately 2+. Although the form of expression differs, feelings of personal inadequacy are reflected on both occasions.

The Rorschach shows a typical shift in terms of a greater number of R and a decrease in the W per cent, with greater emphasis on D. The F per cent, in this instance, indicates slightly greater constriction, and the second record also reflects a decrease in responsiveness to color. The number of core responses, in this instance, is 23; 9 answers are unique to the first record and 22 to the second.

Y2 (pages 86-87) also shows a rise in I.Q. with, in this case, a minor change in the pattern of the scattergram. This is carried by the rise in the Arithmetic score in the second testing; otherwise, the relation of the five subtests remains the same.

In the Szondi, Y2 appears slightly more anxious and tense, but the difference in the two profiles is not marked.

There is an improvement in the Figure Drawing in the sense that now the whole individual is envisaged in the concept, draw a person.

While we may discard as unimportant the increase in the total number of R in the second Rorschach record of Y2 and consider as also unnoteworthy the decrease in W responses and increase in d and dds, the changes from 5 to 11 M, the increase in the F per cent, and the decrease in CF and C cannot be dismissed so readily. Core responses are 27, with 15 answers unique to Record 1 and 38 introduced as unique to Record 2. It would appear, in terms of this new constellation, as if this individual had grown during the year toward greater maturity, less impulsivity and egocentricity. The change is not spectacular but it is in the direction that would be expected assuming that the environment, physical and psychological, in which this individual found himself permitted normal maturation. The only corroborating evidence we have in this case is that Y2's academic grades were better at the time of the second testing.

The scattergram of Y3 (pages 88-89) has a characteristic and distinctive pattern which is retained, except for the rise in the Similarities score, in the second test. Digit Memory proves to be unusually difficult for this individual; conversely, his arithmetical ability is outstanding. A rise of six points in the Similarities is achieved by answers indicating a much more careful and less slap-dash approach to the test situation.

Whereas initially the male figure was drawn without features, and again one may use the word carelessly, there is a marked advance and willingness to be identified, to have a face to present toward the public, in the second attempt. Characteristic of both drawings is the long, fawn-like neck and the fact that only heads are drawn. The line, however, is much firmer and more definite in the second drawing.

The Rorschach shows the expected shift in the direction of fewer W responses, and in the second record two F− answers have dropped out and there are included five animal responses with good movement, which give some liveliness to the record which was previously lacking. The number of core responses is 14, with 37 answers unique to Record 1 and 44 found only in Record 2.

As will be seen from the Work Sheets of Y4 (pages 90-91), we find here the only markedly different scattergram following the year's interval. Scores on the Comprehension have dropped, which is unusual, while the arithmetical problems are handled with ease and rapidity where previously they evoked confusion and anxiety.

The Rorschach record reflects a marked introversial swing, with a rise in the M responses from 2 to 7 and a dropping out of the 2 CF responses obtained in the first record. The core responses, in this instance, were only 8, with 20 answers unique to the first and 35 unique to the second record. The drawings have changed in style and reflect different psychological conflicts, as does the Szondi.

The personal signature of Y5 is written all over his Rorschach record. Both records (pages 92-93) contain an unusually large number of responses. Particularly striking is the perpetuation of his highly individualized mental approach, with its 32 and 31 per cent dds responses. The distribution of the determinants in the psychogram is also very similar after the year's interval. Although in the second year Y5 has lost three of his FC responses, the picture is still an emotionally lively one, the six M responses and the F per cent being sufficiently stabilizing to offset the three CF responses.

Although superficially different, both attempts to draw the female figure are grotesque caricatures which avoid coming to grips with the feminine form in its more natural aspects.

The only real difference in the scattergram is the greater facility in the Digit Memory, which raises this score sufficiently so that the I.Q. of Y5 is now rated in the *Very Superior Group.* This rise in I.Q., and the addition of one M response is sufficient to alter the quantitative rating from 30 to 32.

Despite the unusual number of responses in these records, there are only eight core responses, or responses identical to both. Thus, the essentially similar pattern of psychic reactivity as reflected in the psychogram is repeated with virtually new content one year after the first testing.

Y6 (pages 94-95), one year after the first test, shows his "trademark" clearly in the Szondi, Wechsler and Figure Drawings. The Szondi contains six of the eight original scores, +h, +s, +e, −hy, −k and −m. The sharp drop on the Comprehension in the Wechsler still characterizes the scattergram. Greater facility in handling the arithmetical problems is the sole cause of the improvement in total score.

The concept of the woman, as reflected in the Figure Drawing, has undergone virtually no change. There is a pupil-less eye in the first and an exaggeration of eyelash detail in the second, but the general treatment of the figures is almost identical.

On the Rorschach, however, a genuine change is shown. Y6 has come out of his shell to the extent that in the place of lack of all color responses he now achieves a Sum C of 4.5. He is freer in his associative material and more relaxed; the second record incorporates much of the first but new material is added. Nine of the original 14 Rorschach responses appear again in Record 2.

On the quantitative scale Y6 gains five points, from an OVER-ALL EVALUATION of 26 to 31.

# WORK SHEET

Y₁

#1

## VERBAL I. Q.

| EWS | Info. | Comp. | Digit | Arith. | Sim. |
|-----|-------|-------|-------|--------|------|
| 18 | 25 | 20 | | 14 | 23-24 |
| 17 | 24 | 19 | 17 | 13 | 21-22 |
| 16 | 23 | 18 | 16 | 12 | 20 |
| 15 | 21-22 | 17 | | (11) | 19 |
| 14 | 20 | 16 | 15 | | (17-18) |
| 13 | 18-19 | 15 | 14 | 10 | 16 |
| 12 | 17 | (14) | | 9 | 15 |
| | | | | | |
| 11 | (15-16 | 12-13 | 13 | | 13-14 |
| 10 | (13-14) | 11 | (12 | 8 | 12 |
| 9 | 12 | 10 | (11) | 7 | 11 |
| 8 | 10-11 | 9 | | | 9-10 |
| 7 | 9 | 8 | 10 | 6 | 8 |
| 6 | 7-8 | 7 | 9 | 5 | 7 |
| | | | | | |
| 5 | 6 | 5-6 | | | 5-6 |
| 4 | 4-5 | 4 | 8 | 4 | 4 |
| 3 | 2-3 | 3 | 7 | 3 | 3 |
| 2 | 1 | 2 | 6 | | 1-2 |
| 1 | 0 | 1 | | 2 | 0 |
| 0 | | 0 | 5 | 1 | |

## SZONDI

| SEXUAL | | PAROXYSMAL | | EGO | | CONTACT | |
|--------|--------|------------|--------|--------|--------|---------|--------|
| h | s | e | hy | k | p | d | m |
| | | | | | | | X |
| | | | | | X | | X |
| X | | | | X | X | | X |
| X | X | | | X | X | | X |
| X | X | X | X | X | | X | X |
| X | X | | | X | | X | |
| X | | | | | | | |

## OVER-ALL EVALUATION = 25

| | | | | | |
|--|--|--|--|--|--|
| OVER-ALL RATING | 1 | 2 | 3 | 4 | 5 |
| PRODUCTIVITY | 1 | 2 | (3) | 4 | 5 |
| RELATION TO REALITY | 1 | (2) | 3 | 4 | 5 |
| THOUGHT CONTENT | 1 | 2 | (3) | 4 | 5 |
| CONSTRUCTIVE FANTASY | 1 | 2 | (3) | 4 | 5 |
| DRIVE | 1 | 2 | (3) | 4 | 5 |
| EMOTIONAL TONE | 1 | 2 | (3) | 4 | 5 |
| SOCIAL ATTITUDE | 1 | (2) | 3 | 4 | 5 |
| ANXIETY | 1 | 2 | (3) | 4 | 5 |
| I. Q. RATING  115 | 1 | 2 | (3) | 4 | 5 |

## RORSCHACH

| | | | |
|--|--|--|--|
| R 30 | M 4 | | Fc |
| | FM 3 | F 15 | c 1+3 |
| W% 30 | m 2 | F- | C' |
| D% 53 | k 1 | F% 50 | FC 4 |
| d% 7 | K | | CF +1 |
| Dd%/S 10 | FK | | c +1 |

# WORK SHEET

Y₁

## # 2

### VERBAL I. Q.

| EWS | Info. | Comp. | Digit | Arith. | Sim. |
|-----|-------|-------|-------|--------|------|
| 18 | 25 | 20 | | 14 | 23-24 |
| 17 | 24 | 19 | 17 | 13 | 21-22 |
| 16 | 23 | 18 | 16 | 12 | 20 |
| 15 | 21-22 | 17 | | 11 | 19 |
| 14 | 20 | 16 | 15 | | 17-18 |
| 13 | 18-19 | 15 | 14 | 10 | 16 |
| 12 | 17 | 14 | | 9 | 15 |
| | | | | | |
| 11 | 15-16 | 12-13 | | | 13-14 |
| 10 | 13-14 | 11 | 12 | 8 | 12 |
| 9 | 12 | 10 | 11 | 7 | 11 |
| 8 | 10-11 | 9 | | | 9-10 |
| 7 | 9 | 8 | 10 | 6 | 8 |
| 6 | 7-8 | 7 | 9 | 5 | 7 |
| | | | | | |
| 5 | 6 | 5-6 | | | 5-6 |
| 4 | 4-5 | 4 | 8 | 4 | 4 |
| 3 | 2-3 | 3 | 7 | 3 | 3 |
| 2 | 1 | 2 | 6 | | 1-2 |
| 1 | 0 | 1 | | 2 | 0 |
| 0 | | 0 | 5 | 1 | |

### SZONDI

| SEXUAL | | PAROXYSMAL | | EGO | | CONTACT | |
|--------|---|------------|----|-----|---|---------|---|
| h | s | e | hy | k | p | d | m |
| | | | | | | | X |
| | | | | | X | | X X |
| | | | | | X | | X |
| X | | | | X | X | X | X |
| X | X | | | | | | |
| X | X | X | X | X | X | | X |
| X | X | | X | | | | |
| | | | X | | | | |
| | | | X | | | | |

### OVER-ALL EVALUATION = 29

| | | | | | |
|---|---|---|---|---|---|
| OVER-ALL RATING | 1 | 2 | 3 | 4 | 5 |
| PRODUCTIVITY | 1 | 2 | 3 | ④ | 5 |
| RELATION TO REALITY | 1 | ② | 3 | 4 | 5 |
| THOUGHT CONTENT | 1 | 2 | ③ | 4 | 5 |
| CONSTRUCTIVE FANTASY | 1 | 2 | ③ | 4 | 5 |
| DRIVE | 1 | 2 | ③ | 4 | 5 |
| EMOTIONAL TONE | 1 | 2 | ③ | 4 | 5 |
| SOCIAL ATTITUDE | 1 | 2 | ③ | 4 | 5 |
| ANXIETY | 1 | 2 | ③ | 4 | 5 |
| I. Q. RATING     130 | 1 | 2 | 3 | 4 | ⑤ |

### RORSCHACH

| R | 45 | M | 4 | | | Fc | 1 |
|---|----|---|---|---|---|----|----|
| | | FM | 4 | F | 30 | c | 1+1 |
| W% | 16 | m | 1+1 | F- | | C' | 1 |
| D% | 64 | k | | F% | 67 | FC | 3 |
| d% | 11 | K | | | | CF | |
| Dd% | 9 | FK | | | | C | |
| S | | | | | | | |

# WORK SHEET

½

#1

## VERBAL I. Q.

| EWS | Info. | Comp. | Digit | Arith. | Sim. |
|---|---|---|---|---|---|
| 18 | 25 | 20 | | 14 | 23-24 |
| 17 | 24 | 19 | 17 | 13 | 21-22 |
| 16 | 23 | 18 | 16 | 12 | (20) |
| 15 | 21-22 | 17 | | 11 | 19 |
| 14 | 20 | (16) | (15) | | 17-18 |
| 13 | 18-19 | 15 | 14 | 10 | 16 |
| 12 | 17 | 14 | | 9 | 15 |
| 11 | (15-16) | 12-13 | 13 | | 13-14 |
| 10 | 13-14 | 11 | 12 | (8) | 12 |
| 9 | 12 | 10 | 11 | 7 | 11 |
| 8 | 10-11 | 9 | | | 9-10 |
| 7 | 9 | 8 | 10 | 6 | 8 |
| 6 | 7-8 | 7 | 9 | 5 | 7 |
| 5 | 6 | 5-6 | | | 5-6 |
| 4 | 4-5 | 4 | 8 | 4 | 4 |
| 3 | 2-3 | 3 | 7 | 3 | 3 |
| 2 | 1 | 2 | 6 | | 1-2 |
| 1 | 0 | 1 | | 2 | 0 |
| 0 | | 0 | 5 | 1 | |

## SZONDI

| SEXUAL | | PAROXYSMAL | | EGO | | CONTACT | |
|---|---|---|---|---|---|---|---|
| h | s | e | hy | k | p | d | m |
| | | | | | | | X |
| | | | | X | X | X | X |
| | X | X | X | X | X | X | X |
| X | | X | X | X | | X | X |
| X | | | X | X | | X | |
| | | | X | X | | | |

## OVER-ALL EVALUATION = 31

| | | | | | |
|---|---|---|---|---|---|
| OVER-ALL RATING | 1 | 2 | 3 | 4 | 5 |
| PRODUCTIVITY | 1 | 2 | 3 | (4) | 5 |
| RELATION TO REALITY | 1 | 2 | (3) | 4 | 5 |
| THOUGHT CONTENT | 1 | 2 | (3) | 4 | 5 |
| CONSTRUCTIVE FANTASY | 1 | 2 | (3) | 4 | 5 |
| DRIVE | 1 | 2 | 3 | (4) | 5 |
| EMOTIONAL TONE | 1 | 2 | 3 | (4) | 5 |
| SOCIAL ATTITUDE | 1 | 2 | (3) | 4 | 5 |
| ANXIETY | 1 | 2 | (3) | 4 | 5 |
| I. Q. RATING   121 | 1 | 2 | 3 | (4) | 5 |

## RORSCHACH

| R 42 | M 5 | | Fc 3+1 |
|---|---|---|---|
| | FM 9 | F 10 | c 2+1 |
| W% 40 | m 4+2 | F- | C' |
| D% 52 | k +4 | F% 24 | FC 3 |
| d% 5 | K | | CF 2+1 |
| Dd% 3 S | FK 3+1 | | c 1+1 |

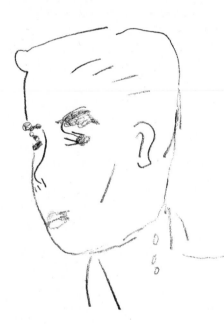

# WORK SHEET
## # 2

Y2

### VERBAL I. Q.

| EWS | Info. | Comp. | Digit | Arith. | Sim. |
|---|---|---|---|---|---|
| 18 | 25 | 20 | | 14 | 23-24 |
| 17 | 24 | 19 | 17 | 13 | 21-22 |
| 16 | 23 | 18 | 16 | 12 | 20 |
| 15 | 21-22 | 17 | | 11 | 19 |
| 14 | 20 | 16 | 15 | | 17-18 |
| 13 | 18-19 | 15 | 14 | 10 | 16 |
| 12 | 17 | 14 | | 9 | 15 |
| 11 | 15-16 | 12-13 | 13 | | 13-14 |
| 10 | 13-14 | 11 | 12 | 8 | 12 |
| 9 | 12 | 10 | 11 | 7 | 11 |
| 8 | 10-11 | 9 | | | 9-10 |
| 7 | 9 | 8 | 10 | 6 | 8 |
| 6 | 7-8 | 7 | 9 | 5 | 7 |
| 5 | 6 | 5-6 | | | 5-6 |
| 4 | 4-5 | 4 | 8 | 4 | 4 |
| 3 | 2-3 | 3 | 7 | 3 | 3 |
| 2 | 1 | 2 | 6 | | 1-2 |
| 1 | 0 | 1 | | 2 | 0 |
| 0 | | 0 | 5 | 1 | |

### SZONDI

| SEXUAL | | PAROXYSMAL | | EGO | | CONTACT | |
|---|---|---|---|---|---|---|---|
| h | s | e | hy | k | p | d | m |
| | | | | | | | X |
| | | | | | | | X |
| | | | | | | | X |
| | X | | | | X | | X |
| X | X | X | | X | X | X | X |
| | | X | X | X | X | X | X |
| | | X | X | X | | X | |
| | | X | | X | | | |

### OVER-ALL EVALUATION = 35

| | 1 | 2 | 3 | 4 | 5 |
|---|---|---|---|---|---|
| OVER-ALL RATING | 1 | 2 | 3 | 4 | 5 |
| PRODUCTIVITY | 1 | 2 | 3 | (4) | 5 |
| RELATION TO REALITY | 1 | 2 | 3 | (4) | 5 |
| THOUGHT CONTENT | 1 | 2 | 3 | (4) | 5 |
| CONSTRUCTIVE FANTASY | 1 | 2 | 3 | 4 | (5) |
| DRIVE | 1 | 2 | 3 | (4) | 5 |
| EMOTIONAL TONE | 1 | 2 | (3) | 4 | 5 |
| SOCIAL ATTITUDE | 1 | 2 | (3) | 4 | 5 |
| ANXIETY | 1 | 2 | (3) | 4 | 5 |
| I. Q. RATING   132 | 1 | 2 | 3 | 4 | (5) |

### RORSCHACH

R 65   M 11   Fc 3

FM 8   F 30   c +1

W% 26   m 5+1   F-   c' +1

D% 52   k +4   F% 46   FC 2

d% 14   K 1   CF 1+1

Dd% 8   FK 4   c +1

S

## WORK SHEET Y3

### # 1

### VERBAL I. Q.

| EWS | Info. | Comp. | Digit | Arith. | Sim. |
|-----|-------|-------|-------|--------|------|
| 18 | 25 | 20 | | 14 | 23-24 |
| 17 | 24 | 19 | 17 | 13 | 21-22 |
| 16 | 23 | 18 | 16 | 12 | 20 |
| 15 | 21-22 | 17 | | 11 | 19 |
| 14 | 20 | 16 | 15 | | 17-18 |
| 13 | 18-19 | 15 | 14 | 10 | 16 |
| 12 | 17 | 14 | | 9 | 15 |
| 11 | 15-16 | 12-13 | 13 | | 13-14 |
| 10 | 13-14 | 11 | 12 | 8 | 12 |
| 9 | 12 | 10 | | 7 | 11 |
| 8 | 10-11 | 9 | | | 9-10 |
| 7 | 9 | 8 | 10 | 6 | 8 |
| 6 | 7-8 | 7 | 9 | 5 | 7 |
| 5 | 6 | 5-6 | | | 5-6 |
| 4 | 4-5 | 4 | 8 | 4 | 4 |
| 3 | 2-3 | 3 | 7 | 3 | 3 |
| 2 | 1 | 2 | 6 | | 1-2 |
| 1 | 0 | 1 | | 2 | 0 |
| 0 | | 0 | 5 | 1 | |

### SZONDI

| SEXUAL | | PAROXYSMAL | | EGO | | CONTACT | |
|---|---|---|---|---|---|---|---|
| h | s | e | hy | k | p | d | m |

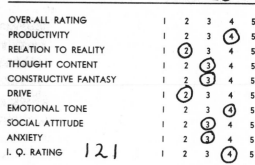

### OVER-ALL EVALUATION = 28

| | 1 | 2 | 3 | 4 | 5 |
|---|---|---|---|---|---|
| OVER-ALL RATING | 1 | 2 | 3 | 4 | 5 |
| PRODUCTIVITY | 1 | 2 | 3 | (4) | 5 |
| RELATION TO REALITY | 1 | (2) | 3 | 4 | 5 |
| THOUGHT CONTENT | 1 | 2 | (3) | 4 | 5 |
| CONSTRUCTIVE FANTASY | 1 | 2 | (3) | 4 | 5 |
| DRIVE | 1 | (2) | 3 | 4 | 5 |
| EMOTIONAL TONE | 1 | 2 | 3 | (4) | 5 |
| SOCIAL ATTITUDE | 1 | 2 | (3) | 4 | 5 |
| ANXIETY | 1 | 2 | (3) | 4 | 5 |
| I. Q. RATING 121 | 1 | 2 | 3 | (4) | 5 |

### RORSCHACH

| R 51 | M 4 | | Fc 7 |
|---|---|---|---|
| | FM 0 | F 28 | c 2 |
| W% 24 | m +4 | F- 2 | C' 3 |
| D% 35 | k | F% 59 | FC 3 |
| d% 22 | K +1 | | CF 2 |
| Dd% 19 | FK | | C |
| S | | | |

# WORK SHEET

## # 2

### VERBAL I. Q.

| EWS | Info. | Comp. | Digit | Arith. | Sim. |
|-----|-------|-------|-------|--------|------|
| 18 | 25 | 20 | | (14) | 23-24 |
| 17 | 24 | 19 | 17 | | (21-22) |
| 16 | 23 | 18 | 16 | 12 | 20 |
| 15 | (21-22) | 17 | | 11 | 19 |
| 14 | 20 | (16) | 15 | | 17-18 |
| 13 | 18-19 | 15 | 14 | 10 | 16 |
| 12 | 17 | 14 | | 9 | 15 |
| | | | | | |
| 11 | 15-16 | 12-13 | 13 | | 13-14 |
| 10 | 13-14 | 11 | (12) | 8 | 12 |
| 9 | 12 | 10 | 11 | 7 | 11 |
| 8 | 10-11 | 9 | | | 9-10 |
| 7 | 9 | 8 | 10 | 6 | 8 |
| 6 | 7-8 | 7 | 9 | 5 | 7 |
| | | | | | |
| 5 | 6 | 5-6 | | | 5-6 |
| 4 | 4-5 | 4 | 8 | 4 | 4 |
| 3 | 2-3 | 3 | 7 | 3 | 3 |
| 2 | 1 | 2 | 6 | | 1-2 |
| 1 | 0 | 1 | | 2 | 0 |
| 0 | | 0 | 5 | 1 | |

### SZONDI

| SEXUAL | | PAROXYSMAL | | EGO | | CONTACT | |
|--------|--------|-----|-----|-----|-----|-----|-----|
| h | s | e | hy | k | p | d | m |
| | | | | | | | |
| X | | | | | | | |
| X | X | | | | X | | |
| X | X | X | X | X | X | X | X |
| X | X | X | | | X | X | X |
| X | X | X | | X | X | X | X |
| | X | | | | | | X |

### OVER-ALL EVALUATION = *31*

| | | | | | |
|---|---|---|---|---|---|
| OVER-ALL RATING | 1 | 2 | 3 | 4 | 5 |
| PRODUCTIVITY | 1 | 2 | 3 | (4) | 5 |
| RELATION TO REALITY | 1 | 2 | (3) | 4 | 5 |
| THOUGHT CONTENT | 1 | 2 | (3) | 4 | 5 |
| CONSTRUCTIVE FANTASY | 1 | 2 | (3) | 4 | 5 |
| DRIVE | 1 | 2 | (3) | 4 | 5 |
| EMOTIONAL TONE | 1 | 2 | 3 | (4) | 5 |
| SOCIAL ATTITUDE | 1 | 2 | (3) | 4 | 5 |
| ANXIETY | 1 | 2 | (3) | 4 | 5 |
| I. Q. RATING *133* | 1 | 2 | 3 | 4 | (5) |

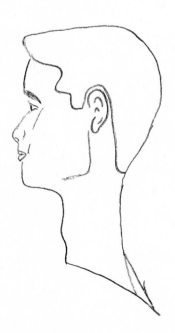

### RORSCHACH

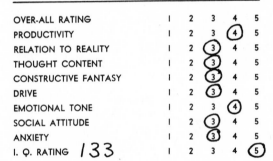

| | | |
|---|---|---|
| R *58* | M *3* | Fc *4* |
| | FM *5* | F *37* | c *+3* |
| W% *5* | m *+2* | F- | C' *2* |
| D% *47* | k | F% *64* | FC *3* |
| d% *26* | K *2* | | CF *2* |
| Dd% *22* | FK | | C |
| S | | |

# WORK SHEET = 1/4

## # 1

## VERBAL I. Q.

| EWS | Info. | Comp. | Digit | Arith. | Sim. |
|---|---|---|---|---|---|
| 18 | 25 | 20 | | 14 | 23-24 |
| 17 | 24 | 19 | 17 | 13 | 21-22 |
| 16 | 23 | 18 | 16 | 12 | 20 |
| 15 | 21-22 | 17 | | 11 | 19 |
| 14 | 20 | 16 | 15 | | 17-18 |
| 13 | 18-19 | 15 | 14 | 10 | 16 |
| 12 | 17 | 14 | | 9 | 15 |
| | | | | | |
| 11 | 15-16 | 12-13 | 13 | | 13-14 |
| 10 | 13-14 | 11 | 12 | 8 | 12 |
| 9 | 12 | 10 | 11 | 7 | 11 |
| 8 | 10-11 | 9 | | | 9-10 |
| 7 | 9 | 8 | 10 | 6 | 8 |
| 6 | 7-8 | 7 | 9 | 5 | 7 |
| | | | | | |
| 5 | 6 | 5-6 | | | 5-6 |
| 4 | 4-5 | 4 | 8 | 4 | 4 |
| 3 | 2-3 | 3 | 7 | 3 | 3 |
| 2 | 1 | 2 | 6 | | 1-2 |
| 1 | 0 | 1 | | 2 | 0 |
| 0 | | 0 | 5 | 1 | |

## SZONDI

| SEXUAL | | PAROXYSMAL | | EGO | | CONTACT | |
|---|---|---|---|---|---|---|---|
| h | s | e | hy | k | p | d | m |
| | | | | | X | | |
| X | X | X | | | X | X | |
| X | X | X | X | | X | X | |
| X | X | X | X | X | | X | X |
| X | X | | X | X | | X | |

### OVER-ALL EVALUATION = 28

| | 1 | 2 | 3 | 4 | 5 |
|---|---|---|---|---|---|
| OVER-ALL RATING | 1 | 2 | ③ | 4 | 5 |
| PRODUCTIVITY | 1 | 2 | ③ | 4 | 5 |
| RELATION TO REALITY | 1 | 2 | ③ | 4 | 5 |
| THOUGHT CONTENT | 1 | 2 | ③ | 4 | 5 |
| CONSTRUCTIVE FANTASY | 1 | ② | 3 | 4 | 5 |
| DRIVE | 1 | 2 | ③ | 4 | 5 |
| EMOTIONAL TONE | 1 | 2 | ③ | 4 | 5 |
| SOCIAL ATTITUDE | 1 | 2 | ③ | 4 | 5 |
| ANXIETY | 1 | 2 | 3 | ④ | 5 |
| I. Q. RATING 127 | 1 | 2 | 3 | ④ | 5 |

### RORSCHACH

R 28     M 2            Fc 2

FM 3     F 13     c 2+2

W% 11     m 2     F-     C'

D% 64     k 1     F% 46     FC 1

d% 4     K     CF 2

Dd% / S 21     FK     c +1

# WORK SHEET

**# 2**

Y4

## VERBAL I. Q.

| EWS | Info. | Comp. | Digit | Arith. | Sim. |
|-----|-------|-------|-------|--------|------|
| 18 | 25 | 20 | | (14) | (23-24) |
| 17 | 24 | 19 | (17) | 13 | 21-22 |
| 16 | 23 | 18 | 16 | 12 | 20 |
| 15 | 21-22 | 17 | | 11 | 19 |
| 14 | (20) | 16 | 15 | | 17-18 |
| 13 | 18-19 | 15 | 14 | 10 | 16 |
| 12 | 17 | 14 | | 9 | 15 |
| | | | | | |
| 11 | 15-16 | (12-13) | 13 | | 13-14 |
| 10 | 13-14 | 11 | 12 | 8 | 12 |
| 9 | 12 | 10 | 11 | 7 | 11 |
| 8 | 10-11 | 9 | | | 9-10 |
| 7 | 9 | 8 | 10 | 6 | 8 |
| 6 | 7-8 | 7 | 9 | 5 | 7 |
| | | | | | |
| 5 | 6 | 5-6 | | | 5-6 |
| 4 | 4-5 | 4 | 8 | 4 | 4 |
| 3 | 2-3 | 3 | 7 | 3 | 3 |
| 2 | 1 | 2 | 6 | | 1-2 |
| 1 | 0 | 1 | 5 | 2 | 0 |
| 0 | | 0 | | 1 | |

## SZONDI

| SEXUAL | | PAROXYSMAL | | EGO | | CONTACT | |
|--------|---|------------|----|-----|---|---------|---|
| h | s | e | hy | k | p | d | m |
| X | X | X | X | | | | X |
| X | X | X | X | | X | X | X |
| | | | X | X | X | X | X |
| | | | | X | X | X | X |
| | | | | X | X | | X |

## OVER-ALL EVALUATION = 30

| | 1 | 2 | 3 | 4 | 5 |
|---|---|---|---|---|---|
| OVER-ALL RATING | 1 | 2 | 3 | 4 | 5 |
| PRODUCTIVITY | 1 | 2 | 3 | (4) | 5 |
| RELATION TO REALITY | 1 | 2 | (3) | 4 | 5 |
| THOUGHT CONTENT | 1 | 2 | (3) | 4 | 5 |
| CONSTRUCTIVE FANTASY | 1 | 2 | 3 | (4) | 5 |
| DRIVE | 1 | 2 | (3) | 4 | 5 |
| EMOTIONAL TONE | 1 | (2) | 3 | 4 | 5 |
| SOCIAL ATTITUDE | 1 | 2 | (3) | 4 | 5 |
| ANXIETY | 1 | 2 | (3) | 4 | 5 |
| I. Q. RATING  137 | 1 | 2 | 3 | 4 | (5) |

## RORSCHACH

| R  40 | M 7 | | Fc 1 |
|-------|------|------|------|
| | FM 1 | F 26 | c |
| W% 8 | m 2 | F- | C' 1 |
| D% 63 | k | F% 65 | FC 2 |
| d% 10 | K | | CF |
| Dd% 19 S | FK | | C |

## WORK SHEET  Y5
1

### VERBAL I. Q. = 127

| EWS | Info. | Comp. | Digit | Arith. | Sim. |
|---|---|---|---|---|---|
| 18 | 25 | 20 | | (14) | 23-24 |
| 17 | 24 | 19 | 17 | 13 | 21-22 |
| 16 | 23 | 18 | 16 | 12 | (20) |
| 15 | 21-22 | (17) | | 11 | 19 |
| 14 | 20 | 16 | 15 | | 17-18 |
| 13 | 18-19 | 15 | 14 | 10 | 16 |
| 12 | (17) | 14 | | 9 | 15 |
| 11 | 15-16 | 12-13 | 3 | | 13-14 |
| 10 | 13-14 | 11 | 12 | 8 | 12 |
| 9 | 12 | 10 | (11) | 7 | 11 |
| 8 | 10-11 | 9 | | | 9-10 |
| 7 | 9 | 8 | 10 | 6 | 8 |
| 6 | 7-8 | 7 | 9 | 5 | 7 |
| 5 | 6 | 5-6 | | | 5-6 |
| 4 | 4-5 | 4 | 8 | 4 | 4 |
| 3 | 2-3 | 3 | 7 | 3 | 3 |
| 2 | 1 | 2 | 6 | | 1-2 |
| 1 | 0 | 1 | | 2 | 0 |
| 0 | | 0 | 5 | 1 | |

### SZONDI

| SEXUAL | | PAROXYSMAL | | EGO | | CONTACT | |
|---|---|---|---|---|---|---|---|
| h | s | e | hy | k | p | d | m |
| | | | | | X | | |
| | | X | | | X | | |
| X | | X | | | X | | X |
| X | | X | | | X | X | X |
| X | X | X | X | X | X | X | X |
| | X | | X | | | | X |
| | X | | | | | | |

### OVER-ALL EVALUATION = 30

| | 1 | 2 | 3 | 4 | 5 |
|---|---|---|---|---|---|
| OVER-ALL RATING | 1 | 2 | 3 | 4 | 5 |
| PRODUCTIVITY | 1 | (2) | 3 | 4 | 5 |
| RELATION TO REALITY | 1 | 2 | 3 | (4) | 5 |
| THOUGHT CONTENT | 1 | 2 | 3 | (4) | 5 |
| CONSTRUCTIVE FANTASY | 1 | 2 | (3) | 4 | 5 |
| DRIVE | 1 | (2) | 3 | 4 | 5 |
| EMOTIONAL TONE | 1 | 2 | 3 | (4) | 5 |
| SOCIAL ATTITUDE | 1 | 2 | (3) | 4 | 5 |
| ANXIETY | 1 | 2 | 3 | (4) | 5 |
| I. Q. RATING = 127 | 1 | 2 | 3 | (4) | 5 |

### RORSCHACH

| | | | |
|---|---|---|---|
| R 74 | M 5 | | Fc 3 |
| | FM 3 | F 38 | c 1 |
| W% 18 | m 3+1 | F- 5 | C' 3 |
| D% 31 | k 2 | F% 58 | FC 5 |
| d% 19 | K | | CF 3 |
| Dd% 32 | FK 2 | | c 1 |
| S | | | |

# WORK SHEET

Y5

2

## VERBAL I. Q. = 132

| EWS | Info. | Comp. | Digit | Arith. | Sim. |
|-----|-------|-------|-------|--------|------|
| 18 | 25 | 20 | | 14 | 23-24 |
| 17 | 24 | 19 | 17 | 13 | 21-22 |
| 16 | 23 | 18 | 16 | 12 | 20 |
| 15 | 21-22 | 17 | | 11 | 19 |
| 14 | 20 | 16 | 15 | | 17-18 |
| 13 | 18-19 | 15 | 14 | 10 | 16 |
| 12 | 17 | 14 | | 9 | 15 |
| 11 | 15-16 | 12-13 | 13 | | 13-14 |
| 10 | 13-14 | 11 | 12 | 8 | 12 |
| 9 | 12 | 10 | 11 | 7 | 11 |
| 8 | 10-11 | 9 | | | 9-10 |
| 7 | 9 | 8 | 10 | 6 | 8 |
| 6 | 7-8 | 7 | 9 | 5 | 7 |

## SZONDI

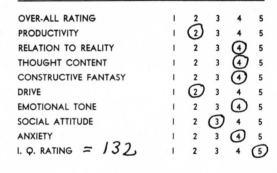

| SEXUAL | | PAROXYSMAL | | EGO | | CONTACT | |
|---|---|---|---|---|---|---|---|
| h | s | e | hy | k | p | d | m |

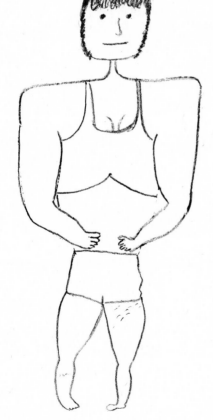

## OVER-ALL EVALUATION = 32

| | 1 | 2 | 3 | 4 | 5 |
|---|---|---|---|---|---|
| OVER-ALL RATING | 1 | 2 | 3 | 4 | 5 |
| PRODUCTIVITY | 1 | (2) | 3 | 4 | 5 |
| RELATION TO REALITY | 1 | 2 | 3 | (4) | 5 |
| THOUGHT CONTENT | 1 | 2 | 3 | (4) | 5 |
| CONSTRUCTIVE FANTASY | 1 | 2 | 3 | (4) | 5 |
| DRIVE | 1 | (2) | 3 | 4 | 5 |
| EMOTIONAL TONE | 1 | 2 | 3 | (4) | 5 |
| SOCIAL ATTITUDE | 1 | 2 | (3) | 4 | 5 |
| ANXIETY | 1 | 2 | 3 | (4) | 5 |
| I. Q. RATING = 132 | 1 | 2 | 3 | 4 | (5) |

## RORSCHACH

| R 71 | M 6 | | Fc 3 |
|---|---|---|---|
| | FM 2 | F 49 | c 2+2 |
| W% 8 | m 4+2 | F- 1 | C' |
| D% 42 | k | F% 69 | FC 2 |
| d% 18 | K | | CF 3 |
| Dd% 31 | FK +1 | | c +1 |
| S | | | |

# WORK SHEET

*Y6*

*1*

## VERBAL I. Q. = 131

| EWS | Info. | Comp. | Digit | Arith. | Sim. |
|-----|-------|-------|-------|--------|------|
| 18 | 25 | 20 | | 14 | 23-24 |
| 17 | 24 | 19 | 17 | 13 | 21-22 |
| 16 | 23 | 18 | 16 | 12 | 20 |
| 15 | 21-22 | 17 | | 11 | 19 |
| 14 | 20 | 16 | 15 | | 17-18 |
| 13 | 18-19 | 15 | 14 | 10 | 16 |
| 12 | 17 | 14 | | 9 | 15 |
| 11 | 15-16 | 12-13 | 13 | | 13-14 |
| 10 | 13-14 | 11 | 12 | 8 | 12 |
| 9 | 12 | 10 | 11 | 7 | 11 |
| 8 | 10-11 | 9 | | | 9-10 |
| 7 | 9 | 8 | 10 | 6 | 8 |
| 6 | 7-8 | 7 | 9 | 5 | 7 |
| 5 | 6 | 5-6 | | | 5-6 |
| 4 | 4-5 | 4 | 8 | 4 | 4 |
| 3 | 2-3 | 3 | 7 | 3 | 3 |
| 2 | 1 | 2 | 6 | | 1-2 |
| 1 | 0 | 1 | | 2 | 0 |
| 0 | | 0 | 5 | 1 | |

## SZONDI

| SEXUAL | | PAROXYSMAL | | EGO | | CONTACT | |
|--------|--------|------------|--------|--------|--------|---------|--------|
| h | s | e | hy | k | p | d | m |
| X | X | | | | | | |
| X | X | X | | | | | |
| X | X | X | X | | X | X | X |
| | X | | X | X | X | X | X |
| | | | X | X | | X | X |
| | | | | X | | | X |

## OVER-ALL EVALUATION = 26

| | | | | | |
|--|--|--|--|--|--|
| OVER-ALL RATING | 1 | 2 | 3 | 4 | 5 |
| PRODUCTIVITY | 1 | (2) | 3 | 4 | 5 |
| RELATION TO REALITY | 1 | 2 | (3) | 4 | 5 |
| THOUGHT CONTENT | 1 | 2 | (3) | 4 | 5 |
| CONSTRUCTIVE FANTASY | 1 | 2 | (3) | 4 | 5 |
| DRIVE | 1 | 2 | (3) | 4 | 5 |
| EMOTIONAL TONE | (1) | 2 | 3 | 4 | 5 |
| SOCIAL ATTITUDE | 1 | 2 | (3) | 4 | 5 |
| ANXIETY | 1 | 2 | (3) | 4 | 5 |
| I. Q. RATING | 1 | 2 | 3 | 4 | (5) |

## RORSCHACH

| R | 14 | M | 4 | | | Fc | 1 |
|---|----|---|---|---|---|----|---|
| | | FM | 4 | F | 2 | c | |
| W% | 43 | m | 1 | F- | | C' | |
| D% | 50 | k | 1 | F% | 14 | FC | |
| d% | 7 | K | 1 | | | CF | |
| Dd% | | FK | | | | c | |
| S | | | | | | | |

# WORK SHEET

Y6

2

## VERBAL I. Q. = 140

| EWS | Info. | Comp. | Digit | Arith. | Sim. |
|-----|-------|-------|-------|--------|------|
| 18 | 25 | 20 | | 14 | 23-24 |
| 17 | 24 | 19 | 17 | 13 | 21-22 |
| 16 | 23 | 18 | 16 | 12 | 20 |
| 15 | 21-22 | 17 | | 11 | 19 |
| 14 | 20 | 16 | 15 | | 17-18 |
| 13 | 18-19 | 15 | 14 | 10 | 16 |
| 12 | 17 | 14 | | 9 | 15 |
| | | | | | |
| 11 | 15-16 | 12-13 | 13 | | 13-14 |
| 10 | 13-14 | 11 | 12 | 8 | 12 |
| 9 | 12 | 10 | 11 | 7 | 11 |
| 8 | 10-11 | 9 | | | 9-10 |
| 7 | 9 | 8 | 10 | 6 | 8 |
| 6 | 7-8 | 7 | 9 | 5 | 7 |
| | | | | | |
| 5 | 6 | 5-6 | | | 5-6 |
| 4 | 4-5 | 4 | 8 | 4 | 4 |
| 3 | 2-3 | 3 | 7 | 3 | 3 |
| 2 | 1 | 2 | 6 | | 1-2 |
| 1 | 0 | 1 | | 2 | 0 |
| 0 | | 0 | 5 | 1 | |

## SZONDI

| SEXUAL | | PAROXYSMAL | | EGO | | CONTACT | |
|---|---|---|---|---|---|---|---|
| h | s | e | hy | k | p | d | m |
| X | | | | | X | | |
| X | X | | | | X | | |
| X | X | X | | | X | | |
| X | X | X | | | X | | |
| | X | X | X | X | | | X |
| | | | X | X | | | X |
| | | | X | X | | | X |
| | | | X | X | | | |

## OVER-ALL EVALUATION = 31

| | | | | | |
|---|---|---|---|---|---|
| OVER-ALL RATING | 1 | 2 | 3 | 4 | 5 |
| PRODUCTIVITY | 1 | 2 | ③ | 4 | 5 |
| RELATION TO REALITY | 1 | 2 | ③ | 4 | 5 |
| THOUGHT CONTENT | 1 | 2 | ③ | 4 | 5 |
| CONSTRUCTIVE FANTASY | 1 | 2 | ③ | 4 | 5 |
| DRIVE | 1 | 2 | ③ | 4 | 5 |
| EMOTIONAL TONE | 1 | 2 | 3 | ④ | 5 |
| SOCIAL ATTITUDE | 1 | 2 | ③ | 4 | 5 |
| ANXIETY | 1 | 2 | 3 | ④ | 5 |
| I. Q. RATING | 1 | 2 | 3 | 4 | ⑤ |

## RORSCHACH

| | | |
|---|---|---|
| R 32 | M 3 | Fc 4 |
| | FM 3+1   F 13 | c |
| W% 16 | m 1+1   F- | C' |
| D% 36 | k   F% 41 | FC 5 |
| d% 13 | K | CF 2 |
| Dd% 16 | FK 1 | c |
| S | | |

Table V shows the distribution of "core" responses and those unique to Records 1 and 2 for these six subjects.

TABLE V.

|  | "Core" Responses | Unique to Record 1 | Unique to Record 2 |
|---|---|---|---|
| Y1 | 23 | 9 | 22 |
| Y2 | 27 | 15 | 38 |
| Y3 | 14 | 37 | 43 |
| Y4 | 8 | 20 | 35 |
| Y5 | 8 | 66 | 63 |
| Y6 | 9 | 5 | 23 |
| Totals | 89 | 152 | 224 |

For comparative purposes we have given some of the TAT material of four of these six subjects. The difference between the first and second performances and the differences between the four subjects can be taken into account for cards 8 BM, 13 MF, 7 BM and 6 BM respectively. Also, for Y1 and Y2, we have recorded the sentence completions from a shortened version of the Holsopple-Miale test. Again, a comparison is possible between the two subjects, or the reactions of either subject one year apart.

STORIES GIVEN TO 8 BM

| Subject | First Test | Second Test |
|---|---|---|
| Y1 | A person has been hurt and possibly killed and the boy has witnessed this and is about to get sick. In the background doctors are examining the man. | A man has been stabbed and two men are leaning over him, one of them removing the knife. The little boy has just witnessed the scene and is rather stunned by the sight. The two gentlemen look rather distinguished and could be doctors. |
| Y2 | Some one has been shot and now they are about to be "butchered." If this happened, or rather this was the scene in a movie as you walked in—I think the boy in the suit merely got in the line of vision. | There has been and possibly still is a fight going on. The men have set their guns down because the man in the supine position has been wounded. They are about to cut him up to remove a bullet, fragment of glass, etc., and then bandage the wound. Perhaps the boy is the man's son and is turning his back and can't stand to watch. |

| Subject | First Test | Second Test |
|---|---|---|

Y3     **First Test:** The boy is daydreaming. In the dream a man has been hurt and his companions are doing their best to aid him. The boy dreams of some day leading an interesting and adventurous life.

**Second Test:** Time: 15 years ago. The picture shows the removal of a bullet from a wounded man by an amateur. It is during the years of war in England. The boy is standing guard. The patient miraculously survives.

Y4     **First Test:** The boy in the foreground with the rifle has accidentally shot the boy on the operating table. The boy has lost much blood. The surgeons are working to save the boy who was shot. One doctor is probing for the bullet, the other is giving the victim blood. The boy on the table seems to be breathing fairly well judging by his chest size. He will be saved.

**Second Test:** The boy in foreground, wearing suit, accidentally shot the person who is lying in background. The wound caused by the shotgun, which is leaning against wall in foreground, has been very extensive and requires the work of a team of surgeons as evidenced by the man standing at patient's head with what could be a blood plasma bottle. The surgeons are apparently working in a private home as a staircase is in background. Since the patient was treated by a skilled surgeon in adequate time, he will make a full recovery.

## Stories Given to 13 MF

Y1     **First Test:** The man in the picture has most likely killed the girl and possibly ravished her, though his clothes look too neat for this to have happened. He is very shocked and despondent over what he has done and will either commit suicide or have a very guilty conscience.

**Second Test:** This man just killed the woman and is feeling very guilty and will turn himself in. He had probably strangled her.

(*or*) The girl could be a patient that the doctor has been working very hard to save and he has just lost a hard battle.

Y2     **First Test:** It appears as if a husband has just returned home, possibly from work, and has found his wife dead in bed. She appears to be nude and possibly has been raped and then killed. The man appears to be almost hysterical.

**Second Test:** A man has been gone from home —possibly to work, etc.—he has returned home and found his wife dead—probably raped and the victim of a sex maniac. The blow is so great to him that he has to turn his face as he weeps in this initial time of great shock. He probably hasn't but will call the police.

| *Subject* | *First Test* | *Second Test* |
|---|---|---|
| Y3 | Here the man and woman have had sex relations and, both being worn out and satisfied, the man is leaving.<br>(*or*) Could be a school boy turning in shame after this act with a prostitute.<br>(*or*) This man has just learned some bad news from woman. | The ages of the two characters and the exposure of the woman's breasts suggest that sex relations have occurred or are being contemplated. The man is a student and the girl is sleeping with him. This diversion has about gotten the best of him. He marries the girl and enjoys ample "diversion." |
| Y4 | The setting of this scene seems to be taking place in a home where the financial condition is rather poor. The woman seems to be a tuberculin type who has, probably due to financial reasons, ostensibly not been under proper medical care. The woman died. | It is Friday night. The married medical student has just finished studying for the night. His wife is asleep and he is very sleepy because he has been studying for four hours now. He is preparing to go to bed and get some rest, and he will do very well on the quiz tomorrow. |

### STORIES GIVEN TO 7 BM

| | | |
|---|---|---|
| Y1 | The younger man has evidently done something wrong and is being counseled by his lawyer. They are awaiting the verdict in the courtroom. He is afraid the verdict will be guilty. | These are two gangsters. The older one has just told the younger to watch his step or given him some sort of threat or other. The younger is infuriated and will later kill or at least seek revenge on the older.<br>(*or*) The older man is a lawyer giving advice to his client in court. The case is going badly against them. |
| Y2 | An older man, possibly the father of the other, is conferring with a younger man. Perhaps it is in a store, perhaps in court. The expressions on their faces seem to be very serious. It appears to me something sinister is about to happen. | These two men are probably blood related as father and son. They are attending a convention and something important, controversial, etc., has just been said. They are counseling with each other about the matter and may stand up to voice their opinion in the matter. Their motives are probably sinister. |

| Subject | First Test | Second Test |
|---|---|---|
| Y3 | Father and son are "in conference." Here the father is advising his son in some matter. The son reluctantly takes his advice and finds it good. | Father is advising his son in a problem of great depth. The son respects his father's wisdom and employs his advice. The problem is solved. |
| Y4 | The boy has reached a point where he must make a crucial decision. The somewhat elderly man seems to be advising the boy in this matter. The question is should he remain in medical school or leave after flunking a course in freshman year. He repeated and did okay. | The young man, after having been asked for an interview at the office of an older doctor, has decided that this is where he will practice medicine. The older doctor is now telling him some of the difficulties he will encounter as this city's new physician. The young physician will establish a very good practice here. |

### Stories Given to 6 BM

| Subject | First Test | Second Test |
|---|---|---|
| Y1 | The man has done something he is ashamed of and is waiting to tell the party he has offended. He will probably apologize. | The man just came and informed the woman of her son's death. The woman has turned away in grief and is trying to control herself. |
| Y2 | It appears as if the man came after his date and has been told she left, that he wouldn't be permitted to see her, or something of similar nature. (or) He has been told of some very unhappy occurrence and is greatly affected. (or) Perhaps they are waiting for a phone call or the report on something in which they are very much interested. | This is probably a mother and her son. The son has just told his mother about his plans to leave immediately to go to some place far off. She has probably scolded him and told him how badly she needs him there to help with expenses, etc. He is angry, yet sad over her feelings toward him in the matter. She is unfair to him. He will leave in spite of her desires. |
| Y3 | Here a mother and son have been talking. They both are somewhat sad—probably a disagreement or bad news. (or) Mother is disappointed in son's actions. Son is somewhat headstrong about his choosings. | Bad news has just been received by this mother and her son. They are lost in worry, but through prayer and faith they resolve the problem. |

| Subject | First Test | Second Test |
|---------|-----------|-------------|
| Y4 | The young man has just told his mother that he was getting married in the near future. His mother, by over-indulging the boy, has spoiled him. She is very unhappy. Adjustment is made; everyone becomes happy. | The young man has just told his mother that he is moving away after getting married. This news has come as a complete surprise to his mother and she is somewhat shocked by his statement to this effect. The young man marries, moves away, and eventually the mother becomes happily adjusted within her circle of friends. |

| Incomplete Sentence | Subject Y1 | Subject Y2 |
|---------------------|-----------|-----------|
| Few children fear. . . | (1) Fire. <br> (2) Fire. | (1) Pets. <br> (2) Animals. |
| When an animal is wild. . . | (1) He is dangerous. <br> (2) It usually fears man. | (1) Kill it. <br> (2) It's best to stay away from it. |
| Compared to dogs, cats are. . . | (1) Lazy. <br> (2) Undemonstrative. | (1) Quieter. <br> (2) More feminine and not as good pets. |
| Fathers should learn that. | (1) Children are individuals. <br> (2) Their children often understand more than they are given credit for. | (1) Children make noise. <br> (2) Children love for their dads to play with them. |
| It is easy to get into trouble when. . . | (1) Under the influence of alcohol. <br> (2) One doesn't think. | (1) A boy. <br> (2) You hang around with the wrong crowd. |
| No one can repair the damage caused by. . . | (1) Death. <br> (2) Thoughtless words. | (1) Fire. <br> (2) The dropping of an egg on a hard floor. |
| Worse than being lonely is. . . | (1) Being desolate. <br> (2) Causing loneliness. | (1) In trouble and alone. <br> (2) To be in love and be away from your lover. |
| If people only knew how much. . . | (1) Being pleasant helps. <br> (2) Better off the world would be without selfishness. | (1) Trouble they cause. <br> (2) They waste daily, they'd be more saving. |
| Children are usually certain that. . . | (1) They are safe at at home. <br> (2) They will have more fun when they grow up. | (1) Love comes from parents. <br> (2) They get enough candy. |

| *Incomplete Sentence* | *Subject Y1* | *Subject Y2* |
|---|---|---|
| The best of mothers may forget. . . | (1) They were once girls also. <br> (2) They were once girls. | (1) They should care for child. <br> (2) Their children want some love and affection daily. |
| Too much distance lies between. . . | (1) Ann and me. <br> (2) Me and my degree. | (1) Continents. <br> (2) The earth and the moon to go in a Model T. |
| The kind of an animal I would like to be. . . Why?. . . | (1) Owner of, is a dog. <br> (2) Is the kind I am. <br> (1) Friendliness, playfulness, protective instinct. <br> (2) Because I like being human. | (1) Dog. <br> (2) Is a bird. <br> (1) Is petted and care taken. <br> (2) Because they can fly and this fascinates me. |
| Nothing is harder to stop than. . . | (1) Radiation. <br> (2) An avalanche. | (1) A train. <br> (2) God's will. |
| He couldn't bear to touch. | (1) Pain. <br> (2) A snake. | (1) A snake. <br> (2) The burned child. |
| Failure may be expected when. . . | (1) One gives up. <br> (2) One is too apprehensive of failure. | (1) A person doesn't try. <br> (2) One is slothful with his money. |
| An effeminate man may. . . | (1) Look masculine. <br> (2) Be that way through too much association with his mother. | (1) Be insulting. problem. <br> (2) Turn into a sexual |
| A mother is more likely than a father to. . . | (1) Live longer. <br> (2) Cry. | (1) Love. <br> (2) Show affection to the kids. |
| It hurts when. . . | (1) You fall. <br> (2) One fails. | (1) You are disappointed. <br> (2) A person burns himself. |

## VII. Two different patterns of growth in siblings. Retesting after four, seven, and eleven years.

The younger of the two sisters, G1, was first tested at the age of 11. The second test battery was given when she was 15, the third at 22.

As was not the case with other individuals whose test records are contained in these pages, a close and continuous relationship has existed between G1, her sister G2, and the writer over the years. Information on their growth and development over the eleven-year period is available from several sources.

Concerning G1 we have, in the first place, her own account of "what it felt like" during these eleven years. We have the parents' impressions, substantiated by reports from school and college. We have the observations of the examiner as a friend and, finally, the comments of the therapist with whom G1 worked intermittently over a five-year period. The therapy in this instance was not considered systematic treatment. In fact, the therapist himself seriously questioned how much of the change which appeared between the second and third testing was due to therapy and how much to time, aging and experience.

Epitomizing in a few sentences what can be gleaned from these various sources, one has, by common consent, the following description: G1 was an unusually bright and attractive youngster who, in late adolescence, ran into a stormy period of confusion and depression and who has now emerged into comparative security, creativeness and personal adjustment.

The first testing dossier on G1 was obtained, interestingly enough, as a "control subject" to her, at that time, somewhat depressed sister. Testing G1 was undertaken with the feeling that perhaps the sister's difficulties could be better understood if the personality structure of the challenging younger child was also assessed. Neither clinically nor from the test picture was it envisaged that G1 herself would run into difficulties.

Five years later, however, this previously sunny individual had run head-on into trouble. For her, indeed, the times were out of joint. Academic problems and problems of personal adjustment in school and subsequently in the college community began piling up on her. Fierce antagonisms developed between her and her parents.

The second testing interview took place at this time in an attempt to gauge the extent and severity of her difficulties. It seemed to have been timed to catch the full impact of the *abrupt* change in the direction of growth.

Emerging from this period of psychological doldrums, G1 is now en route to increasing maturity. Her academic and creative work improved beyond measure, and many tangible achievements bear witness to her competence in her chosen field. As detailed inspection of the content of the Rorschach indicates, she is still confronted with problems inherent in normal living but her vitality and warmth, obscured completely in the period represented by Test Record 2, now stand her in good stead.

The Summary of Test Findings on the following pages shows a sharp regression when the estimates derived from Test Record 1 and those from Test Record 2 are compared, and an equally marked restoration to the previous level when Record 2 is compared with Record 3. This second Summary Sheet corresponds very closely with the estimates given by G1's therapist covering the same period as that included between the second and third testing.

Concerning the Work Sheets: G1 was originally tested by the revised Stanford Binet and obtained a score of 126. This slumped to 112 during the "disturbed" period, and rebounded to approximately the original level at the third testing.

Unusual talent is shown at the eleven-year level in the Figure Drawings. In the second testing, the strange dark head of the male figure is enlightening in terms of the psychological problem facing G1 at that time. A somewhat stylized but much less disturbed production characterizes Record 3.

The Rorschach on Record 2 has lost much of the color and vitality reflected in the first testing and achieved again in the third. The 2 F– responses which make their appearance approach the bizarre; *all color responses have dropped out.* There is a marked rise in the F per cent; the record is colorless and constricted when compared with her achievements on Records 1 and 3. Interestingly enough, several answers which appear in Record 1 involving color reappear in Record 3 in slightly different form. Not a single answer is elaborated in any way in the second Rorschach record. Her verbalization and ideas are stereotyped and abbreviated. In Record 3, as originally found in Record 1, imagination and gaiety are blended in rather piquant fashion. The three sets of answers to Card VIII are given as illustrations:

> *Age 11.* Two polars bears dancing, there is a fire beneath them. A lovely sunset. Two boats with blue sails.
> *Age 15.* Tigers climbing.
> *Age 22.* Here are two bears, and they are climbing a mountain. It's warmer at the bottom of the mountain than at the top. . . .these colors. . . . And there is a river running down the mountain (points to blue). At the top of the mountain there is an animal. At the bottom it's all soft, fluffy and orangey. It's nice.

*Text continued on page 110*

## WORK SHEET

G1

*1*

### REVISED STANFORD-BINET SCALE

TEST SUMMARY

| | Years | Months |
|---|---|---|
| VI | | |
| VII | | |
| VIII | BA | |
| IX | | 10 |
| X | | 10 |
| XI | | 10 |
| XII | | 8 |
| XIII | | 10 |
| XIV | | 12 |
| A.A. | | 10 |
| S.A. I | | 4 |
| S.A. II | | 2 |
| S.A. III | | |
| | 8 | 76 |
| | | |
| Total | 14 | 4 |

OVER-ALL EVALUATION = 30

| | | | | | |
|---|---|---|---|---|---|
| OVER-ALL RATING | I | 2 | 3 | 4 | 5 |
| PRODUCTIVITY | I | ②  | 3 | 4 | 5 |
| RELATION TO REALITY | I | 2 | 3 | ④ | 5 |
| THOUGHT CONTENT | I | 2 | 3 | ④ | 5 |
| CONSTRUCTIVE FANTASY | I | 2 | ③ | 4 | 5 |
| DRIVE | I | 2 | ③ | 4 | 5 |
| EMOTIONAL TONE | I | 2 | ③ | 4 | 5 |
| SOCIAL ATTITUDE | I | 2 | ③ | 4 | 5 |
| ANXIETY | I | 2 | 3 | ④ | 5 |
| I. Q. RATING = 126 | I | 2 | 3 | ④ | 5 |

### RORSCHACH

| | | | | | |
|---|---|---|---|---|---|
| R 17 | M 3 | | | Fc | / |
| | FM 4 | F 5 | | c | |
| W% 53 | m | F- | | C' | |
| D% 47 | k | F% 29 | | FC 3 | |
| d% | K | | | CF | / |
| Dd% | FK | | | c +2 | |
| S | | | | | |

## WORK SHEET

G1

2

VERBAL I. Q. = 112

| EWS | Info. | Comp. | Digit | Arith. | Sim. |
|---|---|---|---|---|---|
| 18 | 25 | 20 | | 14 | 23-24 |
| 17 | 24 | 19 | 17 | 13 | 21-22 |
| 16 | 23 | 18 | 16 | 12 | 20 |
| 15 | 21-22 | 17 | | 11 | 19 |
| 14 | 20 | 16 | 15 | | 17-18 |
| 13 | 18-19 | 15 | 14 | 10 | 16 |
| 12 | 17 | 14 | | 9 | 15 |
| 11 | (15-16) | (12-13) | (13) | | (13-14) |
| 10 | 13-14 | 11 | 12 | (8) | 12 |
| 9 | 12 | 10 | 11 | 7 | 11 |
| 8 | 10-11 | 9 | | | 9-10 |
| 7 | 9 | 8 | 10 | 6 | 8 |
| 6 | 7-8 | 7 | 9 | 5 | 7 |
| 5 | 6 | 5-6 | | | 5-6 |
| 4 | 4-5 | 4 | 8 | 4 | 4 |
| 3 | 2-3 | 3 | 7 | 3 | 3 |
| 2 | 1 | 2 | 6 | | 1-2 |
| 1 | 0 | 1 | | 2 | 0 |
| 0 | | 0 | 5 | 1 | |

### SZONDI

| SEXUAL | | PAROXYSMAL | | EGO | | CONTACT | |
|---|---|---|---|---|---|---|---|
| h | s | e | hy | k | p | d | m |
| | X | X | | | X | X | X |
| X | X | X | | X | X | X | X |
| X | X | X | X | X | | X | X |
| X | X | | X | X | | X | |

OVER-ALL EVALUATION = 20

### RORSCHACH

| | | | |
|---|---|---|---|
| R 19 | M 2 | | Fc |
| | FM 2 | F 11 | c |
| W% 58 | m +1 | F- 2 | C' 2 |
| D% 37 | k | F% 68 | FC |
| d% | K | | CF |
| Dd% 5 | FK | | C |
| S | | | |

**G1**     SUMMARY OF TEST FINDINGS     **1 AND 2**

### MANNER DURING TEST

| (1) Overly distressed | (2) Tense | (3) Indifferent | (4) *Appropriate* | (5) Relaxed and actively interested |
|---|---|---|---|---|
| (1) Hostile | (2) Uneasy | | | |

### I.Q. (Bellevue-Wechsler)

| (1) Below average | (2) Average | (3) High average | (4) *Superior* | (5) Very superior |
|---|---|---|---|---|

### PRODUCTIVITY (Rorschach)

| (1) Impoverished | (2) *Reduced output* | (3) Adequate | (4) Better than average | (5) Rich and well-ordered |
|---|---|---|---|---|
| | (2) Compulsive productivity | | | |

### RELATION TO REALITY (Rorschach, Bellevue-Wechsler, Drawings)

| (1) Loose | (2) Lapses—together with good form | (3) Not noticeably disturbed | (4) *Essentially firm* | (5) Firm and good |
|---|---|---|---|---|

### USUAL-UNUSUAL THOUGHT CONTENT (Rorschach, Unpleasant Concept)

| (1) Bizarre | (2) Tendency toward the bizarre | (3) Adequate | (4) *Original trends* | (5) Outstandingly original |
|---|---|---|---|---|
| (1) Stereotyped | (2) Tendency toward stereotypy | | | |

### CONSTRUCTIVE FANTASY (Rorschach)

| (1) Absent | (2) Barely accessible | (3) *Accessible* | (4) Readily accessible | (5) Active but not hampering |
|---|---|---|---|---|
| (1) Withdrawal into fantasy | | | | |

### DRIVE (Rorschach, Szondi, Unpleasant Concept)

| (1) Overpowering aggression | (2) Over-aggressive | (3) *Adequate* | (4) Clearly sufficient | (5) Sufficient—exceptionally well-directed |
|---|---|---|---|---|
| (1) Hampering passivity | (2) Insufficient drive | | | |

### EMOTIONAL TONE (Rorschach, Szondi)

| (1) Explosive emotions | (2) Getting out of hand | (3) *Trend toward emotional expression* | (4) Warmth available | (5) Warm, readily available |
|---|---|---|---|---|
| (1) Lacking | (2) Indicated but repressed emotions | | | |

### SOCIAL ATTITUDE (T. A. T.)

| (1) Uncontrolled | (2) Constricted or neglected | (3) *Adequate* | (4) Well-regulated | (5) Free and flexible |
|---|---|---|---|---|

### ANXIETY

| (1) Disintegrating | (2) Marked | (3) Moderate | (4) *Not marked* | (5) Lack of evidence of anxiety |
|---|---|---|---|---|

### OVER-ALL EVALUATION

| (1) Markedly disturbed personality | (2) Less than adequate personality with some psychological problems | (3) Adequate personality | (4) *Better than average functioning personality* | (5) Exceptionally well-integrated personality with excellent potential |
|---|---|---|---|---|

## WORK SHEET — G1

3

VERBAL I. Q. = 122

| EWS | Info. | Comp. | Digit | Arith. | Sim. |
|---|---|---|---|---|---|
| 18 | 25 | 20 | | 14 | 23-24 |
| 17 | 24 | 19 | 17 | 13 | 21-22 |
| 16 | 23 | 18 | 16 | 12 | 20 |
| 15 | 21-22 | 17 | | 11 | (19) |
| 14 | 20 | 16 | (15) | | 17-18 |
| 13 | 18-19 | (15) | 14 | (10) | 16 |
| 12 | 17 | 14 | | 9 | 15 |
| 11 | (15-16) | 12-13 | 13 | | 13-14 |
| 10 | 13-14 | 11 | 12 | 8 | 12 |
| 9 | 12 | 10 | 11 | 7 | 11 |

### SZONDI

| SEXUAL | | PAROXYSMAL | | EGO | | CONTACT | |
|---|---|---|---|---|---|---|---|
| h | s | e | hy | k | p | d | m |
| | X | X | X | X | X | | |
| | X | X | X | X | X | X | X |
| X | X | X | X | X | | X | X |
| X | | X | X | | | | |
| X | | | X | | | | |

OVER-ALL EVALUATION = 34

### RORSCHACH

| | | | | | |
|---|---|---|---|---|---|
| R 42 | M 3 | | | Fc 1 | |
| | FM 9 | F 16 | | c 2 | |
| W% 33 | m 1+2 | F- | | C' | |
| D% 52 | k | F% 38 | | FC 5+1 | |
| d% 5 | K +1 | | | CF 3+1 | |
| Dd% 10 | FK 2+1 | | | c | |
| S | | | | | |

**G1**     # SUMMARY OF TEST FINDINGS   **2 AND 3**

## MANNER DURING TEST

| (1) Overly distressed | (2) Tense | (3) *Indifferent* | (4) Appropriate | (5) Relaxed and actively interested |
|---|---|---|---|---|
| (1) Hostile | (2) Uneasy | | | |

## I.Q. (Bellevue-Wechsler)

| (1) Below average | (2) Average | (3) *High average* | (4) Superior | (5) Very superior |
|---|---|---|---|---|

## PRODUCTIVITY (Rorschach)

| (1) Impoverished | (2) *Reduced output* | (3) Adequate | (4) Better than average | (5) Rich and well-ordered |
|---|---|---|---|---|
| | (2) Compulsive productivity | | | |

## RELATION TO REALITY (Rorschach, Bellevue-Wechsler, Drawings)

| (1) Loose | (2) Lapses—together with good form | (3) *Not noticeably disturbed* | (4) Essentially firm | (5) Firm and good |
|---|---|---|---|---|

## USUAL-UNUSUAL THOUGHT CONTENT (Rorschach, Unpleasant Concept)

| (1) Bizarre | (2) Tendency toward the bizarre | (3) Adequate | (4) Original trends | (5) Outstandingly original |
|---|---|---|---|---|
| (1) Stereotyped | (2) *Tendency toward stereotypy* | | | |

## CONSTRUCTIVE FANTASY (Rorschach)

| (1) Absent | (2) *Barely accessible* | (3) Accessible | (4) Readily accessible | (5) Active but not hampering |
|---|---|---|---|---|
| (1) Withdrawal into fantasy | | | | |

## DRIVE (Rorschach, Szondi, Unpleasant Concept)

| (1) Overpowering aggression | (2) Over-aggressive | (3) Adequate | (4) Clearly sufficient | (5) Sufficient—exceptionally well-directed |
|---|---|---|---|---|
| (1) Hampering passivity | (2) *Insufficient drive* | | | |

## EMOTIONAL TONE (Rorschach, Szondi)

| (1) Explosive emotions | (2) Getting out of hand | (3) Trend toward emotional expression | (4) Warmth available | (5) Warm, readily available |
|---|---|---|---|---|
| (1) *Lacking* | (2) Indicated but re-pressed emotions | | | |

## SOCIAL ATTITUDE (T. A. T.)

| (1) Uncontrolled | (2) *Constricted or neglected* | (3) Adequate | (4) Well-regulated | (5) Free and flexible |
|---|---|---|---|---|

## ANXIETY

| (1) Disintegrating | (2) Marked | (3) *Moderate* | (4) Not marked | (5) Lack of evidence of anxiety |
|---|---|---|---|---|

## OVER-ALL EVALUATION

| (1) Markedly disturbed personality | (2) *Less than adequate personality with some psychological problems* | (3) Adequate personality | (4) Better than average functioning personality | (5) Exceptionally well-integrated personality with excellent potential |
|---|---|---|---|---|

# G₁     SUMMARY OF THERAPIST'S FINDINGS

### ESTIMATED INTELLIGENCE LEVEL

| (1) Below average | (2) Average | (3) High average | (4) Superior | (5) Very superior |
|---|---|---|---|---|

### FLOW OF ASSOCIATIVE MATERIAL

| (1) Impoverished | (2) Reduced output | (3) Adequate | (4) Better than average | (5) Rich and well-ordered |
|---|---|---|---|---|
| | (2) Compulsive productivity | | | |

### RELATION TO REALITY

| (1) Loose | (2) Lapses—together with good form | (3) Not noticeably disturbed | (4) Essentially firm | (5) Firm and good |
|---|---|---|---|---|

### USUAL-UNUSUAL THOUGHT CONTENT

| (1) Bizarre | (2) Tendency toward the bizarre | (3) Adequate | (4) Original trends | (5) Outstandingly original |
|---|---|---|---|---|
| (1) Stereotyped | (2) Tendency toward stereotypy | | | |

### CONSTRUCTIVE FANTASY

| (1) Absent | (2) Barely accessible | (3) Accessible | (4) Readily accessible | (5) Active but not hampering |
|---|---|---|---|---|
| (1) Withdrawal into fantasy | | | | |

### DRIVE

| (1) Overpowering aggression | (2) Over-aggressive | (3) Adequate | (4) Clearly sufficient | (5) Sufficient—exceptionally well-directed |
|---|---|---|---|---|
| (1) Hampering passivity | (2) Insufficient drive | | | |

### EMOTIONAL TONE

| (1) Explosive emotions | (2) Getting out of hand | (3) Trend toward emotional expression | (4) Warmth available | (5) Warm, readily available |
|---|---|---|---|---|
| (1) Lacking | (2) Indicated but repressed emotions | | | |

### SOCIAL ATTITUDE

| (1) Uncontrolled | (2) Constricted or neglected | (3) Adequate | (4) Well-regulated | (5) Free and flexible |
|---|---|---|---|---|

### ANXIETY

| (1) Disintegrating | (2) Marked | (3) Moderate | (4) Not marked | (5) Lack of evidence of anxiety |
|---|---|---|---|---|

### OVER-ALL EVALUATION

| (1) Markedly disturbed personality | (2) Less than adequate personality with some psychological problems | (3) Adequate personality | (4) Better than average functioning personality | (5) Exceptionally well-integrated personality with excellent potential |
|---|---|---|---|---|

Card IX gives comparable material:

*Age 11.* Like the griffins in *Alice in Wonderland;* they are dancing over a fire.
*Age 15,* A butterfly with three wings.
*Age 22.* This is like the atomic bomb. And here are witches, with witches' hats on. In the center could be a big face, cheeks and eyes; it's a sort of Mickey Mouse character. Oh, and here's a baby witch, the big witch is spitting fire, the little one is quite passive.

The Sentence Completions given in the second test reflect an antagonistic attitude toward parents and authoritative figures. A softer and more benign approach is shown in this same test on the third occasion, when the storm has abated.

The process of growing up for G2 was, in contrast to G1, essentially all-of-one piece. In terms of clinical observations, reports from environmental sources, and the test findings, there were no sudden breaks in the general pattern of growth. G2 did not pass through a period of "Sturm and Drang"; she progressed relatively smoothly. At all times, what problems she may have had were masked under socially adjusted behavior. More than the average youngster, she engaged in constructive community activities, and recently has found full satisfaction in her maternal role.

As the four TAT stories at the ages of 13, 16, 17 and 24 show, G2 passed through a period of fear that her sister would supplant her as a more important person in the family group, to a point where they could be good "buddies" and, following her marriage, to a place where her sister could be disregarded. The stories told to Card GF9 show the second girl as first "having taken something that the girl behind the tree wants." This animosity reaches a climax in the story where "the two women are bitter enemies." A year later, however, they are getting ready to go off to a picnic together in amicable style, and several years later the second female figure is completely ignored and the projection of G2's own concern with her own family has taken over the scene completely:

*Age 13.* "I think that these two people are looking for each other. The one on the beach is looking for the one behind the tree. The girl who is running has taken something that the girl behind the tree wants, and I don't think they have been down to the beach. The girl who is running looks as if she came from a party in the night."
*Age 16.* "The two women here are bitter enemies. The one in the foreground is jealous of the one running on the beach for she thinks she is trying to steal

her husband away from her, and the woman in the foreground is spying on the other one to see where she is going, to see if she is going to meet her husband. The woman running on the beach feels uneasy as though she knew she were being watched."

*Age 17.* "One day in the Anderson household there was hustle and bustle, and if we looked into the kitchen we would find two girls getting ready to go off to a picnic. Later, when everything was ready, they drove off to the seaside. When they got there they spread out the lunch and then they went into the bathing house to get into their bathing suits and get ready for bathing. The picture is just before they are getting into their bathing suits. Then they all went home tired but happy."

*Age 24.* "Marcia has taken her children down to the beach for the summer. Her husband, John, is expected to meet them there and his train has been delayed. At last she hears he is coming and rushes from the beach to get into her car."

Turning now to the Work Sheets, which have been given for three of the four test batteries, we find greater scatter and a lower I.Q. in the first (I.Q. 108) and a leveling off in the scattergram resulting in an I.Q. of 116 and 120 in subsequent testings.

The Rorschach remains strikingly similar over the many years structurally, in content, and in type of verbalization. It will be noted that there is great consistency in the mental approach, the W to D ratio being heavily weighted in favor of D, a fact closely paralleling G2's essentially practical orientation and her relative lack of interest in intellectual pursuits. Color responses, which make their appearance tentatively on Work Sheet 1, are reinforced and maintained over the subsequent years. Human movement responses show a slight increase in the later records.

The earlier drawings, two of which are shown here, reflect the glamour girl influence to a marked degree. This need to maintain an irreproachable facade has given rise to some difficulties and occasionally stands in G2's way, keeping her from obtaining greater personal satisfaction and from being free to express more spontaneity. Like the "masks" which appear in the Rorschach records, she sometimes has to take refuge behind impeccable grooming. In the latest testing, full-length figures are achieved which reflect less obsessive concern with her facial appearance.*

The OVER-ALL EVALUATION varies only slightly between any one testing and the subsequent one. The trend is consistently toward a fuller and richer production.

---

* All drawings given for G2 are reproduced in their entirety. On Work Sheets 2 and 3, only heads were drawn when the "person" was asked for. On Work Sheet 4, the figure of the man is reduced. It was drawn originally the same size as the woman.

# WORK SHEET 2

*G2*

### VERBAL I. Q. = 108

| EWS | Info. | Comp. | Digit | Arith. | Sim. |
|---|---|---|---|---|---|
| 18 | 25 | 20 |  | 14 | 23-24 |
| 17 | 24 | 19 | 17 | 13 | 21-22 |
| 16 | 23 | 18 | 16 | 12 | 20 |
| 15 | 21-22 | 17 |  | 11 | 19 |
| 14 | 20 | 16 | (15) |  | 17-18 |
| 13 | 18-19 | (15) | 14 | 10 | 16 |
| 12 | 17 | (14) |  | 9 | 15 |
| 11 | (15-16) | 12-13 | 13 |  | 13-14 |
| 10 | 13-14 | 11 | 12 | 8 | 12 |
| 9 | 12 | 10 | 11 | 7 | 11 |
| 8 | 10-11 | 9 |  |  | (9-10) |
| 7 | 9 | 8 | 10 |  | 8 |
| 6 | 7-8 | 7 | 9 | (5) | 7 |
| 5 | 6 | 5-6 |  |  | 5-6 |
| 4 | 4-5 | 4 | 8 | 4 | 4 |
| 3 | 2-3 | 3 | 7 | 3 | 3 |
| 2 | 1 | 2 | 6 |  | 1-2 |
| 1 | 0 | 1 |  | 2 | 0 |
| 0 |  | 0 | 5 | 1 |  |

### SZONDI

| SEXUAL | | PAROXYSMAL | | EGO | | CONTACT | |
|---|---|---|---|---|---|---|---|
| h | s | e | hy | k | p | d | m |
|  |  |  |  |  | X |  | X |
|  |  |  |  | X | X |  | X |
| X | X | X | X | X | X | X | X |
| X | X | X | X | X | X | X | X |
|  | X |  | X |  |  | X |  |
|  |  |  | X |  |  |  |  |
|  |  |  | X |  |  |  |  |

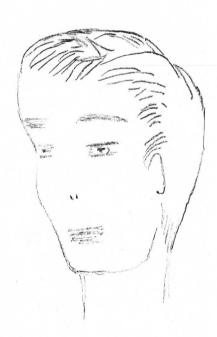

### RORSCHACH

| R 29 | M 4 | | Fc 2 |
|---|---|---|---|
| | FM 3 | F 14 | c |
| W% 14 | m +2 | F- 2 | C' 1+ |
| D% 55 | k 1+1 | F% 55 | FC 1 |
| d% 17 | K | | CF 1+ |
| Dd% 14 | FK | | C |
| S |  |  |  |

# WORK SHEET

G2

3

## VERBAL I. Q. = 116

| EWS | Info. | Comp. | Digit | Arith. | Sim. |
|---|---|---|---|---|---|
| 18 | 25 | 20 | | 14 | 23-24 |
| 17 | 24 | 19 | 17 | 13 | 21-22 |
| 16 | 23 | 18 | 16 | 12 | 20 |
| 15 | 21-22 | 17 | | 11 | 19 |
| 14 | 20 | 16 | 15 | | 17-18 |
| 13 | 18-19 | 15 | 14 | 10 | 16 |
| 12 | 17 | 14 | | 9 | 15 |
| 11 | 15-16 | 12-13 | 13 | | 13-14 |
| 10 | 13-14 | 11 | 12 | 8 | 12 |
| 9 | 12 | 10 | 11 | 7 | 11 |
| 8 | 10-11 | 9 | | | 9-10 |
| 7 | 9 | 8 | 10 | 6 | 8 |
| 6 | 7-8 | 7 | 9 | 5 | 7 |
| 5 | 6 | 5-6 | | | 5-6 |
| 4 | 4-5 | 4 | 8 | 4 | 4 |
| 3 | 2-3 | 3 | 7 | 3 | 3 |
| 2 | 1 | 2 | 6 | | 1-2 |
| 1 | 0 | 1 | | 2 | 0 |
| 0 | | 0 | 5 | 1 | |

## SZONDI

| SEXUAL | | PAROXYSMAL | | EGO | | CONTACT | |
|---|---|---|---|---|---|---|---|
| h | s | e | hy | k | p | d | m |

## RORSCHACH

| R **38** | M **7** | | Fc **2** |
|---|---|---|---|
| | FM **11** | F **10** | c |
| W% **18** | m | F- **2** | C' |
| D% **69** | k | F% **32** | FC **4** |
| d% **10** | K | | CF **1** |
| Dd% **3** | FK **1** | | C |
| S | | | |

=== **WORK SHEET** ===  *G2*

**4**

### VERBAL I. Q. = 120

| EWS | Info. | Comp. | Digit | Arith. | Sim. |
|-----|-------|-------|-------|--------|------|
| 18 | 25 | 20 | | 14 | 23-24 |
| 17 | 24 | 19 | 17 | 13 | 21-22 |
| 16 | 23 | 18 | 16 | 12 | 20 |
| 15 | 21-22 | 17 | | 11 | 19 |
| 14 | 20 | 16 | 15 | | 17-18 |
| 13 | 18-19 | 15 | 14 | 10 | 16 |
| 12 | 17 | 14 | | 9 | 15 |
| 11 | 15-16 | 12-13 | 13 | | 13-14 |
| 10 | 13-14 | 11 | 12 | 8 | 12 |

### SZONDI

| SEXUAL | | PAROXYSMAL | | EGO | | CONTACT | |
|---|---|---|---|---|---|---|---|
| h | s | e | hy | k | p | d | m |

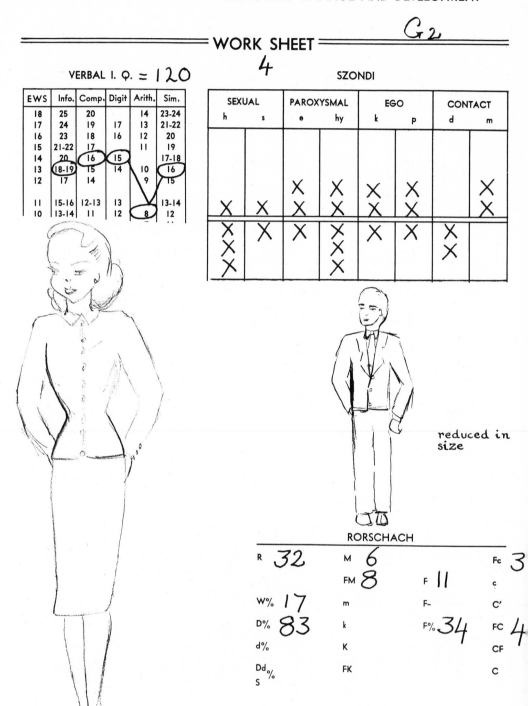

*reduced in size*

### RORSCHACH

| | | | | | |
|---|---|---|---|---|---|
| R | 32 | M | 6 | Fc | 3 |
| | | FM | 8 | F | 11 | c | |
| W% | 17 | m | | F– | | C' | |
| D% | 83 | k | | F% 34 | FC | 4 |
| d% | | K | | | CF | |
| Dd% | | FK | | | C | |
| S | | | | | | |

# G 2     SUMMARY OF TEST FINDINGS   1, 2, 3, 4

## MANNER DURING TEST

| (1) Overly distressed | (2) Tense | (3) Indifferent | (4) Appropriate | (5) Relaxed and actively interested |
|---|---|---|---|---|
| (1) Hostile | (2) Uneasy | | 2, 3, 4 | |

## I.Q. (Bellevue-Wechsler)

| (1) Below average | (2) Average | (3) High average 3 | (4) Superior 4 | (5) Very superior |
|---|---|---|---|---|

## PRODUCTIVITY (Rorschach)

| (1) Impoverished | (2) Reduced output | (3) Adequate | (4) Better than average | (5) Rich and well-ordered |
|---|---|---|---|---|
| | (2) Compulsive productivity | 1 - 2 - 3 - 4 | | |

## RELATION TO REALITY (Rorschach, Bellevue-Wechsler, Drawings)

| (1) Loose | (2) Lapses—together with good form | (3) Not noticeably disturbed | (4) Essentially firm | (5) Firm and good |
|---|---|---|---|---|
| | | | 1 - 2 - 3 - 4 | |

## USUAL-UNUSUAL THOUGHT CONTENT (Rorschach, Unpleasant Concept)

| (1) Bizarre | (2) Tendency toward the bizarre | (3) Adequate | (4) Original trends | (5) Outstandingly original |
|---|---|---|---|---|
| (1) Stereotyped | (2) Tendency toward stereotypy | 1 - 2 - 3 - 4 | | |

## CONSTRUCTIVE FANTASY (Rorschach)

| (1) Absent | (2) Barely accessible | (3) Accessible | (4) Readily accessible | (5) Active but not hampering |
|---|---|---|---|---|
| (1) Withdrawal into fantasy | | | 3 · 4 | |

## DRIVE (Rorschach, Szondi, Unpleasant Concept)

| (1) Overpowering aggression | (2) Over-aggressive | (3) Adequate | (4) Clearly sufficient | (5) Sufficient—exceptionally well-directed |
|---|---|---|---|---|
| (1) Hampering passivity | (2) Insufficient drive | 1 · 2 · 3 · 4 | | |

## EMOTIONAL TONE (Rorschach, Szondi)

| (1) Explosive emotions | (2) Getting out of hand | (3) Trend toward emotional expression | (4) Warmth available | (5) Warm, readily available |
|---|---|---|---|---|
| (1) Lacking | (2) Indicated but re-pressed emotions | | 3 · 4 | |

## SOCIAL ATTITUDE (T. A. T.)

| (1) Uncontrolled | (2) Constricted or neglected | (3) Adequate 3 | (4) Well-regulated 4 | (5) Free and flexible |
|---|---|---|---|---|

## ANXIETY

| (1) Disintegrating | (2) Marked | (3) Moderate | (4) Not marked 4 | (5) Lack of evidence of anxiety |
|---|---|---|---|---|

## OVER-ALL EVALUATION

| (1) Markedly disturbed personality | (2) Less than adequate personality with some psychological problems | (3) Adequate personality | (4) Better than average functioning personality | (5) Exceptionally well-integrated personality with excellent potential |
|---|---|---|---|---|

## VIII. Retesting subsequent to sudden cessation of acute stress.

The initial psychodiagnostic examination of the four women whose test and retest findings are discussed here occurred as the psychologist's contribution to a clinical study of thirty-two patients who had had three or more consecutive, spontaneous abortions. This clinical study by Berle and Javert[3] was undertaken to determine the relation of life stress to the occurrence of repeated abortions, to indicate the nature of the physiologic mechanism operative in such cases, and to investigate a type of therapy which served to interrupt the repeated abortion sequence.

Summarizing their findings these authors state:

"1. Medical, social, and biographic data were obtained in the case of 32 women with primary and secondary habitual abortion. The occurrence of spontaneous abortions was often found to be related in time to periods of stress in these patients' lives. Ultimately, repeated abortion itself was found to be the source of major stress in all patients.

"2. Group intelligence and projective tests were done on 15 patients and revealed a wide range (within expected limits) of intellectual capacity and personality characteristics.

"3. A significant personality disorder was diagnosed in 6 (19 per cent) of the patients studied. The majority of patients were considered by all observers to be free of psychosis or character neurosis.

"4. A combined regimen of medical care and psychotherapy, largely in the hands of the obstetrician, has been outlined.

"5. Under this regimen, 27 conceptions in 24 patients have resulted in 25 live children, or 92.5 per cent success."

The four women who were retested had been successfully treated by this program several years previously and responded with interest to the idea of a follow-up study when approached by the psychologist. All commented spontaneously, in their initial written reply, on the enormous difference successful treatment had made in their lives. Each stated that when first tested she had been experiencing profound discouragement, tension and depression.

The statements of Subject AB1 and Subject AB2 may be given here since they are more telling than attempts to summarize them. Subject AB1, for instance, commented:

"I think the nicest thing is finding I am 'normal.' People were always asking all sorts of private questions so that I began to avoid parties, and I avoided all my friends who had childern. You suddenly have some status when you have a child, and when you have two children you don't get advice at all!

"The great pressure is off. You don't know if you're going to have children. You think of the future all the time. You wonder what you'll do when you're older. You wonder if you'll face life alone. Now that the children are here you live from day to day. Your whole approach is more normal. You don't look for the significant things people might be saying. You look at the whole world differently. It helps you to understand; it's a rewarding experience. I feel more complete as a person. I'm much busier than ever, so is my husband. We are much closer. We're not self-centered any more. We have more interest in the town, in the community. In fact, everything is different. The children ended the 'barren' period for me.

"I was considered a hypochondriac. I became so involved in my body through all that period. I feel healthier even though I'm sure I'm no different. Little children can be trying and I certainly lose my temper, but all the same I've learned to relax. I used to know what it was like to have too much time. I was always worrying; I couldn't even enjoy my leisure. Now I find I can meet all the emergencies.

"The doctor I saw before told me I must not think of myself like a normal woman. I was causing trouble by insisting on trying to have children; I was making a nuisance of myself. When we went to Dr. J. I found he had a personal relationship with his patients that was quite different. He asked pertinent questions but he never told you what to do. I think I altered my outlook through my conversations with him. He had a perspective to life. He taught me. I began to join educational workshops."

Subject AB2 gives the picture from her point of view:

"At that time I had always a scared feeling about everything—even taking that test made me feel tense. It was a tense period for me. I was very ill. I always had pain. Now I feel fulfilled—well, I might put it. I would like more (children) but I've got what I was aiming at. I feel I've come of age. I can take on many more interests now that this one hurdle is taken care of, even though I'm busier. We've become much closer as a family; we've gone through things together, my husband and I, and we look at it all now with interest. There was so much on my mind before—I was sort of caught in a trap, afraid of doing something wrong all the time. I feel younger now, even though I'm four years older. I used to feel ancient."

Although we feel that, as a rule, making composite statements about test findings tends to obscure important individual differences, group characteristics here seem to be sufficiently striking to warrant discussion in this way. In none of the four subjects, for instance, did the retests show a significant change occurring in the I.Q. Three of these patients (AB1, AB2, AB3) were placed initially in the *Superior Group* on the Bellevue-Wechsler, and so remained. The fourth (AB4) was in the *Very Superior Group* and retested at that level.

The Szondi records of all four showed a consistent change in the sexual vector. The findings for Subject AB4 may be taken as representative. During the period of strain, tension and resignation, these patients had all strenuously repressed the h, or tender feeling, factor. Subsequently, however, it seems to have become "safe" to accept this component in the self, and a more essentially feminine picture emerged.

SZONDI

| AB4—1 | | | | | | | | AB4—2 | | | | | | | |
|---|---|---|---|---|---|---|---|---|---|---|---|---|---|---|---|
| Sexual | | Paroxysmal | | Ego | | Contact | | Sexual | | Paroxysmal | | Ego | | Contact | |
| h | s | e | hy | k | p | d | m | h | s | e | hy | k | p | d | m |
|  |  |  |  |  |  |  |  | x |  |  |  |  |  |  |  |
|  |  |  |  |  | x |  |  | x |  |  |  | x |  |  |  |
|  |  | x |  |  | x | x | x | x | x |  |  | x |  |  | x |
|  | x | x | x | x | x | x | x | x | x | x |  | x |  |  | x |
| x | x | x | x | x | x |  |  |  | x | x | x | x |  | x |  |
| x |  |  | x | x |  |  |  |  | x | x | x | x |  | x |  |
| x |  |  | x |  |  |  |  |  |  |  | x | x |  |  |  |
| x |  |  |  |  |  |  |  |  |  |  |  |  |  |  |  |

Striking changes occurred in the Rorschach records of these subjects, particularly the appearance of good FC responses in quantity. The FC responses in the record of Subject AB3 increased from one to nine, in the record of AB4, from one to five, in that of AB1, from one to six. In both instances the record of AB2 showed three good FC responses. The total number of FC responses for the group as a whole rose from five in the first testing to 23 in the second! 

There is also an increase in the number of good human movement responses in the individual records: Subject AB4 shows a rise from seven to 13, Subject AB3, from 10 to 11 (not considered an important rise), in Subject AB1 there is an increase from three to seven, while Subject AB2 shows five human movement responses in both records.

The CAT and TAT responses also showed interesting shifts. Take, for example, the TAT picture responded to in the following way by AB4:

> "This child is rather bored because it is Sunday afternoon. She's all dressed up in her best clothes, visiting her aunt. Instead of being able to play outdoors as she wants, she is listening while her aunt reads "Little People Under the Sea," a book which her aunt enjoyed in her youth but which the child considers old-fashioned and dull. As a treat she has been allowed to play with her grandmother's doll which she is holding disinterestedly because she has outgrown such childish toys."

Here the female figure is the aunt, not the mother, and the child's holding up the doll disinterestedly reflects this individual's depression and disinterest to which her whole struggle to have a child of her own had brought her. Four years later this picture was responded to as follows:

"This is a picture of a mother and a daughter and the daughter is now hold-ing and playing with her favorite doll. The mother is reading to the child as she used to when her daughter was younger. The daughter is about to go away to school, and this hour that they have together is symbolic of the childhood days and the start of a new life."

Here we have a "mother" instead of an "aunt" and the child now looks on the doll as her favorite.

In the Sentence Completion Test AB4 answered: "The kind of animal I would most like to be . . . ." with, "A bird, to get away from it all into the air." Four years later, however, the elephant is chosen be-cause it has "the longest life." A consistent theme in the discussions of these four subjects was the fact that so many things now were found valuable and fun to do that they needed more time, where before time had hung heavy on their hands.

A shift in attitude also occurs in regard to what things are the most important. One subject, for whom orderliness had been shown to be of the utmost importance in the initial testing, replied in the second test to the sentence: "The best of mothers may forget that . . . ." with, "It is more important to let the household chores be undone in order to have more time to play with the children and be unrushed with them." In the same way, there is mutual participation of the parents in the business of child-rearing, as seen in the sentence: "Fathers should learn that . . . ." "They have a tremendous influence in molding their children with love and discipline, and that it takes a good father, for instance, even to make a good woman."

An interesting change occurred in the Drawings, as exemplified by Figures 8 and 9. With these subjects we had asked not for individual figure drawings but for drawings of a family. Initially, in the period fraught with anxiety and depression, the family was portrayed by all of them as three isolated individuals, whereas all patients subsequently portrayed the family in close groups.

These four cases seem to indicate a change in the test battery con-sistent with, and in line with, the objective findings. We know that a major stress had been removed, and that with the advent of the child (and in two cases children), real fulfillment of life goals had been achieved. The spontaneous comments of these individuals in terms of the greater richness, gaiety and fulfillment of their lives is reflected in the startling rise in FC responses.

At the same time, the fulfillment of the common life goal does not

FIG. 8.   DRAWING OF THE FAMILY, FIRST TESTING.

FIG. 9.   DRAWING OF THE FAMILY, SECOND TESTING.

# SUMMARY OF TEST FINDINGS *AB 1*

## MANNER DURING TEST

| (1) Overly distressed | (2) Tense | (3) Indifferent | (4) Appropriate | (5) Relaxed and actively interested |
|---|---|---|---|---|
| (1) Hostile | (2) Uneasy | | | |

## I.Q. (Bellevue-Wechsler)

| (1) Below average | (2) Average | (3) High average | (4) *Superior* | (5) Very superior |
|---|---|---|---|---|

## PRODUCTIVITY (Rorschach)

| (1) Impoverished | (2) Reduced output | (3) *Adequate* | (4) Better than average | (5) Rich and well-ordered |
|---|---|---|---|---|
| | (2) Compulsive productivity | | | |

## RELATION TO REALITY (Rorschach, Bellevue-Wechsler, Drawings)

| (1) Loose | (2) Lapses—together with good form | (3) *Not noticeably disturbed* | (4) Essentially firm | (5) Firm and good |
|---|---|---|---|---|

## USUAL-UNUSUAL THOUGHT CONTENT (Rorschach, Unpleasant Concept)

| (1) Bizarre | (2) Tendency toward the bizarre | (3) *Adequate* | (4) Original trends | (5) Outstandingly original |
|---|---|---|---|---|
| (1) Stereotyped | (2) Tendency toward stereotypy | | | |

## CONSTRUCTIVE FANTASY (Rorschach)

| (1) Absent | (2) Barely accessible | (3) *Accessible* | (4) Readily accessible | (5) Active but not hampering |
|---|---|---|---|---|
| (1) Withdrawal into fantasy | | | | |

## DRIVE (Rorschach, Szondi, Unpleasant Concept)

| (1) Overpowering aggression | (2) Over-aggressive | (3) Adequate | (4) Clearly sufficient | (5) Sufficient—exceptionally well-directed |
|---|---|---|---|---|
| (1) Hampering passivity | (2) *Insufficient drive* | | | |

## EMOTIONAL TONE (Rorschach, Szondi)

| (1) Explosive emotions | (2) Getting out of hand | (3) Trend toward emotional expression | (4) Warmth available | (5) Warm, readily available |
|---|---|---|---|---|
| (1) *Lacking* | (2) Indicated but repressed emotions | | | |

## SOCIAL ATTITUDE (T. A. T.)

| (1) Uncontrolled | (2) *Constricted or neglected* | (3) Adequate | (4) Well-regulated | (5) Free and flexible |
|---|---|---|---|---|

## ANXIETY

| (1) Disintegrating | (2) Marked | (3) *Moderate* | (4) Not marked | (5) Lack of evidence of anxiety |
|---|---|---|---|---|

## OVER-ALL EVALUATION

| (1) Markedly disturbed personality | (2) *Less than adequate personality with some psychological problems* | (3) Adequate personality | (4) Better than average functioning personality | (5) Exceptionally well-integrated personality with excellent potential |
|---|---|---|---|---|

mask the specific individuality of each of these patients. The good form-color responses which come into the second record are added to individual psychograms which differ in each case. For example, there is an originality, an intellectual drive reflected in both Rorschach records of Subject AB4 not found in the other patients. The range and scope of AB4's intellectual interests are at a different level from the others, yet within their respective frames of reference each finds herself increasingly busy and happy, with added time for interests despite the increase in activity on the home front.

The Summary Chart of AB1 has been given in full, the quantitative findings being 24 for the first test battery and 33 for the second. The quantitative scores for AB2, AB3 and AB4 are, respectively, 23:30, 25:35, 28:38.

## IX. Retesting following gradual reduction in stress.

Subject L1, married, and now in his middle thirties, was first tested shortly after his arrival in this country and retested subsequent to a five-year interval. His case is included here since it is representative of those individuals whose psychological growth and development may reasonably be supposed to have been furthered by the cessation of long-standing stress and by concommitant intrenchment in a new physical and psychological environment of greater opportunity and freedom. L1 had struggled through difficult conditions during the war years and did not have an easy time on immediate arrival in this country. Asked to describe what had been happening to him during the five-year interval between the first and second testing, he wrote as follows:

> "I believe that the results of the first test must have shown a subnormal or contracted self. I would like to explain this. Lack of funds forced me to work first (before going into his chosen career) and I hoped to get a suitable job. Once I arrived, however, things didn't work out so well because of citizenship status, and all I could get was a badly paid factory job. It was impossible to save anything, and when the year was up it was clear that I had to keep on working and postpone my studies indefinitely.
>
> "During the second year, still working in a factory, things went from bad to worse financially and around the time that I was tested there seemed to be 'no exit' to my situation. My education was yet insufficient to get a job in my chosen field, and I had little chance to find other work. Two years in factories was a deadening experience, especially because for some time there seemed to be no way out at all. None of my capacities or skills or education was used, and I remained on the lowest level of the totem pole at the factory where I worked. I hardly had a chance to read, much less an opportunity to live in the kind of community of educated people I was used to. Without going into too many details, the result was that I felt 'dried up' intellectually and contracted emotionally. Subsequent to the testing, things seemed to be getting better—my chance to study, my contact with X. But these were still vague changes. I was out of money altogether, and many other attempts to get out of my situation had previously failed.
>
> "Five years later, by the time of the second test, everything had completely changed. I was using what I had and what I was. I loved my studies. I was involved in the kind of community and with the kind of people I felt at home with. Things had, in a way, become normal again, but also it was almost more than normal. I was undertaking a task I could finish and could handle. I was doing something in which I was totally involved myself and could apply all I had. My life was once again meaningful because I did what I wanted rather than simply subsist, as previously. All this, I feel, enables me to unfold again—slowly, at first, but now steadily. All things are going in a positive direction. I can solve my own emotional problems and get to know myself better. At the time of the second test some of the growth beyond this normal self may have be-

gun to show. Who would not grow when he is happy in his work, feels a worthy challenge, finds direction in his life, and finds what he is and does and has, applied usefully in a worthwhile manner?"

In the light of the foregoing statement, a comparison of the Work Sheets is interesting. In the Bellevue-Wechsler the scattergram has changed in shape and Subject L1 now has gained 28 points in I.Q., passing from the *Average* to the *Very Superior Group* of the total population.

Despite the passage of five years the Szondi pattern, however, is almost identical. At neither time was any marked disturbance shown. The only change, namely, the open k, +p distribution, shows greater abandonment in work and satisfaction than did the –k, open p of the first testing.

The Figure Drawings have changed remarkably. Instead of the weak and scrawny old man drawn in response to the request for a male figure, there is one which shows vitality and aliveness. It is a contemporary figure, a vigorous youth rather than an emaciated figure. Previously, the attempt to draw a woman had failed after four distorted profiles had been tried. At the second testing there is, again, vitality in the figure which is drawn.

Although the Rorschach record has not gained much in terms of productivity, it has been enormously enriched within the same framework. Human movement responses have risen from three to eight, the FM from two to eleven. Of great importance is the appearance of the four FC responses, with a 4:2:1 ratio of FC to CF to C. The five disturbed F– responses have dropped from the record. There is a gaiety and animation here which renders the second record almost unrecognizable as the companion of the first.

The Sentence Completion Tests cover much of the same material on the first and second presentation. There is, however, some modification in the direction of less desperation. While "Worse than being lonely is . . ." was originally answered by "being hated," it has become, in the second record, "not being loved." At the time of the first testing, feelings of dissatisfaction had reached a point where the world seemed actively unkind and the individual the butt of many misfortunes.

The Most Unpleasant Concept, which in both instances dealt with deprivation and war, is drawn in the second instance with feeling and expression as opposed to the few stark lines and the minimal involvement that was carried in the first drawing.

This individual started out on the quantitative scale with a score of 23 and rises to 34 at the second testing.

## WORK SHEET

*L 1*

*1*

### VERBAL I. Q. = 111

| EWS | Info. | Comp. | Digit | Arith. | Sim. |
|---|---|---|---|---|---|
| 18 | 25 | 20 |  | 14 | 23-24 |
| 17 | 24 | 19 | 17 | 13 | 21-22 |
| 16 | 23 | 18 | 16 | 12 | 20 |
| 15 | 21-22 | 17 |  | 11 | 19 |
| 14 | 20 | 16 | 15 |  | 17-18 |
| 13 | 18-19 | 15 | 14 | 10 | 16 |
| 12 | 17 | 14 |  | 9 | 15 |
|  |  |  |  |  |  |
| 11 | 15-16 | 12-13 | 13 |  | 13-14 |
| 10 | 13-14 | 11 | 12 | 8 | 12 |
| 9 | 12 | 10 | 11 | 7 | 11 |
| 8 | 10-11 | 9 |  |  | 9-10 |
| 7 | 9 | 8 | 10 | 6 | 8 |
| 6 | 7-8 | 7 | 9 | 5 | 7 |
|  |  |  |  |  |  |
| 5 | 6 | 5-6 |  |  | 5-6 |
| 4 | 4-5 | 4 | 8 | 4 | 4 |
| 3 | 2-3 | 3 | 7 | 3 | 3 |
| 2 | 1 | 2 | 6 |  | 1-2 |
| 1 | 0 | 1 |  | 2 | 0 |
| 0 |  | 0 | 5 | 1 |  |

### SZONDI

| SEXUAL | | PAROXYSMAL | | EGO | | CONTACT | |
|---|---|---|---|---|---|---|---|
| h | s | e | hy | k | p | d | m |

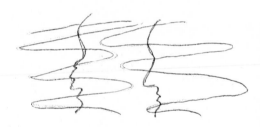

OVER-ALL EVALUATION = 23

### RORSCHACH

| R | 30 | M | 3 | | | Fc | 1 |
|---|---|---|---|---|---|---|---|
| | | FM | 2 | F | 15 | c | 1 |
| W% | 40 | m | 1+1 | F- | 5 | C' | +2 |
| D% | 47 | k | +1 | F% | 67 | FC | |
| d% | 7 | K | | | | CF | 1 |
| Dd% | 6 | FK | 1 | | | C | |
| S | | | | | | | |

# WORK SHEET
## 2

*L1*

### VERBAL I. Q. = 130

| EWS | Info. | Comp. | Digit | Arith. | Sim. |
|---|---|---|---|---|---|
| 18 | 25 | 20 |  | 14 | 23-24 |
| 17 | 24 | 19 | 17 | 13 | 21-22 |
| 16 | 23 | 18 | 16 | 12 | 20 |
| 15 | 21-22 | 17 |  | 11 | 19 |
| 14 | 20 | 16 | 15 |  | 17-18 |
| 13 | 18-19 | 15 | 14 | 10 | 16 |
| 12 | 17 | 14 |  | 9 | 15 |
|  |  |  |  |  |  |
| 11 | 15-16 | 12-13 | 13 |  | 13-14 |
| 10 | 13-14 | 11 | 12 | 8 | 12 |
| 9 | 12 | 10 | 11 | 7 | 11 |
| 8 | 10-11 | 9 |  |  | 9-10 |
| 7 | 9 | 8 | 10 | 6 | 8 |
| 6 | 7-8 | 7 | 9 | 5 | 7 |
|  |  |  |  |  |  |
| 5 | 6 | 5-6 |  |  | 5-6 |
| 4 | 4-5 | 4 | 8 | 4 | 4 |
| 3 | 2-3 | 3 | 7 | 3 | 3 |
| 2 | 1 | 2 | 6 |  | 1-2 |
| 1 | 0 | 1 |  | 2 | 0 |
| 0 |  | 0 | 5 | 1 |  |

### SZONDI

| SEXUAL | | PAROXYSMAL | | EGO | | CONTACT | |
|---|---|---|---|---|---|---|---|
| h | s | e | hy | k | p | d | m |
|  |  |  |  |  |  |  | X |
|  |  |  |  |  |  |  | X X |
| X |  |  |  |  | X |  | X X |
| X | X | X | X |  | X | X | X X |
| X | X | X | X | X |  | X |  |
| X | X |  | X |  |  | X X |  |
|  | X X |  |  |  |  | X |  |

OVER-ALL EVALUATION = 34

### RORSCHACH

| | | | | | |
|---|---|---|---|---|---|
| R | 36 | M | 8 | Fc | +2 |
|  |  | FM | 11 | F | 5 | c | 2 |
| W% | 36 | m | 1+1 | F- |  | C' | 1+1 |
| D% | 58 | k |  | F% | 14 | FC | 4 |
| d% | 6 | K | 1+1 |  |  | CF | 2+1 |
| Dd% |  | FK |  |  |  | c | 1+2 |
| S |  |  |  |  |  |  |  |

# SUMMARY OF TEST FINDINGS  *L1*

## MANNER DURING TEST

| | | | | |
|---|---|---|---|---|
| **(1)** Overly distressed | **(2)** Tense | **(3)** Indifferent | **(4)** Appropriate | **(5)** Relaxed and actively interested |
| **(1)** Hostile | **(2)** Uneasy | | | |

## I.Q. (Bellevue-Wechsler)

| | | | | |
|---|---|---|---|---|
| **(1)** Below average | **(2)** Average | **(3)** High average | **(4)** Superior | **(5)** Very superior |

## PRODUCTIVITY (Rorschach)

| | | | | |
|---|---|---|---|---|
| **(1)** Impoverished | **(2)** Reduced output | **(3)** Adequate | **(4)** Better than average | **(5)** Rich and well-ordered |
| | **(2)** Compulsive productivity | | | |

## RELATION TO REALITY (Rorschach, Bellevue-Wechsler, Drawings)

| | | | | |
|---|---|---|---|---|
| **(1)** Loose | **(2)** Lapses—together with good form | **(3)** Not noticeably disturbed | **(4)** Essentially firm | **(5)** Firm and good |

## USUAL-UNUSUAL THOUGHT CONTENT (Rorschach, Unpleasant Concept)

| | | | | |
|---|---|---|---|---|
| **(1)** Bizarre | **(2)** Tendency toward the bizarre | **(3)** Adequate | **(4)** Original trends | **(5)** Outstandingly original |
| **(1)** Stereotyped | **(2)** Tendency toward stereotypy | | | |

## CONSTRUCTIVE FANTASY (Rorschach)

| | | | | |
|---|---|---|---|---|
| **(1)** Absent | **(2)** Barely accessible | **(3)** Accessible | **(4)** Readily accessible | **(5)** Active but not hampering |
| **(1)** Withdrawal into fantasy | | | | |

## DRIVE (Rorschach, Szondi, Unpleasant Concept)

| | | | | |
|---|---|---|---|---|
| **(1)** Overpowering aggression | **(2)** Over-aggressive | **(3)** Adequate | **(4)** Clearly sufficient | **(5)** Sufficient— exceptionally well-directed |
| **(1)** Hampering passivity | **(2)** Insufficient drive | | | |

## EMOTIONAL TONE (Rorschach, Szondi)

| | | | | |
|---|---|---|---|---|
| **(1)** Explosive emotions | **(2)** Getting out of hand | **(3)** Trend toward emotional expression | **(4)** Warmth available | **(5)** Warm, readily available |
| **(1)** Lacking | **(2)** Indicated but repressed emotions | | | |

## SOCIAL ATTITUDE (T. A. T.)

| | | | | |
|---|---|---|---|---|
| **(1)** Uncontrolled | **(2)** Constricted or neglected | **(3)** Adequate | **(4)** Well-regulated | **(5)** Free and flexible |

## ANXIETY

| | | | | |
|---|---|---|---|---|
| **(1)** Disintegrating | **(2)** Marked | **(3)** Moderate | **(4)** Not marked | **(5)** Lack of evidence of anxiety |

## OVER-ALL EVALUATION

| | | | | |
|---|---|---|---|---|
| **(1)** Markedly disturbed personality | **(2)** Less than adequate personality with some psychological problems | **(3)** Adequate personality | **(4)** Better than average functioning personality | **(5)** Exceptionally well-integrated personality with excellent potential |

## X. Retesting following long-term analytic therapy.

The ten cases discussed here have in common the fact that they have all been in long-term, orthodox analytic treatment. With the exception of A7 and A10, all were treated by different analysts. All were tested just prior to entering therapy, but there was some variation in the time interval that had elapsed subsequent to the termination of therapy. The analysts in all cases were still in touch with their former patients, so that up-to-date reports were obtainable; however, the second clinical assessment reflects the patient's status at the time of termination of treatment.

A1 was tested before entering therapy and retested seven years later, after five years of intensive analytic treatment. At the time of the initial referral for a psychodiagnostic evaluation the following information was available: "The patient's chief complaint is headaches, which he has had since grade school. Mild ones may last a week; severe ones are of shorter duration and are arrested by aspirin. In recent years they have been diminishing in intensity but not in frequency. The pain is sometimes throbbing, sometimes dull. They may be unilateral, generalized or sub-occipital. They are increased by any push, jar or noise. The only aura is a vague feeling of fullness in the head. There are no oculomotor or general or localized motor or sensory disturbances, and no visual disturbances suggestive of a true migraine."

Two other physiologic symptoms were mentioned at this time as part of the general complaint, and such psychological difficulties as being acutely uneasy in social situations and having periods of depression. The diagnostic impression was: "This is a psychoneurotic depression with a certain amount of diffuse phobic anxiety, and with foci of psychosomatic, spasmogenic disturbances. There is no sign of any concurrent malignant process, either organic or psychological."

At the termination of therapy the analyst assessed this patient as having shown considerable improvement. On the OVER-ALL EVALUATION, he classifies him as having reached the level described on the 5-point scale as an *Adequate personality* from the previous position of *Less than adequate personality with some psychological problems*. However, in specific areas, improvement was considered more marked.

The patient, discussing his therapeutic experience, concluded:

"I considered it a tremendous investment of time and a great deal of help. Looking back, I realized at what a low point I was. Since then I know I am greatly improved. I understand myself much better. I didn't get what I wanted completely out of the treatment. I had to compromise. But I do have a much

# WORK SHEET
*1*

## VERBAL I. Q.

| EWS | Info. | Comp. | Digit | Arith. | Sim. |
|---|---|---|---|---|---|
| 18 | 25 | 20 |  | 14 | 23-24 |
| 17 | 24 | 19 | 17 | 13 | 21-22 |
| 16 | 23 | 18 | 16 | 12 | 20 |
| 15 | 21-22 | 17 |  | 11 | 19 |
| 14 | 20 | 16 | 15 |  | 17-18 |
| 13 | 18-19 | 15 | 14 | 10 | 16 |
| 12 | 17 | 14 |  | 9 | 15 |
| 11 | 15-16 | 12-13 | 13 |  | 13-14 |
| 10 | 13-14 | 11 | 12 | 8 | 12 |
| 9 | 12 | 10 | 11 | 7 | 11 |
| 8 | 10-11 | 9 |  |  | 9-10 |
| 7 | 9 | 8 | 10 | 6 | 8 |
| 6 | 7-8 | 7 | 9 | 5 | 7 |
| 5 | 6 | 5-6 |  |  | 5-6 |
| 4 | 4-5 | 4 | 8 | 4 | 4 |
| 3 | 2-3 | 3 | 7 | 3 | 3 |
| 2 | 1 | 2 | 6 | 2 | 1-2 |
| 1 | 0 | 1 |  | 2 | 0 |
| 0 |  | 0 | 5 | 1 |  |

## SZONDI

| SEXUAL | | PAROXYSMAL | | EGO | | CONTACT | |
|---|---|---|---|---|---|---|---|
| h | s | e | hy | k | p | d | m |
|  |  |  |  |  |  |  | X |
|  | X | X |  |  | X | X | X |
| X | X | X |  |  | X | X | X |
| X |  | X | X | X | X | X |  |
|  |  |  | X | X | X | X |  |
|  |  |  | X | X |  |  |  |

## RORSCHACH

| R | 33 | M | 1 | | | Fc | 2 |
|---|---|---|---|---|---|---|---|
|  |  | FM | 5 | F | 18 | c |  |
| W% | 24 | m |  | F- | 6 | C' |  |
| D% | 39 | k |  | F% | 73 | FC | 1 |
| d% | 30 | K |  |  |  | CF |  |
| Dd% / S | 7 | FK |  |  |  | C |  |

# WORK SHEET 2

## VERBAL I. Q.

| EWS | Info. | Comp. | Digit | Arith. | Sim. |
|-----|-------|-------|-------|--------|------|
| 18 | 25 | 20 | | 14 | 23-24 |
| 17 | 24 | 19 | 17 | 13 | 21-22 |
| 16 | 23 | 18 | 16 | 12 | 20 |
| 15 | 21-22 | 17 | | 11 | 19 |
| 14 | 20 | 16 | 15 | | 17-18 |
| 13 | 18-19 | 15 | 14 | 10 | 16 |
| 12 | 17 | 14 | | 9 | 15 |
| | | | | | |
| 11 | 15-16 | 12-13 | 13 | | 13-14 |
| 10 | 13-14 | 11 | 12 | 8 | 12 |
| 9 | 12 | 10 | 11 | 7 | 11 |
| 8 | 10-11 | 9 | | | 9-10 |
| 7 | 9 | 8 | 10 | 6 | 8 |
| 6 | 7-8 | 7 | 9 | 5 | 7 |
| | | | | | |
| 5 | 6 | 5-6 | | | 5-6 |
| 4 | 4-5 | 4 | 8 | 4 | 4 |
| 3 | 2-3 | 3 | 7 | 3 | 3 |
| 2 | 1 | 2 | 6 | | 1-2 |
| 1 | 0 | 1 | | 2 | 0 |
| 0 | | 0 | 5 | 1 | |

## SZONDI

| SEXUAL | | PAROXYSMAL | | EGO | | CONTACT | |
|---|---|---|---|---|---|---|---|
| h | s | e | hy | k | p | d | m |
| | | | | | | | X |
| | | | | | | | X |
| | | | | | X | | X |
| X | X | X | X | X | X | X | X |
| X | X | X | X | X | X | X | X |
| | | | X | X | X | | |
| | | | X | | | | |

## RORSCHACH

| | | | | | |
|---|---|---|---|---|---|
| R 57 | M 6 | | | Fc 2 | |
| | FM 5 | | F 34 | c | |
| W% 26 | m 1 | | F- 5 | C' +1 | |
| D% 37 | k | | F% 68 | FC 2 | |
| d% 19 | K 1 | | | CF | |
| Dd% 18 | FK 1 | | | C | |
| S | | | | | |

## SUMMARY OF TEST FINDINGS $A_1$

### MANNER DURING TEST

| (1) Overly distressed | (2) Tense | (3) Indifferent | (4) Appropriate | (5) Relaxed and actively interested |
|---|---|---|---|---|
| (1) Hostile | (2) Uneasy | | | |

### I.Q. (Bellevue-Wechsler)

| (1) Below average | (2) Average | (3) High average | (4) Superior | (5) Very superior |
|---|---|---|---|---|

### PRODUCTIVITY (Rorschach)

| (1) Impoverished | (2) Reduced output | (3) Adequate | (4) Better than average | (5) Rich and well-ordered |
|---|---|---|---|---|
| | (2) Compulsive productivity | | | |

### RELATION TO REALITY (Rorschach, Bellevue-Wechsler, Drawings)

| (1) Loose | (2) Lapses—together with good form | (3) Not noticeably disturbed | (4) Essentially firm | (5) Firm and good |
|---|---|---|---|---|

### USUAL-UNUSUAL THOUGHT CONTENT (Rorschach, Unpleasant Concept)

| (1) Bizarre | (2) Tendency toward the bizarre | (3) Adequate | (4) Original trends | (5) Outstandingly original |
|---|---|---|---|---|
| (1) Stereotyped | (2) Tendency toward stereotypy | | | |

### CONSTRUCTIVE FANTASY (Rorschach)

| (1) Absent | (2) Barely accessible | (3) Accessible | (4) Readily accessible | (5) Active but not hampering |
|---|---|---|---|---|
| (1) Withdrawal into fantasy | | | | |

### DRIVE (Rorschach, Szondi, Unpleasant Concept)

| (1) Overpowering aggression | (2) Over-aggressive | (3) Adequate | (4) Clearly sufficient | (5) Sufficient—exceptionally well-directed |
|---|---|---|---|---|
| (1) Hampering passivity | (2) Insufficient drive | | | |

### EMOTIONAL TONE (Rorschach, Szondi)

| (1) Explosive emotions | (2) Getting out of hand | (3) Trend toward emotional expression | (4) Warmth available | (5) Warm, readily available |
|---|---|---|---|---|
| (1) Lacking | (2) Indicated but re-pressed emotions | | | |

### SOCIAL ATTITUDE (T. A. T.)

| (1) Uncontrolled | (2) Constricted or neglected | (3) Adequate | (4) Well-regulated | (5) Free and flexible |
|---|---|---|---|---|

### ANXIETY

| (1) Disintegrating | (2) Marked | (3) Moderate | (4) Not marked | (5) Lack of evidence of anxiety |
|---|---|---|---|---|

### OVER-ALL EVALUATION

| (1) Markedly disturbed personality | (2) Less than adequate personality with some psychological problems | (3) Adequate personality | (4) Better than average functioning personality | (5) Exceptionally well-integrated personality with excellent potential |
|---|---|---|---|---|

## SUMMARY OF THERAPIST'S FINDINGS   *A₁*

### ESTIMATED INTELLIGENCE LEVEL

| (1) Below average | (2) Average | (3) High average | (4) Superior | (5) Very superior |
|---|---|---|---|---|

### FLOW OF ASSOCIATIVE MATERIAL

| (1) Impoverished | (2) Reduced output | (3) Adequate | (4) Better than average | (5) Rich and well-ordered |
|---|---|---|---|---|
| | (2) Compulsive productivity | | | |

### RELATION TO REALITY

| (1) Loose | (2) Lapses—together with good form | (3) Not noticeably disturbed | (4) Essentially firm | (5) Firm and good |
|---|---|---|---|---|

### USUAL-UNUSUAL THOUGHT CONTENT

| (1) Bizarre | (2) Tendency toward the bizarre | (3) Adequate | (4) Original trends | (5) Outstandingly original |
|---|---|---|---|---|
| (1) Stereotyped | (2) Tendency toward stereotypy | | | |

### CONSTRUCTIVE FANTASY

| (1) Absent | (2) Barely accessible | (3) Accessible | (4) Readily accessible | (5) Active but not hampering |
|---|---|---|---|---|
| (1) Withdrawal into fantasy | | | | |

### DRIVE

| (1) Overpowering aggression | (2) Over-aggressive | (3) Adequate | (4) Clearly sufficient | (5) Sufficient—exceptionally well-directed |
|---|---|---|---|---|
| (1) Hampering passivity | (2) Insufficient drive | | | |

### EMOTIONAL TONE

| (1) Explosive emotions | (2) Getting out of hand | (3) Trend toward emotional expression | (4) Warmth available | (5) Warm, readily available |
|---|---|---|---|---|
| (1) Lacking | (2) Indicated but repressed emotions | | | |

### SOCIAL ATTITUDE

| (1) Uncontrolled | (2) Constricted or neglected | (3) Adequate | (4) Well-regulated | (5) Free and flexible |
|---|---|---|---|---|

### ANXIETY

| (1) Disintegrating | (2) Marked | (3) Moderate | (4) Not marked | (5) Lack of evidence of anxiety |
|---|---|---|---|---|

### OVER-ALL EVALUATION

| (1) Markedly disturbed personality | (2) Less than adequate personality with some psychological problems | (3) Adequate personality | (4) Better than average functioning personality | (5) Exceptionally well-integrated personality with excellent potential |
|---|---|---|---|---|

better understanding of myself. While I still get sometimes depressed, I can look and see what's the peg on which I should hang it. My headaches, however, are not improved at all."

The changes, as reflected in the test material, are consistent though not spectacular. Three items are particulary noteworthy: In the first place, there is change in the quality of the Figure Drawings. Both technically (where this individual's artistic ability has begun to show itself) and in the change of mood (repose rather than anxiety), the second drawings are clearly superior. Then there is a rise in the human movement responses from one to six, which is encouraging in this total personality structure since, on the whole, it has been on the constricted side. Finally, there is a very real change in abstract thinking (Similarities) where near-bizarre responses have dropped out and a neutral and objective approach within this subtest has been achieved.

It is interesting, in this instance, to make a detailed comparison between the summaries obtained from the therapist and the test findings. A1 had an I.Q. of 125 when first tested, and on retesting, obtained a score of 139, which took him out of the *Superior Group* (score of 4) and put him into the *Very Superior Group* of the total population (score of 5). As was mentioned before, the marked change occurs in the relevance that is found in the abstract thinking: his replies no longer indicate a tendency to a bizarre approach toward the world.

The therapist initially rated this individual's INTELLIGENCE as *Below average* (score of 1), and at the termination of treatment rated him as *Superior* (score of 4). A special note from the therapist on this point calls attention to the fact that this patient gave the impression of an inferior intellectual status because of the inhibiting effect of his disintegrating anxiety.

The change in the FLOW OF ASSOCIATIVE MATERIAL (PRODUCTIVITY) passes from *Adequate* (3) to *Better than average* (4) according to the test findings and the therapist's estimate. Both methods of appraisal assess this individual at the start of therapy as having a RELATION TO REALITY which we have called *Lapses—together with good form* (2). In view of the changed performance in the Figure Drawing and the increased accuracy in the abstract thinking, the second testing places this patient in the classification *Essentially firm* (4), while his therapist finds him at the termination of treatment as having a RELATION TO REALITY of *Firm and good* (5). The slightly inferior rating on the test results is based on the five F— responses that persist in Record 2.

Change in terms of THOUGHT CONTENT is greater according to the therapist's estimate (1 to 5) than on the tests but, as was pointed out, the patient was initially rated as more inhibited and stereotyped in the clinical setting than the test showed. In the same way, there is a wider swing in the estimate of CONSTRUCTIVE FANTASY. Whereas in the test the transition is from a score of 2 to 4, the therapist estimates this patient as from 1 to 5.

Where the category of DRIVE is concerned, *Hampering passivity* was not an essential characteristic of the test findings but did color the clinical picture. Thus, the test estimates in both instances are considered in the *Adequate* range (3), a stage which, as far as the therapist's estimate is concerned, the patient reached only at the end of treatment.

According to our quantitative system we can bring the patient only from a score of 1 to 2 in terms of EMOTIONAL TONE (from 1 to 2 FC responses), whereas his therapist charts him from a score of 2 to 4.

In terms of SOCIAL ATTITUDE, both the tests and the therapist found this individual initially *Constricted* (2). The change that took place occurred in the same direction clinically and according to the tests, but was considered more marked by the therapist. There is a wider swing also in the category of ANXIETY in that the therapist estimates this individual's anxiety as initially being *Disintegrating* (1), whereas in terms of the test it appeared to be *Marked* (2) but in no degree as extreme as that of many patients who have been assessed.

Interestingly enough, despite the fact that there is more change noted in the therapist's itemized estimates than in the comparable ones for the test findings, the clinical OVER-ALL EVALUATION still leaves the patient at *Adequate personality* (3), whereas, according to the quantitative system, the tests have shown sufficient improvement to take him into the category of *Better than average functioning personality* (4).

The total quantitative scores are as follows: The first test, 21; the second test, 30; the therapist's first evaluation, 14; the therapist's second evaluation, 37. Despite these differences in quantitative scores, the picture here is essentially the same when the *direction of change* is considered. Independent estimates by the therapist and the psychologist show no conflict on this. It is important to note, however, that the patient did not lose his headaches and that there still remains a somewhat tense and constricted picture in terms of the Rorschach scores.

A2, male, was between the ages of 25 and 30 and unmarried at the time of the first testing. Two therapists estimated him as at level 1, or a *Markedly disturbed personality*, at the start of therapy, and at level 2 at its termination. The therapist with whom he had worked had considerable reservation about including him in a group of patients designated as

## WORK SHEET

A2

1

### VERBAL I. Q. = 130

| EWS | Info. | Comp. | Digit | Arith. | Sim. |
|-----|-------|-------|-------|--------|------|
| 18 | 25 | 20 | | 14 | 23-24 |
| 17 | 24 | 19 | 17 | 13 | 21-22 |
| 16 | 23 | 18 | 16 | 12 | 20 |
| 15 | 21-22 | 17 | 15 | 11 | 19 |
| 14 | 20 | 16 | 14 | | 7-18 |
| 13 | 18-19 | 15 | | 10 | 16 |
| 12 | 17 | 14 | | 9 | 15 |
| | | | | | |
| 11 | 15-16 | 12-13 | 13 | | 13-14 |
| 10 | 13-14 | 11 | 12 | 8 | 12 |
| 9 | 12 | 10 | 11 | 7 | 11 |
| 8 | 10-11 | 9 | | | 9-10 |
| 7 | 9 | 8 | 10 | 6 | 8 |
| 6 | 7-8 | 7 | 9 | 5 | 7 |
| | | | | | |
| 5 | 6 | 5-6 | | | 5-6 |
| 4 | 4-5 | 4 | 8 | 4 | 4 |
| 3 | 2-3 | 3 | 7 | 3 | 3 |
| 2 | 1 | 2 | 6 | | 1-2 |
| 1 | 0 | 1 | | 2 | 0 |
| 0 | | 0 | 5 | 1 | |

### SZONDI

| SEXUAL | | PAROXYSMAL | | EGO | | CONTACT | |
|--------|--------|--------|--------|--------|--------|--------|--------|
| h | s | e | hy | k | p | d | m |
| | | | | | | | |
| | | X | X | X | X | | |
| X | X | X | X | XX | XX | X | X |
| X | X | X | X | X | | X | X |
| | X | X | X | | | | X |

### OVER-ALL EVALUATION = 22

| | 1 | 2 | 3 | 4 | 5 |
|---|---|---|---|---|---|
| OVER-ALL RATING | 1 | 2 | 3 | 4 | 5 |
| PRODUCTIVITY | 1 | ②ⓧ | 3 | 4 | 5 |
| RELATION TO REALITY | 1 | ② | 3 | 4 | 5 |
| THOUGHT CONTENT | 1 | 2 | ③ | 4 | 5 |
| CONSTRUCTIVE FANTASY | 1 | ② | 3 | 4 | 5 |
| DRIVE | 1 | ② | 3 | 4 | 5 |
| EMOTIONAL TONE | 1 | ② | 3 | 4 | 5 |
| SOCIAL ATTITUDE | 1 | ② | 3 | 4 | 5 |
| ANXIETY | 1 | ② | 3 | 4 | 5 |
| I. Q. RATING   130 | 1 | 2 | 3 | 4 | ⑤ |

### RORSCHACH

| R | 14 | M | 1 | | | Fc | 1 |
|---|----|---|---|---|---|----|---|
| | | FM | 1 | F | 2 | c | |
| W% | 64 | m | 1+1 | F- | 2 | C' | |
| D% | 36 | k | 1 | F% | 29 | FC | 1 |
| d% | | K | | | | CF | 2 |
| Dd% | | FK | | | | c | 2+ |
| S | | | | | | | |

# WORK SHEET

*A2*

2

## VERBAL I. Q. = 136

| EWS | Info. | Comp. | Digit | Arith. | Sim. |
|-----|-------|-------|-------|--------|------|
| 18 | 25 | 20 | | 14 | 23-24 |
| 17 | 24 | 19 | 17 | 13 | 21-22 |
| 16 | 23 | 18 | 16 | 12 | 20 |
| 15 | 21-22 | 17 | | 11 | 19 |
| 14 | 20 | 16 | 15 | | 17-18 |
| 13 | 18-19 | 15 | 14 | 10 | 16 |
| 12 | 17 | 14 | | 9 | 15 |
| | | | | | |
| 11 | 15-16 | 12-13 | 13 | | 13-14 |
| 10 | 13-14 | 11 | 12 | 8 | 12 |
| 9 | 12 | 10 | 11 | 7 | 11 |
| 8 | 10-11 | 9 | | | 9-10 |
| 7 | 9 | 8 | 10 | 6 | 8 |
| 6 | 7-8 | 7 | 9 | 5 | 7 |
| | | | | | |
| 5 | 6 | 5-6 | | | 5-6 |
| 4 | 4-5 | 4 | 8 | 4 | 4 |
| 3 | 2-3 | 3 | 7 | 3 | 3 |
| 2 | 1 | 2 | 6 | | 1-2 |
| 1 | 0 | 1 | | 2 | 0 |
| 0 | | 0 | 5 | 1 | |

## SZONDI

| SEXUAL | | PAROXYSMAL | | EGO | | CONTACT | |
|--------|--|------------|--|-----|--|---------|--|
| h | s | e | hy | k | p | d | m |

## OVER-ALL EVALUATION = 32

| | | | | | |
|---|---|---|---|---|---|
| OVER-ALL RATING | 1 | 2 | 3 | 4 | 5 |
| PRODUCTIVITY | 1 | 2 | ③ | 4 | 5 |
| RELATION TO REALITY | 1 | 2 | ③ | 4 | 5 |
| THOUGHT CONTENT | 1 | 2 | ③ | 4 | 5 |
| CONSTRUCTIVE FANTASY | 1 | 2 | 3 | ④ | 5 |
| DRIVE | 1 | 2 | 3 | ④ | 5 |
| EMOTIONAL TONE | 1 | 2 | 3 | ④ | 5 |
| SOCIAL ATTITUDE | 1 | 2 | ③ | 4 | 5 |
| ANXIETY | 1 | 2 | ③ | 4 | 5 |
| I. Q. RATING = 136 | 1 | 2 | 3 | 4 | ⑤ |

## RORSCHACH

R 38     M 6(2-)          Fc 2+1

         FM 6      F 7     c 1

W% 42    m 3+1    F-       C' +1

D% 47    k 3      F% 18    FC 4

d% 11    K                 CF 3

Dd%      FK 1             c 2

S

# SUMMARY OF TEST FINDINGS  A₂

## MANNER DURING TEST

| (1) Overly distressed | (2) Tense | (3) Indifferent | (4) Appropriate | (5) Relaxed and actively interested |
|---|---|---|---|---|
| (1) Hostile | (2) Uneasy | | | |

## I.Q. (Bellevue-Wechsler)

| (1) Below average | (2) Average | (3) High average | (4) Superior | (5) Very superior |
|---|---|---|---|---|

## PRODUCTIVITY (Rorschach)

| (1) Impoverished | (2) Reduced output | (3) Adequate | (4) Better than average | (5) Rich and well-ordered |
|---|---|---|---|---|
| | (2) Compulsive productivity | | | |

## RELATION TO REALITY (Rorschach, Bellevue-Wechsler, Drawings)

| (1) Loose | (2) Lapses—together with good form | (3) Not noticeably disturbed | (4) Essentially firm | (5) Firm and good |
|---|---|---|---|---|

## USUAL-UNUSUAL THOUGHT CONTENT (Rorschach, Unpleasant Concept)

| (1) Bizarre | (2) Tendency toward the bizarre | (3) Adequate | (4) Original trends | (5) Outstandingly original |
|---|---|---|---|---|
| (1) Stereotyped | (2) Tendency toward stereotypy | | | |

## CONSTRUCTIVE FANTASY (Rorschach)

| (1) Absent | (2) Barely accessible | (3) Accessible | (4) Readily accessible | (5) Active but not hampering |
|---|---|---|---|---|
| (1) Withdrawal into fantasy | | | | |

## DRIVE (Rorschach, Szondi, Unpleasant Concept)

| (1) Overpowering aggression | (2) Over-aggressive | (3) Adequate | (4) Clearly sufficient | (5) Sufficient—exceptionally well-directed |
|---|---|---|---|---|
| (1) Hampering passivity | (2) Insufficient drive | | | |

## EMOTIONAL TONE (Rorschach, Szondi)

| (1) Explosive emotions | (2) Getting out of hand | (3) Trend toward emotional expression | (4) Warmth available | (5) Warm, readily available |
|---|---|---|---|---|
| (1) Lacking | (2) Indicated but repressed emotions | | | |

## SOCIAL ATTITUDE (T. A. T.)

| (1) Uncontrolled | (2) Constricted or neglected | (3) Adequate | (4) Well-regulated | (5) Free and flexible |
|---|---|---|---|---|

## ANXIETY

| (1) Disintegrating | (2) Marked | (3) Moderate | (4) Not marked | (5) Lack of evidence of anxiety |
|---|---|---|---|---|

## OVER-ALL EVALUATION

| (1) Markedly disturbed personality | (2) Less than adequate personality with some psychological problems | (3) Adequate personality | (4) Better than average functioning personality | (5) Exceptionally well-integrated personality with excellent potential |
|---|---|---|---|---|

## SUMMARY OF THERAPIST'S FINDINGS        *A2,*

### ESTIMATED INTELLIGENCE LEVEL

| (1) Below average | (2) Average | (3) High average | (4) Superior | (5) Very superior |
|---|---|---|---|---|

*(5) Very superior is circled)*

### FLOW OF ASSOCIATIVE MATERIAL

| (1) Impoverished | (2) Reduced output | (3) Adequate | (4) Better than average | (5) Rich and well-ordered |
|---|---|---|---|---|
| | (2) Compulsive productivity | | | |

*(3) Adequate is circled*

### RELATION TO REALITY

| (1) Loose | (2) Lapses—together with good form | (3) Not noticeably disturbed | (4) Essentially firm | (5) Firm and good |
|---|---|---|---|---|

*(4) Essentially firm is circled*

### USUAL-UNUSUAL THOUGHT CONTENT

| (1) Bizarre | (2) Tendency toward the bizarre | (3) Adequate | (4) Original trends | (5) Outstandingly original |
|---|---|---|---|---|
| (1) Stereotyped | (2) Tendency toward stereotypy | | | |

*(4) Original trends is circled*

### CONSTRUCTIVE FANTASY

| (1) Absent | (2) Barely accessible | (3) Accessible | (4) Readily accessible | (5) Active but not hampering |
|---|---|---|---|---|
| (1) Withdrawal into fantasy | | ? | | |

### DRIVE

| (1) Overpowering aggression | (2) Over-aggressive | (3) Adequate | (4) Clearly sufficient | (5) Sufficient—exceptionally well-directed |
|---|---|---|---|---|
| (1) Hampering passivity | (2) Insufficient drive | | | |

*(1) Hampering passivity is circled*

### EMOTIONAL TONE

| (1) Explosive emotions | (2) Getting out of hand | (3) Trend toward emotional expression | (4) Warmth available | (5) Warm, readily available |
|---|---|---|---|---|
| (1) Lacking | (2) Indicated but repressed emotions | | | |

*(2) Getting out of hand is circled*

### SOCIAL ATTITUDE

| (1) Uncontrolled | (2) Constricted or neglected | (3) Adequate | (4) Well-regulated | (5) Free and flexible |
|---|---|---|---|---|

*(2) Constricted or neglected is circled*

### ANXIETY

| (1) Disintegrating | (2) Marked | (3) Moderate | (4) Not marked | (5) Lack of evidence of anxiety |
|---|---|---|---|---|

*(2) Marked is circled with arrow to (3) Moderate*

### OVER-ALL EVALUATION

| (1) Markedly disturbed personality | (2) Less than adequate personality with some psychological problems | (3) Adequate personality | (4) Better than average functioning personality | (5) Exceptionally well-integrated personality with excellent potential |
|---|---|---|---|---|

*(1) Markedly disturbed personality is circled with arrow to (2)*

showing definite improvement. At the time of the second testing, however, several years had elapsed since the long-term analytic therapy had ended, and our findings seem to indicate that improvement can take place subsequent to the termination of therapy; thus, we are inclined to think that the greater degree of change reflected in the test findings represents his present status.

This patient spoke freely about his own feelings in regard to his previous and present condition. By no means did he feel that analytic therapy had been completely successful, although he did feel himself to have been helped in many areas. Some of the old difficulties, he claimed, still persisted, although his over-all feeling was one of encouragement and that the experience had been worthwhile.

A comparison of the subtests in the Bellevue-Wechsler reveals a slightly altered pattern in the psychogram although his score places him in the *Very Superior Group* of the total population both times. On the Szondi, the shift from –m to ambivalent m is perhaps the most favorable change. There would also appear to be a greater mobilization of energy, a greater capacity to work indicated in the –h +s scores. One of the positive results of therapy mentioned by this patient was the fact that he had been able to get going and work better since his treatment. The ego picture remains the same.

Although there is much in the second set of Drawings that can be considered still ineffectual, those produced in Test 2 are at least attempts at full-length figures. In Test 1 the entire page had been taken up with a sketchy and inadequate head and shoulders. The concept of the person as a whole has emerged in Test 2, even though it is still an individual lacking hands or feet and without proper facial features.

The Rorschach can be said to show genuine improvement although some identical and quite disturbed color responses still remain. Three good FC responses have found their way into the record, and the total of human movement answers is now six as opposed to one. There is also greater vitality in the animal movement responses, which have risen quantitatively in the same way.

Previously, of the three F responses given, two were F–, and profoundly disturbed at that. The second record shows a different form level; the F– responses have dropped out, although in over-reaching himself somewhat in the realm of fancy, as will be noted, two of the M responses are minus ones.

The OVER-ALL EVALUATION in the second record is a total score of 32, whereas at the start of treatment the patient was estimated at 22. The Summary Sheet of the therapist's findings shows considerably less movement in the direction of a richer personality than do the tests. On the other hand, it should be pointed out that the original clinical estimate in certain areas was higher. Clinically, for instance, this individual showed a more adequate flow of associative material; did not demonstrate, in the initial therapeutic sessions, the deviations from a firm relationship to reality which he did in the tests; and showed more originality in thinking than could be found from the tests alone. There is agreement on the shift toward greater drive both in the therapist's estimate and in the tests.

A3, an unmarried girl in her early twenties at the time of the initial psychodiagnostic testing, was seen for the second assessment after some eight years of analytic treatment with two therapists. The initial rating by the first therapist on the OVER-ALL EVALUATION was 1; the estimate of the second therapist at the time of testing brought her up to 3, an *Adequate personality*. Some excerpts from the material in the case history at the time of the first testing read as follows:

> "From high school years, A3 has had violent homosexual attachments. With these she has become so obsessionally preoccupied at times that she can barely think of anything else, night or day. Yet she has never had an overt homosexual experience, beyond the most casual and rare gestures of affection. Furthermore, in her obsessional sexual preoccupation her fantasies are always of masochistic, heterosexual perversions involving gangsters, rescues by young brave fathers, etc.
>
> "In her relationships with men she has been compulsively promiscuous; and in these unhappy experiences she feels compelled to behave coarsely and obscenely with the deliberate intent of alienating the man. She is caught between an incessant compulsion to become involved with men and an immediate compulsion to rid herself of them. She has never been engaged and is repelled and frightened at the thought of marriage. She becomes involved with eligible young men again and again, and then flees the situation through this unhappy device.
>
> "On top of this she suffers from severe insomnia, a chronic state of anxiety, bouts of diarrhea, and recurring nightmares from which she awakens screaming."

Elsewhere, the therapist stated:

> "Much of the facade of her personality is a screen behind which she hides. She wears a front of sweetness, gaiety, warmth, and interest in the world and in people around her. Actually, this covers a good deal of bitterness, a resentful depression which in the past she masked even from herself, some obsessional morbid fantasies, a limited interest in things outside of herself, and a tendency to lapse into a world of make-believe not unlike that of a child. Because she is young and attractive, she has been able to hide much of this throughout school and college: but such masking devices as she has used never continue to work

# WORK SHEET
1

## VERBAL I. Q. = 124

| EWS | Info. | Comp. | Digit | Arith. | Sim. |
|-----|-------|-------|-------|--------|------|
| 18 | 25 | 20 | | 14 | 23-24 |
| 17 | 24 | 19 | 17 | 13 | 21-22 |
| 16 | 23 | 18 | 16 | 12 | 20 |
| 15 | 21-22 | 17 | | 11 | 19 |
| 14 | 20 | 16 | 15 | | 17-18 |
| 13 | 18-19 | 15 | 14 | 10 | 16 |
| 12 | 17 | 14 | | 9 | 15 |
| 11 | 15-16 | 12-13 | 13 | | 13-14 |
| 10 | 13-14 | 11 | 12 | 8 | 12 |
| 9 | 12 | 10 | 11 | 7 | 11 |
| 8 | 10-11 | 9 | | | 9-10 |
| 7 | 9 | 8 | 10 | 6 | 8 |
| 6 | 7-8 | 7 | 9 | 5 | 7 |
| 5 | 6 | 5-6 | | | 5-6 |
| 4 | 4-5 | 4 | 8 | 4 | 4 |
| 3 | 2-3 | 3 | 7 | 3 | 3 |
| 2 | 1 | 2 | 6 | | 1-2 |
| 1 | 0 | 1 | | 2 | 0 |
| 0 | | 0 | 5 | 1 | |

## SZONDI

| | SEXUAL | | PAROXYSMAL | | EGO | | CONTACT | |
|---|---|---|---|---|---|---|---|---|
| | h | s | e | hy | k | p | d | m |
| | | | | | | X | | X |
| | | | | | | X | | X |
| | X | X | X | X | X | X | X | X |
| | X | X | | X | X | X | X | |
| | X | X | | X | X | X | X | |
| | | | | | X | | | |
| | | | | | | | | |

## OVER-ALL EVALUATION = 22

| | | | | | |
|---|---|---|---|---|---|
| OVER-ALL RATING | 1 | 2 | 3 | 4 | 5 |
| PRODUCTIVITY | 1 | 2 | 3 | (4) | 5 |
| RELATION TO REALITY | 1 | (2) | 3 | 4 | 5 |
| THOUGHT CONTENT | 1 | (2) | 3 | 4 | 5 |
| CONSTRUCTIVE FANTASY | 1 | 2 | (3) | 4 | 5 |
| DRIVE | 1 | (2) | 3 | 4 | 5 |
| EMOTIONAL TONE | (1) | 2 | 3 | 4 | 5 |
| SOCIAL ATTITUDE | (1) | 2 | 3 | 4 | 5 |
| ANXIETY | 1 | 2 | (3) | 4 | 5 |
| I. Q. RATING  124 | 1 | 2 | 3 | (4) | 5 |

## RORSCHACH

| | | | | | |
|---|---|---|---|---|---|
| R 40 | M 6 (3-) | | | Fc 2 | |
| | FM 1 | F 9 | | c 1+ | |
| W% 40 | m 1 +1 | F- 5 | | C' | |
| D% 55 | k 1 | F% 35 | | FC 2 | |
| d% 3 | K | | | CF 8 | |
| Dd% 2 | FK 2 | | | c 2 | |
| S | | | | | |

# WORK SHEET 2

## VERBAL I. Q. = 139

| EWS | Info. | Comp. | Digit | Arith. | Sim. |
|-----|-------|-------|-------|--------|------|
| 18 | 25 | 20 | | 14 | 23-24 |
| 17 | 24 | 19 | 17 | 13 | 21-22 |
| 16 | 23 | 18 | 16 | 12 | 20 |
| 15 | 21-22 | 17 | | 11 | 19 |
| 14 | 20 | 16 | 15 | | 17-18 |
| 13 | 18-19 | 15 | 14 | 10 | 16 |
| 12 | 17 | 14 | | 9 | 15 |
| | | | | | |
| 11 | 15-16 | 12-13 | 13 | | 13-14 |
| 10 | 13-14 | 11 | 12 | 8 | 12 |
| 9 | 12 | 10 | 11 | 7 | 11 |
| 8 | 10-11 | 9 | | | 9-10 |
| 7 | 9 | 8 | 10 | 6 | 8 |
| 6 | 7-8 | 7 | 9 | 5 | 7 |
| | | | | | |
| 5 | 6 | 5-6 | | | 5-6 |
| 4 | 4-5 | 4 | 8 | 4 | 4 |
| 3 | 2-3 | 3 | 7 | 3 | 3 |
| 2 | 1 | 2 | 6 | | 1-2 |
| 1 | 0 | 1 | | 2 | 0 |
| 0 | | 0 | 5 | 1 | |

## SZONDI

| SEXUAL | | PAROXYSMAL | | EGO | | CONTACT | |
|--------|---|------------|----|-----|---|---------|---|
| h | s | e | hy | k | p | d | m |

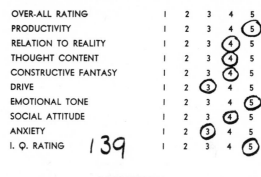

## OVER-ALL EVALUATION = 37

| | | | | | |
|---|---|---|---|---|---|
| OVER-ALL RATING | 1 | 2 | 3 | 4 | 5 |
| PRODUCTIVITY | 1 | 2 | 3 | 4 | ⑤ |
| RELATION TO REALITY | 1 | 2 | 3 | ④ | 5 |
| THOUGHT CONTENT | 1 | 2 | 3 | ④ | 5 |
| CONSTRUCTIVE FANTASY | 1 | 2 | 3 | ④ | 5 |
| DRIVE | 1 | 2 | ③ | 4 | 5 |
| EMOTIONAL TONE | 1 | 2 | 3 | 4 | ⑤ |
| SOCIAL ATTITUDE | 1 | 2 | 3 | ④ | 5 |
| ANXIETY | 1 | 2 | ③ | 4 | 5 |
| I. Q. RATING 139 | 1 | 2 | 3 | 4 | ⑤ |

## RORSCHACH

| R | 52 | M | 7 | | | Fc | 4+1 |
|---|----|---|----|---|----|----|-----|
| | | FM | 1 | F | 23 | c | 3 |
| W% | 25 | m | +4 | F- | | C' | +1 |
| D% | 58 | k | | F% | 43 | FC | 7 |
| d% | 9 | K | | | | CF | 4 |
| Dd% S | 8 | FK | 1 | | | C | 2 |

## SUMMARY OF TEST FINDINGS    A 3

### MANNER DURING TEST

| (1) Overly distressed | (2) Tense | (3) Indifferent | (4) Appropriate | (5) Relaxed and actively interested |
|---|---|---|---|---|
| (1) Hostile | (2) Uneasy | | | |

### I.Q. (Bellevue-Wechsler)

| (1) Below average | (2) Average | (3) High average | (4) Superior | (5) Very superior |
|---|---|---|---|---|

### PRODUCTIVITY (Rorschach)

| (1) Impoverished | (2) Reduced output | (3) Adequate | (4) Better than average | (5) Rich and well-ordered |
|---|---|---|---|---|
| | (2) Compulsive productivity | | | |

### RELATION TO REALITY (Rorschach, Bellevue-Wechsler, Drawings)

| (1) Loose | (2) Lapses—together with good form | (3) Not noticeably disturbed | (4) Essentially firm | (5) Firm and good |
|---|---|---|---|---|

### USUAL-UNUSUAL THOUGHT CONTENT (Rorschach, Unpleasant Concept)

| (1) Bizarre | (2) Tendency toward the bizarre | (3) Adequate | (4) Original trends | (5) Outstandingly original |
|---|---|---|---|---|
| (1) Stereotyped | (2) Tendency toward stereotypy | | | |

### CONSTRUCTIVE FANTASY (Rorschach)

| (1) Absent | (2) Barely accessible | (3) Accessible | (4) Readily accessible | (5) Active but not hampering |
|---|---|---|---|---|
| (1) Withdrawal into fantasy | | | | |

### DRIVE (Rorschach, Szondi, Unpleasant Concept)

| (1) Overpowering aggression | (2) Over-aggressive | (3) Adequate | (4) Clearly sufficient | (5) Sufficient—exceptionally well-directed |
|---|---|---|---|---|
| (1) Hampering passivity | (2) Insufficient drive | | | |

### EMOTIONAL TONE (Rorschach, Szondi)

| (1) Explosive emotions | (2) Getting out of hand | (3) Trend toward emotional expression | (4) Warmth available | (5) Warm, readily available |
|---|---|---|---|---|
| (1) Lacking | (2) Indicated but repressed emotions | | | |

### SOCIAL ATTITUDE (T. A. T.)

| (1) Uncontrolled | (2) Constricted or neglected | (3) Adequate | (4) Well-regulated | (5) Free and flexible |
|---|---|---|---|---|

### ANXIETY

| (1) Disintegrating | (2) Marked | (3) Moderate | (4) Not marked | (5) Lack of evidence of anxiety |
|---|---|---|---|---|

### OVER-ALL EVALUATION

| (1) Markedly disturbed personality | (2) Less than adequate personality with some psychological problems | (3) Adequate personality | (4) Better than average functioning personality | (5) Exceptionally well-integrated personality with excellent potential |
|---|---|---|---|---|

## SUMMARY OF THERAPIST'S FINDINGS A3

### ESTIMATED INTELLIGENCE LEVEL

| (1) Below average | (2) Average | (3) High average | (4) Superior ⟵(circled) | (5) Very superior |
|---|---|---|---|---|

### FLOW OF ASSOCIATIVE MATERIAL

| (1) Impoverished | (2) Reduced output | (3) Adequate | (4) Better than average | (5) Rich and well-ordered |
|---|---|---|---|---|
| | (2) Compulsive productivity (circled) → | | | |

### RELATION TO REALITY

| (1) Loose | (2) Lapses—together with good form (circled) → | (3) Not noticeably disturbed | (4) Essentially firm | (5) Firm and good |
|---|---|---|---|---|

### USUAL-UNUSUAL THOUGHT CONTENT

| (1) Bizarre | (2) Tendency toward the bizarre | (3) Adequate (circled) → | (4) Original trends | (5) Outstandingly original |
|---|---|---|---|---|
| (1) Stereotyped | (2) Tendency toward stereotypy | | | |

### CONSTRUCTIVE FANTASY

| (1) Absent | (2) Barely accessible | (3) Accessible (circled) | (4) Readily accessible | (5) Active but not hampering |
|---|---|---|---|---|
| (1) Withdrawal into fantasy | | | | |

### DRIVE

| (1) Overpowering aggression | (2) Over-aggressive | (3) Adequate | (4) Clearly sufficient | (5) Sufficient—exceptionally well-directed |
|---|---|---|---|---|
| (1) Hampering passivity | (2) Insufficient drive (circled) → | | | |

### EMOTIONAL TONE

| (1) Explosive emotions | (2) Getting out of hand | (3) Trend toward emotional expression | (4) Warmth available | (5) Warm, readily available |
|---|---|---|---|---|
| (1) Lacking | (2) Indicated but repressed emotions (circled) → | | | |

### SOCIAL ATTITUDE

| (1) Uncontrolled | (2) Constricted or neglected | (3) Adequate (circled) → | (4) Well-regulated | (5) Free and flexible |
|---|---|---|---|---|

### ANXIETY

| (1) Disintegrating | (2) Marked | (3) Moderate (circled) | (4) Not marked | (5) Lack of evidence of anxiety |
|---|---|---|---|---|

### OVER-ALL EVALUATION

| (1) Markedly disturbed personality | (2) Less than adequate personality with some psychological problems | (3) Adequate personality (circled) | (4) Better than average functioning personality | (5) Exceptionally well-integrated personality with excellent potential |
|---|---|---|---|---|

[dashed box] 1ST THERAPIST

indefinitely. Furthermore, these same tendencies influence her relationships with both her contemporaries and older people. As a matter of fact, it is the ease with which she can substitute fantasies and day dreams for vigorous and sustained interests in either activities or people which threatens her most seriously."

Turning to a comparison of Work Sheets 1 and 2, one finds not only a marked rise in I.Q., from 124 to 139, but a very different type of scattergram. The erraticness and scatter seen in the first performance is virtually absent in the second.

More situational anxiety is reflected in the Szondi taken in the second testing; the +m has risen considerably. The patient, interestingly enough, commented that she was, so to speak, on her mettle and that she felt that there was more tension in regard to the test on the second occasion. At the present time, it may be said that she cares what others think of her and about the impression she makes socially, whereas at the time of the initial testing she rather enjoyed her erraticness.

The Figure Drawings bear a highly idiosyncratic stamp. It is as if this individual could only caricature, rather than portray, a facet of womanhood with which she was concerned at the time. Comparison of test and clinical material reveals that the initial drawing paralleled material which came to the surface in clinical sessions concerning her acute embarrassment, as a child, at what she considered the unshapeliness of her own body. At the time of the second testing, there was considerable identification with an aesthetic mother figure, which would seem to have influenced the second drawing.

A structural comparison of the Rorschach scores does not reflect the great differences between the records. The increase in the total number of R is insignificant, but the change in type and quality of the human movement response is striking. The six human movement responses in the initial record included three bizarre and warped concepts.

On the color side, a tremendous difference has taken place even at the structural level. This gifted, ambi-equal girl now produces responses having a ratio of 7 FC:4 CF:2 C, whereas previously the explosive and primitive emotions completely colored the affectual picture, 2 FC:8 CF: 2 C.

The quality of the responses is so markedly different in the two records that several answers are recorded for comparative purposes. In Rorschach 1, there are grotesque concepts and masochistic fantasies of the following kind: (Card II) "Two clowns, clapping hands, and blood all around. It really looks like blood. It looks as if they have been whipped, bruised and bloody underneath. They've got little goatees and noses made long by theatrical putty. Here, it's suggestive of the underside of the cow, with udders, teats and blood all around. There's a tail in the red part. The clothes of the clowns are torn off their backs—the whip has torn the cloth away." Or take the responses to Card IV: "This is a frightful one, all distorted. The trunk of a tree, a roughly hewn log. And here is a bear nailed, while alive, to this thing by a man, his body chopped off, his arms chopped off, membranes still hanging, with the boots left on. There are parts of it all ragged from its being beaten." Or take again, the answer to Card IX: "Here is an embryo of a newborn baby, but it's a very sick baby. They have to keep it alive by some apparatus—a tube all around it, and machines. The green is a rubber bag. The baby has to breathe through this to get any air. It has to defecate and urinate into the same rubber bag. Its functions won't work unless they are produced artificially. Here is a rubber rod inserted into his stomach."

The subsequent answer to Card II has by no means lost its highly charged affective characteristics, but the picture is an infinitely more controlled one: "A drop of blood on a white-tiled floor. Two witches playing pat-a-cake. They have teeth and fang-like lips. Two Greek gods with hooked noses, hair, a goatee. The drawings of the north wind or the south wind blowing. There are reddish bruises on the witches." To Card IV, we now have: "A person with amputated limbs, large boots, a velvet flap or crown, an old one, pockmarked with age." and to Card IX: "Like a map showing terrain in a geography book. The green might indicate a forest, the orange might be swampy water and the red, mountains. Or it could be a faded old coat and a man fishing, sitting there leaning against a rock. The green is his wife and she comes along. She is angry and pushes him into the water; he's in the act of falling."

Some of the most interesting aspects of this individual's test findings are the changes exhibited in the Sentence Completion. The shortened version of the Holsopple-Miale test which was used throughout these investigations is given here, with the answers from the first and second tests arranged for comparative purposes:

| *Incomplete Sentences* | *Completions* |
| --- | --- |
| Children are usually certain that. . . | (1) They'll be spanked if they spill ashes. |
|  | (2) It's fun to eat. |
| People are praised when. . . | (1) They've done good. |
|  | (2) They do good. |
| A large crowd. . . | (1) Gathered to watch the hanging. |
|  | (2) Gathered on opening night. |

| *Incomplete Sentences* | *Completions* |
|---|---|
| A person is most helpless when. . . | (1) A baby. |
| | (2) He is sick and poor. |
| When an animal is wild. . . | (1) It will kill you. |
| | (2) Some people like to hunt it. |
| The hardest decisions are. . . | (1) The worst. |
| | (2) When all alternatives have about equal appeal. |
| The easiest way to get money. . . | (1) Is to steal. |
| | (2) Is to inherit it. |
| Twenty years from now. . . | (1) God knows. |
| | (2) I hope I'll still be alive and happy. |
| Parents would worry less. . . | (1) If children weren't people. |
| | (2) If they had more confidence in themselves as parents. |
| When fire starts. . . | (1) Everyone runs. |
| | (2) Call the fire department. |
| Compared with dogs, cats are. . . | (1) Nicer. |
| | (2) Quieter, cleaner but not so friendly. |
| Fathers should learn that. . . | (1) They, too, have a part in bringing up the child other than just beating it. |
| | (2) They are as important to the child as the mother. |
| It is easy to get into trouble when. . . | (1) You don't know which way you're going. |
| | (2) You don't know what the trouble is. |
| Few children fear. . . | (1) Little. |
| | (2) Bugs. |
| At the end of the road. . . | (1) There's nothing. |
| | (2) Lies no one knows where. |
| He drew back from the touch of. . . | (1) Her hand. |
| | (2) His teacher's moist hand. |
| The white girl who married the colored man. . . | (1) Was too attracted to move away. |
| | (2) Had difficulty adjusting to a new life. |
| The most pleasant dreams. . . | (1) Occur least often. |
| | (2) Occur during the day. |
| No one can repair the damage caused by. . . | (1) Parents. |
| | (2) War. |
| The nicest thing about being a child. . . | (1) Is lack of responsibility. |
| | (2) Is how fresh everything seems to us. |
| There is hardly any. . . | (1) Rose without thorns. |
| | (2) Achievement without effort. |
| To be without shame. . . | (1) Is to be happy. |
| | (2) Is to be free. |
| Worse than being lonely is. . . | (1) Being really all alone. |
| | (2) Being neurotic. |
| When a person is ill. . . | (1) *Sometimes* he's taken care of. |
| | (2) It's best to seek help. |

| *Incomplete Sentences* | *Completions* |
|---|---|
| The best thing about old age. . . | (1) You're going to die very soon. |
| | (2) Is how experienced you are. |
| If people only knew how much. . . | (1) There is to learn. |
| | (2) Love other people want, they wouldn't feel so loveless themselves. |
| People refrain from murder only because. | (1) They're scared. |
| | (2) The training against killing is so strong. |
| The finger pointed. . . | (1) At me. |
| | (2) At the soldier looking at the recruiting sign. |
| A naked man. . . | (1) Walks differently. |
| | (2) Can be beautiful. |
| A woman's body. . . | (1) Was found naked and bloodstained. |
| | (2) Is as lovely. |
| The kind of animal I would most like to be is. . . | (1) A tiger. |
| | (2) A bird. |
| Why. . . | (1) Fierce and powerful. King of the jungle. Able to kill. |
| | (2) The idea of freedom of flight. |

The macabre streak which runs through the initial test findings has vanished from the second. There is also a pessimism found in the first record which is greatly minimized later. The masochistic preoccupation with being beaten, which gave rise to some of the grotesquely flavored Rorschach responses as well, has now subsided and is replaced by healthier attitudes. To highlight some of these changes, we could point to such initial statements concerned with mutilation and beating as: "A woman's body . . . was found naked and bloodstained." "Fathers should learn that . . . they, too, have a part in bringing up the child other than beating it." "The kind of animal I would most like to be . . . a tiger." Why? . . . "Able to kill."

Indications of depression came through in such sentences as: "The best thing about old age . . . you're going to die very soon." "At the end of the road . . . there is nothing." "Twenty years from now . . . God knows." "When a person is ill . . . *sometimes* he's taken care of." Psychopathic traits also found their way into the first test: "The easiest way to get money . . . is to steal it"; and considerable guilt: "The finger pointed . . . at me."

The different orientation can be seen in the fact that none of these sentences recur. In general, in the total test pattern, A3 has developed a more positive and healthier orientation to life. On the OVER-ALL EVALUATION this patient starts with a score of 22 and ends with 37.

The clinical assessment made by the patient's second therapist is available for comparison with the test findings. It should be pointed out, however, that A3 was initially tested at a time when the first therapist's estimate of her was *Markedly disturbed personality,* a considerably more disturbed picture than the chart which is now included on the basis of the second therapist's evaluation. The dotted lines show how she was assessed by the first therapist at the time of the first psychological evaluation. On this count, A3 had already progressed five points on the quantitative scale before being assessed by the second therapist.

A4 was in his early twenties when first seen for psychodiagnostic testing. He was retested seven years later, after five years of intensive analytic treatment. The original referring physician gave him an OVER-ALL EVALUATION rating of between 1 and 2, but by the time he reached the second therapist with whom he worked over the five-year period he was already assessed as a *Better than average personality.* At the termination of treatment, the second therapist rated A4 as an *Exceptionally well-integrated personality with excellent potential.*

A4 himself spoke enthusiastically about changes which he had experienced subsequent to therapy. He considered it a completely worthwhile experience and rated himself as greatly improved, although he was realistically aware of some remaining difficulties and problems. At the time of the retesting, he had been married for two years and had a child.

An evaluation of the subtests on the Bellevue-Wechsler reveals a flattening out of the curve to an almost perfect distribution on the second testing. Although A4 was originally rated in the *Very Superior Group* of the total population, there was nevertheless some unevenness in his initial production. Freed from personal problems which had crept into his handling of the Comprehension and Similarities and prevented an objective assessment of the questions involved, the score improved qualitatively as well as quantitatively.

In the first testing there were glaring areas of tension in the Szondi, notably the exaggerated need for love and affection (the loaded $+h$ factor) and the childish dependency reflected in the strong $-d$. The ego picture, open in both vectors, suggested an unformed and amorphous personality structure. The second picture shows considerably greater maturity and adult orientation.

While the jester which A4 draws in the second test is meant to portray a feeling of gaiety, it is not completely successful and there is a forced element to the merriment. Nonetheless, when one compares the expansive stance with the huddled and inadequate figure drawn at the first testing, a greater freedom and spontaneity is reflected.

The comparison between the Rorschach records may be said to show an individual who has blossomed from initial promise. The expansion and changes toward greater freedom are reflected in both the structural properties of the record and in the content. Most striking is the wealth of good form-color responses which are now available, and the addition of four good human movement answers reflecting various kinds of identification not achieved in the first record. That the number of Fc responses has risen to nine may be considered by some as reflecting undue sensitivity, but the total record gives the impression of excellent balance, and the nuances of refinement of feeling in conjunction with the full-blooded color responses do not appear to be indications of an inability to react directly and spontaneously. It is interesting that the mental approach, despite the lapse of seven years and the doubling of the total number of responses, remains essentially the same.

The quantitative score achieved by this individual at the start is 28, at the termination of treatment, 36. An even more enthusiastic picture is given from the clinical side. There is no question but that A1, A3, and A4 show change in a constructive direction. (Patient A4's records are shown on the next four pages.)

The therapist's estimate of A5, a girl in her early twenties, was that of a *Markedly disturbed personality* at the start of therapy. At its termination, she was rated clinically as an *Adequate personality* with the potential for *Better than average* adjustment, a rating somewhere between 3 and 4 on our scale. Her therapist further described her as, "A warm, friendly, bright person who is well-liked. She still has difficulty in asserting herself and will have to work at establishing more well-rounded relationships with her peers."

Summarizing the therapist's full report, one finds the following: A5 entered therapy initially with considerable suspicion and was quite uncommunicative at first. Rapport had to be established under unfavorable circumstances. The patient had been very much involved with both her parents in a masochistic way. During treatment, the therapist states, there was no attempt made to modify the environment; the parents were never contacted because of the deep, basic distrust the patient had of the therapist at the start of treatment. Therapy was felt to be an attack and that the analyst was "attacking mother."

Because her individuation was so poor, the patient was encouraged to find some identification with the analyst. A5 was a twin, and this difficult relationship complicated the identification with the mother. After a period in which the patient was helped to develop her own individuality, the emphasis of the analysis fell on the working out of her

# WORK SHEET

1

## VERBAL I. Q. = 141

| EWS | Info. | Comp. | Digit | Arith. | Sim. |
|-----|-------|-------|-------|--------|------|
| 18 | 25 | 20 | | ⟨14⟩ | 23-24 |
| 17 | 24 | 19 | ⟨17⟩ | 13 | 21-22 |
| 16 | ⟨23⟩ | 18 | 16 | 12 | 20 |
| 15 | 21-22 | ⟨17⟩ | | 11 | 19 |
| 14 | 20 | 16 | 15 | | ⟨17-18⟩ |
| 13 | 18-19 | 15 | 14 | 10 | 16 |
| 12 | 17 | 14 | | 9 | 15 |
| | | | | | |
| 11 | 15-16 | 12-13 | 13 | | 13-14 |
| 10 | 13-14 | 11 | 12 | 8 | 12 |
| 9 | 12 | 10 | 11 | 7 | 11 |
| 8 | 10-11 | 9 | | | 9-10 |
| 7 | 9 | 8 | 10 | 6 | 8 |
| 6 | 7-8 | 7 | 9 | 5 | 7 |
| | | | | | |
| 5 | 6 | 5-6 | | | 5-6 |
| 4 | 4-5 | 4 | 8 | 4 | 4 |
| 3 | 2-3 | 3 | 7 | 3 | 3 |
| 2 | 1 | 2 | 6 | | 1-2 |
| 1 | 0 | 1 | 5 | 2 | 0 |
| 0 | | 0 | | 1 | |

## SZONDI

| SEXUAL | | PAROXYSMAL | | EGO | | CONTACT | |
|--------|---|------------|----|-----|---|---------|---|
| h | s | e | hy | k | p | d | m |
| X | | | | | | | |
| X | | | | | | | X |
| X | | | | | | | |
| X | X | X | X | X | X | X | X |
| X | X | X | X | | X | X | X |
| X | | | X | | | X | |
| | | | | | | X | |
| | | | | | | X | |

## OVER-ALL EVALUATION = 28

| | 1 | 2 | 3 | 4 | 5 |
|---|---|---|---|---|---|
| OVER-ALL RATING | 1 | 2 | 3 | 4 | 5 |
| PRODUCTIVITY | 1 | 2 | ③ | 4 | 5 |
| RELATION TO REALITY | 1 | 2 | ③ | 4 | 5 |
| THOUGHT CONTENT | 1 | 2 | ③ | 4 | 5 |
| CONSTRUCTIVE FANTASY | 1 | 2 | ③ | 4 | 5 |
| DRIVE | 1 | 2 | ③ | 4 | 5 |
| EMOTIONAL TONE | 1 | ② | 3 | 4 | 5 |
| SOCIAL ATTITUDE | 1 | 2 | ③ | 4 | 5 |
| ANXIETY | 1 | 2 | ③ | 4 | 5 |
| I. Q. RATING  141 | 1 | 2 | 3 | 4 | ⑤ |

## RORSCHACH

| R 37 | M 4 | | Fc 4 |
|------|------|------|------|
| | FM 8 | F 14 | c |
| W% 18 | m | F- 4 | C' 1 |
| D% 66 | k | F% 49 | FC 2 |
| d% | K | | CF |
| Dd% 16 S | FK | | C |

## WORK SHEET 2

### VERBAL I. Q. = 146

| EWS | Info. | Comp. | Digit | Arith. | Sim. |
|---|---|---|---|---|---|
| 18 | 25 | 20 | | 14 | 23-24 |
| 17 | 24 | 19 | 17 | 13 | 21-22 |
| 16 | 23 | 18 | 16 | 12 | 20 |
| 15 | 21-22 | 17 | | 11 | 19 |
| 14 | 20 | 16 | 15 | | 17-18 |
| 13 | 18-19 | 15 | 14 | 10 | 16 |
| 12 | 17 | 14 | | 9 | 15 |
| | | | | | |
| 11 | 15-16 | 12-13 | 13 | | 13-14 |
| 10 | 13-14 | 11 | 12 | 8 | 12 |
| 9 | 12 | 10 | 11 | 7 | 11 |
| 8 | 10-11 | 9 | | | 9-10 |
| 7 | 9 | 8 | 10 | 6 | 8 |
| 6 | 7-8 | 7 | 9 | 5 | 7 |
| | | | | | |
| 5 | 6 | 5-6 | | | 5-6 |
| 4 | 4-5 | 4 | 8 | 4 | 4 |
| 3 | 2-3 | 3 | 7 | 3 | 3 |
| 2 | 1 | 2 | 6 | | 1-2 |
| 1 | 0 | 1 | | 2 | 0 |
| 0 | | 0 | 5 | 1 | |

### SZONDI

| SEXUAL | | PAROXYSMAL | | EGO | | CONTACT | |
|---|---|---|---|---|---|---|---|
| h | s | e | hy | k | p | d | m |

OVER-ALL EVALUATION = 36

| | | | | | |
|---|---|---|---|---|---|
| OVER-ALL RATING | 1 | 2 | 3 | 4 | 5 |
| PRODUCTIVITY | 1 | 2 | 3 | 4 | (5) |
| RELATION TO REALITY | 1 | 2 | 3 | (4) | 5 |
| THOUGHT CONTENT | 1 | 2 | 3 | (4) | 5 |
| CONSTRUCTIVE FANTASY | 1 | 2 | 3 | (4) | 5 |
| DRIVE | 1 | 2 | (3) | 4 | 5 |
| EMOTIONAL TONE | 1 | 2 | 3 | (4) | 5 |
| SOCIAL ATTITUDE | 1 | 2 | (3) | 4 | 5 |
| ANXIETY | 1 | 2 | 3 | (4) | 5 |
| I. Q. RATING 146 | 1 | 2 | 3 | 4 | (5) |

### RORSCHACH

| | | | | | |
|---|---|---|---|---|---|
| R 77 | M 8 | | | | Fc 9 |
| | FM 7 | | F 36 | | c 1 |
| W% 16 | m 1+1 | | F- 5 | | C' |
| D% 52 | k | | F% 53 | | FC 9 |
| d% 12 | K +1 | | | | CF 1 |
| Dd% S 20 | FK | | | | C |

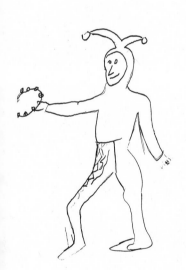

# SUMMARY OF TEST FINDINGS   *A4*

## MANNER DURING TEST

| (1) Overly distressed | (2) Tense | (3) Indifferent | (4) Appropriate | (5) Relaxed and actively interested |
|---|---|---|---|---|
| (1) Hostile | (2) Uneasy | | | |

## I.Q. (Bellevue-Wechsler)

| (1) Below average | (2) Average | (3) High average | (4) Superior | (5) Very superior |
|---|---|---|---|---|

## PRODUCTIVITY (Rorschach)

| (1) Impoverished | (2) Reduced output | (3) Adequate | (4) Better than average | (5) Rich and well-ordered |
|---|---|---|---|---|
| | (2) Compulsive productivity | | | |

## RELATION TO REALITY (Rorschach, Bellevue-Wechsler, Drawings)

| (1) Loose | (2) Lapses—together with good form | (3) Not noticeably disturbed | (4) Essentially firm | (5) Firm and good |
|---|---|---|---|---|

## USUAL-UNUSUAL THOUGHT CONTENT (Rorschach, Unpleasant Concept)

| (1) Bizarre | (2) Tendency toward the bizarre | (3) Adequate | (4) Original trends | (5) Outstandingly original |
|---|---|---|---|---|
| (1) Stereotyped | (2) Tendency toward stereotypy | | | |

## CONSTRUCTIVE FANTASY (Rorschach)

| (1) Absent | (2) Barely accessible | (3) Accessible | (4) Readily accessible | (5) Active but not hampering |
|---|---|---|---|---|
| (1) Withdrawal into fantasy | | | | |

## DRIVE (Rorschach, Szondi, Unpleasant Concept)

| (1) Overpowering aggression | (2) Over-aggressive | (3) Adequate | (4) Clearly sufficient | (5) Sufficient—exceptionally well-directed |
|---|---|---|---|---|
| (1) Hampering passivity | (2) Insufficient drive | | | |

## EMOTIONAL TONE (Rorschach, Szondi)

| (1) Explosive emotions | (2) Getting out of hand | (3) Trend toward emotional expression | (4) Warmth available | (5) Warm, readily available |
|---|---|---|---|---|
| (1) Lacking | (2) Indicated but repressed emotions | | | |

## SOCIAL ATTITUDE (T. A. T.)

| (1) Uncontrolled | (2) Constricted or neglected | (3) Adequate | (4) Well-regulated | (5) Free and flexible |
|---|---|---|---|---|

## ANXIETY

| (1) Disintegrating | (2) Marked | (3) Moderate | (4) Not marked | (5) Lack of evidence of anxiety |
|---|---|---|---|---|

## OVER-ALL EVALUATION

| (1) Markedly disturbed personality | (2) Less than adequate personality with some psychological problems | (3) Adequate personality | (4) Better than average functioning personality | (5) Exceptionally well-integrated personality with excellent potential |
|---|---|---|---|---|

## SUMMARY OF THERAPIST'S FINDINGS A4

### ESTIMATED INTELLIGENCE LEVEL

| (1) Below average | (2) Average | (3) High average | (4) Superior | (5) Very superior |
|---|---|---|---|---|

### FLOW OF ASSOCIATIVE MATERIAL

| (1) Impoverished | (2) Reduced output | (3) Adequate | (4) Better than average | (5) Rich and well-ordered |
|---|---|---|---|---|
| | (2) Compulsive productivity | | | |

### RELATION TO REALITY

| (1) Loose | (2) Lapses—together with good form | (3) Not noticeably disturbed | (4) Essentially firm | (5) Firm and good |
|---|---|---|---|---|

### USUAL-UNUSUAL THOUGHT CONTENT

| (1) Bizarre | (2) Tendency toward the bizarre | (3) Adequate | (4) Original trends | (5) Outstandingly original |
|---|---|---|---|---|
| (1) Stereotyped | (2) Tendency toward stereotypy | | | |

### CONSTRUCTIVE FANTASY

| (1) Absent | (2) Barely accessible | (3) Accessible | (4) Readily accessible | (5) Active but not hampering |
|---|---|---|---|---|
| (1) Withdrawal into fantasy | | | | |

### DRIVE

| (1) Overpowering aggression | (2) Over-aggressive | (3) Adequate | (4) Clearly sufficient | (5) Sufficient— exceptionally well-directed |
|---|---|---|---|---|
| (1) Hampering passivity | (2) Insufficient drive | | | |

### EMOTIONAL TONE

| (1) Explosive emotions | (2) Getting out of hand | (3) Trend toward emotional expression | (4) Warmth available | (5) Warm, readily available |
|---|---|---|---|---|
| (1) Lacking | (2) Indicated but re-pressed emotions | | | |

### SOCIAL ATTITUDE

| (1) Uncontrolled | (2) Constricted or neglected | (3) Adequate | (4) Well-regulated | (5) Free and flexible |
|---|---|---|---|---|

### ANXIETY

| (1) Disintegrating | (2) Marked | (3) Moderate | (4) Not marked | (5) Lack of evidence of anxiety |
|---|---|---|---|---|

### OVER-ALL EVALUATION

| (1) Markedly disturbed personality | (2) Less than adequate personality with some psychological problems | (3) Adequate personality | (4) Better than average functioning personality | (5) Exceptionally well-integrated personality with excellent potential |
|---|---|---|---|---|

⌐ ¬ = 1ˢᵀ THERAPIST

relationship with her mother, or, more explicitly, enabling her to accept the lack of the identification which she had felt. For a long time the patient could only see it as "mother's fault, her complete oversight of me as a person," and could only slowly accept her own part, namely, her own withdrawal as the simpler solution in the face of her own aggression.

When this was worked through, it was easy for her to look at the much more guilt-laden relationship with her twin sister. She had had to be her twin's protector and mother, and much libido had been directed toward the twin. This made relationships with boys very difficult, and she constantly repeated her twin relationship with her boy friends. Frequently these relationships were terminated by her out of fear of her own aggression and her castrative wishes. She would assuage her guilt feelings about this by "letting them sleep with her."

Due to her twin relationship, the problems of individuation and personalization were of particular importance in therapy. A5 had constantly tried to overcome her sibling rivalry by "giving up mother" to her twin, while still trying to hold on to her father. She constantly divided the parents between them: mother belongs to the twin, father is mine.

At one point, there came a very traumatic moment: "There is no room for me under the coat." She had run to her mother who had, in a protective gesture, put her coat round the sister but A5, arriving a moment later, could not find room enough inside.

For several months, approximately at the age of three or four, the patient felt herself to be a boy and the twin to be the girl. Patient A5 was the active, dominant and aggressive one of the twins, playing outdoors whenever possible, suggesting games and exploring in their sexual play. However, she was also the giving, unselfish one, looking out for the twin and protecting her. At all times there seems to have been very close identification, one with the other; they would watch each other's pain, pleasure, guilt and anger.

The strong bond between the twins, and the weak relationship to the mother, gave the whole ego an appearance of flatness. There had grown up, in relationships with others, an over-compensation expressed by an artificial show of emotion. The patient was only able to throw this off after she gained strength of her own and more realization of herself.

The patient had escaped into over-activity to deal with her aggressive and hostile feelings, while her identification with her twin made up for the lack of fulfillment of emotional needs by her parents.

The first work done in therapy was aimed toward the strengthening of ego feelings, which were extremely weak, and toward drawing the patient out from her corner—"When mother and I were in the same room she took up all the space. There was no room left for me."—and getting her over her fear of sitting inactively and talking rather than running around.

In the light of the therapist's comments it is worthwhile to consider the test findings in detail. The extent of A5's disturbance and at the same time, in our opinion, her potential for responding to therapy can be seen from the test battery.

On the first test battery there is marked scatter on the Wechsler; the full bodies of the figures cannot be attempted; productivity on the Rorschach is far below the potential for an individual whose I.Q. places her in the *Superior Group* of the population. Moreover, within this small output the percentage of M's reflect marked withdrawal; there are definite bizarre qualities to the thinking process; there is failure in the face of Card VI and other disturbed features to the record.

In the light of the twin relationship, the second answer to Card 1, "Two little pixies facing each other, a well between them," suggests both their closeness and feeling of isolation.

The very disturbed answer on Card IV, "Somebody's father, decomposed; no one I cared about but at whose house I once stayed," gives a picture loaded with oedipal problems which have had no chance at ventilation.

The answer to Card X, "It's seen in parts, someone trying to hold these things apart. Things coming in on him, green legs," reflects the inroads of her disturbance into the thinking and reality testing area. The repetition of "masks" in two of the ten answers reinforces the picture of lack of personalization.

A5, however, shows her originality in her answer to Card III: "It's a car ad. Two very exaggerated butlers on either side, saying, 'For those who care for the best'." There is also a lively human movement response on Card VII: "Two little old ladies gossiping, lots of teeth, very interested in what the other one is saying."

As might be expected at this point, the whole problem of feminine identification is the area of maximum tension, and this is reflected in the ambivalent score in the h factor in the Szondi test. This individual's too facile withdrawal into her own fantasy is shown in the open k, +p ego distribution. Though not in any way a greatly disturbed record, the Szondi is not inconsistent with the type of difficulties shown in the Rorschach and reported by the therapist. Rather, it indicates, along with the good human movement responses in Card III, a potential for readjustment. That the Szondi does not give a more disturbed picture at this stage is, in our opinion, an encouraging sign.

The contrast between Record 1 and Record 2 allows us to make note of considerable improvement in several areas, although some unsolved

# WORK SHEET

A5

1

## VERBAL I. Q. = 126

| EWS | Info. | Comp. | Digit | Arith. | Sim. |
|---|---|---|---|---|---|
| 18 | 25 | 20 |  | 14 | 23-24 |
| 17 | 24 | 19 | 17 | 13 | 21-22 |
| 16 | 23 | 18 | 16 | 12 | 20 |
| 15 | 21-22 | 17 |  | 11 | 19 |
| 14 | 20 | 16 | 15 |  | 17-18 |
| 13 | 18-19 | 15 | 14 | 10 | 16 |
| 12 | 17 | 14 |  | 9 | 15 |
| 11 | 15-16 | 12-13 | 13 |  | 13-14 |
| 10 | 13-14 | 11 | 12 | 8 | 12 |
| 9 | 12 | 10 | 11 | 7 | 11 |
| 8 | 10-11 | 9 |  |  | 9-10 |
| 7 | 9 | 8 | 10 | 6 | 8 |
| 6 | 7-8 | 7 | 9 | 5 | 7 |
| 5 | 6 | 5-6 |  |  | 5-6 |
| 4 | 4-5 | 4 | 8 | 4 | 4 |
| 3 | 2-3 | 3 | 7 | 3 | 3 |
| 2 | 1 | 2 | 6 |  | 1-2 |
| 1 | 0 | 1 |  | 2 | 0 |
| 0 |  | 0 | 5 | 1 |  |

## SZONDI

| SEXUAL | | PAROXYSMAL | | EGO | | CONTACT | |
|---|---|---|---|---|---|---|---|
| h | s | e | hy | k | p | d | m |

## OVER-ALL EVALUATION = 21

| | | | | | |
|---|---|---|---|---|---|
| OVER-ALL RATING | 1 | 2 | 3 | 4 | 5 |
| PRODUCTIVITY | 1 | (2) | 3 | 4 | 5 |
| RELATION TO REALITY | 1 | (2) | 3 | 4 | 5 |
| THOUGHT CONTENT | 1 | (2) | 3 | 4 | 5 |
| CONSTRUCTIVE FANTASY | 1 | 2 | (3) | 4 | 5 |
| DRIVE | 1 | (2) | 3 | 4 | 5 |
| EMOTIONAL TONE | 1 | (2) | 3 | 4 | 5 |
| SOCIAL ATTITUDE | 1 | (2) | 3 | 4 | 5 |
| ANXIETY | 1 | (2) | 3 | 4 | 5 |
| I. Q. RATING = 126 | 1 | 2 | 3 | (4) | 5 |

## RORSCHACH

| R  12 | M  5(1-) | | Fc |
|---|---|---|---|
| | FM  1 | F  2 | c |
| W%  67 | m  1+1 | F-  2 | C' |
| D%  33 | k | F%  33 | FC |
| d% | K | | CF  1 |
| Dd% | FK | | C |
| S | | | |

===== **WORK SHEET** ===== A5

2

## VERBAL I. Q. = 135

| EWS | Info. | Comp. | Digit | Arith. | Sim. |
|-----|-------|-------|-------|--------|------|
| 18 | 25 | 20 | | 14 | 23-24 |
| 17 | 24 | 19 | 17 | 13 | 21-22 |
| 16 | 23 | 18 | 16 | 12 | 20 |
| 15 | 21-22 | 17 | | 11 | 19 |
| 14 | 20 | 16 | 15 | | 17-18 |
| 13 | 18-19 | 15 | 14 | 10 | 16 |
| 12 | 17 | 14 | | 9 | 15 |
| | | | | | |
| 11 | 15-16 | 12-13 | 13 | | 13-14 |
| 10 | 13-14 | 11 | 12 | 8 | 12 |
| 9 | 12 | 10 | 11 | 7 | 11 |
| 8 | 10-11 | 9 | | | 9-10 |
| 7 | 9 | 8 | 10 | 6 | 8 |
| 6 | 7-8 | 7 | 9 | 5 | 7 |
| | | | | | |
| 5 | 6 | 5-6 | | | 5-6 |
| 4 | 4-5 | 4 | 8 | 4 | 4 |
| 3 | 2-3 | 3 | 7 | 3 | 3 |
| 2 | 1 | 2 | 6 | | 1-2 |
| 1 | 0 | 1 | | 2 | 0 |
| 0 | | 0 | 5 | 1 | |

### SZONDI

| SEXUAL | | PAROXYSMAL | | EGO | | CONTACT | |
|--------|---|------------|----|-----|---|---------|---|
| h | s | e | hy | k | p | d | m |

OVER-ALL EVALUATION = 35

| | I | 2 | 3 | 4 | 5 |
|---|---|---|---|---|---|
| OVER-ALL RATING | I | 2 | 3 | 4 | 5 |
| PRODUCTIVITY | I | 2 | 3 | 4 | (5) |
| RELATION TO REALITY | I | (2) | 3 | 4 | 5 |
| THOUGHT CONTENT | I | 2 | 3 | (4) | 5 |
| CONSTRUCTIVE FANTASY | I | 2 | 3 | 4 | (5) |
| DRIVE | I | (2) | 3 | 4 | 5 |
| EMOTIONAL TONE | I | 2 | 3 | (4) | 5 |
| SOCIAL ATTITUDE | I | 2 | 3 | (4) | 5 |
| ANXIETY | I | 2 | 3 | (4) | 5 |
| I. Q. RATING 135 | I | 2 | 3 | 4 | (5) |

### RORSCHACH

R 59      M 17 (3-)      Fc 1+1

FM 4      F 25      c

W% 24      m +2      F- 3      C'

D% 55      k      F% 47      FC 4+4

d% 7      K      CF 3+1

Dd% 14      FK 1      c 1
S

# SUMMARY OF TEST FINDINGS

A5

### MANNER DURING TEST

| (1) Overly distressed | (2) Tense | (3) Indifferent | (4) Appropriate | (5) Relaxed and actively interested |
|---|---|---|---|---|
| (1) Hostile | (2) Uneasy | | | |

### I.Q. (Bellevue-Wechsler)

| (1) Below average | (2) Average | (3) High average | (4) Superior | (5) Very superior |
|---|---|---|---|---|

### PRODUCTIVITY (Rorschach)

| (1) Impoverished | (2) Reduced output | (3) Adequate | (4) Better than average | (5) Rich and well-ordered |
|---|---|---|---|---|
| | (2) Compulsive productivity | | | |

### RELATION TO REALITY (Rorschach, Bellevue-Wechsler, Drawings)

| (1) Loose | (2) Lapses—together with good form | (3) Not noticeably disturbed | (4) Essentially firm | (5) Firm and good |
|---|---|---|---|---|

### USUAL-UNUSUAL THOUGHT CONTENT (Rorschach, Unpleasant Concept)

| (1) Bizarre | (2) Tendency toward the bizarre | (3) Adequate | (4) Original trends | (5) Outstandingly original |
|---|---|---|---|---|
| (1) Stereotyped | (2) Tendency toward stereotypy | | | |

### CONSTRUCTIVE FANTASY (Rorschach)

| (1) Absent | (2) Barely accessible | (3) Accessible | (4) Readily accessible | (5) Active but not hampering |
|---|---|---|---|---|
| (1) Withdrawal into fantasy | | | | |

### DRIVE (Rorschach, Szondi, Unpleasant Concept)

| (1) Overpowering aggression | (2) Over-aggressive | (3) Adequate | (4) Clearly sufficient | (5) Sufficient—exceptionally well-directed |
|---|---|---|---|---|
| (1) Hampering passivity | (2) Insufficient drive | | | |

### EMOTIONAL TONE (Rorschach, Szondi)

| (1) Explosive emotions | (2) Getting out of hand | (3) Trend toward emotional expression | (4) Warmth available | (5) Warm, readily available |
|---|---|---|---|---|
| (1) Lacking | (2) Indicated but repressed emotions | | | |

### SOCIAL ATTITUDE (T. A. T.)

| (1) Uncontrolled | (2) Constricted or neglected | (3) Adequate | (4) Well-regulated | (5) Free and flexible |
|---|---|---|---|---|

### ANXIETY

| (1) Disintegrating | (2) Marked | (3) Moderate | (4) Not marked | (5) Lack of evidence of anxiety |
|---|---|---|---|---|

### OVER-ALL EVALUATION

| (1) Markedly disturbed personality | (2) Less than adequate personality with some psychological problems | (3) Adequate personality | (4) Better than average functioning personality | (5) Exceptionally well-integrated personality with excellent potential |
|---|---|---|---|---|

## SUMMARY OF THERAPIST'S FINDINGS

AS

### ESTIMATED INTELLIGENCE LEVEL

| (1) Below average | (2) Average | (3) High average | (4) Superior | (5) Very superior |
|---|---|---|---|---|

### FLOW OF ASSOCIATIVE MATERIAL

| (1) Impoverished | (2) Reduced output<br>(2) Compulsive productivity | (3) Adequate | (4) Better than average | (5) Rich and well-ordered |
|---|---|---|---|---|

### RELATION TO REALITY

| (1) Loose | (2) Lapses—together with good form | (3) Not noticeably disturbed | (4) Essentially firm | (5) Firm and good |
|---|---|---|---|---|

### USUAL-UNUSUAL THOUGHT CONTENT

| (1) Bizarre | (2) Tendency toward the bizarre | (3) Adequate | (4) Original trends | (5) Outstandingly original |
|---|---|---|---|---|
| (1) Stereotyped | (2) Tendency toward stereotypy | | | |

### CONSTRUCTIVE FANTASY

| (1) Absent | (2) Barely accessible | (3) Accessible | (4) Readily accessible | (5) Active but not hampering |
|---|---|---|---|---|
| (1) Withdrawal into fantasy | | | | |

### DRIVE

| (1) Overpowering aggression | (2) Over-aggressive | (3) Adequate | (4) Clearly sufficient | (5) Sufficient—exceptionally well-directed |
|---|---|---|---|---|
| (1) Hampering passivity | (2) Insufficient drive | | | |

### EMOTIONAL TONE

| (1) Explosive emotions | (2) Getting out of hand . | (3) Trend toward emotional expression | (4) Warmth available | (5) Warm, readily available |
|---|---|---|---|---|
| (1) Lacking | (2) Indicated but repressed emotions | | | |

### SOCIAL ATTITUDE

| (1) Uncontrolled | (2) Constricted or neglected | (3) Adequate | (4) Well-regulated | (5) Free and flexible |
|---|---|---|---|---|

### ANXIETY

| (1) Disintegrating | (2) Marked | (3) Moderate | (4) Not marked | (5) Lack of evidence of anxiety |
|---|---|---|---|---|

### OVER-ALL EVALUATION

| (1) Markedly disturbed personality | (2) Less than adequate personality with some psychological problems | (3) Adequate personality | (4) Better than average functioning personality | (5) Exceptionally well-integrated personality with excellent potential |
|---|---|---|---|---|

problems remain. The major work of analysis was over at the time of the second testing, but the patient was still seeing the analyst occasionally.

As far as the Bellevue-Wechsler is concerned, this individual now achieves a rating in the *Very Superior* adult group. The Comprehension score in particular, even though it rises only three points on the weighted scale, indicates a solidarity and a realism not shown so markedly in the first performance. The scatter has leveled off, and the inroads of anxiety in the test situation are not so great, with both the Digit Memory and the Arithmetic handled better than previously.

The Szondi profile is practically unchanged and is again one that carries no suggestion of disturbance of any magnitude. One might expect that as further growth takes place, a +h would characterize this individual's more complete acceptance of herself in a woman's role.

Change and improvement are shown in the Rorschach, the richness and originality now reflected being in startling contrast to the first record. Although problems remain—the first answer to Card IV, for instance, shows the patient still to be concerned with her relationship to her father —it is clear that an individual capable of giving the second Rorschach record is also able to handle such problems in a more effective manner. Her relationship to her father, incidentally, was explored very late in the analysis and it is the therapist's feeling that if A5 were retested once more, the tests would register the progress that she has since made in this area.

In the Figure Drawings, still somewhat unsure of her feminine role, A5 depicts herself in slacks but is willing now to portray a "whole" individual.

## A5 RORSCHACH RESPONSES

| RORSCHACH 1 | RORSCHACH 2 |
|---|---|
| *Card I* | *Card I* |
| 1. A mask. | 1. Two elves here, playing, balancing against a bell somehow. Have tails. |
| 2. Two little pixies facing each other— a well between them. | 2. Figure in here, figure of woman balancing blanket on head. Her arms are up. |
| | 3. Halloween mask of a cat. |
| | 4. Woman's face on either side, old ladies looking in old-fashioned mirrors. Have hats with pompoms on them. |
| *Card II* | *Card II* |
| 1. Mongolians. Hands up between them. Heads included. | 1. Two figures, Russian dancers with red turbans on. They are down on one |

RORSCHACH 1

RORSCHACH 2

knee clicking heels which creates an impact. They may be challenging each other—bumped their heads, too. Have knapsacks on backs.
2. Two elephants.
3. Rooster.
4. An old man with potbelly, looking off over here.
5. Two monks dancing. They are leaping off into space on either side.

*Card III*

1. A car ad. Two very exaggerated butlers on either side. "For those who care for the best."

*Card III*

1. This is a poster advertising a car—rather abstract thing. Two butlers with car in middle, wide and low. Wide windshield. Butlers wearing high heels, starched waist fronts. Also balancing each other by "opposing strains."
2. Bow tie in middle.
3. Bloody parts on side.
4. Poster in process of being made. Paint cans upset.
5. Soft-headed monster.
6. African natives, heads project in back.
7. Hoofs

*Card IV*

1. The "Heep"—a comic-book character vegetated in earth and decomposed.

2. Someone's father, decomposed; no one I cared about but at whose house I stayed once.

*Card IV*

1. Caricature of middle-aged man sitting on toilet—big stomach, rumpled clothes, feet sticking forward and big floppy penis about as big as he is. He's a washout.
2. Horses.
3. Moose.
4. Camel's nose.
5. French nuns, worshipping something in middle.
6. Witches.

*Card V*

1. A bug, wings spread, landed, or about to take off.

*Card V*

1. A bat, facing the other way.

2. Stamen from a flower.
3. A rabbit.
4. Two women facing the other way.

RORSCHACH 1

RORSCHACH 2

They are covered by bearskin rugs. Both women have peg legs. "Two are better than one."

*Card VI*

1. Don't know what this is.

*Card VI*

1. O.K. this is a penis—vague—get this over with.
2. Aerial view of a canal.
3. Bedpost.
4. Candlestick.
5. Wings.
6. Cat's whiskers.
7. Two old men sitting back to back with arms high up, pointing. Egotistical individuals.
8. Ice tongs.

*Card VII*

1. Two little old ladies gossiping, lots of teeth—very interested in what the other one is saying.

*Card VII*

1. Two old ladies talking in rocking chairs, speaking so eagerly.

2. Elephants.

*Card VIII*

1. Clown's mask or just his face made up.

*Card VIII*

1. Clown's mask.
2. Pink rats—mice's ears—not very vicious.
3. Candlestick.
4. Mask, illustrated—the unhappy one.
5. Insect.
6. A fox terrier's head.
7. Albino antelope.

*Card IX*

1. I see things in pairs—two seahorses facing each other.

*Card IX*

1. There are two pink elephants— knocked heads together. You can see concussion of their impact.
2. Two old lobsters offering up their old claws to each other to say "hello." Trying to be gruff and old but kicking up heels.
3. Sweet young thing kissing herself in mirror. She's green—she's in shadow.
4. Two pregnant sea lions, male. The male sea lion carries babies.
5. Old man with beard. Just wrenched beard away from the other one.
6. Madonna.

RORSCHACH 1

*Card X*

1. Well, seen in parts, someone trying to hold these things apart. Things coming on him, green legs.

RORSCHACH 2

*Card X*

1. I remember—man in middle with green pants, loin cloth on, Turkish slippers, full blouse, earphones. No face, it's not here.
2. Blue crabs.
3. Eiffel tower.
4. Torch.
5. Deep sea crabs.
6. Soft-shelled crabs.
7. Flying mice leaping at this thing here.
8. Man—doesn't fit into any form— holding up these pink clowns who are blowing bubbles. Pink structures are being shifted.
9. Rats struggling to get in.
10. Torches are being brought by women to attack rats.

A6 was in his early twenties and unmarried when first tested by this examiner. He had previously taken psychological tests, however, some five years before, at what may be considered the height of his disturbance. It has been possible to record some aspects of this first psychological testing by way of the dotted lines on the Test Summary. At the time of the first testing by this examiner, A6 was about to embark on additional therapy.

The therapist's OVER-ALL EVALUATION at the time this patient entered therapy was that he presented a *Markedly disturbed personality*. At the time of termination of treatment, this assessment had progressed to grade 2, a *Less than adequate personality with psychological problems*, while the test findings gave a rating of 3, *Adequate personality*. The therapist commented, "I confined myself to an evaluation of the patient in the therapeutic situation. This may possibly account for the apparent discrepancy, since there does not seem to be the same clinical improvement observable except for a somewhat lessened tendency toward explosive emotional reactions and a slight improvement in the intensity and duration of regressive phenomena. I have the impression, however, that these phenomena are related to the transference, and there is occasional evidence that there has been some improvement in this patient's business and social life, which is consistent with the discrepancy to be found between his performance in the tests and his behavior in the therapeutic situation."

## WORK SHEET === A 6

### 1

### VERBAL I. Q. = 137

| EWS | Info. | Comp. | Digit | Arith. | Sim. |
|---|---|---|---|---|---|
| 18 | 25 | 20 | | 14 | 23-24 |
| 17 | 24 | 19 | 17 | 13 | 21-22 |
| 16 | 23 | 18 | 16 | 12 | 20 |
| 15 | 21-22 | 17 | | 11 | 19 |
| 14 | 20 | 16 | 15 | | 17-18 |
| 13 | 18-19 | 15 | 14 | 10 | 16 |
| 12 | 17 | 14 | | 9 | 15 |
| | | | | | |
| 11 | 15-16 | 12-13 | 13 | | 13-14 |
| 10 | 13-14 | 11 | 12 | 8 | 12 |
| 9 | 12 | 10 | 11 | 7 | 11 |
| 8 | 10-11 | 9 | | | 9-10 |
| 7 | 9 | 8 | 10 | 6 | 8 |
| 6 | 7-8 | 7 | 9 | 5 | 7 |
| | | | | | |
| 5 | 6 | 5-6 | | | 5-6 |
| 4 | 4-5 | 4 | 8 | 4 | 4 |
| 3 | 2-3 | 3 | 7 | 3 | 3 |
| 2 | 1 | 2 | 6 | | 1-2 |
| 1 | 0 | 1 | | 2 | 0 |
| 0 | | 0 | 5 | 1 | |

### SZONDI

| SEXUAL | | PAROXYSMAL | | EGO | | CONTACT | |
|---|---|---|---|---|---|---|---|
| h | s | e | hy | k | p | d | m |
| | | | | | X | | |
| X | | | | | X | | |
| X | | | | | X | | X |
| X | | X | | X | X | X | X |
| X | | X | X | X | | X | X |
| X | | | X | X | | | X |
| | | | X | | | | |
| | | | X | | | | |

### OVER-ALL EVALUATION = 25

| | 1 | 2 | 3 | 4 | 5 |
|---|---|---|---|---|---|
| OVER-ALL RATING | 1 | 2 | 3 | 4 | 5 |
| PRODUCTIVITY | 1 | (2) | 3 | 4 | 5 |
| RELATION TO REALITY | 1 | 2 | 3 | (4) | 5 |
| THOUGHT CONTENT | 1 | 2 | (3) | 4 | 5 |
| CONSTRUCTIVE FANTASY | 1 | (2) | 3 | 4 | 5 |
| DRIVE | 1 | 2 | (3) | 4 | 5 |
| EMOTIONAL TONE | 1 | (2) | 3 | 4 | 5 |
| SOCIAL ATTITUDE | 1 | (2) | 3 | 4 | 5 |
| ANXIETY | 1 | (2) | 3 | 4 | 5 |
| I. Q. RATING   137 | 1 | 2 | 3 | 4 | (5) |

### RORSCHACH

R 12    M 2        Fc 1

FM 3    F 2    c

W% 34    m +2    F-    C' 1

D% 66    k    F% 17    FC

d%    K 1+1    CF 1

Dd%    FK    c 1
S

## WORK SHEET

A6

2

### VERBAL I. Q. = 143

| EWS | Info. | Comp. | Digit | Arith. | Sim. |
|---|---|---|---|---|---|
| 18 | 25 | 20 | | 14 | 23-24 |
| 17 | 24 | 19 | 17 | 13 | 21-22 |
| 16 | 23 | 18 | 16 | 12 | 20 |
| 15 | 21-22 | 17 | 15 | 11 | 19 |
| 14 | 20 | 16 | 15 | | 17-18 |
| 13 | 18-19 | 15 | 14 | 10 | 16 |
| 12 | 17 | 14 | | 9 | 15 |
| | | | | | |
| 11 | 15-16 | 12-13 | 13 | | 13-14 |
| 10 | 13-14 | 11 | 12 | 8 | 12 |
| 9 | 12 | 10 | 11 | 7 | 11 |
| 8 | 10-11 | 9 | | | 9-10 |
| 7 | 9 | 8 | 10 | 6 | 8 |
| 6 | 7-8 | 7 | 9 | 5 | 7 |
| | | | | | |
| 5 | 6 | 5-6 | | | 5-6 |
| 4 | 4-5 | 4 | 8 | 4 | 4 |
| 3 | 2-3 | 3 | 7 | 3 | 3 |
| 2 | 1 | 2 | 6 | | 1-2 |
| 1 | 0 | 1 | | 2 | 0 |
| 0 | | 0 | 5 | 1 | |

### SZONDI

| SEXUAL | | PAROXYSMAL | | EGO | | CONTACT | |
|---|---|---|---|---|---|---|---|
| h | s | e | hy | k | p | d | m |

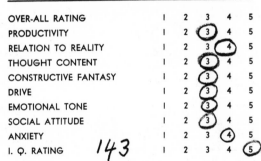

### OVER-ALL EVALUATION = 31

| | | | | | |
|---|---|---|---|---|---|
| OVER-ALL RATING | 1 | 2 | 3 | 4 | 5 |
| PRODUCTIVITY | 1 | 2 | ③ | 4 | 5 |
| RELATION TO REALITY | 1 | 2 | 3 | ④ | 5 |
| THOUGHT CONTENT | 1 | 2 | ③ | 4 | 5 |
| CONSTRUCTIVE FANTASY | 1 | 2 | ③ | 4 | 5 |
| DRIVE | 1 | 2 | ③ | 4 | 5 |
| EMOTIONAL TONE | 1 | 2 | ③ | 4 | 5 |
| SOCIAL ATTITUDE | 1 | 2 | ③ | 4 | 5 |
| ANXIETY | 1 | 2 | 3 | ④ | 5 |
| I. Q. RATING  143 | 1 | 2 | 3 | 4 | ⑤ |

### RORSCHACH

| | | | | |
|---|---|---|---|---|
| R 24 | M 4 | | | Fc 3 |
| | FM 3 | F 5 | | c 1 |
| W% 39 | m 1+1 | F- 2 | | C' |
| D% 61 | k | F% 29 | | FC 2 |
| d% | K +1 | | | CF 2 |
| Dd% | FK 1 | | | C |
| S | | | | |

# SUMMARY OF TEST FINDINGS    *A 6*

## MANNER DURING TEST

| (1) Overly distressed | (2) Tense | (3) Indifferent | (4) Appropriate | (5) Relaxed and actively interested |
|---|---|---|---|---|
| (1) **Hostile** | (2) Uneasy | | | |

## I.Q. (Bellevue-Wechsler)

| (1) Below average | (2) Average | (3) High average | (4) Superior | (5) **Very superior** |
|---|---|---|---|---|

## PRODUCTIVITY (Rorschach)

| (1) Impoverished | (2) **Reduced output** | (3) Adequate | (4) Better than average | (5) Rich and well-ordered |
|---|---|---|---|---|
| | (2) Compulsive productivity | | | |

## RELATION TO REALITY (Rorschach, Bellevue-Wechsler, Drawings)

| (1) Loose | (2) Lapses—together with good form | (3) Not noticeably disturbed | (4) **Essentially firm** | (5) Firm and good |
|---|---|---|---|---|

## USUAL-UNUSUAL THOUGHT CONTENT (Rorschach, Unpleasant Concept)

| (1) Bizarre | (2) Tendency toward the bizarre | (3) **Adequate** | (4) Original trends | (5) Outstandingly original |
|---|---|---|---|---|
| (1) Stereotyped | (2) Tendency toward stereotypy | | | |

## CONSTRUCTIVE FANTASY (Rorschach)

| (1) Absent | (2) **Barely accessible** | (3) Accessible | (4) Readily accessible | (5) Active but not hampering |
|---|---|---|---|---|
| (1) Withdrawal into fantasy | | | | |

## DRIVE (Rorschach, Szondi, Unpleasant Concept)

| (1) Overpowering aggression | (2) Over-aggressive | (3) **Adequate** | (4) Clearly sufficient | (5) Sufficient—exceptionally well-directed |
|---|---|---|---|---|
| (1) Hampering passivity | (2) Insufficient drive | | | |

## EMOTIONAL TONE (Rorschach, Szondi)

| (1) Explosive emotions | (2) **Getting out of hand** | (3) Trend toward emotional expression | (4) Warmth available | (5) Warm, readily available |
|---|---|---|---|---|
| (1) Lacking | (2) Indicated but re-pressed emotions | | | |

## SOCIAL ATTITUDE (T. A. T.)

| (1) Uncontrolled | (2) **Constricted or neglected** | (3) Adequate | (4) Well-regulated | (5) Free and flexible |
|---|---|---|---|---|

## ANXIETY

| (1) Disintegrating | (2) **Marked** | (3) Moderate | (4) Not marked | (5) Lack of evidence of anxiety |
|---|---|---|---|---|

## OVER-ALL EVALUATION

| (1) Markedly disturbed personality | (2) **Less than adequate personality with some psychological problems** | (3) Adequate personality | (4) Better than average functioning personality | (5) Exceptionally well-integrated personality with excellent potential |
|---|---|---|---|---|

# SUMMARY OF THERAPIST'S FINDINGS A6

### ESTIMATED INTELLIGENCE LEVEL

| (1) Below average | (2) Average | (3) High average | (4) Superior | (5) **Very superior** |
|---|---|---|---|---|

### FLOW OF ASSOCIATIVE MATERIAL

| (1) Impoverished | (2) **Reduced output** | (3) Adequate | (4) Better than average | (5) Rich and well-ordered |
|---|---|---|---|---|
| | (2) Compulsive productivity | | | |

### RELATION TO REALITY

| (1) Loose | (2) **Lapses—together with good form** | (3) Not noticeably disturbed | (4) Essentially firm | (5) Firm and good |
|---|---|---|---|---|

### USUAL-UNUSUAL THOUGHT CONTENT

| (1) Bizarre | (2) **Tendency toward the bizarre** | (3) Adequate | (4) Original trends | (5) Outstandingly original |
|---|---|---|---|---|
| (1) Stereotyped | (2) Tendency toward stereotypy | | | |

### CONSTRUCTIVE FANTASY

| (1) Absent | (2) **Barely accessible** | (3) Accessible | (4) Readily accessible | (5) Active but not hampering |
|---|---|---|---|---|
| (1) Withdrawal into fantasy | | | | |

### DRIVE

| (1) Overpowering aggression | (2) **Over-aggressive** | (3) Adequate | (4) Clearly sufficient | (5) Sufficient—exceptionally well-directed |
|---|---|---|---|---|
| (1) Hampering passivity | (2) Insufficient drive | | | |

### EMOTIONAL TONE

| (1) Explosive emotions | (2) **Getting out of hand** | (3) Trend toward emotional expression | (4) Warmth available | (5) Warm, readily available |
|---|---|---|---|---|
| (1) Lacking | (2) Indicated but repressed emotions | | | |

### SOCIAL ATTITUDE

| (1) Uncontrolled | (2) **Constricted or neglected** | (3) Adequate | (4) Well-regulated | (5) Free and flexible |
|---|---|---|---|---|

### ANXIETY

| (1) Disintegrating | (2) Marked | (3) **Moderate** | (4) Not marked | (5) Lack of evidence of anxiety |
|---|---|---|---|---|

### OVER-ALL EVALUATION

| (1) Markedly disturbed personality | (2) **Less than adequate personality with some psychological problems** | (3) Adequate personality | (4) Better than average functioning personality | (5) Exceptionally well-integrated personality with excellent potential |
|---|---|---|---|---|

There is over-all improvement in the test findings, slight in degree but consistent. On the scattergram, for instance, there is less of a discrepancy between the Comprehension score and the rest of the subtests. In essence, this individual has somewhat overcome his personalized approach to the world around him and is seen to be in greater communication and rapport with others.

On the Szondi, there is a reversal in the ego picture but it is of questionable significance. Greater control is clearly exerted over aggressive impulses, however, as seen in the $+$e, open s constellation as opposed to the $+$s, open e on the original record.

The Drawings bear the stamp of individualization to a high degree. An asthenic nude figure in both instances suggests an aloofness and sensitivity, but within this framework there is a slightly greater expansiveness in the second drawing; the figure is drawn as making a gesture with the right hand away from the body and toward others. A similar delicate change was carried in the drawing of the male.

The Rorschach has expanded in the number of responses, in the quantity and quality of the M responses, and in the addition of two FC's and one CF. Moreover, the pure C response has dropped out in the second record. Although there are now two F– responses, these can better be absorbed in the total R than they could have earlier.

The TAT when first taken by this patient was handled with almost complete evasion; he could not commit himself or become involved in the task posed by the test. In the second testing, we see his willingness to make his problems known through the test material:

|  |  |
|---|---|
| First Testing | Second Testing |

**Picture 13 MF**

| First Testing | Second Testing |
|---|---|
| I don't find it sufficiently interesting to tell a story—too obvious. | I guess he's supposed to be expressing sudden perception of a problem. I see I'm stalling for time. He's having an affair with this young lady and he has feelings, as he's getting up and getting dressed. Somehow, other girls he's known . . . . he's built up a relationship. It represents lost opportunity for pursuing relationship. |

**Picture 6 BM**

| First Testing | Second Testing |
|---|---|
| I think that . . . . one of these lines of thought, well, . . . . maybe it isn't . . . . well, . . . . maybe it's supposed to provoke some line of thought involving disappointment. | This is the woman's son. He's been in business with his father. They've had an argument. He's going to leave this business this time and go somewhere else. He doesn't like to have to do this but the |

FIRST TESTING

SECOND TESTING

deteriorating nature of the situation has forced him to.

*Picture 7 BM*

This picture could obviously evoke no story because it's too bland. It's a young man who becomes progressively enraged, then he's suddenly dismayed. Now he's suddenly apprehensive or nostalgic.

The boy's family has been hurt in some way. He feels he knows who's done it. He just has general ideas of revenge and he's presenting a solution to the older friend whose nature is such that, in a hardheaded way, he may be of some help.

The OVER-ALL EVALUATION when this patient was first tested by this examiner was 25. If one assesses the picture so as to include material from the earlier test, made five years previously, one might say his base line is quantitatively 20. When retested for a second time in our series the quantitative score had reached 31.

A7, married and with children, was first tested when in his middle fifties and retested subsequent to several years of analytic treatment. He was assessed by his therapist as being a *Less than adequate personality with psychological problems* at the start of treatment, and was considered to have moved to the OVER-ALL EVALUATION of *Adequate personality* at its termination. He sought treatment at a time when he was on the verge of a depression. This individual had been deeply traumatized by life circumstances, including death of loved ones and serious physical sickness. Even so, his activities had been spectacularly successful in many areas.

A comparison of the Wechsler subtests reveals that, despite the high I.Q. of 137 achieved on the first testing, there is an important change for the better in Record 2. The abstract thinking, which at first contained several too personalized answers, has leveled off to a near-perfect score.

The Szondi reflects a change toward greater aggressiveness, toward unthwarted activity, in the +s response. Were this unaccompanied by the important increase of three FC responses in the Rorschach, such a change might be thought to indicate too aggressive or ruthless an orien-

# WORK SHEET — A7

VERBAL I. Q. = 137

| EWS | Info. | Comp. | Digit | Arith. | Sim. |
|---|---|---|---|---|---|
| 18 | (25) | 20 | | 14 | 23-24 |
| 17 | 24 | 19 | 17 | (13) | 21-22 |
| 16 | 23 | 18 | 16 | 12 | 20 |
| 15 | 21-22 | (17) | | 11 | 19 |
| 14 | 20 | 16 | (15) | | 17-18 |
| 13 | 18-19 | 15 | 14 | 10 | (16) |
| 12 | 17 | 14 | | 9 | 15 |
| 11 | 15-16 | 12-13 | 13 | | 13-14 |
| 10 | 13-14 | 11 | 12 | 8 | 12 |
| 9 | 12 | 10 | 11 | 7 | 11 |
| 8 | 10-11 | 9 | | | 9-10 |
| 7 | 9 | 8 | 10 | 6 | 8 |
| 6 | 7-8 | 7 | 9 | 5 | 7 |
| 5 | 6 | 5-6 | | | 5-6 |
| 4 | 4-5 | 4 | 8 | 4 | 4 |
| 3 | 2-3 | 3 | 7 | 3 | 3 |
| 2 | 1 | 2 | 6 | | 1-2 |
| 1 | 0 | 1 | | 2 | 0 |
| 0 | | 0 | 5 | 1 | |

## SZONDI

| SEXUAL | | PAROXYSMAL | | EGO | | CONTACT | |
|---|---|---|---|---|---|---|---|
| h | s | e | hy | k | p | d | m |
| | | | | | X | | |
| X | X | | | | X | | X |
| X | X | X | X | X | X | | X |
| X | X | | X | X | X | X | |
| X | X | | X | X | | X | |
| | | | X | | | | |

OVER-ALL EVALUATION = 30

| | | | | | |
|---|---|---|---|---|---|
| OVER-ALL RATING | 1 | 2 | 3 | 4 | 5 |
| PRODUCTIVITY | 1 | 2 | ③ | 4 | 5 |
| RELATION TO REALITY | 1 | ② | 3 | 4 | 5 |
| THOUGHT CONTENT | 1 | 2 | 3 | ④ | 5 |
| CONSTRUCTIVE FANTASY | 1 | 2 | 3 | ④ | 5 |
| DRIVE | 1 | 2 | ③ | 4 | 5 |
| EMOTIONAL TONE | 1 | ② | 3 | 4 | 5 |
| SOCIAL ATTITUDE | 1 | 2 | 3 | ④ | 5 |
| ANXIETY | 1 | 2 | ③ | 4 | 5 |
| I. Q. RATING   137 | 1 | 2 | 3 | 4 | ⑤ |

## RORSCHACH

| R 36 | M 8 | | Fc 2 |
|---|---|---|---|
| | FM 4 | F 13 | c |
| W% 31 | m | F- 6 | C' |
| D% 56 | k | F% 53 | FC |
| d% 11 | K 1 | | CF 2+ |
| Dd% 2 S | FK | | C |

## WORK SHEET

A7

2

### VERBAL I. Q. = 144

| EWS | Info. | Comp. | Digit | Arith. | Sim. |
|-----|-------|-------|-------|--------|------|
| 18 | (25) | 20 | | (14) | 23-24 |
| 17 | 24 | (19) | 17 | 13 | (21-22) |
| 16 | 23 | 18 | 16 | 12 | 20 |
| 15 | 21-22 | 17 | | 11 | 19 |
| 14 | 20 | 16 | (15) | | 17-18 |
| 13 | 18-19 | 15 | 14 | 10 | 16 |
| 12 | 17 | 14 | | 9 | 15 |
| 11 | 15-16 | 12-13 | 13 | | 13-14 |
| 10 | 13-14 | 11 | 12 | 8 | 12 |
| 9 | 12 | 10 | 11 | 7 | 11 |
| 8 | 10-11 | 9 | | | 9-10 |
| 7 | 9 | 8 | 10 | 6 | 8 |
| 6 | 7-8 | 7 | 9 | 5 | 7 |
| 5 | 6 | 5-6 | | | 5-6 |
| 4 | 4-5 | 4 | 8 | 4 | 4 |
| 3 | 2-3 | 3 | 7 | 3 | 3 |
| 2 | 1 | 2 | 6 | | 1-2 |
| 1 | 0 | 1 | | 2 | 0 |
| 0 | | 0 | 5 | 1 | |

### SZONDI

| SEXUAL | | PAROXYSMAL | | EGO | | CONTACT | |
|--------|---|------------|----|-----|---|---------|---|
| h | s | e | hy | k | p | d | m |

### OVER-ALL EVALUATION = 36

| | | | | | |
|--|--|--|--|--|--|
| OVER-ALL RATING | 1 | 2 | 3 | 4 | 5 |
| PRODUCTIVITY | 1 | 2 | (3) | 4 | 5 |
| RELATION TO REALITY | 1 | 2 | 3 | 4 | (5) |
| THOUGHT CONTENT | 1 | 2 | 3 | (4) | 5 |
| CONSTRUCTIVE FANTASY | 1 | 2 | 3 | (4) | 5 |
| DRIVE | 1 | 2 | (3) | 4 | 5 |
| EMOTIONAL TONE | 1 | 2 | 3 | (4) | 5 |
| SOCIAL ATTITUDE | 1 | 2 | 3 | (4) | 5 |
| ANXIETY | 1 | 2 | 3 | (4) | 5 |
| I. Q. RATING  *144* | 1 | 2 | 3 | 4 | (5) |

### RORSCHACH

| | | | | | |
|--|--|--|--|--|--|
| R 37 | M 8 | | | Fc 3 |
| | FM 1 | F 19 | c | |
| W% 27 | m 1 | F- | C' | |
| D% 54 | k | F% 51 | FC 3 | |
| d% 14 | K +1 | | CF 2 | |
| Dd% 5 | FK | | C | |
| S | | | | |

# SUMMARY OF TEST FINDINGS    A 7

## MANNER DURING TEST

| (1) Overly distressed | (2) Tense | (3) Indifferent | (4) Appropriate | (5) Relaxed and actively interested |
|---|---|---|---|---|
| (1) Hostile | (2) Uneasy | | | |

## I.Q. (Bellevue-Wechsler)

| (1) Below average | (2) Average | (3) High average | (4) Superior | (5) Very superior |
|---|---|---|---|---|

## PRODUCTIVITY (Rorschach)

| (1) Impoverished | (2) Reduced output | (3) Adequate | (4) Better than average | (5) Rich and well-ordered |
|---|---|---|---|---|
| | (2) Compulsive productivity | | | |

## RELATION TO REALITY (Rorschach, Bellevue-Wechsler, Drawings)

| (1) Loose | (2) Lapses—together with good form | (3) Not noticeably disturbed | (4) Essentially firm | (5) Firm and good |
|---|---|---|---|---|

## USUAL-UNUSUAL THOUGHT CONTENT (Rorschach, Unpleasant Concept)

| (1) Bizarre | (2) Tendency toward the bizarre | (3) Adequate | (4) Original trends | (5) Outstandingly original |
|---|---|---|---|---|
| (1) Stereotyped | (2) Tendency toward stereotypy | | | |

## CONSTRUCTIVE FANTASY (Rorschach)

| (1) Absent | (2) Barely accessible | (3) Accessible | (4) Readily accessible | (5) Active but not hampering |
|---|---|---|---|---|
| (1) Withdrawal into fantasy | | | | |

## DRIVE (Rorschach, Szondi, Unpleasant Concept)

| (1) Overpowering aggression | (2) Over-aggressive | (3) Adequate | (4) Clearly sufficient | (5) Sufficient—exceptionally well-directed |
|---|---|---|---|---|
| (1) Hampering passivity | (2) Insufficient drive | | | |

## EMOTIONAL TONE (Rorschach, Szondi)

| (1) Explosive emotions | (2) Getting out of hand | (3) Trend toward emotional expression | (4) Warmth available | (5) Warm, readily available |
|---|---|---|---|---|
| (1) Lacking | (2) Indicated but re-pressed emotions | | | |

## SOCIAL ATTITUDE (T. A. T.)

| (1) Uncontrolled | (2) Constricted or neglected | (3) Adequate | (4) Well-regulated | (5) Free and flexible |
|---|---|---|---|---|

## ANXIETY

| (1) Disintegrating | (2) Marked | (3) Moderate | (4) Not marked | (5) Lack of evidence of anxiety |
|---|---|---|---|---|

## OVER-ALL EVALUATION

| (1) Markedly disturbed personality | (2) Less than adequate personality with some psychological problems | (3) Adequate personality | (4) Better than average functioning personality | (5) Exceptionally well-integrated personality with excellent potential |
|---|---|---|---|---|

## SUMMARY OF THERAPIST'S FINDINGS  A7

### ESTIMATED INTELLIGENCE LEVEL

| (1) Below average | (2) Average | (3) High average | (4) Superior | (5) Very superior |
|---|---|---|---|---|

### FLOW OF ASSOCIATIVE MATERIAL

| (1) Impoverished | (2) Reduced output | (3) Adequate | (4) Better than average | (5) Rich and well-ordered |
|---|---|---|---|---|
| | (2) Compulsive productivity | | | |

### RELATION TO REALITY

| (1) Loose | (2) Lapses—together with good form | (3) Not noticeably disturbed | (4) Essentially firm | (5) Firm and good |
|---|---|---|---|---|

### USUAL-UNUSUAL THOUGHT CONTENT

| (1) Bizarre | (2) Tendency toward the bizarre | (3) Adequate | (4) Original trends | (5) Outstandingly original |
|---|---|---|---|---|
| (1) Stereotyped | (2) Tendency toward stereotypy | | | |

### CONSTRUCTIVE FANTASY

| (1) Absent | (2) Barely accessible | (3) Accessible | (4) Readily accessible | (5) Active but not hampering |
|---|---|---|---|---|
| (1) Withdrawal into fantasy | | | | |

### DRIVE

| (1) Overpowering aggression | (2) Over-aggressive | (3) Adequate | (4) Clearly sufficient | (5) Sufficient—exceptionally well-directed |
|---|---|---|---|---|
| (1) Hampering passivity | (2) Insufficient drive | | | |

### EMOTIONAL TONE

| (1) Explosive emotions | (2) Getting out of hand | (3) Trend toward emotional expression | (4) Warmth available | (5) Warm, readily available |
|---|---|---|---|---|
| (1) Lacking | (2) Indicated but re-pressed emotions | | | |

### SOCIAL ATTITUDE

| (1) Uncontrolled | (2) Constricted or neglected | (3) Adequate | (4) Well-regulated | (5) Free and flexible |
|---|---|---|---|---|

### ANXIETY

| (1) Disintegrating | (2) Marked | (3) Moderate | (4) Not marked | (5) Lack of evidence of anxiety |
|---|---|---|---|---|

### OVER-ALL EVALUATION

| (1) Markedly disturbed personality | (2) Less than adequate personality with some psychological problems | (3) Adequate personality | (4) Better than average functioning personality | (5) Exceptionally well-integrated personality with excellent potential |
|---|---|---|---|---|

tation. This change is paralleled by increased ease and achievement in work and business as reported from external sources as well as from the patient's own assessment. The shift from –k, +p to open k, ambivalent p, cannot be interpreted as indicating an important difference within the ego. This individual still remains somewhat conflicted in his interpersonal relationships, as shown in the ambivalent m score.

The startling discrepancy between the graphic material and the very high level of intellectual achievement is still as vividly portrayed in Record 2 as in Record 1. Within the total setting of the excellent intelligence and the giftedness as reflected in the Rorschach, however, we were inclined to interpret such Figure Drawings in terms of a specific defect in translating a concept rather than as suggesting the type of basic disturbance that could be deduced from such figures were they part of a totally different personality gestalt. A discussion with the patient's therapist on this issue revealed this hypothesis to have been correct. The therapist used the words, "a defect comparable to color blindness"—a defect, incidentally, which had caused the patient considerable distress in his earlier years.

The Rorschach in this instance is a rich one on both occasions, with unusually original and lively human movement responses. Record 2 reveals a marked improvement in reality testing. The six disturbed F–responses are not found in the second record and, as previously commented, there are introduced in Record 2, three bona fide FC responses not found previously.

A8 was in her forties when first tested and was unmarried. This patient was estimated by the therapist as a *Markedly disturbed personality* (1) at the time she entered treatment, and was assessed as a *Better than average functioning personality* (4) at its termination. Most striking on the Summary Sheet submitted by the therapist has been the movement occurring in the categories FLOW OF ASSOCIATIVE MATERIAL and DRIVE. However, positive and significant change is reported by the therapist in all areas. The therapist further comments that this individual has made tremendous strides in the professional field in which she works, making a very positive contribution along tangible and well-recognized lines. It is further stated: "She still lives a life that is too socially isolated, which was not true in her earlier years. She no longer has paralyzing depressions but does have occasional bouts of anxiety when excessive emotional demands are made on her. Her total health has improved enormously, and her sense of humor has helped revive her contentment with life." This patient was in therapy for five years but has remained in close contact with the therapist over an eleven-year period. The testing and retesting occurred with an interval of ten years between.

Turning now to the Work Sheets, comparison of the Wechsler subtests reveals an important change in pattern as well as level. It is most striking that in the Comprehension, Reasoning and Judgment this individual gains 8 points on the weighted scale, rising from 9 to 17. Her initial performance in this subtest had been very poor, indicating that this woman lived in a highly unrealistic world and related inadequately to the practical problems arising in ordinary daily life. This gain epitomizes her more realistic orientation at the time of the second testing. The changes in the Digit Memory and Arithmetic scores, gains and losses which essentially counterbalance each other, do not appear to be particularly significant. However, both quantitatively and qualitatively the change in the Comprehension is a remarkable one.

Since this individual was so isolated from others, as exemplified by many aspects of the first test performance, the change in the ego picture in the Szondi is an encouraging one. Originally walled off, in terms of the +k, open p constellation, the –k, +p change would suggest greater identification with others, at least at some levels of her experience, although, as the Contact Vector shows, there is still a basic pessimism concerning the pleasurable rewards from human relationships.

The change in the Figure Drawings is also in the direction of a more realistic adjustment. Sketchy, inadequate and fraught with anxiety as the drawing of the man in the second testing is, it is nonetheless a drawing of a creature who is a part of this society rather than the combination of sheik and prophet which was first portrayed. The original drawing of a figure swathed in veils and flowing robes has now given place to the concept of the male in realistic garb.

The initial Rorschach record is virtually impossible to score, or perhaps it is more accurate to say that scoring does not carry its flavor, which is one essentially of atmospheric comment rather than interpretation. Such answers as: "A shadow on water," "Something malignant," "Something sloppy," "Not clearcut or neat," "An expanse seen from a plane at night," "Well defined and neat," "Chopped, separated, going into some-

## WORK SHEET   A8

VERBAL I. Q. = 120

| EWS | Info. | Comp. | Digit | Arith. | Sim. |
|---|---|---|---|---|---|
| 18 | 25 | 20 |  | 14 | 23-24 |
| 17 | 24 | 19 | 17 | 13 | 21-22 |
| 16 | 23 | 18 | 16 | 12 | 20 |
| 15 | 21-22 | 17 |  | 11 | 19 |
| 14 | 20 | 16 | 15 |  | 17-18 |
| 13 | 18-19 | 15 | 14 | 10 | 16 |
| 12 | 17 | 14 |  | 9 | 15 |
|  |  |  |  |  |  |
| 11 | 15-16 | 12-13 | 13 |  | 13-14 |
| 10 | 13-14 | 11 | 12 | 8 | 12 |
| 9 | 12 | 10 | 11 | 7 | 11 |
| 8 | 10-11 | 9 |  |  | 9-10 |
| 7 | 9 | 8 | 10 | 6 | 8 |
| 6 | 7-8 | 7 | 9 | 5 | 7 |
|  |  |  |  |  |  |
| 5 | 6 | 5-6 |  |  | 5-6 |
| 4 | 4-5 | 4 | 8 | 4 | 4 |
| 3 | 2-3 | 3 | 7 | 3 | 3 |
| 2 | 1 | 2 | 6 |  | 1-2 |
| 1 | 0 | 1 |  | 2 | 0 |
| 0 |  | 0 | 5 | 1 |  |

SZONDI

| SEXUAL | | PAROXYSMAL | | EGO | | CONTACT | |
|---|---|---|---|---|---|---|---|
| h | s | e | hy | k | p | d | m |
| X |  |  |  | X |  |  |  |
| X |  | X |  | X |  | X |  |
| X |  | X |  | X | X | X | X |
| X | X | X | X | X | X |  | X |
|  |  | X | X |  |  |  | X |
|  |  | X | X |  |  |  |  |

OVER-ALL EVALUATION = 20

## WORK SHEET

A8

2

### VERBAL I. Q. 131

| EWS | Info. | Comp. | Digit | Arith. | Sim. |
|-----|-------|-------|-------|--------|------|
| 18 | 25 | 20 | | 14 | 23-24 |
| 17 | 24 | 19 | 17 | 13 | 21-22 |
| 16 | 23 | 18 | 16 | 12 | 20 |
| 15 | 21-22 | 17 | | 11 | 19 |
| 14 | 20 | 16 | 15 | | 17-18 |
| 13 | 18-19 | 15 | 14 | 10 | 16 |
| 12 | 17 | 14 | | 9 | 15 |
| 11 | 15-16 | 12-13 | 13 | | 13-14 |
| 10 | 13-14 | 11 | 12 | 8 | 12 |
| 9 | 12 | 10 | 11 | 7 | 11 |
| 8 | 10-11 | 9 | | | 9-10 |
| 7 | 9 | 8 | 10 | 6 | 8 |
| 6 | 7-8 | 7 | 9 | 5 | 7 |
| 5 | 6 | 5-6 | | | 5-6 |
| 4 | 4-5 | 4 | 8 | 4 | 4 |
| 3 | 2-3 | 3 | 7 | 3 | 3 |
| 2 | 1 | 2 | 6 | | 1-2 |
| 1 | 0 | 1 | | 2 | 0 |
| 0 | | 0 | 5 | 1 | |

### SZONDI

| SEXUAL | | PAROXYSMAL | | EGO | | CONTACT | |
|--------|---|------------|----|-----|---|---------|---|
| h | s | e | hy | k | p | d | m |
| | | | | | X | | |
| | | | | | X | | |
| X | | X | | | X | | |
| X | X | X | X | | X | X | X |
| X | | X | X | X | X | X | X |
| | | X | X | X | | | X |
| | | | X | | | | |

### OVER-ALL EVALUATION = 29

| | 1 | 2 | 3 | 4 | 5 |
|---|---|---|---|---|---|
| OVER-ALL RATING | 1 | 2 | 3 | 4 | 5 |
| PRODUCTIVITY | 1 | 2 | ③ | 4 | 5 |
| RELATION TO REALITY | 1 | 2 | ③ | 4 | 5 |
| THOUGHT CONTENT | 1 | 2 | ③ | 4 | 5 |
| CONSTRUCTIVE FANTASY | 1 | 2 | ③ | 4 | 5 |
| DRIVE | 1 | 2 | ③ | 4 | 5 |
| EMOTIONAL TONE | 1 | 2 | ③ | 4 | 5 |
| SOCIAL ATTITUDE | 1 | 2 | ③ | 4 | 5 |
| ANXIETY | 1 | 2 | ③ | 4 | 5 |
| I. Q. RATING 131 | 1 | 2 | 3 | 4 | ⑤ |

### RORSCHACH

| R 21 | M 4 | | Fc 3+1 |
|------|-----|---|--------|
| | FM 5 | F 5 | c |
| W% 48 | m +2 | F- | C' |
| D% 52 | k | F% 24 | FC 3+2 |
| d% | K | | CF 1 |
| Dd% | FK | | C |
| S | | | |

# SUMMARY OF TEST FINDINGS

## MANNER DURING TEST

| | | | | |
|---|---|---|---|---|
| (1) Overly distressed | (2) Tense | (3) Indifferent | (4) Appropriate | (5) Relaxed and actively interested |
| (1) Hostile | (2) Uneasy | | | |

## I.Q. (Bellevue-Wechsler)

| | | | | |
|---|---|---|---|---|
| (1) Below average | (2) Average | (3) High average | (4) Superior | (5) Very superior |

## PRODUCTIVITY (Rorschach)

| | | | | |
|---|---|---|---|---|
| (1) Impoverished | (2) Reduced output | (3) Adequate | (4) Better than average | (5) Rich and well-ordered |
| | (2) Compulsive productivity | | | |

## RELATION TO REALITY (Rorschach, Bellevue-Wechsler, Drawings)

| | | | | |
|---|---|---|---|---|
| (1) Loose | (2) Lapses—together with good form | (3) Not noticeably disturbed | (4) Essentially firm | (5) Firm and good |

## USUAL-UNUSUAL THOUGHT CONTENT (Rorschach, Unpleasant Concept)

| | | | | |
|---|---|---|---|---|
| (1) Bizarre | (2) Tendency toward the bizarre | (3) Adequate | (4) Original trends | (5) Outstandingly original |
| (1) Stereotyped | (2) Tendency toward stereotypy | | | |

## CONSTRUCTIVE FANTASY (Rorschach)

| | | | | |
|---|---|---|---|---|
| (1) Absent | (2) Barely accessible | (3) Accessible | (4) Readily accessible | (5) Active but not hampering |
| (1) Withdrawal into fantasy | | | | |

## DRIVE (Rorschach, Szondi, Unpleasant Concept)

| | | | | |
|---|---|---|---|---|
| (1) Overpowering aggression | (2) Over-aggressive | (3) Adequate | (4) Clearly sufficient | (5) Sufficient— exceptionally well-directed |
| (1) Hampering passivity | (2) Insufficient drive | | | |

## EMOTIONAL TONE (Rorschach, Szondi)

| | | | | |
|---|---|---|---|---|
| (1) Explosive emotions | (2) Getting out of hand | (3) Trend toward emotional expression | (4) Warmth available | (5) Warm, readily available |
| (1) Lacking | (2) Indicated but repressed emotions | | | |

## SOCIAL ATTITUDE (T. A. T.)

| | | | | |
|---|---|---|---|---|
| (1) Uncontrolled | (2) Constricted or neglected | (3) Adequate | (4) Well-regulated | (5) Free and flexible |

## ANXIETY

| | | | | |
|---|---|---|---|---|
| (1) Disintegrating | (2) Marked | (3) Moderate | (4) Not marked | (5) Lack of evidence of anxiety |

## OVER-ALL EVALUATION

| | | | | |
|---|---|---|---|---|
| (1) Markedly disturbed personality | (2) Less than adequate personality with some psychological problems | (3) Adequate personality | (4) Better than average functioning personality | (5) Exceptionally well-integrated personality with excellent potential |

## SUMMARY OF THERAPIST'S FINDINGS     *A8*

### ESTIMATED INTELLIGENCE LEVEL

| (1) Below average | (2) Average | (3) High average | (4) Superior | (5) Very superior |
|---|---|---|---|---|

### FLOW OF ASSOCIATIVE MATERIAL

| (1) Impoverished | (2) Reduced output | (3) Adequate | (4) Better than average | (5) Rich and well-ordered |
|---|---|---|---|---|
|  | (2) Compulsive productivity |  |  |  |

### RELATION TO REALITY

| (1) Loose | (2) Lapses—together with good form | (3) Not noticeably disturbed | (4) Essentially firm | (5) Firm and good |
|---|---|---|---|---|

### USUAL-UNUSUAL THOUGHT CONTENT

| (1) Bizarre | (2) Tendency toward the bizarre | (3) Adequate | (4) Original trends | (5) Outstandingly original |
|---|---|---|---|---|
| (1) Stereotyped | (2) Tendency toward stereotypy |  |  |  |

### CONSTRUCTIVE FANTASY

| (1) Absent | (2) Barely accessible | (3) Accessible | (4) Readily accessible | (5) Active but not hampering |
|---|---|---|---|---|
| (1) Withdrawal into fantasy |  |  |  |  |

### DRIVE

| (1) Overpowering aggression | (2) Over-aggressive | (3) Adequate | (4) Clearly sufficient | (5) Sufficient—exceptionally well-directed |
|---|---|---|---|---|
| (1) Hampering passivity | (2) Insufficient drive |  |  |  |

### EMOTIONAL TONE

| (1) Explosive emotions | (2) Getting out of hand | (3) Trend toward emotional expression | (4) Warmth available | (5) Warm, readily available |
|---|---|---|---|---|
| (1) Lacking | (2) Indicated but repressed emotions |  |  |  |

### SOCIAL ATTITUDE

| (1) Uncontrolled | (2) Constricted or neglected | (3) Adequate | (4) Well-regulated | (5) Free and flexible |
|---|---|---|---|---|

### ANXIETY

| (1) Disintegrating | (2) Marked | (3) Moderate | (4) Not marked | (5) Lack of evidence of anxiety |
|---|---|---|---|---|

### OVER-ALL EVALUATION

| (1) Markedly disturbed personality | (2) Less than adequate personality with some psychological problems | (3) Adequate personality | (4) Better than average functioning personality | (5) Exceptionally well-integrated personality with excellent potential |
|---|---|---|---|---|

thing," "Diffusion, lack of organization" epitomize this type of answer. Even where a solid percept is achieved, it is clothed in atmospheric statements: "A bat, very malignant; I contrast the dainty feet with the big malignant wings."*

Although such answers have not been completely eliminated from Record 2, they are fewer and, much more important, they are incidental to a solid framework of bona fide responses. In Record 2, good human movement and color responses are both available, and where impressionistic responses, or responses embedded in feeling, do occur, they do not deal with the disrupting and menacing forces which this individual originally felt within her, but, instead, have a pleasing quality. For example: "This is essentially feminine, delicacy in coloring; it could be a necklace, beautiful and fragile; a piece of good workmanship. I like the shading." This is the whole response to Card VII. Or again, in dealing with genuine color responses: "This suggests a flower, beautiful and exotic, one that blooms rather rarely."

On Card X, which previously looked like "diffusion and lack of organization," one finds this type of response: "The total immediate impression is a pleasant one. The whole thing has a flowerlike quality, many flowers." There is also gaiety and movement: "There is a suggestion of seahorses. The big ones are sucking on something and they are trying to catch this little yellow thing. The crabs have already caught something. This does not have cohesion."

What was experienced before as a paralyzing lack of organization, while admittedly still lacking "cohesiveness," is now infinitely less disturbing.

In the original record the only human movement response was, "Two harpies looking unpleasant, quarreling." Record 2 produces: "A fulsome female figure with old-fashioned hipline and busts and hands upraised." "Two clowns playing pat-a-cake in a bar after the show is over." "Two wrestlers locked knee to knee. It is an amiable match." The "extremely disturbing, sloppy, not clearcut or neat" of Card IV on Record I now indicates a nice attempt to grapple with the potentially disrupting instinctual drive: "A gorilla with his hands outstretched coming toward me. The eyes are not particularly animal, perhaps they're more human. The rest of his face is obscured but he is dancing rather than walking. He's up on his toes a bit. He *should* (laughing) be more menacing."

These changes result in a quantitative shift on the OVER-ALL EVALUATION from 20 to 29. They are unquestionably in the direction of greater

---

*The full drawing of the man has been included on the Work Sheet since formal Rorschach scoring seemed impossible.

realism in many areas. This individual now seems to be free to utilize the extreme sensitivity which previously paralyzed her, and while not having yet achieved close emotional relationship of a very intimate nature and while still reflecting some resignation and pessimism, she appears to have reached a point at which life can be enjoyed and participated in, rather than fled from.

A9 was in his middle forties when initially tested; the second evaluation followed nine years after the first.

The therapist's evaluation of this patient was at the level of *Adequate personality* at the start of treatment and was rated at a lower level of the scale, *Less than adequate personality with psychological problems* at its termination, an unusual finding. Explaining the lack of progress, or the presence of even greater disturbance, the analyst commented: "A9 showed rigid and strong defenses against what must be extremely frightening unconscious fantasies, or possibly unusually painful reality events in his early life. He gave the impression that he was protecting not only himself but someone else from exposure to himself and to the analyst. Analytic work had to be extremely careful and tentative, and it was recommended that he discontinue his analysis since he was getting no benefit, and since it was feared that disturbing his defenses might result in more serious difficulties for him."

A9, himself, commented on the fact that he felt he had received no benefit from his long-term analytic treatment (with several therapists). Modifying this, he admitted that perhaps one symptom had been alleviated but stated that, in essence, he felt himself equally frustrated, if not more so, than at the start of treatment.

There is much good potential here, as shown by Record 1, and this case remains genuinely puzzling as to why so little progress was made; yet, the tests mirror this lack of progress undeniably.

The I.Q. and the scattergram are beyond reproach in both tests and the Szondi does not indicate any profound disturbance on either recording. While the Figure Drawings unquestionably portray rigidity, they do not have bizarre qualities and cannot be considered as in any way essentially different from those of many patients who have shown unmistakable change for the better following treatment.

The second Rorschach record reflects the increased sense of frustration experienced by this individual and must be classified as a deteriorated

## WORK SHEET — A9

1

### VERBAL I. Q. = 144

| EWS | Info. | Comp. | Digit | Arith. | Sim. |
|---|---|---|---|---|---|
| 18 | 25 | 20 | | (14) | 23-24 |
| 17 | 24 | (19) | (17) | 13 | 21-22 |
| 16 | (23) | 18 | 16 | 12 | (20) |
| 15 | 21-22 | 17 | | 11 | 19 |
| 14 | 20 | 16 | 15 | | 17-18 |
| 13 | 18-19 | 15 | 14 | 10 | 16 |
| 12 | 17 | 14 | | 9 | 15 |
| | | | | | |
| 11 | 15-16 | 12-13 | 13 | | 13-14 |
| 10 | 13-14 | 11 | 12 | 8 | 12 |
| 9 | 12 | 10 | 11 | 7 | 11 |
| 8 | 10-11 | 9 | | | 9-10 |
| 7 | 9 | 8 | 10 | 6 | 8 |
| 6 | 7-8 | 7 | 9 | 5 | 7 |
| | | | | | |
| 5 | 6 | 5-6 | | | 5-6 |
| 4 | 4-5 | 4 | 8 | 4 | 4 |
| 3 | 2-3 | 3 | 7 | 3 | 3 |
| 2 | 1 | 2 | 6 | | 1-2 |
| 1 | 0 | 1 | | 2 | 0 |
| 0 | | 0 | 5 | 1 | |

### SZONDI

| SEXUAL | | PAROXYSMAL | | EGO | | CONTACT | |
|---|---|---|---|---|---|---|---|
| h | s | e | hy | k | p | d | m |

### OVER-ALL EVALUATION = 27

| | | | | | |
|---|---|---|---|---|---|
| OVER-ALL RATING | 1 | 2 | 3 | 4 | 5 |
| PRODUCTIVITY | 1 | (2) | 3 | 4 | 5 |
| RELATION TO REALITY | 1 | 2 | (3) | 4 | 5 |
| THOUGHT CONTENT | 1 | 2 | (3) | 4 | 5 |
| CONSTRUCTIVE FANTASY | 1 | (2) | 3 | 4 | 5 |
| DRIVE | 1 | 2 | (3) | 4 | 5 |
| EMOTIONAL TONE | 1 | 2 | (3) | 4 | 5 |
| SOCIAL ATTITUDE | 1 | 2 | (3) | 4 | 5 |
| ANXIETY | 1 | 2 | (3) | 4 | 5 |
| I. Q. RATING   144 | 1 | 2 | 3 | 4 | (5) |

### RORSCHACH

| | | | | | |
|---|---|---|---|---|---|
| R 16 | M 2 | | | | Fc 1 |
| | FM 2 | | F 7 | | c |
| W% 63 | m | | F- 1 | | C' |
| D% 37 | k | | F% 50 | | FC 1 |
| d% | K | | | | CF |
| Dd% S | FK | | | | c 1 |

# WORK SHEET A9

2

## VERBAL I. Q. = 144

| EWS | Info. | Comp. | Digit | Arith. | Sim. |
|-----|-------|-------|-------|--------|------|
| 18 | 25 | 20 | | (14) | 23-24 |
| 17 | (24) | 19 | (17) | 13 | (21-22) |
| 16 | 23 | (18) | 16 | 12 | 20 |
| 15 | 21-22 | 17 | | 11 | 19 |
| 14 | 20 | 16 | 15 | | 17-18 |
| 13 | 18-19 | 15 | 14 | 10 | 16 |
| 12 | 17 | 14 | | 9 | 15 |
| | | | | | |
| 11 | 15-16 | 12-13 | 13 | | 13-14 |
| 10 | 13-14 | 11 | 12 | 8 | 12 |
| 9 | 12 | 10 | 11 | 7 | 11 |
| 8 | 10-11 | 9 | | | 9-10 |
| 7 | 9 | 8 | 10 | 6 | 8 |
| 6 | 7-8 | 7 | 9 | 5 | 7 |
| | | | | | |
| 5 | 6 | 5-6 | | | 5-6 |
| 4 | 4-5 | 4 | 8 | 4 | 4 |
| 3 | 2-3 | 3 | 7 | 3 | 3 |
| 2 | 1 | 2 | 6 | | 1-2 |
| 1 | 0 | 1 | | 2 | 0 |
| 0 | | 0 | 5 | 1 | |

## SZONDI

| SEXUAL | | PAROXYSMAL | | EGO | | CONTACT | |
|--------|---|------------|----|-----|---|---------|---|
| h | s | e | hy | k | p | d | m |

(Szondi profile markings with X symbols in various cells)

## OVER-ALL EVALUATION = 23

| | | | | | |
|---|---|---|---|---|---|
| OVER-ALL RATING | 1 | 2 | 3 | 4 | 5 |
| PRODUCTIVITY | 1 | (2) | 3 | 4 | 5 |
| RELATION TO REALITY | 1 | (2) | 3 | 4 | 5 |
| THOUGHT CONTENT | 1 | 2 | (3) | 4 | 5 |
| CONSTRUCTIVE FANTASY | 1 | (2) | 3 | 4 | 5 |
| DRIVE | 1 | (2) | 3 | 4 | 5 |
| EMOTIONAL TONE | (1) | 2 | 3 | 4 | 5 |
| SOCIAL ATTITUDE | 1 | 2 | (3) | 4 | 5 |
| ANXIETY | 1 | 2 | (3) | 4 | 5 |
| I. Q. RATING 144 | 1 | 2 | 3 | 4 | (5) |

## RORSCHACH

| | | | | | |
|---|---|---|---|---|---|
| R 17 | M 1 | | | | Fc |
| | FM 1 | F 5 | | | c |
| W% 47 | m +1 | F- 4 | | | C' |
| D% 53 | k | F% 53 | | | FC |
| d% | K | | | | CF 2 |
| Dd% | FK | | | | C 4 |
| S | | | | | |

## SUMMARY OF TEST FINDINGS  *Aq*

### MANNER DURING TEST

| (1) Overly distressed | (2) Tense | (3) Indifferent | (4) Appropriate | (5) Relaxed and actively interested |
|---|---|---|---|---|
| (1) Hostile | (2) Uneasy | | | |

### I.Q. (Bellevue-Wechsler)

| (1) Below average | (2) Average | (3) High average | (4) Superior | (5) Very superior |
|---|---|---|---|---|

### PRODUCTIVITY (Rorschach)

| (1) Impoverished | (2) Reduced output | (3) Adequate | (4) Better than average | (5) Rich and well-ordered |
|---|---|---|---|---|
| | (2) Compulsive productivity | | | |

### RELATION TO REALITY (Rorschach, Bellevue-Wechsler, Drawings)

| (1) Loose | (2) Lapses—together with good form | (3) Not noticeably disturbed | (4) Essentially firm | (5) Firm and good |
|---|---|---|---|---|

### USUAL-UNUSUAL THOUGHT CONTENT (Rorschach, Unpleasant Concept)

| (1) Bizarre | (2) Tendency toward the bizarre | (3) Adequate | (4) Original trends | (5) Outstandingly original |
|---|---|---|---|---|
| (1) Stereotyped | (2) Tendency toward stereotypy | | | |

### CONSTRUCTIVE FANTASY (Rorschach)

| (1) Absent | (2) Barely accessible | (3) Accessible | (4) Readily accessible | (5) Active but not hampering |
|---|---|---|---|---|
| (1) Withdrawal into fantasy | | | | |

### DRIVE (Rorschach, Szondi, Unpleasant Concept)

| (1) Overpowering aggression | (2) Over-aggressive | (3) Adequate | (4) Clearly sufficient | (5) Sufficient—exceptionally well-directed |
|---|---|---|---|---|
| (1) Hampering passivity | (2) Insufficient drive | | | |

### EMOTIONAL TONE (Rorschach, Szondi)

| (1) Explosive emotions | (2) Getting out of hand | (3) Trend toward emotional expression | (4) Warmth available | (5) Warm, readily available |
|---|---|---|---|---|
| (1) Lacking | (2) Indicated but repressed emotions | | | |

### SOCIAL ATTITUDE (T. A. T.)

| (1) Uncontrolled | (2) Constricted or neglected | (3) Adequate | (4) Well-regulated | (5) Free and flexible |
|---|---|---|---|---|

### ANXIETY

| (1) Disintegrating | (2) Marked | (3) Moderate | (4) Not marked | (5) Lack of evidence of anxiety |
|---|---|---|---|---|

### OVER-ALL EVALUATION

| (1) Markedly disturbed personality | (2) Less than adequate personality with some psychological problems | (3) Adequate personality | (4) Better than average functioning personality | (5) Exceptionally well-integrated personality with excellent potential |
|---|---|---|---|---|

## SUMMARY OF THERAPIST'S FINDINGS A9

### ESTIMATED INTELLIGENCE LEVEL

| (1) Below average | (2) Average | (3) High average | (4) **Superior** | (5) Very superior |
|---|---|---|---|---|

### FLOW OF ASSOCIATIVE MATERIAL

| (1) **Impoverished** | (2) Reduced output | (3) Adequate | (4) Better than average | (5) Rich and well-ordered |
|---|---|---|---|---|
| | (2) Compulsive productivity | | | |

### RELATION TO REALITY

| (1) Loose | (2) Lapses—together with good form | (3) **Not noticeably disturbed** | (4) Essentially firm | (5) Firm and good |
|---|---|---|---|---|

### USUAL-UNUSUAL THOUGHT CONTENT

| (1) Bizarre | (2) Tendency toward the bizarre | (3) Adequate | (4) Original trends | (5) Outstandingly original |
|---|---|---|---|---|
| (1) Stereotyped | (2) Tendency toward stereotypy | | | |

### CONSTRUCTIVE FANTASY

| (1) **Absent** | (2) Barely accessible | (3) Accessible | (4) Readily accessible | (5) Active but not hampering |
|---|---|---|---|---|
| (1) Withdrawal into fantasy | | | | |

### DRIVE

| (1) Overpowering aggression | (2) Over-aggressive | (3) **Adequate** | (4) Clearly sufficient | (5) Sufficient—exceptionally well-directed |
|---|---|---|---|---|
| (1) Hampering passivity | (2) Insufficient drive | | | |

### EMOTIONAL TONE

| (1) Explosive emotions | (2) Getting out of hand | (3) Trend toward emotional expression | (4) Warmth available | (5) Warm, readily available |
|---|---|---|---|---|
| (1) Lacking | (2) **Indicated but re-pressed emotions** | | | |

### SOCIAL ATTITUDE

| (1) Uncontrolled | (2) Constricted or neglected | (3) **Adequate** | (4) Well-regulated | (5) Free and flexible |
|---|---|---|---|---|

### ANXIETY

| (1) Disintegrating | (2) Marked | (3) **Moderate** | (4) Not marked | (5) Lack of evidence of anxiety |
|---|---|---|---|---|

### OVER-ALL EVALUATION

| (1) Markedly disturbed personality | (2) Less than adequate personality with some psychological problems | (3) **Adequate personality** | (4) Better than average functioning personality | (5) Exceptionally well-integrated personality with excellent potential |
|---|---|---|---|---|

or less good performance. There is a decrease in the number of human movement responses, an increase in the F−, and a sizable increase in explosive, primitive and unmodified emotions. This individual appears to be getting considerably less satisfaction out of life and to be reacting to this through the discharge of highly explosive emotional material.

The OVER-ALL EVALUATION on a quantitative basis from the test findings nets this individual 27 at the start of the treatment and 23 at the time of retesting.

Unlike A9, concerning whom both therapist and psychologist agree that regressive features characterize the assessment at the later date, A10 has been rated as showing marked improvement by his therapist, an improvement which the test findings do not reflect. The apparent discrepancy, however, was subsequently explained when therapist and psychologist compared notes on the dates of the testing periods, and a check was made on the patient's actual condition at the time of the second psychological assessment.

A10 was in his middle twenties when first evaluated psychologically. He was rated by his therapist as a *Markedly disturbed personality* at the start of treatment, and to have reached stage 4, a *Better than average functioning personality*, at its termination.

A comparison of the Work Sheets reveals considerably greater scatter in the second Bellevue-Wechsler, and a drop in the total I.Q. from 135 to 124. Qualitatively, the drop in the Comprehension was accounted for by the intrusion of personal problems into areas which should be handled objectively.

The Szondi indicated that this individual was attempting, at the time of the second testing, to exert rigid control on his aggressiveness. The s factor, overloaded in the first test, is reversed and, combined with the strong +e, reflects the exaggerated effort at control.

The Rorschach total scores have decreased, in this instance, as have also the M and FM responses. The all-important FC achieved in Record 1 has now been lost.

This individual denies his drawing of the female figure with even greater vehemence on the second testing and the figure itself has become cruder during the interval of time. On our scale, these drawings would have been classified as belonging to different levels and would not have been thought to have been done by the same individual. The drawing of the male became reduced, in the second attempt, to about one-quarter of the original size but is otherwise identical.

As mentioned, a discussion between therapist and psychologist revealed that the second therapeutic estimate reflected the individual's condition when he left analytic therapy, whereas at the time of the retesting session, he was spiraling into a period of fierce resentment against the world. An unsatisfactory engagement had led to his self-esteem being temporarily jeopardized.

A10's records are shown on the next four pages.

# WORK SHEET *A10*

## VERBAL I. Q. = *135*

*1*

| EWS | Info. | Comp. | Digit | Arith. | Sim. |
|-----|-------|-------|-------|--------|------|
| 18 | 25 | 20 | | 14 | 23-24 |
| 17 | 24 | 19 | 17 | 13 | 21-22 |
| 16 | 23 | 18 | 16 | 12 | 20 |
| 15 | 21-22 | 17 | | 11 | 19 |
| 14 | 20 | 16 | 15 | | 17-18 |
| 13 | 18-19 | 15 | 14 | 10 | 16 |
| 12 | 17 | 14 | | 9 | 15 |
| | | | | | |
| 11 | 15-16 | 12-13 | 13 | | 13-14 |
| 10 | 13-14 | 11 | 12 | 8 | 12 |
| 9 | 12 | 10 | 11 | 7 | 11 |
| 8 | 10-11 | 9 | | | 9-10 |
| 7 | 9 | 8 | 10 | 6 | 8 |
| 6 | 7-8 | 7 | 9 | 5 | 7 |
| | | | | | |
| 5 | 6 | 5-6 | | | 5-6 |
| 4 | 4-5 | 4 | 8 | 4 | 4 |
| 3 | 2-3 | 3 | 7 | 3 | 3 |
| 2 | 1 | 2 | 6 | | 1-2 |
| 1 | 0 | 1 | | 2 | 0 |
| 0 | | 0 | 5 | 1 | |

## SZONDI

| SEXUAL | | PAROXYSMAL | | EGO | | CONTACT | |
|--------|--------|-----------|--------|--------|--------|--------|--------|
| h | s | e | hy | k | p | d | m |

## RORSCHACH

| | | | | | |
|---|---|---|---|---|---|
| R | *28* | M | *9* | | Fc | *1* |
| | | FM | *6* | F | *9* | c | |
| W% | *39* | m | | F- | | C' | *1* |
| D% | *61* | k | | F% | *32* | FC | *1* |
| d% | | K | *+1* | | | CF | *1+* |
| Dd% | | FK | *+1* | | | C | |
| S | | | | | | | |

# WORK SHEET

A10

2

## VERBAL I. Q. = 124

| EWS | Info. | Comp. | Digit | Arith. | Sim. |
|-----|-------|-------|-------|--------|------|
| 18 | 25 | 20 | | 14 | 23-24 |
| 17 | 24 | 19 | 17 | 13 | 21-22 |
| 16 | 23 | 18 | 16 | 12 | 20 |
| 15 | 21-22 | 17 | | 11 | 19 |
| 14 | 20 | 16 | 15 | | 17-18 |
| 13 | 18-19 | 15 | 14 | 10 | 16 |
| 12 | 17 | 14 | | 9 | 15 |
| 11 | 15-16 | 12-13 | 13 | | 13-14 |
| 10 | 13-14 | 11 | 12 | 8 | 12 |
| 9 | 12 | 10 | 11 | 7 | 11 |
| 8 | 10-11 | 9 | | | 9-10 |
| 7 | 9 | 8 | 10 | 6 | 8 |
| 6 | 7-8 | 7 | 9 | 5 | 7 |
| 5 | 6 | 5-6 | | | 5-6 |
| 4 | 4-5 | 4 | 8 | 4 | 4 |
| 3 | 2-3 | 3 | 7 | 3 | 3 |

## SZONDI

| SEXUAL | | PAROXYSMAL | | EGO | | CONTACT | |
|--------|--------|--------|--------|--------|--------|--------|--------|
| h | s | e | hy | k | p | d | m |
| | | X | | | | | |
| | | X | X | | X | | |
| | | X | X | | X | | |
| X | X | X | X | | X | X | X |
| X | X | | X | X | X | X | |
| X | X | | X | X | | | |
| X | X | | | | | | |

OVER-ALL EVALUATION = 26

## RORSCHACH

| | | | | | |
|---|---|---|---|---|---|
| R | 21 | M | 5 | Fc | |
| | | FM | 3 | F | 11 | c | |
| W% | 29 | m | | F- | | c' | +1 |
| D% | 67 | k | | F% | 57 | FC | |
| d% | | K | 1+1 | | | CF | +1 |
| Dd% | 4 | FK | | | | C | |
| S | | | | | | | |

# SUMMARY OF TEST FINDINGS A10

## MANNER DURING TEST

| (1) Overly distressed | (2) Tense | (3) Indifferent | (4) Appropriate | (5) Relaxed and actively interested |
|---|---|---|---|---|
| (1) Hostile | (2) Uneasy | | | |

## I.Q. (Bellevue-Wechsler)

| (1) Below average | (2) Average | (3) High average | (4) Superior | (5) Very superior |
|---|---|---|---|---|

## PRODUCTIVITY (Rorschach)

| (1) Impoverished | (2) Reduced output | (3) Adequate | (4) Better than average | (5) Rich and well-ordered |
|---|---|---|---|---|
| | (2) Compulsive productivity | | | |

## RELATION TO REALITY (Rorschach, Bellevue-Wechsler, Drawings)

| (1) Loose | (2) Lapses—together with good form | (3) Not noticeably disturbed | (4) Essentially firm | (5) Firm and good |
|---|---|---|---|---|

## USUAL-UNUSUAL THOUGHT CONTENT (Rorschach, Unpleasant Concept)

| (1) Bizarre | (2) Tendency toward the bizarre | (3) Adequate | (4) Original trends | (5) Outstandingly original |
|---|---|---|---|---|
| (1) Stereotyped | (2) Tendency toward stereotypy | | | |

## CONSTRUCTIVE FANTASY (Rorschach)

| (1) Absent | (2) Barely accessible | (3) Accessible | (4) Readily accessible | (5) Active but not hampering |
|---|---|---|---|---|
| (1) Withdrawal into fantasy | | | | |

## DRIVE (Rorschach, Szondi, Unpleasant Concept)

| (1) Overpowering aggression | (2) Over-aggressive | (3) Adequate | (4) Clearly sufficient | (5) Sufficient— exceptionally well-directed |
|---|---|---|---|---|
| (1) Hampering passivity | (2) Insufficient drive | | | |

## EMOTIONAL TONE (Rorschach, Szondi)

| (1) Explosive emotions | (2) Getting out of hand | (3) Trend toward emotional expression | (4) Warmth available | (5) Warm, readily available |
|---|---|---|---|---|
| (1) Lacking | (2) Indicated but repressed emotion | | | |

## SOCIAL ATTITUDE (T. A. T.)

| (1) Uncontrolled | (2) Constricted or neglected | (3) Adequate | (4) Well-regulated | (5) Free and flexible |
|---|---|---|---|---|

## ANXIETY

| (1) Disintegrating | (2) Marked | (3) Moderate | (4) Not marked | (5) Lack of evidence of anxiety |
|---|---|---|---|---|

## OVER-ALL EVALUATION

| (1) Markedly disturbed personality | (2) Less than adequate personality with some psychological problems | (3) Adequate personality | (4) Better than average functioning personality | (5) Exceptionally well-integrated personality with excellent potential |
|---|---|---|---|---|

## SUMMARY OF THERAPIST'S FINDINGS

### ESTIMATED INTELLIGENCE LEVEL

| (1) Below average | (2) Average | (3) High average | (4) Superior | (5) Very superior |
|---|---|---|---|---|

### FLOW OF ASSOCIATIVE MATERIAL

| (1) Impoverished | (2) Reduced output | (3) Adequate | (4) Better than average | (5) Rich and well-ordered |
|---|---|---|---|---|
| | (2) Compulsive productivity | | | |

### RELATION TO REALITY

| (1) Loose | (2) Lapses—together with good form | (3) Not noticeably disturbed | (4) Essentially firm | (5) Firm and good |
|---|---|---|---|---|

### USUAL-UNUSUAL THOUGHT CONTENT

| (1) Bizarre | (2) Tendency toward the bizarre | (3) Adequate | (4) Original trends | (5) Outstandingly original |
|---|---|---|---|---|
| (1) Stereotyped | (2) Tendency toward stereotypy | | | |

### CONSTRUCTIVE FANTASY

| (1) Absent | (2) Barely accessible | (3) Accessible | (4) Readily accessible | (5) Active but not hampering |
|---|---|---|---|---|
| (1) Withdrawal into fantasy | | | | |

### DRIVE

| (1) Overpowering aggression | (2) Over-aggressive | (3) Adequate | (4) Clearly sufficient | (5) Sufficient—exceptionally well-directed |
|---|---|---|---|---|
| (1) Hampering passivity | (2) Insufficient drive | | | |

### EMOTIONAL TONE

| (1) Explosive emotions | (2) Getting out of hand | (3) Trend toward emotional expression | (4) Warmth available | (5) Warm, readily available |
|---|---|---|---|---|
| (1) Lacking | (2) Indicated but repressed emotions | | | |

### SOCIAL ATTITUDE

| (1) Uncontrolled | (2) Constricted or neglected | (3) Adequate | (4) Well-regulated | (5) Free and flexible |
|---|---|---|---|---|

### ANXIETY

| (1) Disintegrating | (2) Marked | (3) Moderate | (4) Not marked | (5) Lack of evidence of anxiety |
|---|---|---|---|---|

### OVER-ALL EVALUATION

| (1) Markedly disturbed personality | (2) Less than adequate personality with some psychological problems | (3) Adequate personality | (4) Better than average functioning personality | (5) Exceptionally well-integrated personality with excellent potential |
|---|---|---|---|---|

## XI. Retesting following long-term psychotherapy.

As stated earlier, it has not been our primary concern in this volume to determine the different degrees of impact of various forms of psychotherapy on retest material. For purposes of organizing our results more efficiently, however, we have differentiated three techniques here and arranged the cases accordingly: the orthodox analytic approach, dynamically oriented (long-term) psychotherapy, and brief psychotherapy with long-term follow-up.

In this chapter we have grouped together six patients who were not in orthodox analysis but whose therapists were admittedly analytically oriented and for whom, with the possible exception of PT1, psychotherapy was dynamically centered. Other than PT5, whose treatment lasted just less than one year, long-term therapy refers to periods of several years. PT4 was in therapy eight years, the others more than two.

PT1, a girl in her early teens, was rated by her therapist as a *Markedly disturbed personality* at the start of treatment and was considered to have improved to the level of a *Less than adequate personality with some psychological problems* at its termination. Comparing the test material of PT1 at the start of therapy and at the time of retesting three years later, the Work Sheets show that the outstanding change is a rise of 20 points in the I.Q. This increase in score comes about almost exclusively from her better handling of the "on-the-spot" tests, i.e., in the Digit Memory and the Arithmetic, PT1 now makes a reasonable showing instead of a very poor one. What she seems to have gained from her therapeutic sessions is the capacity to utilize what very limited resources she possesses. Perhaps these resources in themselves have scarcely changed, but certainly what she can do with her psychological equipment is much greater.

Improvement is also noticed in her ability to relate meaningfully to the testing situation through the Sentence Completion. When first tested, this child reacted in a haphazard and arbitrary way to many of the sentences in this test. For example, to the sentence: "Few children fear . . ." she replied with the one word, "Sadly." To the sentence: "It hurts when . . ." she replied with the meaningless, "When you get it." She completed the sentence: "Fathers should learn that . . ." with the word, "Stupid," and replied to the sentence: "When fire starts . . ." with, "It never ends."

In the second test she replied to the sentence: "Few children fear . . ." with the more meaningful, "Cats," and to the sentence: "When fire starts . . ." with the appropriate, "Send in an alarm." This time she replied to: "It hurts when . . ." with, "You cut yourself." These are, of course, circumscribed and unrevealing answers but at least they are sensible completions.

It cannot be said that great strides are reflected in the Rorschach record except for the introduction of 2 FC responses, which reinforce the picture of a greater amenability and relatedness to the environment. Failure on Card VI, however, suggests that sexual problems may now be coming to the forefront. Previously she had responded without delay to this card with two adequate responses.

The Szondi also indicates that a socializing process has taken place. When first tested, the two completely open factors spoke for the diagnosis of a psychotic condition; Deri and others have called attention to this as reflecting a seriously disturbed individual. There is a lessening of the loaded +s in the second test which, though slight, is along the direction indicated by the other test material, i.e., PT1 has become less turbulently destructive and is somewhat more aware of the demands made on her by the world in which she lives.

A comparison of the summaries from the test findings and the therapist reveals essentially similar appraisals. Independent assessments by the parents also note genuine improvement in reference to PT1's manageability and increased social adaptation. Her records follow on the next four pages.

## WORK SHEET  *PT₁*

1

### VERBAL I. Q. = 68

| EWS | Info. | Comp. | Digit | Arith. | Sim. |
|-----|-------|-------|-------|--------|------|
| 18  | 25    | 20    |       | 14     | 23-24 |
| 17  | 24    | 19    | 17    | 13     | 21-22 |
| 16  | 23    | 18    | 16    | 12     | 20   |
| 15  | 21-22 | 17    |       | 11     | 19   |
| 14  | 20    | 16    | 15    |        | 17-18 |
| 13  | 18-19 | 15    | 14    | 10     | 16   |
| 12  | 17    | 14    |       | 9      | 15   |
|     |       |       |       |        |      |
| 11  | 15-16 | 12-13 | 13    |        | 13-14 |
| 10  | 13-14 | 11    | 12    | 8      | 12   |
| 9   | 12    | 10    | 11    | 7      | 11   |
| 8   | 10-11 | 9     |       |        | 9-10 |
| 7   | 9     | 8     | 10    | 6      | 8    |
| 6   | 7-8   | 7     | 9     | 5      | 7    |
|     |       |       |       |        |      |
| 5   | 6     | 5-6   |       |        | 5-6  |
| 4   | 4-5   | 4     | 8     | 4      | 4    |
| 3   | 2-3   | 3     | 7     | 3      | 3    |
| 2   | 1     | 2     | 6     |        | 1-2  |
| 1   | 0     | 1     |       | 2      | 0    |
| 0   |       | 0     | 5     | 1      |      |

### SZONDI

| SEXUAL | | PAROXYSMAL | | EGO | | CONTACT | |
|--------|---|-----------|----|-----|---|---------|---|
| h | s | e | hy | k | p | d | m |

### OVER-ALL EVALUATION = 13

| | 1 | 2 | 3 | 4 | 5 |
|---|---|---|---|---|---|
| OVER-ALL RATING | 1 | 2 | 3 | 4 | 5 |
| PRODUCTIVITY | 1 | ②| 3 | 4 | 5 |
| RELATION TO REALITY | ① | 2 | 3 | 4 | 5 |
| THOUGHT CONTENT | ① | 2 | 3 | 4 | 5 |
| CONSTRUCTIVE FANTASY | 1 | 2 | ③| 4 | 5 |
| DRIVE | ① | 2 | 3 | 4 | 5 |
| EMOTIONAL TONE | ① | 2 | 3 | 4 | 5 |
| SOCIAL ATTITUDE | ① | 2 | 3 | 4 | 5 |
| ANXIETY | 1 | ②| 3 | 4 | 5 |
| I. Q. RATING   68 | ① | 2 | 3 | 4 | 5 |

### RORSCHACH

| | | | | | |
|---|---|---|---|---|---|
| R | 13 | M | 3(1-) | | Fc |
| | | FM | 3(1-) | F  5 | c |
| W% | 46 | m | +1 | F- 2 | C' |
| D% | 46 | k | | F% 54 | FC |
| d% | | K | | | CF |
| Dd% | 8 | FK | | | C |
| S | | | | | |

# WORK SHEET

PT 1

2

## VERBAL I. Q. = 88

| EWS | Info. | Comp. | Digit | Arith. | Sim. |
|---|---|---|---|---|---|
| 18 | 25 | 20 |  | 14 | 23-24 |
| 17 | 24 | 19 | 17 | 13 | 21-22 |
| 16 | 23 | 18 | 16 | 12 | 20 |
| 15 | 21-22 | 17 |  | 11 | 19 |
| 14 | 20 | 16 | 15 |  | 17-18 |
| 13 | 18-19 | 15 | 14 | 10 | 16 |
| 12 | 17 | 14 |  | 9 | 15 |
|  |  |  |  |  |  |
| 11 | 15-16 | 12-13 | 13 |  | 13-14 |
| 10 | 13-14 | 11 | 12 | 8 | 12 |
| 9 | 12 | 10 | 11 | 7 | 11 |
| 8 | 10-11 | 9 |  |  | 9-10 |
| 7 | 9 | 8 | 10 | 6 | 8 |
| 6 | 7-8 | 7 | 9 | 5 | 7 |
|  |  |  |  |  |  |
| 5 | 6 | 5-6 |  |  | 5-6 |
| 4 | 4-5 | 4 | 8 | 4 | 4 |
| 3 | 2-3 | 3 | 7 | 3 | 3 |
| 2 | 1 | 2 | 6 |  | 1-2 |
| 1 | 0 | 1 |  | 2 | 0 |
| 0 |  | 0 | 5 | 1 |  |

## SZONDI

| SEXUAL | | PAROXYSMAL | | EGO | | CONTACT | |
|---|---|---|---|---|---|---|---|
| h | s | e | hy | k | p | d | m |

## OVER-ALL EVALUATION = 16

| | | | | | |
|---|---|---|---|---|---|
| OVER-ALL RATING | 1 | 2 | 3 | 4 | 5 |
| PRODUCTIVITY | 1 | (2) | 3 | 4 | 5 |
| RELATION TO REALITY | 1 | (2) | 3 | 4 | 5 |
| THOUGHT CONTENT | (1) | 2 | 3 | 4 | 5 |
| CONSTRUCTIVE FANTASY | (1) | 2 | 3 | 4 | 5 |
| DRIVE | 1 | (2) | 3 | 4 | 5 |
| EMOTIONAL TONE | 1 | (2) | 3 | 4 | 5 |
| SOCIAL ATTITUDE | 1 | (2) | 3 | 4 | 5 |
| ANXIETY | 1 | 2 | (3) | 4 | 5 |
| I. Q. RATING   88 | (1) | 2 | 3 | 4 | 5 |

## RORSCHACH

| | | |
|---|---|---|
| R   11 | M | Fc |
|  | FM 6 | F 2 |
| W% 36 | m | F- 1 |
| D% 64 | k | F% 27   FC 2 |
| d% | K | CF |
| Dd% | FK | C |
| S | | |

# SUMMARY OF TEST FINDINGS   *PT1*

## MANNER DURING TEST

| (1) Overly distressed | (2) Tense | (3) Indifferent | (4) Appropriate | (5) Relaxed and actively interested |
|---|---|---|---|---|
| (1) **Hostile** | (2) Uneasy | | | |

## I.Q. (Bellevue-Wechsler)

| (1) **Below average** | (2) Average | (3) High average | (4) Superior | (5) Very superior |
|---|---|---|---|---|

## PRODUCTIVITY (Rorschach)

| (1) Impoverished | (2) **Reduced output** | (3) Adequate | (4) Better than average | (5) Rich and well-ordered |
|---|---|---|---|---|
| | (2) Compulsive productivity | | | |

## RELATION TO REALITY (Rorschach, Bellevue-Wechsler, Drawings)

| (1) **Loose** | (2) Lapses—together with good form | (3) Not noticeably disturbed | (4) Essentially firm | (5) Firm and good |
|---|---|---|---|---|

## USUAL-UNUSUAL THOUGHT CONTENT (Rorschach, Unpleasant Concept)

| (1) **Bizarre** | (2) Tendency toward the bizarre | (3) Adequate | (4) Original trends | (5) Outstandingly original |
|---|---|---|---|---|
| (1) Stereotyped | (2) Tendency toward stereotypy | | | |

## CONSTRUCTIVE FANTASY (Rorschach)

| (1) Absent | (2) Barely accessible | (3) **Accessible** | (4) Readily accessible | (5) Active but not hampering |
|---|---|---|---|---|
| (1) Withdrawal into fantasy | | | | |

## DRIVE (Rorschach, Szondi, Unpleasant Concept)

| (1) **Overpowering aggression** | (2) Over-aggressive | (3) Adequate | (4) Clearly sufficient | (5) Sufficient—exceptionally well-directed |
|---|---|---|---|---|
| (1) Hampering passivity | (2) Insufficient drive | | | |

## EMOTIONAL TONE (Rorschach, Szondi)

| (1) **Explosive emotions** | (2) Getting out of hand | (3) Trend toward emotional expression | (4) Warmth available | (5) Warm, readily available |
|---|---|---|---|---|
| (1) Lacking | (2) Indicated but repressed emotions | | | |

## SOCIAL ATTITUDE (T. A. T.)

| (1) **Uncontrolled** | (2) Constricted or neglected | (3) Adequate | (4) Well-regulated | (5) Free and flexible |
|---|---|---|---|---|

## ANXIETY

| (1) Disintegrating | (2) **Marked** | (3) Moderate | (4) Not marked | (5) Lack of evidence of anxiety |
|---|---|---|---|---|

## OVER-ALL EVALUATION

| (1) **Markedly disturbed personality** | (2) Less than adequate personality with some psychological problems | (3) Adequate personality | (4) Better than average functioning personality | (5) Exceptionally well-integrated personality with excellent potential |
|---|---|---|---|---|

## SUMMARY OF THERAPIST'S FINDINGS    *PT 1*

### ESTIMATED INTELLIGENCE LEVEL

| (1) Below average | (2) Average | (3) High average | (4) Superior | (5) Very superior |
|---|---|---|---|---|

### FLOW OF ASSOCIATIVE MATERIAL

| (1) Impoverished | (2) Reduced output | (3) Adequate | (4) Better than average | (5) Rich and well-ordered |
|---|---|---|---|---|
| | (2) Compulsive productivity | | | |

### RELATION TO REALITY

| (1) Loose | (2) Lapses—together with good form | (3) Not noticeably disturbed | (4) Essentially firm | (5) Firm and good |
|---|---|---|---|---|

### USUAL-UNUSUAL THOUGHT CONTENT

| (1) Bizarre | (2) Tendency toward the bizarre | (3) Adequate | (4) Original trends | (5) Outstandingly original |
|---|---|---|---|---|
| (1) Stereotyped | (2) Tendency toward stereotypy | | | |

### CONSTRUCTIVE FANTASY

| (1) Absent | (2) Barely accessible | (3) Accessible | (4) Readily accessible | (5) Active but not hampering |
|---|---|---|---|---|
| (1) Withdrawal into fantasy | | | | |

### DRIVE

| (1) Overpowering aggression | (2) Over-aggressive | (3) Adequate | (4) Clearly sufficient | (5) Sufficient—exceptionally well-directed |
|---|---|---|---|---|
| (1) Hampering passivity | (2) Insufficient drive | | | |

### EMOTIONAL TONE

| (1) Explosive emotions | (2) Getting out of hand | (3) Trend toward emotional expression | (4) Warmth available | (5) Warm, readily available |
|---|---|---|---|---|
| (1) Lacking | (2) Indicated but repressed emotions | | | |

### SOCIAL ATTITUDE

| (1) Uncontrolled | (2) Constricted or neglected | (3) Adequate | (4) Well-regulated | (5) Free and flexible |
|---|---|---|---|---|

### ANXIETY

| (1) Disintegrating | (2) Marked | (3) Moderate | (4) Not marked | (5) Lack of evidence of anxiety |
|---|---|---|---|---|

### OVER-ALL EVALUATION

| (1) Markedly disturbed personality | (2) Less than adequate personality with some psychological problems | (3) Adequate personality | (4) Better than average functioning personality | (5) Exceptionally well-integrated personality with excellent potential |
|---|---|---|---|---|

PT2 was eleven years old when first tested and thirteen at the time of retesting after two years of psychotherapy. The therapist estimated this boy at the second over-all level of adjustment at the start of treatment and, although considerable improvement was noted, which has been charted according to the areas in which it was reflected, the therapist nevertheless felt that the over-all level of adjustment was unchanged at the termination of treatment. His records are shown on pages 202-205.

A comparison of the two Work Sheets reveals a considerably improved Bellevue-Wechsler scattergram with a somewhat different pattern. The Arithmetic, which presented a major problem in the first test, is handled much better in the second. Comprehension, Reasoning and Judgment has risen considerably, and an important few points have been added to the Information. (The WISC was used for the first testing.)

The Szondi on both occasions is unusual, but some improvement can be seen in the retest in the loss of the completely open d factor, –d, –m being a less desolate picture than that reflected in the open d, –m. The ambivalent s, the appearance of some capacity to sublimate in the area of aggression, also is an advance.

The Figure Drawings have increased in size, and although the male figure is now set at an angle, indicating that this child still experiences pressures sufficiently strong to tilt him over, the drawing can be considered a better attempt than the previous one.

Genuine improvement can be found in the Rorschach where, for the first time, some much needed awareness and responsiveness to others is reflected in the two FC's and an additional CF response. That this individual is in danger of withdrawing into his own fantasy world is still reflected in the high number of M responses, although they are qualitatively much superior in the second record.

The Most Unpleasant Concept given on the first testing is this child in his own coffin. Still preoccupied with death on the retest, he nonetheless has shifted the emphasis and is less personally involved, since the Most Unpleasant Concept in the second testing is of a prisoner in a concentration camp being hanged.

The OVER-ALL EVALUATION based on the quantitative estimate of the test findings gives PT2 an initial score of 19 points, whereas on the second testing he rates 28. An identical difference exists between the therapist's two assessments, with PT2 rating 19 on the first therapeutic estimate and 28 on the second.

According to his parents, this boy is adjusting much better both in school and at home. They give unqualified praise to the psychotherapeutic efforts.

PT3, in her middle twenties and married when first examined psychologically, was retested after two years of psychotherapy. Her therapist rated PT3 as a *Less than adequate personality* who progressed, following the two years of psychotherapy, to the *Adequate* level.

Comparing the Work Sheets of PT3, commencing with the Bellevue-Wechsler, one finds much less scatter and a rise in I.Q. from 112 to 130. This takes this patient out of the *High Average Group* and places her in the *Very Superior*.

Relatively little change has occurred on the Szondi. There is greater structuring in the ego, with a –k replacing the previously completely open factor. This individual also accepts her feminine role with less conflict as evidenced by the distributions in the h and s factors.

The drawings make quite an impact since they pass from a truly bizarre type of expression, as seen in Record 1, to a much more normal attempt. The transparency has gone, and the pumpkin-like face is replaced by a genuine attempt to draw the human features. Although the arms are pinned to the side and no hands have been attempted, they are much more functional units than the appendages attached without any look of reality in the first drawing.

A quantitative estimate shows this individual to have increased her scores from 17 on the first testing to 31 on the second. Originally estimated at 26 on the therapist's scale (that is, assessed as less disturbed by the therapist than from the initial test findings), she progresses to 32 at the second clinical evaluation.

(Records for PT3 will be found on pages 206-209.)

=== **WORK SHEET** === *PT 2*

## VERBAL I. Q. = 96

| EWS | Info. | Comp. | Digit | Arith. | Sim. |
|---|---|---|---|---|---|
| 18 | 25 | 20 |  | 14 | 23-24 |
| 17 | 24 | 19 | 17 | 13 | 21-22 |
| 16 | 23 | 18 | 16 | 12 | 20 |
| 15 | 21-22 | 17 |  | 11 | 19 |
| 14 | 20 | 16 | 15 |  | 17-18 |
| 13 | 18-19 | 15 | 14 | 10 | 16 |
| 12 | 17 | 14 |  | 9 | 15 |
|  |  |  |  |  |  |
| 11 | 15-16 | 12-13 | 13 |  | 13-14 |
| 10 | 13-14 | 11 | 12 | 8 | 12 |
| 9 | 12 | 10 | 11 | 7 | 11 |
| 8 | 10-11 | 9 |  |  | 9-10 |
| 7 | 9 | 8 | 10 | 6 | 8 |
| 6 | 7-8 | 7 | 9 | 5 | 7 |
|  |  |  |  |  |  |
| 5 | 6 | 5-6 |  |  | 5-6 |
| 4 | 4-5 | 4 | 8 | 4 | 4 |
| 3 | 2-3 | 3 | 7 |  | 3 |
| 2 | 1 | 2 | 6 |  | 1-2 |
| 1 | 0 | 1 |  | 2 | 0 |
| 0 |  | 0 | 5 | 1 |  |

### SZONDI

| SEXUAL | | PAROXYSMAL | | EGO | | CONTACT | |
|---|---|---|---|---|---|---|---|
| h | s | e | hy | k | p | d | m |

### RORSCHACH

| | | | | | |
|---|---|---|---|---|---|
| R | 14 | M | 5 | | Fc |
| | | FM | 2 | F | 4 | c |
| W% | 64 | m | +1 | F- | 1 | C' |
| D% | 36 | k | | F% | 36 | FC |
| d% | | K | 1 | | | CF |
| Dd% | | FK | | | | C |
| S | | | | | | |

# WORK SHEET

PT2

2

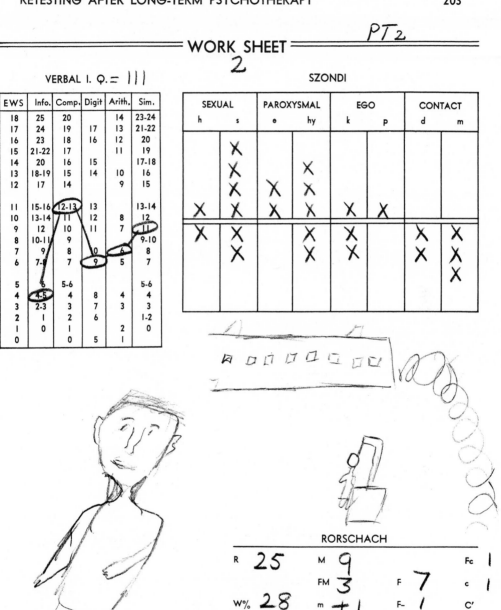

VERBAL I. Q. = 111

| EWS | Info. | Comp. | Digit | Arith. | Sim. |
|-----|-------|-------|-------|--------|------|
| 18 | 25 | 20 | | 14 | 23-24 |
| 17 | 24 | 19 | 17 | 13 | 21-22 |
| 16 | 23 | 18 | 16 | 12 | 20 |
| 15 | 21-22 | 17 | | 11 | 19 |
| 14 | 20 | 16 | 15 | | 17-18 |
| 13 | 18-19 | 15 | 14 | 10 | 16 |
| 12 | 17 | 14 | | 9 | 15 |
| 11 | 15-16 | 12-13 | 13 | | 13-14 |
| 10 | 13-14 | 11 | 12 | 8 | 12 |
| 9 | 12 | 10 | 11 | 7 | 11 |
| 8 | 10-11 | 9 | | | 9-10 |
| 7 | 9 | 8 | | 6 | 8 |
| 6 | 7-8 | 7 | 9 | 5 | 7 |
| 5 | 6 | 5-6 | | | 5-6 |
| 4 | 4-5 | 4 | 8 | 4 | 4 |
| 3 | 2-3 | 3 | 7 | 3 | 3 |
| 2 | 1 | 2 | 6 | | 1-2 |
| 1 | 0 | 1 | | 2 | 0 |
| 0 | | 0 | 5 | 1 | |

SZONDI

| SEXUAL | | PAROXYSMAL | | EGO | | CONTACT | |
|---|---|---|---|---|---|---|---|
| h | s | e | hy | k | p | d | m |

RORSCHACH

| R | 25 | M | 9 | | | Fc | 1 |
|---|----|---|---|---|---|----|---|
| | | FM | 3 | F | 7 | c | 1 |
| W% | 28 | m | +1 | F- | 1 | C' | |
| D% | 68 | k | | F% | 32 | FC | 2 |
| d% | 4 | K | 1+1 | | | CF | +1 |
| Dd% | | FK | | | | C | |
| S | | | | | | | |

# SUMMARY OF TEST FINDINGS *PT2*

### MANNER DURING TEST

| (1) Overly distressed | (2) *Tense* | (3) Indifferent | (4) Appropriate | (5) Relaxed and actively interested |
|---|---|---|---|---|
| (1) Hostile | (2) Uneasy | | | |

### I.Q. (Bellevue-Wechsler)

| (1) Below average | (2) *Average* | (3) High average | (4) Superior | (5) Very superior |
|---|---|---|---|---|

### PRODUCTIVITY (Rorschach)

| (1) Impoverished | (2) *Reduced output* | (3) Adequate | (4) Better than average | (5) Rich and well-ordered |
|---|---|---|---|---|
| | (2) Compulsive productivity | | | |

### RELATION TO REALITY (Rorschach, Bellevue-Wechsler, Drawings)

| (1) Loose | (2) Lapses—together with good form | (3) *Not noticeably disturbed* | (4) Essentially firm | (5) Firm and good |
|---|---|---|---|---|

### USUAL-UNUSUAL THOUGHT CONTENT (Rorschach, Unpleasant Concept)

| (1) Bizarre | (2) *Tendency toward the bizarre* | (3) Adequate | (4) Original trends | (5) Outstandingly original |
|---|---|---|---|---|
| (1) Stereotyped | (2) Tendency toward stereotypy | | | |

### CONSTRUCTIVE FANTASY (Rorschach)

| (1) Absent | (2) Barely accessible | (3) *Accessible* | (4) Readily accessible | (5) Active but not hampering |
|---|---|---|---|---|
| (1) Withdrawal into fantasy | | | | |

### DRIVE (Rorschach, Szondi, Unpleasant Concept)

| (1) Overpowering aggression | (2) *Over-aggressive* | (3) Adequate | (4) Clearly sufficient | (5) Sufficient—exceptionally well-directed |
|---|---|---|---|---|
| (1) Hampering passivity | (2) Insufficient drive | | | |

### EMOTIONAL TONE (Rorschach, Szondi)

| (1) Explosive emotions | (2) Getting out of hand | (3) Trend toward emotional expression | (4) Warmth available | (5) Warm, readily available |
|---|---|---|---|---|
| (1) *Lacking* | (2) Indicated but repressed emotions | | | |

### SOCIAL ATTITUDE (T. A. T.)

| (1) Uncontrolled | (2) *Constricted or neglected* | (3) Adequate | (4) Well-regulated | (5) Free and flexible |
|---|---|---|---|---|

### ANXIETY

| (1) Disintegrating | (2) *Marked* | (3) Moderate | (4) Not marked | (5) Lack of evidence of anxiety |
|---|---|---|---|---|

### OVER-ALL EVALUATION

| (1) Markedly disturbed personality | (2) *Less than adequate personality with some psychological problems* | (3) Adequate personality | (4) Better than average functioning personality | (5) Exceptionally well-integrated personality with excellent potential |
|---|---|---|---|---|

## SUMMARY OF THERAPIST'S FINDINGS

### ESTIMATED INTELLIGENCE LEVEL

| (1) Below average | (2) Average | (3) High average | (4) Superior | (5) Very superior |
|---|---|---|---|---|

### FLOW OF ASSOCIATIVE MATERIAL

| (1) Impoverished | (2) Reduced output | (3) Adequate | (4) Better than average | (5) Rich and well-ordered |
|---|---|---|---|---|
|  | (2) Compulsive productivity |  |  |  |

### RELATION TO REALITY

| (1) Loose | (2) Lapses—together with good form | (3) Not noticeably disturbed | (4) Essentially firm | (5) Firm and good |
|---|---|---|---|---|

### USUAL-UNUSUAL THOUGHT CONTENT

| (1) Bizarre | (2) Tendency toward the bizarre | (3) Adequate | (4) Original trends | (5) Outstandingly original |
|---|---|---|---|---|
| (1) Stereotyped | (2) Tendency toward stereotypy |  |  |  |

### CONSTRUCTIVE FANTASY

| (1) Absent | (2) Barely accessible | (3) Accessible | (4) Readily accessible | (5) Active but not hampering |
|---|---|---|---|---|
| (1) Withdrawal into fantasy |  |  |  |  |

### DRIVE

| (1) Overpowering aggression | (2) Over-aggressive | (3) Adequate | (4) Clearly sufficient | (5) Sufficient—exceptionally well-directed |
|---|---|---|---|---|
| (1) Hampering passivity | (2) Insufficient drive |  |  |  |

### EMOTIONAL TONE

| (1) Explosive emotions | (2) Getting out of hand | (3) Trend toward emotional expression | (4) Warmth available | (5) Warm, readily available |
|---|---|---|---|---|
| (1) Lacking | (2) Indicated but repressed emotions |  |  |  |

### SOCIAL ATTITUDE

| (1) Uncontrolled | (2) Constricted or neglected | (3) Adequate | (4) Well-regulated | (5) Free and flexible |
|---|---|---|---|---|

### ANXIETY

| (1) Disintegrating | (2) Marked | (3) Moderate | (4) Not marked | (5) Lack of evidence of anxiety |
|---|---|---|---|---|

### OVER-ALL EVALUATION

| (1) Markedly disturbed personality | (2) Less than adequate personality with ▬▬ psychological problems | (3) Adequate personality | (4) Better than average functioning personality | (5) Exceptionally well-integrated personality with excellent potential |
|---|---|---|---|---|

# WORK SHEET

*PT3*

**I**

### VERBAL I. Q. = 112

| EWS | Info. | Comp. | Digit | Arith. | Sim. |
|-----|-------|-------|-------|--------|------|
| 18 | 25 | 20 | | 14 | 23-24 |
| 17 | 24 | 19 | 17 | 13 | 21-22 |
| 16 | 23 | 18 | 16 | 12 | 20 |
| 15 | 21-22 | 17 | | 11 | 19 |
| 14 | 20 | 16 | 15 | | 17-18 |
| 13 | 18-19 | 15 | 14 | 10 | 16 |
| 12 | 17 | 14 | | 9 | 15 |
| 11 | 15-16 | 12-13 | 13 | | 13-14 |
| 10 | 13-14 | 11 | 12 | 8 | 12 |
| 9 | 12 | 10 | 11 | 7 | 11 |
| 8 | 10-11 | 9 | | | 9-10 |
| 7 | 9 | | 10 | 6 | 8 |
| 6 | 7-8 | 7 | 9 | 5 | 7 |
| 5 | 6 | 5-6 | | | 5-6 |
| 4 | 4-5 | 4 | 8 | 4 | 4 |
| 3 | 2-3 | 3 | 7 | 3 | 3 |
| 2 | 1 | 2 | 6 | | 1-2 |
| 1 | 0 | 1 | | 2 | 0 |
| 0 | | 0 | 5 | 1 | |

## SZONDI

| SEXUAL | | PAROXYSMAL | | EGO | | CONTACT | |
|--------|---|-----------|----|-----|---|---------|---|
| h | s | e | hy | k | p | d | m |

## OVER-ALL EVALUATION = 17

| | | | | | |
|---|---|---|---|---|---|
| OVER-ALL RATING | 1 | 2 | 3 | 4 | 5 |
| PRODUCTIVITY | ①| 2 | 3 | 4 | 5 |
| RELATION TO REALITY | 1 | ② | 3 | 4 | 5 |
| THOUGHT CONTENT | 1 | ② | 3 | 4 | 5 |
| CONSTRUCTIVE FANTASY | 1 | ② | 3 | 4 | 5 |
| DRIVE | 1 | ② | 3 | 4 | 5 |
| EMOTIONAL TONE | ① | 2 | 3 | 4 | 5 |
| SOCIAL ATTITUDE | 1 | ② | 3 | 4 | 5 |
| ANXIETY | 1 | ② | 3 | 4 | 5 |
| I. Q. RATING  112 | 1 | 2 | ③ | 4 | 5 |

## RORSCHACH

| R | 10 | M | 2 | | | Fc | |
|---|----|---|---|---|---|----|--|
| | | FM | 1 | F | 6 | c | |
| W% | 50 | m | | F- | 1 | C' | |
| D% | 40 | k | | F% | 70 | FC | |
| d% | | K | | | | CF | |
| Dd% S | 10 | FK | | | | C | |

# WORK SHEET

PT3

## VERBAL I. Q. = 130

| EWS | Info. | Comp. | Digit | Arith. | Sim. |
|-----|-------|-------|-------|--------|------|
| 18 | 25 | 20 | | 14 | 23-24 |
| 17 | 24 | 19 | 17 | 13 | 21-22 |
| 16 | 23 | 18 | 16 | 12 | 20 |
| 15 | 21-22 | 17 | | 11 | 19 |
| 14 | 20 | 16 | 15 | | 17-18 |
| 13 | 18-19 | 15 | 14 | 10 | 16 |
| 12 | 17 | 14 | | 9 | 15 |
| 11 | 15-16 | 12-13 | | | 13-14 |
| 10 | 13-14 | 11 | 12 | 8 | 12 |
| 9 | 12 | 10 | 11 | 7 | 11 |
| 8 | 10-11 | 9 | | | 9-10 |
| 7 | 9 | 8 | 10 | 6 | 8 |
| 6 | 7-8 | 7 | 9 | 5 | 7 |
| 5 | 6 | 5-6 | | | 5-6 |
| 4 | 4-5 | 4 | 8 | 4 | 4 |
| 3 | 2-3 | 3 | 7 | 3 | 3 |
| 2 | 1 | 2 | 6 | | 1-2 |
| 1 | 0 | 1 | | 2 | 0 |
| 0 | | 0 | 5 | 1 | |

2

## SZONDI

| SEXUAL | | PAROXYSMAL | | EGO | | CONTACT | |
|--------|--------|------------|--------|-----|--------|---------|--------|
| h | s | e | hy | k | p | d | m |
| | | X | | | | | X |
| | | X | | | | X | X X |
| X | X | X | X | | X | X | X |
| X | X | X | X | X | X | X | |
| X | X | | X | X | | X | |

### OVER-ALL EVALUATION = 31

| | 1 | 2 | 3 | 4 | 5 |
|---|---|---|---|---|---|
| OVER-ALL RATING | 1 | 2 | 3 | 4 | 5 |
| PRODUCTIVITY | 1 | 2 | 3 | ④ | 5 |
| RELATION TO REALITY | 1 | 2 | ③ | 4 | 5 |
| THOUGHT CONTENT | 1 | 2 | 3 | ④ | 5 |
| CONSTRUCTIVE FANTASY | 1 | ② | 3 | 4 | 5 |
| DRIVE | 1 | 2 | ③ | 4 | 5 |
| EMOTIONAL TONE | 1 | 2 | 3 | ④ | 5 |
| SOCIAL ATTITUDE | 1 | 2 | ③ | 4 | 5 |
| ANXIETY | 1 | 2 | ③ | 4 | 5 |
| I. Q. RATING  130 | 1 | 2 | 3 | 4 | ⑤ |

### RORSCHACH

| R | 43 | M | 2 | | | Fc | 2 |
|---|----|---|---|---|----|----|---|
| | | FM | 4 | F | 22 | c | 1 |
| W% | 20 | m | | F– | | C' | |
| D% | 58 | k | | F% | 51 | FC | 3 |
| d% | 20 | K | 3 | | | CF | 4 |
| Dd% | 2 | FK | | | | c | 2 |
| S | | | | | | | |

# SUMMARY OF TEST FINDINGS

PT3

### MANNER DURING TEST

| (1) Overly distressed | (2) Tense | (3) Indifferent | (4) Appropriate | (5) Relaxed and actively interested |
|---|---|---|---|---|
| (1) Hostile | (2) Uneasy | | | |

### I.Q. (Bellevue-Wechsler)

| (1) Below average | (2) Average | (3) High average | (4) Superior | (5) Very superior |
|---|---|---|---|---|

### PRODUCTIVITY (Rorschach)

| (1) Impoverished | (2) Reduced output | (3) Adequate | (4) Better than average | (5) Rich and well-ordered |
|---|---|---|---|---|
| | (2) Compulsive productivity | | | |

### RELATION TO REALITY (Rorschach, Bellevue-Wechsler, Drawings)

| (1) Loose | (2) Lapses—together with good form | (3) Not noticeably disturbed | (4) Essentially firm | (5) Firm and good |
|---|---|---|---|---|

### USUAL-UNUSUAL THOUGHT CONTENT (Rorschach, Unpleasant Concept)

| (1) Bizarre | (2) Tendency toward the bizarre | (3) Adequate | (4) Original trends | (5) Outstandingly original |
|---|---|---|---|---|
| (1) Stereotyped | (2) Tendency toward stereotypy | | | |

### CONSTRUCTIVE FANTASY (Rorschach)

| (1) Absent | (2) Barely accessible | (3) Accessible | (4) Readily accessible | (5) Active but not hampering |
|---|---|---|---|---|
| (1) Withdrawal into fantasy | | | | |

### DRIVE (Rorschach, Szondi, Unpleasant Concept)

| (1) Overpowering aggression | (2) Over-aggressive | (3) Adequate | (4) Clearly sufficient | (5) Sufficient—exceptionally well-directed |
|---|---|---|---|---|
| (1) Hampering passivity | (2) Insufficient drive | | | |

### EMOTIONAL TONE (Rorschach, Szondi)

| (1) Explosive emotions | (2) Getting out of hand | (3) Trend toward emotional expression | (4) Warmth available | (5) Warm, readily available |
|---|---|---|---|---|
| (1) Lacking | (2) Indicated but repressed emotions | | | |

### SOCIAL ATTITUDE (T. A. T.)

| (1) Uncontrolled | (2) Constricted or neglected | (3) Adequate | (4) Well-regulated | (5) Free and flexible |
|---|---|---|---|---|

### ANXIETY

| (1) Disintegrating | (2) Marked | (3) Moderate | (4) Not marked | (5) Lack of evidence of anxiety |
|---|---|---|---|---|

### OVER-ALL EVALUATION

| (1) Markedly disturbed personality | (2) Less than adequate personality with some psychological problems | (3) Adequate personality | (4) Better than average functioning personality | (5) Exceptionally well-integrated personality with excellent potential |
|---|---|---|---|---|

## SUMMARY OF THERAPIST'S FINDINGS   *PT.3*

### ESTIMATED INTELLIGENCE LEVEL

| (1) Below average | (2) Average | (3) High average *(circled)* | (4) Superior | (5) Very superior |
|---|---|---|---|---|

### FLOW OF ASSOCIATIVE MATERIAL

| (1) Impoverished | (2) Reduced output *(circled, arrow →)* | (3) Adequate | (4) Better than average | (5) Rich and well-ordered |
|---|---|---|---|---|
| | (2) Compulsive productivity | | | |

### RELATION TO REALITY

| (1) Loose | (2) Lapses—together with good form | (3) Not noticeably disturbed | (4) Essentially firm *(circled)* | (5) Firm and good |
|---|---|---|---|---|

### USUAL-UNUSUAL THOUGHT CONTENT

| (1) Bizarre | (2) Tendency toward the bizarre | (3) Adequate *(circled)* | (4) Original trends | (5) Outstandingly original |
|---|---|---|---|---|
| (1) Stereotyped | (2) Tendency toward stereotypy | | | |

### CONSTRUCTIVE FANTASY

| (1) Absent | (2) Barely accessible | (3) Accessible *(circled)* | (4) Readily accessible | (5) Active but not hampering |
|---|---|---|---|---|
| (1) Withdrawal into fantasy | | | | |

### DRIVE

| (1) Overpowering aggression | (2) Over-aggressive | (3) Adequate *(circled, arrow →)* | (4) Clearly sufficient | (5) Sufficient—exceptionally well-directed |
|---|---|---|---|---|
| (1) Hampering passivity | (2) Insufficient drive | | | |

### EMOTIONAL TONE

| (1) Explosive emotions | (2) Getting out of hand | (3) Trend toward emotional expression | (4) Warmth available | (5) Warm, readily available |
|---|---|---|---|---|
| (1) Lacking | (2) Indicated but repressed emotions *(circled, arrow →)* | | | |

### SOCIAL ATTITUDE

| (1) Uncontrolled | (2) Constricted or neglected | (3) Adequate *(circled, arrow →)* | (4) Well-regulated | (5) Free and flexible |
|---|---|---|---|---|

### ANXIETY

| (1) Disintegrating | (2) Marked | (3) Moderate *(circled, arrow →)* | (4) Not marked | (5) Lack of evidence of anxiety |
|---|---|---|---|---|

### OVER-ALL EVALUATION

| (1) Markedly disturbed personality | (2) Less than adequate personality with some psychological problems *(circled, arrow →)* | (3) Adequate personality | (4) Better than average functioning personality | (5) Exceptionally well-integrated personality with excellent potential |
|---|---|---|---|---|

PT4 was unmarried and in her middle twenties at the time of the first psychological examination. She spent eight years in psychotherapy and was retested at the termination of treatment, at which time she was engaged to be married.

The therapist rated her at the start of therapy on the OVER-ALL EVALUATION as *Less than adequate* and at the termination of therapy as an individual considered *Better than average functioning personality.*

Comparing the two Work Sheets, we find this patient to be one of those whose Bellevue-Wechsler performance, both qualitatively and quantitatively, improves remarkably over the period of years between tests, the scores in essence telling the story of a much more realistic approach to life. The low score in the Comprehension in Test Record 1 contains answers of an obviously disturbed type. These drop out of the material completely in the retesting eight years later. When they were read to the patient and she was asked to comment on them, she found it almost unbelievable that they could have been her own productions eight years previously. The abstract thinking has also improved in an important way. These two low scores on Record 1 gave a scattergram typical of individuals perilously perched in terms of their reality orientation, but, with the second testing, bona fide and genuine change is reflected here.

The Szondi, on the other hand, has scarcely changed at all. After eight years this patient still shows the same areas of tension as before. True, the −s is a little less loaded, as is also the exaggerated +m, but the characteristics of the profiles are identical.

The Figure Drawings, too, hardly suggest that eight years have elapsed between them. They are recognizably the same and would promptly be identified as the work of the same person. The second drawing is a little sketchier, but beyond that, nothing has changed.

The Rorschach shows some important changes, and yet it too bears an individual stamp and many of the core responses remain the same. The addition of three good FC responses and the loss of two bizarre CF's are certainly steps in the right direction. Delicate and sensitive Fc responses have been added so that this now scores five as opposed to one. The F− responses have dropped from ten to six, and the total of F+ has risen from twelve to seventeen. Much needed vitality has come into the record through the appearance of six additional, lively FM responses.

Speaking in over-all terms, the therapist found this patient to have lost all the major presenting symptoms. She no longer had frequent weeping spells, psychosomatic symptoms had decreased, and her interpersonal relationships were greatly improved, to the point where she had become engaged. At the same time, she was manifestly happier and could stand her ground so that people did not walk over her. Of primary importance, her therapist felt, was the fact that she had been able to fall in love.

This patient was seen by her therapist three times a week for several years and then went on a reduced schedule of approximately one session every two weeks. At all times, treatment was flexible, the therapist saying in reference to it, "I went at it from all sides." PT4's records are shown on the next four pages.

PT5, a woman of middle age, is an excellent example of some of the more dramatic changes brought about by intensive psychotherapy over a period of time. This patient sought help reluctantly but out of necessity, psychological difficulties of long standing having suddenly gotten to a point where they could no longer be coped with following a peculiarly traumatic situation. She was first tested just prior to entering treatment. Her records are shown on pages 216-219.

Both the psychological tests and the therapist initially assessed this individual as being in category 2 on the OVER-ALL EVALUATION, and both placed her in category 4 at its termination. It will be seen from the summaries by the therapist and from the test findings that the progress occurred in very similar areas.

The patient's manner during the tests changed dramatically. Initially quite distressed, she was able, at the time of retesting, to discuss her previous feelings and look closely at the test findings to study those aspects of the material which mirrored her particular difficulties.

Although the therapist estimates this individual's intelligence twice as being at the very superior level, the Wechsler shows that at the first testing she was unable to do herself justice. The most striking change in the Bellevue-Wechsler on the second test, as will be seen from the Work Sheet, is the rise in the Comprehension scores and a gain of 12 points over-all.

In terms of PRODUCTIVITY, the number of responses on the Rorschach has risen from 14 to 24, bringing this patient out of the *Reduced output* category and placing her in that described as *Adequate*. A change in a similar direction occurs in terms of ASSOCIATIVE MATERIAL, according to the therapist, although this was rated as *Adequate* to begin with.

Concerning RELATION TO REALITY, there is a shift of one point in both the clinical and psychological assessment, the shift in each being in the same direction. The tests, however, had to assess this individual somewhat more severely than the therapist initially because of the grossly inadequate concept of the human being—the snow man—which was first

# WORK SHEET

PT4

1

## VERBAL I. Q. = | | |

| EWS | Info. | Comp. | Digit | Arith. | Sim. |
|---|---|---|---|---|---|
| 18 | 25 | 20 | | 14 | 23-24 |
| 17 | 24 | 19 | 17 | 13 | 21-22 |
| 16 | 23 | 18 | 16 | 12 | 20 |
| 15 | 21-22 | 17 | | 11 | 19 |
| 14 | 20 | 16 | 15 | | 17-18 |
| 13 | 18-19 | 15 | 14 | 10 | 16 |
| 12 | 17 | 14 | | 9 | 15 |
| | | | | | |
| 11 | 15-16 | 12-13 | 13 | | 13-14 |
| 10 | 13-14 | 11 | 12 | 8 | 12 |
| 9 | 12 | 10 | 11 | 7 | 11 |
| 8 | 10-11 | 9 | | | 9-10 |
| 7 | 9 | 8 | 10 | 6 | 8 |
| 6 | 7-8 | 7 | 9 | 5 | 7 |
| | | | | | |
| 5 | 6 | 5-6 | | | 5-6 |
| 4 | 4-5 | 4 | 8 | 4 | 4 |
| 3 | 2-3 | 3 | 7 | 3 | 3 |
| 2 | 1 | 2 | 6 | | 1-2 |
| 1 | 0 | 1 | 5 | 2 | 0 |
| 0 | | 0 | | 1 | |

## SZONDI

| SEXUAL | | PAROXYSMAL | | EGO | | CONTACT | |
|---|---|---|---|---|---|---|---|
| h | s | e | hy | k | p | d | m |

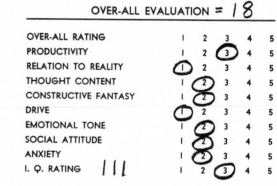

OVER-ALL EVALUATION = 18

| | 1 | 2 | 3 | 4 | 5 |
|---|---|---|---|---|---|
| OVER-ALL RATING | 1 | 2 | 3 | 4 | 5 |
| PRODUCTIVITY | 1 | 2 | ③ | 4 | 5 |
| RELATION TO REALITY | ① | 2 | 3 | 4 | 5 |
| THOUGHT CONTENT | 1 | ② | 3 | 4 | 5 |
| CONSTRUCTIVE FANTASY | 1 | ② | 3 | 4 | 5 |
| DRIVE | ① | 2 | 3 | 4 | 5 |
| EMOTIONAL TONE | 1 | ② | 3 | 4 | 5 |
| SOCIAL ATTITUDE | 1 | ② | 3 | 4 | 5 |
| ANXIETY | 1 | ② | 3 | 4 | 5 |
| I. Q. RATING   | | | 1 | 2 | ③ | 4 | 5 |

I. Q. RATING | | |

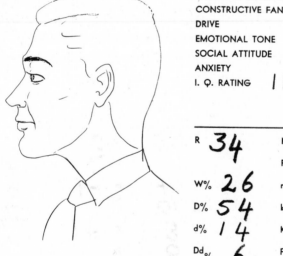

## RORSCHACH

| R | 34 | M | 3 | | | Fc | 1 |
|---|---|---|---|---|---|---|---|
| | | FM | 1 | F | 12 | c | 2 |
| W% | 26 | m | 1 | F- | 10 | C' | |
| D% | 54 | k | | F% | 65 | FC | |
| d% | 14 | K | | | | CF | 2⁻ |
| Dd% | 6 | FK | 2⁻ | | | C | |
| S | | | | | | | |

=== WORK SHEET === *PT4*

**2**

## VERBAL I. Q. = 128

| EWS | Info. | Comp. | Digit | Arith. | Sim. |
|---|---|---|---|---|---|
| 18 | 25 | 20 |  | 14 | 23-24 |
| 17 | 24 | 19 | 17 | 13 | 21-22 |
| 16 | 23 | 18 | 16 | 12 | 20 |
| 15 | (21-22) | 17 |  | (11) | 19 |
| 14 | 20 | (16) | (15) |  | 17-18 |
| 13 | 18-19 | 15 | 14 | 10 | (16) |
| 12 | 17 | 14 |  | 9 | (15) |
|  |  |  |  |  |  |
| 11 | 15-16 | 12-13 | 13 |  | 13-14 |
| 10 | 13-14 | 11 | 12 | 8 | 12 |
| 9 | 12 | 10 | 11 | 7 | 11 |
| 8 | 10-11 | 9 |  |  | 9-10 |
| 7 | 9 | 8 | 10 | 6 | 8 |
| 6 | 7-8 | 7 | 9 | 5 | 7 |
|  |  |  |  |  |  |
| 5 | 6 | 5-6 |  |  | 5-6 |
| 4 | 4-5 | 4 | 8 | 4 | 4 |
| 3 | 2-3 | 3 | 7 | 3 | 3 |
| 2 | 1 | 2 | 6 |  | 1-2 |
| 1 | 0 | 1 |  | 2 | 0 |
| 0 |  | 0 | 5 | 1 |  |

## SZONDI

| SEXUAL | | PAROXYSMAL | | EGO | | CONTACT | |
|---|---|---|---|---|---|---|---|
| h | s | e | hy | k | p | d | m |
|  |  |  |  |  |  |  | X |
|  |  | X |  |  |  |  | X |
|  |  | X |  |  |  |  | X |
|  | X | X | X | X | X | X | X |
| X | X | X | X |  |  | X X | X |
|  | X |  | X |  |  | X |  |
|  | X |  |  |  |  |  |  |
|  | X |  |  |  |  |  |  |
|  | X |  |  |  |  |  |  |

## OVER-ALL EVALUATION = 29

| | 1 | 2 | 3 | 4 | 5 |
|---|---|---|---|---|---|
| OVER-ALL RATING | 1 | 2 | 3 | 4 | 5 |
| PRODUCTIVITY | 1 | 2 | 3 | (4) | 5 |
| RELATION TO REALITY | 1 | 2 | (3) | 4 | 5 |
| THOUGHT CONTENT | 1 | 2 | (3) | 4 | 5 |
| CONSTRUCTIVE FANTASY | 1 | 2 | (3) | 4 | 5 |
| DRIVE | 1 | 2 | (3) | 4 | 5 |
| EMOTIONAL TONE | 1 | (2) | 3 | 4 | 5 |
| SOCIAL ATTITUDE | 1 | 2 | (3) | 4 | 5 |
| ANXIETY | 1 | 2 | (3) | 4 | 5 |
| I. Q. RATING  128 | 1 | 2 | 3 | 4 | (5) |

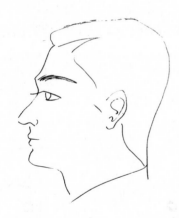

## RORSCHACH

| | | | | | |
|---|---|---|---|---|---|
| R 43 | M 3 | | | Fc 5 | |
| | FM 7 | | F 17 | c 1 | |
| W% 14 | m +1 | | F– 6 | C' | |
| D% 70 | k 1 | | F% 54 | FC 3 | |
| d% 8 | K +1 | | | CF | |
| Dd% 8 | FK | | | C | |
| S | | | | | |

# SUMMARY OF TEST FINDINGS    PT 4

### MANNER DURING TEST

| (1) (Overly distressed) | (2) Tense | (3) Indifferent | (4) Appropriate | (5) Relaxed and actively interested |
|---|---|---|---|---|
| (1) Hostile | (2) Uneasy | | | |

### I.Q. (Bellevue-Wechsler)

| (1) Below average | (2) Average | (3) High average | (4) Superior | (5) Very superior |
|---|---|---|---|---|

### PRODUCTIVITY (Rorschach)

| (1) Impoverished | (2) Reduced output | (3) Adequate | (4) Better than average | (5) Rich and well-ordered |
|---|---|---|---|---|
| | (2) Compulsive productivity | | | |

### RELATION TO REALITY (Rorschach, Bellevue-Wechsler, Drawings)

| (1) Loose | (2) Lapses—together with good form | (3) Not noticeably disturbed | (4) Essentially firm | (5) Firm and good |
|---|---|---|---|---|

### USUAL-UNUSUAL THOUGHT CONTENT (Rorschach, Unpleasant Concept)

| (1) Bizarre | (2) Tendency toward the bizarre | (3) Adequate | (4) Original trends | (5) Outstandingly original |
|---|---|---|---|---|
| (1) Stereotyped | (2) Tendency toward stereotypy | | | |

### CONSTRUCTIVE FANTASY (Rorschach)

| (1) Absent | (2) Barely accessible | (3) Accessible | (4) Readily accessible | (5) Active but not hampering |
|---|---|---|---|---|
| (1) Withdrawal into fantasy | | | | |

### DRIVE (Rorschach, Szondi, Unpleasant Concept)

| (1) Overpowering aggression | (2) Over-aggressive | (3) Adequate | (4) Clearly sufficient | (5) Sufficient— exceptionally well-directed |
|---|---|---|---|---|
| (1) Hampering passivity | (2) Insufficient drive | | | |

### EMOTIONAL TONE (Rorschach, Szondi)

| (1) Explosive emotions | (2) Getting out of hand | (3) Trend toward emotional expression | (4) Warmth available | (5) Warm, readily available |
|---|---|---|---|---|
| (1) Lacking | (2) Indicated but repressed emotions | | | |

### SOCIAL ATTITUDE (T. A. T.)

| (1) Uncontrolled | (2) Constricted or neglected | (3) Adequate | (4) Well-regulated | (5) Free and flexible |
|---|---|---|---|---|

### ANXIETY

| (1) Disintegrating | (2) Marked | (3) Moderate | (4) Not marked | (5) Lack of evidence of anxiety |
|---|---|---|---|---|

### OVER-ALL EVALUATION

| (1) Markedly disturbed personality | (2) Less than adequate personality with some psychological problems | (3) Adequate personality | (4) Better than average functioning personality | (5) Exceptionally well-integrated personality with excellent potential |
|---|---|---|---|---|

## SUMMARY OF THERAPIST'S FINDINGS     *PT4*

### ESTIMATED INTELLIGENCE LEVEL   *NOT RATED*

| (1) Below average | (2) Average | (3) High average | (4) Superior | (5) Very superior |
|---|---|---|---|---|

### FLOW OF ASSOCIATIVE MATERIAL

| (1) Impoverished | (2) Reduced output | (3) Adequate | (4) Better than average | (5) Rich and well-ordered |
|---|---|---|---|---|
| | (2) Compulsive productivity | | | |

### RELATION TO REALITY

| (1) Loose | (2) Lapses—together with good form | (3) Not noticeably disturbed | (4) Essentially firm | (5) Firm and good |
|---|---|---|---|---|

### USUAL-UNUSUAL THOUGHT CONTENT

| (1) Bizarre | (2) Tendency toward the bizarre | (3) Adequate | (4) Original trends | (5) Outstandingly original |
|---|---|---|---|---|
| (1) Stereotyped | (2) Tendency toward stereotypy | | | |

### CONSTRUCTIVE FANTASY

| (1) Absent | (2) Barely accessible | (3) Accessible | (4) Readily accessible | (5) Active but not hampering |
|---|---|---|---|---|
| (1) Withdrawal into fantasy | | | | |

### DRIVE

| (1) Overpowering aggression | (2) Over-aggressive | (3) Adequate | (4) Clearly sufficient | (5) Sufficient—exceptionally well-directed |
|---|---|---|---|---|
| (1) Hampering passivity | (2) Insufficient drive | | | |

### EMOTIONAL TONE

| (1) Explosive emotions | (2) Getting out of hand | (3) Trend toward emotional expression | (4) Warmth available | (5) Warm, readily available |
|---|---|---|---|---|
| (1) Lacking | (2) Indicated but repressed emotions | | | |

### SOCIAL ATTITUDE

| (1) Uncontrolled | (2) Constricted or neglected | (3) Adequate | (4) Well-regulated | (5) Free and flexible |
|---|---|---|---|---|

### ANXIETY

| (1) Disintegrating | (2) Marked | (3) Moderate | (4) Not marked | (5) Lack of evidence of anxiety |
|---|---|---|---|---|

### OVER-ALL EVALUATION

| (1) Markedly disturbed personality | (2) Less than adequate personality with some psychological problems | (3) Adequate personality | (4) Better than average functioning personality | (5) Exceptionally well-integrated personality with excellent potential |
|---|---|---|---|---|

## WORK SHEET #1

### VERBAL I. Q. = 120

| EWS | Info. | Comp. | Digit | Arith. | Sim. |
|-----|-------|-------|-------|--------|------|
| 18 | 25 | 20 | | 14 | 23-24 |
| 17 | 24 | 19 | 17 | 13 | 21-22 |
| 16 | 23 | 18 | 16 | 12 | 20 |
| 15 | 21-22 | 17 | | 11 | 19 |
| 14 | 20 | 16 | 15 | | 17-18 |
| 13 | 18-19 | 15 | 14 | 10 | 16 |
| 12 | 17 | 14 | | 9 | 15 |
| | | | | | |
| 11 | 15-16 | 12-13 | 13 | | 13-14 |
| 10 | 13-14 | 11 | 12 | 8 | 12 |
| 9 | 12 | 10 | 11 | 7 | 11 |
| 8 | 10-11 | 9 | | | 9-10 |
| 7 | 9 | 8 | 10 | 6 | 8 |
| 6 | 7-8 | 7 | 9 | 5 | 7 |
| | | | | | |
| 5 | 6 | 5-6 | | | 5-6 |
| 4 | 4-5 | 4 | 8 | 4 | 4 |
| 3 | 2-3 | 3 | 7 | 3 | 3 |
| 2 | 1 | 2 | 6 | | 1-2 |
| 1 | 0 | 1 | | 2 | 0 |
| 0 | | 0 | 5 | 1 | |

### SZONDI

| SEXUAL | | PAROXYSMAL | | EGO | | CONTACT | |
|--------|---|-----------|----|-----|---|--------|---|
| h | s | e | hy | k | p | d | m |
| | | | | | | | |
| | | X | | | | | |
| | X | X | | | X | | X |
| X | X | X | | X | X | X | X |
| X | X | X | X | X | X | X | X |
| X | | | | | | X | X |
| | | | | | | X | |

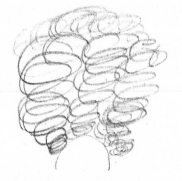

### RORSCHACH

| | | | | |
|---|---|---|---|---|
| R 14 | M 3 | | Fc 2 | |
| | FM 2 | F 4 | c | |
| W% 43 | m | F- 1 | C' | |
| D% 57 | k | F% 36 | FC | |
| d% | K | | CF | |
| Dd% | FK 2 | | c | |
| S | | | | |

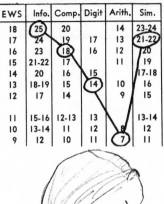

| EWS | Info. | Comp. | Digit | Arith. | Sim. |
|---|---|---|---|---|---|
| 18 | 25 | 20 | | 14 | 23-24 |
| 17 | 24 | 19 | 17 | 13 | 21-22 |
| 16 | 23 | 18 | 16 | 12 | 20 |
| 15 | 21-22 | 17 | | 11 | 19 |
| 14 | 20 | 16 | 15 | | 17-18 |
| 13 | 18-19 | 15 | 14 | 10 | 16 |
| 12 | 17 | 14 | | 9 | 15 |
| 11 | 15-16 | 12-13 | 13 | | 13-14 |
| 10 | 13-14 | 11 | 12 | 8 | 12 |
| 9 | 12 | 10 | 11 | 7 | 11 |

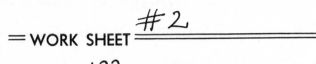

= WORK SHEET =     #2

VERBAL I. Q. = 133     SZONDI

| SEXUAL | | PAROXYSMAL | | EGO | | CONTACT | |
|---|---|---|---|---|---|---|---|
| h | s | e | hy | k | p | d | m |
| | | | | | | | X |
| | | X | X | | X | | X |
| X | X | X | X | | X | X | X |
| X | X | X | X | X | X | X | X |
| | | | | X | X | X | |
| | | | | | | X | |

MOST UNPLEASANT CONCEPT

### RORSCHACH

| R | 24 | M | 4 | | | Fc | 1 |
|---|---|---|---|---|---|---|---|
| | | FM | 6 | F | 6 | c | |
| W% | 25 | m | | F- | | C' | |
| D% | 75 | k | | F% | 25 | FC | 4 |
| d% | | K | 1 | | | CF | 2 |
| Dd% | | FK | | | | C | |
| S | | | | | | | |

## SUMMARY OF TEST FINDINGS    PT5

### MANNER DURING TEST

| | | | | |
|---|---|---|---|---|
| (1) (Overly distressed) | (2) Tense | (3) Indifferent | (4) Appropriate | (5) Relaxed and actively interested |
| (1) Hostile | (2) Uneasy | | | |

### I.Q. (Bellevue-Wechsler)

| | | | | |
|---|---|---|---|---|
| (1) Below average | (2) Average | (3) High average | (4) (Superior) | (5) Very superior |

### PRODUCTIVITY (Rorschach)

| | | | | |
|---|---|---|---|---|
| (1) Impoverished | (2) (Reduced output) | (3) Adequate | (4) Better than average | (5) Rich and well-ordered |
| | (2) Compulsive productivity | | | |

### RELATION TO REALITY (Rorschach, Bellevue-Wechsler, Drawings)

| | | | | |
|---|---|---|---|---|
| (1) Loose | (2) Lapses—together with good form | (3) (Not noticeably disturbed) | (4) Essentially firm | (5) Firm and good |

### USUAL-UNUSUAL THOUGHT CONTENT (Rorschach, Unpleasant Concept)

| | | | | |
|---|---|---|---|---|
| (1) Bizarre | (2) Tendency toward the bizarre | (3) (Adequate) | (4) Original trends | (5) Outstandingly original |
| (1) Stereotyped | (2) Tendency toward stereotypy | | | |

### CONSTRUCTIVE FANTASY (Rorschach)

| | | | | |
|---|---|---|---|---|
| (1) Absent | (2) Barely accessible | (3) (Accessible) | (4) Readily accessible | (5) Active but not hampering |
| (1) Withdrawal into fantasy | | | | |

### DRIVE (Rorschach, Szondi, Unpleasant Concept)

| | | | | |
|---|---|---|---|---|
| (1) Overpowering aggression | (2) Over-aggressive | (3) Adequate | (4) Clearly sufficient | (5) Sufficient—exceptionally well-directed |
| (1) Hampering passivity | (2) (Insufficient drive) | | | |

### EMOTIONAL TONE (Rorschach, Szondi)

| | | | | |
|---|---|---|---|---|
| (1) Explosive emotions | (2) Getting out of hand | (3) Trend toward emotional expression | (4) Warmth available | (5) Warm, readily available |
| (1) (Lacking) | (2) Indicated but repressed emotions | | | |

### SOCIAL ATTITUDE (T. A. T.)

| | | | | |
|---|---|---|---|---|
| (1) Uncontrolled | (2) (Constricted or neglected) | (3) Adequate | (4) Well-regulated | (5) Free and flexible |

### ANXIETY

| | | | | |
|---|---|---|---|---|
| (1) Disintegrating | (2) (Marked) | (3) Moderate | (4) Not marked | (5) Lack of evidence of anxiety |

### OVER-ALL EVALUATION

| | | | | |
|---|---|---|---|---|
| (1) Markedly disturbed personality | (2) (Less than adequate personality with some psychological problems) | (3) Adequate personality | (4) Better than average functioning personality | (5) Exceptionally well-integrated personality with excellent potential |

## SUMMARY OF THERAPIST'S FINDINGS        *PT 5*

### ESTIMATED INTELLIGENCE LEVEL

| (1) Below average | (2) Average | (3) High average | (4) Superior | (5) **Very superior** ⟵ (circled) |
|---|---|---|---|---|

### FLOW OF ASSOCIATIVE MATERIAL

| (1) Impoverished | (2) Reduced output | (3) **Adequate** (circled) ⟶ | (4) Better than average | (5) Rich and well-ordered |
|---|---|---|---|---|
| | (2) Compulsive productivity | | | |

### RELATION TO REALITY

| (1) Loose | (2) Lapses—together with good form | (3) Not noticeably disturbed | (4) **Essentially firm** (circled) ⟶ | (5) Firm and good |
|---|---|---|---|---|

### USUAL-UNUSUAL THOUGHT CONTENT

| (1) Bizarre | (2) Tendency toward the bizarre | (3) Adequate | (4) Original trends | (5) Outstandingly original |
|---|---|---|---|---|
| (1) **Stereotyped** (circled) ⟶ | (2) Tendency toward stereotypy | | | |

### CONSTRUCTIVE FANTASY

| (1) Absent | (2) **Barely accessible** (circled) ⟶ | (3) Accessible | (4) Readily accessible | (5) Active but not hampering |
|---|---|---|---|---|
| (1) Withdrawal into fantasy | | | | |

### DRIVE

| (1) Overpowering aggression | (2) Over-aggressive | (3) Adequate | (4) Clearly sufficient | (5) Sufficient—exceptionally well-directed |
|---|---|---|---|---|
| (1) Hampering passivity | (2) **Insufficient drive** (circled) | | | |

### EMOTIONAL TONE

| (1) Explosive emotions | (2) Getting out of hand | (3) Trend toward emotional expression | (4) Warmth available | (5) Warm, readily available |
|---|---|---|---|---|
| (1) Lacking | (2) **Indicated but repressed emotions** (circled) ⟶ | | | |

### SOCIAL ATTITUDE

| (1) Uncontrolled | (2) **Constricted or neglected** (circled) ⟶ | (3) Adequate | (4) Well-regulated | (5) Free and flexible |
|---|---|---|---|---|

### ANXIETY

| (1) Disintegrating | (2) **Marked** (circled) ⟶ | (3) Moderate | (4) Not marked | (5) Lack of evidence of anxiety |
|---|---|---|---|---|

### OVER-ALL EVALUATION

| (1) Markedly disturbed personality | (2) **Less than adequate personality with some psychological problems** (circled) ⟶ | (3) Adequate personality | (4) Better than average functioning personality | (5) Exceptionally well-integrated personality with excellent potential |
|---|---|---|---|---|

drawn. The fact that what was drawn in response to the instruction to draw a person the second time was a human being with genuine flesh and blood characteristics, in both the male and female drawings, constituted one of the most striking changes.

In terms of THOUGHT CONTENT, both frames of reference assess this patient as belonging to category 3 at the close of therapy. A somewhat more stereotyped approach was presented in the therapeutic sessions than that which broke through in the test material.

In the category, CONSTRUCTIVE FANTASY, there is a shift of one point in the therapist's evaluation. The addition of one good M response (from 3 to 4) clearly indicates the same trend as far as the tests are concerned but is not sufficient to constitute a change on the Summary Sheet.

The tests are a little more lenient in the second appraisal in estimating DRIVE than is the therapist, by virtue of six strong FM responses as opposed to the weak and highly tentative two that had been given before.

The most striking change, both for the therapist and on the test findings, occurs in the category of EMOTIONAL TONE. The second Rorschach record contains 4 good FC responses and 2 CF's where previously there was nothing on the color side. This patient "jumped" on our test Summary Sheet from *Lacking* to *Warmth available. Warmth available* is also the final estimate by the therapist.

The same degree of change is noted by both the therapist and on the test in regard to SOCIAL ATTITUDE. An identical change occurs, also, in terms of ANXIETY and, finally, as mentioned previously, in the OVER-ALL EVALUATION. This is a very close correspondence between findings arrived at from two different frames of reference.

The changes in the test findings are exemplified in several ways. On Card VII in the Rorschach, for example, there is the dropping out of the one F− response, "A face with a horn in the forehead," and an anxiety-ridden answer, "A view from an aeroplane of islands and water." In the second testing this becomes, "This has a pleasant circus quality. There's a lion-like creature balancing on its head. It's kicking its legs gaily in the air." On Card VIII, although in a formal sense the same response is given, there are important modifications. Originally the animals that are seen are apologized for: "I have just been reading a book on animals. I must see humans pretty soon." On the second test this becomes: "That's pretty. It's an animal, certainly. It's small, furry, and stepping from land to land across the water."

Cards IX and X indicate a concreteness where evasion and disinterestedness were reflected before. Card IX originally was seen as, "A design with holes." On the second testing, there is a very lively description of two lobsters ("the color of cooked lobsters") "emerging out of green water. They are supposed to be alive and moving their claws." Card X, which was previously a failure, becomes, "Oh, that's very pretty. There are sea horses, crabs, two sets of crabs, a very pretty flower (described), two little chicks putting their heads together, a goldfish, and the total thing makes up the kind of design you could see on the seashore."

As can be seen in the reproduction on the Work Sheet, the snow man gives way to a realistic figure. Equally impressive, however, was the change in the female drawing, which passes from "a paper doll" to another realistic human portrayal.

This individual has also emerged from the overpowering depression and anxiety reflected in the Most Unpleasant Concept to a point where she can handle and look at the originally disturbing phenomenon. The original drawing was described as "black nothingness." At the time of the second testing, although a comparable figure was drawn, a humorous approach to it is now possible: "This is a slightly manic depression. Two-thirds of the mouth is depressed but one-third is showing some optimism."

The initial quantitative assessment from the tests was 22; the final one, 32. The clinician's quantitative values are 23 for the first assessment and 33 for the second.

PT6, also a middle-aged woman, is selected because of the lack of improvement either in the test findings or observed by the therapist despite several years of treatment.

A detailed assessment by the therapist is not available for this patient, but the therapist did record the fact that little or no improvement had been shown and that the initial level of adjustment was low on the scale, somewhere between 1 and 2 in terms of our OVER-ALL EVALUATION.

The Summary of Test Findings indicates that this individual remained at essentially the same level except for minor changes. While it is true there is less scatter on the Bellevue-Wechsler at the time of the second testing, the I.Q. has actually dropped from 114 to 107.

The Drawings on both occasions would be rated between 1 and 2 on our scale, with the second showing perhaps a little less of the primitive, bizarre quality.

The Rorschach has decreased in productiveness, has lost some emotional liveliness, but has, on the other hand, gained a human movement response and the tendency toward poor form answers has decreased.

The over-all picture, here, confirms the clinical impression that virtually no change has taken place despite therapeutic efforts.

## WORK SHEET

PT 6

1

### VERBAL I. Q. = 114

| EWS | Info. | Comp. | Digit | Arith. | Sim. |
|---|---|---|---|---|---|
| 18 | 25 | 20 | | 14 | 23-24 |
| 17 | 24 | 19 | 17 | 13 | 21-22 |
| 16 | 23 | 18 | 16 | 12 | 20 |
| 15 | 21-22 | 17 | | 11 | 19 |
| 14 | 20 | 16 | (15) | | 17-18 |
| 13 | 18-19 | 15 | 14 | 10 | 16 |
| 12 | 17 | 14 | | 9 | (15) |
| | | | | | |
| 11 | 15-16 | 12-13 | 13 | | 13-14 |
| 10 | (13-14) | 11 | 12 | 8 | 12 |
| 9 | 12 | 10 | 11 | 7 | 11 |
| 8 | 10-11 | (9) | | | 9-10 |
| 7 | 9 | (8) | 10 | (6) | 8 |
| 6 | 7-8 | 7 | 9 | 5 | 7 |
| | | | | | |
| 5 | 6 | 5-6 | | | 5-6 |
| 4 | 4-5 | 4 | 8 | 4 | 4 |
| 3 | 2-3 | 3 | 7 | 3 | 3 |
| 2 | 1 | 2 | 6 | | 1-2 |
| 1 | 0 | 1 | | 2 | 0 |
| 0 | | 0 | 5 | 1 | |

### SZONDI

| SEXUAL | | PAROXYSMAL | | EGO | | CONTACT | |
|---|---|---|---|---|---|---|---|
| h | s | e | hy | k | p | d | m |
| X | | | | | | | X |
| X | | | X | X | | | X |
| X | | X | X | X | | X | X |
| | | X | X | X | X | X | X |
| | | | X | X | X | X | |
| | | | X | X | | | |
| | | X | X | | | | |

### OVER-ALL EVALUATION = 20

| | | | | | |
|---|---|---|---|---|---|
| OVER-ALL RATING | 1 | 2 | 3 | 4 | 5 |
| PRODUCTIVITY | 1 | 2 | (3) | 4 | 5 |
| RELATION TO REALITY | 1 | (2) | 3 | 4 | 5 |
| THOUGHT CONTENT | 1 | (2) | 3 | 4 | 5 |
| CONSTRUCTIVE FANTASY | (1) | 2 | 3 | 4 | 5 |
| DRIVE | 1 | (2) | 3 | 4 | 5 |
| EMOTIONAL TONE | 1 | (2) | 3 | 4 | 5 |
| SOCIAL ATTITUDE | 1 | (2) | 3 | 4 | 5 |
| ANXIETY | 1 | 2 | (3) | 4 | 5 |
| I. Q. RATING  114 | 1 | 2 | (3) | 4 | 5 |

### RORSCHACH

| | | | | | |
|---|---|---|---|---|---|
| R | 22 | M | | Fc | |
| | | FM 5 | F 9 | c | |
| W% | 32 | m | F- 5 | C' | |
| D% | 63 | k | F% 64 | FC | 2 |
| d% | 5 | K | | CF | 1 |
| Dd% | | FK | | C | |
| S | | | | | |

## WORK SHEET 2

PT 6

### VERBAL I. Q. = 107

| EWS | Info. | Comp. | Digit | Arith. | Sim. |
|----|------|------|------|-------|-----|
| 18 | 25 | 20 |  | 14 | 23-24 |
| 17 | 24 | 19 | 17 | 13 | 21-22 |
| 16 | 23 | 18 | 16 | 12 | 20 |
| 15 | 21-22 | 17 |  | 11 | 19 |
| 14 | 20 | 16 | 15 |  | 17-18 |
| 13 | 18-19 | 15 | 14 | 10 | 16 |
| 12 | 17 | 14 |  | 9 | 15 |
| 11 | 15-16 | 12-13 | 13 |  | 13-14 |
| 10 | 13-14 | 11 | 12 | 8 | 12 |
| 9 | 12 | 10 | 11 | 7 | 11 |
| 8 | 10-11 | 9 |  |  | 9-10 |
| 7 | 9 | 8 | 10 | 6 | 8 |
| 6 | 7-8 | 7 | 9 | 5 | 7 |
| 5 | 6 | 5-6 |  |  | 5-6 |
| 4 | 4-5 | 4 | 8 | 4 | 4 |
| 3 | 2-3 | 3 | 7 | 3 | 3 |
| 2 | 1 | 2 | 6 |  | 1-2 |
| 1 | 0 | 1 |  | 2 | 0 |
| 0 |  | 0 | 5 | 1 |  |

### SZONDI

| SEXUAL | | PAROXYSMAL | | EGO | | CONTACT | |
|---|---|---|---|---|---|---|---|
| h | s | e | hy | k | p | d | m |
|  |  | X |  |  |  |  |  |
| X | X | X |  |  |  | X | X |
| X | X | X |  |  | X | X | X |
| | | | | | | | |
|  | X | X | X | X | X | X | X |
|  | X | X |  | X |  | X |  |
|  |  |  |  | X |  |  |  |

### OVER-ALL EVALUATION = 18

| | | | | | |
|---|---|---|---|---|---|
| OVER-ALL RATING | 1 | 2 | 3 | 4 | 5 |
| PRODUCTIVITY | 1 | ② | 3 | 4 | 5 |
| RELATION TO REALITY | 1 | ② | 3 | 4 | 5 |
| THOUGHT CONTENT | 1 | ② | 3 | 4 | 5 |
| CONSTRUCTIVE FANTASY | 1 | ② | 3 | 4 | 5 |
| DRIVE | 1 | ② | 3 | 4 | 5 |
| EMOTIONAL TONE | ① | 2 | 3 | 4 | 5 |
| SOCIAL ATTITUDE | 1 | ② | 3 | 4 | 5 |
| ANXIETY | 1 | 2 | ③ | 4 | 5 |
| I. Q. RATING  107 | 1 | ② | 3 | 4 | 5 |

### RORSCHACH

| | | | |
|---|---|---|---|
| R | 15 | M | 1 | Fc | 1 |
| | | FM | 2 | F | 7 | c | 1 |
| W% | 33 | m | | F- | 2 | C' | |
| D% | 47 | k | | F% | 60 | FC | 1 |
| d% | 20 | K | | | CF | |
| Dd% | | FK | | | C | |
| S | | | | |

## SUMMARY OF TEST FINDINGS   *PT 6*

### MANNER DURING TEST

| (1) Overly distressed | (2) Tense | (3) Indifferent | (4) Appropriate | (5) Relaxed and actively interested |
|---|---|---|---|---|
| (1) Hostile | (2) Uneasy | | | |

### I.Q. (Bellevue-Wechsler)

| (1) Below average | (2) Average | (3) High average | (4) Superior | (5) Very superior |
|---|---|---|---|---|

### PRODUCTIVITY (Rorschach)

| (1) Impoverished | (2) Reduced output | (3) Adequate | (4) Better than average | (5) Rich and well-ordered |
|---|---|---|---|---|
| | (2) Compulsive productivity | | | |

### RELATION TO REALITY (Rorschach, Bellevue-Wechsler, Drawings)

| (1) Loose | (2) Lapses—together with good form | (3) Not noticeably disturbed | (4) Essentially firm | (5) Firm and good |
|---|---|---|---|---|

### USUAL-UNUSUAL THOUGHT CONTENT (Rorschach, Unpleasant Concept)

| (1) Bizarre | (2) Tendency toward the bizarre | (3) Adequate | (4) Original trends | (5) Outstandingly original |
|---|---|---|---|---|
| (1) Stereotyped | (2) Tendency toward stereotypy | | | |

### CONSTRUCTIVE FANTASY (Rorschach)

| (1) Absent | (2) Barely accessible | (3) Accessible | (4) Readily accessible | (5) Active but not hampering |
|---|---|---|---|---|
| (1) Withdrawal into fantasy | | | | |

### DRIVE (Rorschach, Szondi, Unpleasant Concept)

| (1) Overpowering aggression | (2) Over-aggressive | (3) Adequate | (4) Clearly sufficient | (5) Sufficient—exceptionally well-directed |
|---|---|---|---|---|
| (1) Hampering passivity | (2) Insufficient drive | | | |

### EMOTIONAL TONE (Rorschach, Szondi)

| (1) Explosive emotions | (2) Getting out of hand | (3) Trend toward emotional expression | (4) Warmth available | (5) Warm, readily available |
|---|---|---|---|---|
| (1) Lacking | (2) Indicated but re-pressed emotions | | | |

### SOCIAL ATTITUDE (T. A. T.)

| (1) Uncontrolled | (2) Constricted or neglected | (3) Adequate | (4) Well-regulated | (5) Free and flexible |
|---|---|---|---|---|

### ANXIETY

| (1) Disintegrating | (2) Marked | (3) Moderate | (4) Not marked | (5) Lack of evidence of anxiety |
|---|---|---|---|---|

### OVER-ALL EVALUATION

| (1) Markedly disturbed personality | (2) Less than adequate personality with some psychological problems | (3) Adequate personality | (4) Better than average functioning personality | (5) Exceptionally well-integrated personality with excellent potential |
|---|---|---|---|---|

## XII. Retesting following brief psychotherapy. Successful cases.

The eight patients whose records are grouped together here were selected from a total of fifty cases referred by the same therapist for testing and retesting. This therapist, as a part of his own procedure, rates the patient's over-all status on a 5-point scale at the start of treatment, at its termination, and subsequent to a follow-up study four years later. Although worded somewhat differently, this 5-point scale corresponds sufficiently well to that which we have employed throughout as to be transposable.

Patients SA1 through SA8 were considered to have reacted favorably to the therapeutic treatment and to have reached the status of *Adequate personality* or better. The OVER-ALL EVALUATION rating given by the therapist relates, primarily, to the effect of treatment on the patient's capacity to *function successfully* in life. We also have, for this group, a detailed follow-up on the "fate" of the various presenting symptoms. Although, in accordance with the need to minimize the danger of individuals being identified, specific symptoms have not been enumerated here, we have commented in some instances as to whether or not a symptom had been alleviated to the point where it no longer hindered functioning.

SA1 was in his middle twenties and unmarried at the start of treatment. He was rated by the therapist at that time as a *Less than adequate personality with some psychological problems.* After treatment, the OVER-ALL EVALUATION was *Adequate personality,* and this same assessment held four years later at the time a follow-up study was made.

Of the two symptoms which caused SA1 to seek therapeutic help, one remained unchanged, the other improved markedly, to the point where his capacity to function had been radically affected.

A comparison of the Work Sheets, 1 and 2, reveals a slight point gain on the Bellevue-Wechsler, a rise in I.Q. from 133 to 138, with essentially the same pattern in the scattergram. Comparison of the two Szondi profiles would suggest that in the second, the ego is more structured and there is indication of less concern with clinging dependency and self-assertive aggression (a lessening of the loaded −d and +s).

The Figure Drawing of the male reflects the achievement of freedom from the tyranny of a stern father, and a more realistic concept of the role this individual should play as a man. This finding parallels the clinical comments available for this patient.

The Rorschach showed extremely little change in all aspects except

# WORK SHEET
1

## VERBAL I. Q.

| EWS | Info. | Comp. | Digit | Arith. | Sim. |
|-----|-------|-------|-------|--------|------|
| 18 | 25 | 20 | | (14) | 23-24 |
| 17 | 24 | 19 | 17 | 13 | 21-22 |
| 16 | (23) | 18 | 16 | 12 | 20 |
| 15 | 21-22 | 17 | | 11 | (19) |
| 14 | 20 | 16 | 15 | | 17-18 |
| 13 | 18-19 | (15) | (14) | 10 | 16 |
| 12 | 17 | 14 | | 9 | 15 |
| | | | | | |
| 11 | 15-16 | 12-13 | 13 | | 13-14 |
| 10 | 13-14 | 11 | 12 | 8 | 12 |
| 9 | 12 | 10 | 11 | 7 | 11 |
| 8 | 10-11 | 9 | | | 9-10 |
| 7 | 9 | 8 | 10 | 6 | 8 |
| 6 | 7-8 | 7 | 9 | 5 | 7 |
| | | | | | |
| 5 | 6 | 5-6 | | | 5-6 |
| 4 | 4-5 | 4 | 8 | 4 | 4 |
| 3 | 2-3 | 3 | 7 | 3 | 3 |
| 2 | 1 | 2 | 6 | | 1-2 |
| 1 | 0 | 1 | | 2 | 0 |
| 0 | | 0 | 5 | 1 | |

## SZONDI

| SEXUAL | | PAROXYSMAL | | EGO | | CONTACT | |
|--------|---|------------|----|-----|---|---------|---|
| h | s | e | hy | k | p | d | m |
| | X | | | | | | X |
| | X | | | | | | X |
| X | X | X | X | X | X | X | X |
| X | | X | X | X | | X | |
| X | | X | X | | | X | |
| | | | X | | | X | |
| | | | | | | X | |

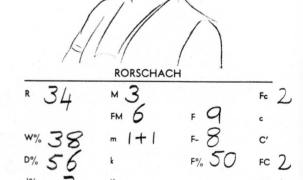

## RORSCHACH

| | | | | | |
|---|---|---|---|---|---|
| R | 34 | M | 3 | Fc | 2 |
| | | FM | 6 | F | 9 | c | |
| W% | 38 | m | 1+1 | F- | 8 | C' | |
| D% | 56 | k | | F% | 50 | FC | 2 |
| d% | 3 | K | | | | CF | 1 |
| Dd% | 3 | FK | | | | c | 2 |
| S | | | | | | | |

# WORK SHEET

## 2

### VERBAL I. Q.

| EWS | Info. | Comp. | Digit | Arith. | Sim. |
|---|---|---|---|---|---|
| 18 | (25) | 20 | | (14) | 23-24 |
| 17 | 24 | 19 | 17 | 13 | (21-22) |
| 16 | 23 | 18 | 16 | 12 | 20 |
| 15 | 21-22 | 17 | | 11 | 19 |
| 14 | 20 | 16 | 15 | | 17-18 |
| 13 | 18-19 | (15) | (14) | 10 | 16 |
| 12 | 17 | 14 | | 9 | 15 |
| 11 | 15-16 | 12-13 | 13 | | 13-14 |
| 10 | 13-14 | 11 | 12 | 8 | 12 |
| 9 | 12 | 10 | 11 | 7 | 11 |
| 8 | 10-11 | 9 | | | 9-10 |
| 7 | 9 | 8 | 10 | 6 | 8 |
| 6 | 7-8 | 7 | 9 | 5 | 7 |
| 5 | 6 | 5-6 | | | 5-6 |
| 4 | 4-5 | 4 | 8 | 4 | 4 |
| 3 | 2-3 | 3 | 7 | 3 | 3 |
| 2 | 1 | 2 | 6 | | 1-2 |
| 1 | 0 | 1 | | 2 | 0 |
| 0 | | 0 | 5 | | 1 |

### SZONDI

| SEXUAL | | PAROXYSMAL | | EGO | | CONTACT | |
|---|---|---|---|---|---|---|---|
| h | s | e | hy | k | p | d | m |
| | | | | | | | |
| | | | | X | | | X |
| | | | X | X | | | X |
| X | | X | X | X | X | X | X |
| X | X | X | X | X | X | X | |
| X | | | X | X | | X | |
| | | | X | | | | |

### RORSCHACH

| | | | | | |
|---|---|---|---|---|---|
| R | 34 | M | 6 | Fc | 3 |
| | | FM | 6 | F 13 | c +1 |
| W% | 35 | m | | F- 2 | C' |
| D% | 56 | k | | F% 44 | FC 1 |
| d% | 3 | K 1 | | | CF 1 |
| Dd% | 6 | FK | | | c 1+1 |
| S | | | | | |

# SUMMARY OF TEST FINDINGS  $SA_1$

## MANNER DURING TEST

| (1) Overly distressed | (2) Tense | (3) Indifferent | (4) Appropriate | (5) Relaxed and actively interested |
|---|---|---|---|---|
| (1) Hostile | (2) Uneasy | | | |

## I.Q. (Bellevue-Wechsler)

| (1) Below average | (2) Average | (3) High average | (4) Superior | (5) Very superior |
|---|---|---|---|---|

## PRODUCTIVITY (Rorschach)

| (1) Impoverished | (2) Reduced output | (3) Adequate | (4) Better than average | (5) Rich and well-ordered |
|---|---|---|---|---|
| | (2) Compulsive productivity | | | |

## RELATION TO REALITY (Rorschach, Bellevue-Wechsler, Drawings)

| (1) Loose | (2) Lapses—together with good form | (3) Not noticeably disturbed | (4) Essentially firm | (5) Firm and good |
|---|---|---|---|---|

## USUAL-UNUSUAL THOUGHT CONTENT (Rorschach, Unpleasant Concept)

| (1) Bizarre | (2) Tendency toward the bizarre | (3) Adequate | (4) Original trends | (5) Outstandingly original |
|---|---|---|---|---|
| (1) Stereotyped | (2) Tendency toward stereotypy | | | |

## CONSTRUCTIVE FANTASY (Rorschach)

| (1) Absent | (2) Barely accessible | (3) Accessible | (4) Readily accessible | (5) Active but not hampering |
|---|---|---|---|---|
| (1) Withdrawal into fantasy | | | | |

## DRIVE (Rorschach, Szondi, Unpleasant Concept)

| (1) Overpowering aggression | (2) Over-aggressive | (3) Adequate | (4) Clearly sufficient | (5) Sufficient—exceptionally well-directed |
|---|---|---|---|---|
| (1) Hampering passivity | (2) Insufficient drive | | | |

## EMOTIONAL TONE (Rorschach, Szondi)

| (1) Explosive emotions | (2) Getting out of hand | (3) Trend toward emotional expression | (4) Warmth available | (5) Warm, readily available |
|---|---|---|---|---|
| (1) Lacking | (2) Indicated but repressed emotions | | | |

## SOCIAL ATTITUDE (T. A. T.)

| (1) Uncontrolled | (2) Constricted or neglected | (3) Adequate | (4) Well-regulated | (5) Free and flexible |
|---|---|---|---|---|

## ANXIETY

| (1) Disintegrating | (2) Marked | (3) Moderate | (4) Not marked | (5) Lack of evidence of anxiety |
|---|---|---|---|---|

## OVER-ALL EVALUATION

| (1) Markedly disturbed personality | (2) Less than adequate personality with some psychological problems | (3) Adequate personality | (4) Better than average functioning personality | (5) Exceptionally well-integrated personality with excellent potential |
|---|---|---|---|---|

## SUMMARY OF THERAPIST'S FINDINGS   *SA 1*

### ESTIMATED INTELLIGENCE LEVEL

| (1) Below average | (2) Average | (3) High average | (4) (Superior) | (5) Very superior |
|---|---|---|---|---|

### FLOW OF ASSOCIATIVE MATERIAL

| (1) Impoverished | (2) Reduced output | (3) (Adequate) | (4) Better than average | (5) Rich and well-ordered |
|---|---|---|---|---|
|  | (2) Compulsive productivity |  |  |  |

### RELATION TO REALITY

| (1) Loose | (2) Lapses—together with good form | (3) (Not noticeably disturbed) | (4) Essentially firm | (5) Firm and good |
|---|---|---|---|---|

### USUAL-UNUSUAL THOUGHT CONTENT

| (1) Bizarre | (2) Tendency toward the bizarre | (3) (Adequate) | (4) Original trends | (5) Outstandingly original |
|---|---|---|---|---|
| (1) Stereotyped | (2) Tendency toward stereotypy |  |  |  |

### CONSTRUCTIVE FANTASY

| (1) Absent | (2) Barely accessible | (3) (Accessible) | (4) Readily accessible | (5) Active but not hampering |
|---|---|---|---|---|
| (1) Withdrawal into fantasy |  |  |  |  |

### DRIVE

| (1) Overpowering aggression | (2) Over-aggressive | (3) Adequate | (4) Clearly sufficient | (5) Sufficient—exceptionally well-directed |
|---|---|---|---|---|
| (1) Hampering passivity | (2) (Insufficient drive) |  |  |  |

### EMOTIONAL TONE

| (1) Explosive emotions | (2) Getting out of hand | (3) Trend toward emotional expression | (4) Warmth available | (5) Warm, readily available |
|---|---|---|---|---|
| (1) Lacking | (2) (Indicated but repressed emotions) |  |  |  |

### SOCIAL ATTITUDE

| (1) Uncontrolled | (2) Constricted or neglected | (3) (Adequate) | (4) Well-regulated | (5) Free and flexible |
|---|---|---|---|---|

### ANXIETY

| (1) Disintegrating | (2) (Marked) | (3) Moderate | (4) Not marked | (5) Lack of evidence of anxiety |
|---|---|---|---|---|

### OVER-ALL EVALUATION

| (1) Markedly disturbed personality | (2) Less than adequate personality with some psychological problems | (3) (Adequate personality) | (4) Better than average functioning personality | (5) Exceptionally well-integrated personality with excellent potential |
|---|---|---|---|---|

one important one—the reduction in F− responses, their number decreasing from eight to two. Aside from this, the changes do not appear to be significant. The total R is identical, as is the mental approach in both instances. While three M responses have been gained, one good FC has been lost, and the appearance of a K response suggests more experienced anxiety on the second testing. The significant change seems to center in the more realistic approach, the improved reality testing. Perhaps one might also say that undiluted impulsive behavior, as expressed in the two pure C responses in Record 1, has become slightly modified, in the second, by the use of pure color as an additional response rather than as a main determinant.

In terms of points accrued on the OVER-ALL EVALUATION, this individual who started with 28 is assessed at 31 at the second testing, hardly a significant change.

SA2, married and in his early forties, was rated by the therapist at stage 3 on the OVER-ALL EVALUATION scale at the start of therapy, progressing to 4 at its termination, and to have reached stage 5, *Exceptionally well-integrated personality with excellent potential*, five years later.

In this instance, the six presenting symtoms were either resolved or markedly improved at the termination of treatment, and in the opinion of the therapist, this case exemplifies the maximum achievement of a short-term therapy technique.

The subsequent work and professional achievements of this individual were startling. He rose rapidly to prominence in an important field.

Comparing the test items in detail, as shown on the Work Sheets, one finds small but important changes on the Wechsler pattern. SA2, with an initial tendency to a too-individualized approach to life, bettered his Comprehension and Similarities scores by two and four points respectively. In both instances, the improved score resulted from the fact that highly personalized thinking no longer invaded neutral areas. It is true that these two subtests still fall below the expected level, particularly the Comprehension, but the change is unquestionably in the right direction.

The inappropriate, loaded +h is lessened in Szondi 2, and a much needed concern with the tangible and realistic is suggested by the +d score. Neither profile can be considered to show an individual who has reached a state of optimal adjustment. Change there is, however, and it is not a detrimental one within the total balance of forces.

The important change in the second Rorschach record is the appearance of an emotional responsiveness barely indicated in Record 1. Both protocols bear the stamp of the gifted, introverted individual, and it is highly questionable whether therapy could, or should, alter this basic personality pattern. It is our feeling, however, that the introduction or the liberation of warmth, as carried by the increased number of color responses, though in itself a small change, makes a marked difference in the functioning of this potentially fantasy-locked individual.

Those tests not reproduced here—the Most Unpleasant Concept and the Sentence Completion—carry pronounced changes in attitudes. The Figure Drawings may be said to show change in the direction of action, from a stance that indicated only preparedness for action. In the second drawing, the discus thrower has launched out, whereas originally he was frozen at the starting point.

This case well illustrates the possible hazards involved in any attempts at quantitative measurement. There is actually only a six-point change on the quantitative scale, a change which is indeed slight in comparison with the vital change that has taken place in this individual's mode of living and subjective experience. It has been borne in on us by this study, and Schafer[25] has also pointed out this same thing, that small changes in test findings occasionally parallel marked changes in function. This raises the question of whether there is a time lag before behavior patterns leading toward greater adjustment become stabilized and subsequently find their way into the medium of the projective material. There is some evidence to this effect, as we shall show in a later chapter.

The Rorschach records of Subject SA2 are included here in their entirety.

## RORSCHACH RECORDS OF SA2

### RECORD 1

*Card I*

1. Two controversial soldiers at Valley Forge, bringing wood in for the fire, striding along.
2. Two observers behind a barricade, looking.
3. A queer, caudal region of the skeleton, prehistoric, prehensile.
4. A small sea animal burping its way along.

### RECORD 2

*Card I*

1. Two Frenchmen of 17th century with powdered wigs, arrogantly discussing something of no importance.
2. The Nike of Samothrace.
3. A single Australian honey bear, the head.
4. A portrait of Abraham Lincoln.
5. Profile of the great stone face in N. H.
6. Picture of a little child, with its head enveloped with a cloth and his hand out.

*Rorschach records continued on page 236.*

# WORK SHEET = *SA2*

I

## VERBAL I. Q. = 125

| EWS | Info. | Comp. | Digit | Arith. | Sim. |
|-----|-------|-------|-------|--------|------|
| 18 | 25 | 20 | | 14 | 23-24 |
| 17 | 24 | 19 | 17 | 13 | 21-22 |
| 16 | 23 | 18 | 16 | 12 | 20 |
| 15 | 21-22 | 17 | | 11 | 19 |
| 14 | 20 | 16 | 15 | | 17-18 |
| 13 | 18-19 | 15 | 14 | 10 | 16 |
| 12 | 17 | 14 | | 9 | 15 |
| 11 | 15-16 | 12-13 | 13 | | 13-14 |
| 10 | 13-14 | 11 | 12 | 8 | 12 |
| 9 | 12 | 10 | 11 | 7 | 11 |
| 8 | 10-11 | 9 | | | 9-10 |
| 7 | 9 | 8 | 10 | 6 | 8 |
| 6 | 7-8 | 7 | 9 | 5 | 7 |

## SZONDI

| SEXUAL | | PAROXYSMAL | | EGO | | CONTACT | |
|--------|--------|------------|--------|--------|--------|---------|--------|
| h | s | e | hy | k | p | d | m |
| X | | | | | X | | |
| X | | | | | X | | X |
| X | X | | | | X | | |
| X | X | | | X | X | | X |
| X | | X | X | X | X | X | X |
| | | | X | X | | | |
| | | | X | X | | | |
| | | | X | | | | |

## OVER-ALL EVALUATION = 30

| | 1 | 2 | 3 | 4 | 5 |
|---|---|---|---|---|---|
| OVER-ALL RATING | 1 | 2 | 3 | 4 | 5 |
| PRODUCTIVITY | 1 | 2 | ③ | 4 | 5 |
| RELATION TO REALITY | 1 | 2 | ③ | 4 | 5 |
| THOUGHT CONTENT | 1 | 2 | ③ | 4 | 5 |
| CONSTRUCTIVE FANTASY | 1 | 2 | 3 | 4 | ⑤ |
| DRIVE | 1 | 2 | 3 | ④ | 5 |
| EMOTIONAL TONE | ① | 2 | 3 | 4 | 5 |
| SOCIAL ATTITUDE | 1 | 2 | ③ | 4 | 5 |
| ANXIETY | 1 | 2 | 3 | ④ | 5 |
| I. Q. RATING  125 | 1 | 2 | 3 | ④ | 5 |

## RORSCHACH

| R 30 | M 12 (1-) | | Fc |
|------|-----------|---|-----|
| | FM 10 | F 5 | c +1 |
| W% 30 | m | F- 1 | C' +1 |
| D% 47 | k | F% 20 | FC 1 |
| d% | K | | CF |
| Dd% 23 | FK 1 | | C |
| S | | | |

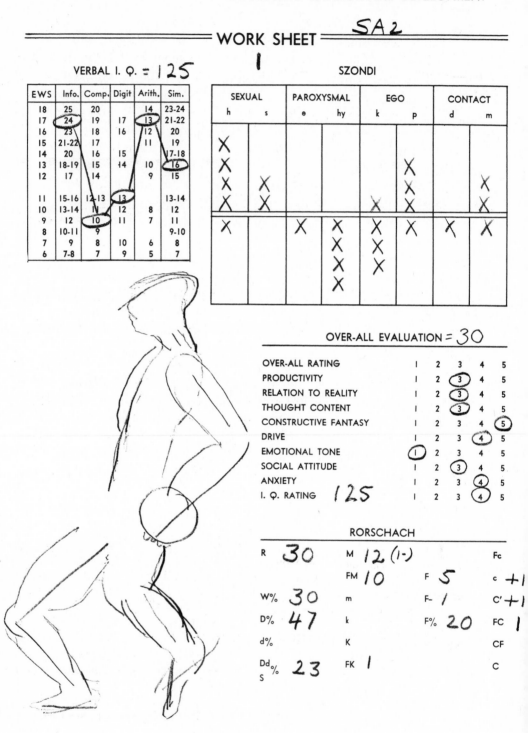

# WORK SHEET       *SA2*

2

## VERBAL I. Q. = 133

| EWS | Info. | Comp. | Digit | Arith. | Sim. |
|-----|-------|-------|-------|--------|------|
| 18 | (25) | 20 | | 14 | 23-24 |
| 17 | 24 | 19 | 17 | 13 | 21-22 |
| 16 | 23 | 18 | 16 | (12) | (20) |
| 15 | 21-22 | 17 | | 11 | 19 |
| 14 | 20 | 16 | 15 | | 17-18 |
| 13 | 18-19 | 15 | (14) | 10 | 16 |
| 12 | 17 | 14 | | 9 | 15 |
| | | | | | |
| 11 | 15-16 | (12-13) | 13 | | 13-14 |
| 10 | 13-14 | 11 | 12 | 8 | 12 |
| 9 | 12 | 10 | 11 | 7 | 11 |
| 8 | 10-11 | 9 | | | 9-10 |
| 7 | 9 | 8 | 10 | 6 | 8 |
| 6 | 7-8 | 7 | 9 | 5 | 7 |
| | | | | | |
| 5 | 6 | 5-6 | | | 5-6 |
| 4 | 4-5 | 4 | 8 | 4 | 4 |
| 3 | 2-3 | 3 | 7 | 3 | 3 |
| 2 | 1 | 2 | 6 | | 1-2 |
| 1 | 0 | 1 | | 2 | 0 |
| 0 | | 0 | 5 | 1 | |

## SZONDI

| SEXUAL | | PAROXYSMAL | | EGO | | CONTACT | |
|---|---|---|---|---|---|---|---|
| h | s | e | hy | k | p | d | m |
| | | | | | X | X | |
| | | | | | X | X | |
| | | | | | X | X | |
| X | | | | | X | X | X |
| X | X | | | | X | X | |
| X | X | X | X | X | X | X | X |
| | | X | X | | | | |
| | | X | X | | | | |

## OVER-ALL EVALUATION = 36

| | 1 | 2 | 3 | 4 | 5 |
|---|---|---|---|---|---|
| OVER-ALL RATING | | | | | |
| PRODUCTIVITY | 1 | 2 | 3 | (4) | 5 |
| RELATION TO REALITY | 1 | 2 | 3 | (4) | 5 |
| THOUGHT CONTENT | 1 | 2 | 3 | (4) | 5 |
| CONSTRUCTIVE FANTASY | 1 | 2 | 3 | 4 | (5) |
| DRIVE | 1 | 2 | 3 | (4) | 5 |
| EMOTIONAL TONE | 1 | 2 | (3) | 4 | 5 |
| SOCIAL ATTITUDE | 1 | 2 | (3) | 4 | 5 |
| ANXIETY | 1 | 2 | 3 | (4) | 5 |
| I. Q. RATING  133 | 1 | 2 | 3 | 4 | (5) |

## RORSCHACH

| R 49 | M 16 | | Fc +2 |
|------|------|------|------|
| | FM 14 | F 13 | c +1 |
| W% 29 | m 2+2 | F- | C' +2 |
| D% 57 | k | F% 27 | FC 1 |
| d% 2 | K | | CF 2+2 |
| Dd% 12 S | FK 1 | | c +1 |

## SUMMARY OF TEST FINDINGS    *SA 2*

### MANNER DURING TEST

| (1) Overly distressed | (2) Tense | (3) Indifferent | (4) Appropriate | (5) Relaxed and actively interested |
|---|---|---|---|---|
| (1) Hostile | (2) Uneasy | | | |

### I.Q. (Bellevue-Wechsler)

| (1) Below average | (2) Average | (3) High average | (4) Superior | (5) Very superior |
|---|---|---|---|---|

### PRODUCTIVITY (Rorschach)

| (1) Impoverished | (2) Reduced output | (3) Adequate | (4) Better than average | (5) Rich and well-ordered |
|---|---|---|---|---|
| | (2) Compulsive productivity | | | |

### RELATION TO REALITY (Rorschach, Bellevue-Wechsler, Drawings)

| (1) Loose | (2) Lapses—together with good form | (3) Not noticeably disturbed | (4) Essentially firm | (5) Firm and good |
|---|---|---|---|---|

### USUAL-UNUSUAL THOUGHT CONTENT (Rorschach, Unpleasant Concept)

| (1) Bizarre | (2) Tendency toward the bizarre | (3) Adequate | (4) Original trends | (5) Outstandingly original |
|---|---|---|---|---|
| (1) Stereotyped | (2) Tendency toward stereotypy | | | |

### CONSTRUCTIVE FANTASY (Rorschach)

| (1) Absent | (2) Barely accessible | (3) Accessible | (4) Readily accessible | (5) Active but not hampering |
|---|---|---|---|---|
| (1) Withdrawal into fantasy | | | | |

### DRIVE (Rorschach, Szondi, Unpleasant Concept)

| (1) Overpowering aggression | (2) Over-aggressive | (3) Adequate | (4) Clearly sufficient | (5) Sufficient—exceptionally well-directed |
|---|---|---|---|---|
| (1) Hampering passivity | (2) Insufficient drive | | | |

### EMOTIONAL TONE (Rorschach, Szondi)

| (1) Explosive emotions | (2) Getting out of hand | (3) Trend toward emotional expression | (4) Warmth available | (5) Warm, readily available |
|---|---|---|---|---|
| (1) Lacking | (2) Indicated but re-pressed emotions | | | |

### SOCIAL ATTITUDE (T. A. T.)

| (1) Uncontrolled | (2) Constricted or neglected | (3) Adequate | (4) Well-regulated | (5) Free and flexible |
|---|---|---|---|---|

### ANXIETY

| (1) Disintegrating | (2) Marked | (3) Moderate | (4) Not marked | (5) Lack of evidence of anxiety |
|---|---|---|---|---|

### OVER-ALL EVALUATION

| (1) Markedly disturbed personality | (2) Less than adequate personality with some psychological problems | (3) Adequate personality | (4) Better than average functioning personality | (5) Exceptionally well-integrated personality with excellent potential |
|---|---|---|---|---|

## SUMMARY OF THERAPIST'S FINDINGS  *SA 2*

### ESTIMATED INTELLIGENCE LEVEL

| (1) Below average | (2) Average | (3) High average | (4) Superior | (5) (Very superior) |
|---|---|---|---|---|

### FLOW OF ASSOCIATIVE MATERIAL

| (1) Impoverished | (2) Reduced output | (3) (Adequate) | (4) Better than average | (5) Rich and well-ordered |
|---|---|---|---|---|
| | (2) Compulsive productivity | | | |

### RELATION TO REALITY

| (1) Loose | (2) (Lapses—together with good form) | (3) Not noticeably disturbed | (4) Essentially firm | (5) Firm and good |
|---|---|---|---|---|

### USUAL-UNUSUAL THOUGHT CONTENT

| (1) Bizarre | (2) (Tendency toward the bizarre) | (3) Adequate | (4) Original trends | (5) Outstandingly original |
|---|---|---|---|---|
| (1) Stereotyped | (2) Tendency toward stereotypy | | | |

### CONSTRUCTIVE FANTASY

| (1) Absent | (2) Barely accessible | (3) (Accessible) | (4) Readily accessible | (5) Active but not hampering |
|---|---|---|---|---|
| (1) Withdrawal into fantasy | | | | |

### DRIVE

| (1) Overpowering aggression | (2) Over-aggressive | (3) (Adequate) | (4) Clearly sufficient | (5) Sufficient—exceptionally well-directed |
|---|---|---|---|---|
| (1) Hampering passivity | (2) Insufficient drive | | | |

### EMOTIONAL TONE

| (1) Explosive emotions | (2) Getting out of hand | (3) (Trend toward emotional expression) | (4) Warmth available | (5) Warm, readily available |
|---|---|---|---|---|
| (1) Lacking | (2) Indicated but re-pressed emotions | | | |

### SOCIAL ATTITUDE

| (1) Uncontrolled | (2) Constricted or neglected | (3) (Adequate) | (4) Well-regulated | (5) Free and flexible |
|---|---|---|---|---|

### ANXIETY

| (1) Disintegrating | (2) Marked | (3) (Moderate) | (4) Not marked | (5) Lack of evidence of anxiety |
|---|---|---|---|---|

### OVER-ALL EVALUATION

| (1) Markedly dis-turbed personality | (2) Less than adequate personality with some psycholog-ical problems | (3) (Adequate personality) | (4) Better than average function-ing personality | (5) Exceptionally well-integrated person-ality with excellent potential |
|---|---|---|---|---|

RECORD 1

RECORD 2

7. Picture of a girl, probably a chorus girl, with her hair very elaborately done; there are two of them.
8. Picture of a man with a coonskin hat on, who is pretty tall and drinks a great deal and is inclined to be cruel.
9. Remnant of a prehistoric crustation; it has prehensile claws; a fossil.
10. Two old ladies dressed in long coats and striding in opposite directions carrying large bundles. They walk very vigorously and seem in a hurry. They try to get away from this prehensile animal and they lift their skirts to be able to go more quickly.
11. These two women could be shamans in ceremonial costumes fanning a fire; in their arms the big branches.

*Card II*

1. Two walruses with their heads together and their tails in the air doing a trained act in the circus.
2. Card II upside down: Two Helen Hokinson females staring very bitterly. My seals are also convertibles, the seals attempting to do a trick too.

*Card II*

1. Two overdressed women, rapidly discussing nothing at all, waving their hands.
2. Two baboons idly chewing food.
3. Two little dogs, French poodles, playfully struggling for a toy. Their feet are raised, ears back, their noses held against the toy.
4. Two elephants at a circus, doing a pas de deux, trunks together.
5. Two dogs, this time they are French poodles behaving very well.
6. Eruption of a volcano; the rocks are boiling; smoke comes up but in the very center fire comes through.

*Card III*

1. Two men dressed in full evening dress being very polite as if doing an act or part of an act.
2. Two sea horses being playful in the water by diving downwards.
3. Two doll-looking men with their heads together wondering what's going on on the map of the estuaries which is below them.

*Card III*

1. Two witches with their hair done very high on their heads (upper red). They dance about a caldron (middle red) singing out their witchery.
2. Two doctors, elderly, slim, who normally stand upright, dressed very correctly, and discussing a cadaver, arguing about some obscure point.

RECORD 1

RECORD 2

3. Two comic figures of men, heads, neck, shouting out a song, probably slightly bawdy.
4. Two tropical fish with long tails swimming in a bowl (white space).
5. Two bare dancers from the Indian tribes doing one of their dances.
6. A plunging neckline brassiere.
7. Two Chimpanzees looking over their shoulders (upper red) to their long tails.

*Card IV*

1. Some one's bad tanning job of a steer. It's pretty gruesome so he's put the head in.

*Card IV*

1. Two nuns kneeling before an altar dressed in black, the robes covering their heads.
2. Picture in a medical book of the female sexual organs.
3. Picture of Louis XIV with his tremendous periwig on.
4. Picture of a jet-propelled airplane with wings sharply swept back.
5. Figure of a great man sitting in a chair, barber chair, grotesquely foreshortened.
6. An owl in its nest.

*Card V*

1. Mephistopheles poised in flight on a terrifying mission. He's wrapped in his black robe, his wings to accomplish this end, a terrifying figure.

*Card V*

1. Figure of a man in a fancy dress costume of a bat.
2. A statesman making a speech in an assembly.

*Card VI*

1. Tribal goddess of a prehistoric or primitive tribe, arms outstretched like someone who has many arms (the top part of the card).
2. Two polar bears.
3. If I could look at it upside down, I would see two eagles looking at their young in a nest.
4. Airplane view of a straight row of vegetation. It would suggest a road in some part of a hollow of land because of the vegetational characteristics which becomes barren and then goes up into wooded hills.

*Card VI*

1. A totem pole.
2. A shack on a small, deserted island, little house.

*Card VII*

1. Two cute girls, very pert, their hair done up in a curious way. They are somewhat sophisticated and theatrical because their job is to be cute.

*Card VIII*

1. Very familiar animals who feed on pine leaves but who are somewhat out of place because they have aggressive looking hind feet and should not be eating that type of food.
2. Two fox terriers with their ears cocked, which makes them look like the Victor Talking Machine Co.

*Card IX*

1. Two clowns at play with baggy trousers and hats. They are playing games with their hands.
2. A contemptuous octopus.
3. Very fat little old man with hair like Einstein, a face like a cute man wearing glasses, eating an ice cream cone.
4. Two thoughtful gentlemen talking from a reclining position with their hands in their lapels.
   Do I say everything I see?
5. I see an indelicate picture of a woman with her legs apart.

*Card X*

1. An insect carnival, has queer little unreal insects who belong. They're playing, doing tricks, and working in the ampitheater.
2. Couple of costumed preying mantises. They have green worms who feel they should look an astounded rabbit in the eye.
3. Two French poodles.
4. Two knights in armor.

*Card VII*

1. Two little girls merely discussing some light affair.
2. Two dogs hastily meeting two other dogs. They are two expensive dogs and meet probably outside an expensive apartment house, smelling, well groomed, expensively cut.

*Card VII*

(I remember this)

1. Two little mild, gentle animals; they eat fruit; their legs don't correspond with the front part, the hind part more of vigorous, carniverous animals.
2. This is the tree on which they are looking for food.
3. Butterfly.
4. A garden with flower arrangements.

*Card IX*

1. Two dressed-up clowns doing a trick which involves having little animals attached to their hips forming a part of the trick.
2. Housewife doing some cleaning.
3. A fountain of pink water, flowing over a malachite base.

*Card X*

1. I see the same thing I saw last time— a circus of animals.
2. Jumping goats.
3. French poodles doing a trick.
4. Two more French poodles doing a trick.
5. Birds with their heads together.
6. A rabbit holding his paws over his eyes because he is so astonished about the performance he sees.
7. Two elaborately gowned women holding yellow pieces of silk round their arms.
8. Two sea horses.

SA3 was in his thirties and single at the time of the first and second testing. The four-year follow-up revealed that he had achieved a happily adjusted marriage shortly after the termination of therapy.

The therapist's rating at the time of the first testing was at the level of 3 on the OVER-ALL EVALUATION scale; at the time of retesting, 4, and at the reassessment four years later this level of 4 had been maintained.

Comparison of the subtests on the Wechsler reveals an identical scattergram, with the I.Q. therefore also remaining the same.*

The Szondi is also remarkably similar; no improvement can be considered to have occurred here. Nor would one rate the Drawings in the retest superior to those in the first assessment. SA3, at the time of retesting, may be said to be turning his back on his problems just as does the figure which he draws. The level of the drawings in test and retest can be classified as inadequate but not bizarre.

The increase in the total number of R in the Rorschach, though it places the patient numerically in a different rating group, does not appear significant. There is, moreover, a loss of two of the good FC's and an increase in the more impulsive, uncontrolled type of response. Anxiety is also evidenced in the appearance of two K responses. The C' and the m reinforce this impression of greater turbulence and distress in the second record. Our feeling here is that this individual is caught too soon after the therapeutic process for change in a consistent direction to have registered. There is some change but it has not assumed a positive direction.

It is interesting, in this connection, to notice that some individuals who are receiving long-term therapy and who are tested in the early stages of therapy show records indicating more acute disturbance.† From the retest findings, it would seem that SA3 fails to show the improvement which was reported clinically at that time. On the over-all quantitative scale SA3 starts and ends with a score of 26.

---

* It is true that there is a one point difference in the Digit scores, but in such cases we do not hesitate to speak in terms of the general distribution rather than call attention to distracting minutiae.

† See Chapter II.

## WORK SHEET

SA3

*1*

### VERBAL I. Q. = 133

| EWS | Info. | Comp. | Digit | Arith. | Sim. |
|-----|-------|-------|-------|--------|------|
| 18 | 25 | 20 | | 14 | 23-24 |
| 17 | 24 | 19 | 17 | 13 | 21-22 |
| 16 | 23 | 18 | 16 | 12 | 20 |
| 15 | 21-22 | 17 | | 11 | 19 |
| 14 | 20 | 16 | 15 | | 17-18 |
| 13 | 18-19 | 15 | 14 | 10 | 16 |
| 12 | 17 | 14 | | 9 | 15 |

### SZONDI

| SEXUAL | | PAROXYSMAL | | EGO | | CONTACT | |
|---|---|---|---|---|---|---|---|
| h | s | e | hy | k | p | d | m |
| X | | X | | | | | |
| X | X | X | | X | | | |
| X | X | X | X | X | | | X |
| X | | X | X | | | X | X |
| X | | | X | | | X | X |
| | | | X | | | X | |
| | | | | | | X | |

### RORSCHACH

| | | | | | |
|---|---|---|---|---|---|
| R | 19 | M | | Fc | 1 |
| | | FM | 5 (1-) | F | 4 | c | |
| W% | 42 | m | | F- | 1 | C' | |
| D% | 47 | k | 1 | F% | 26 | FC | 3 |
| d% | | K | | | | CF | 1 |
| Dd% / S | 11 | FK | 3 | | | C | |

## WORK SHEET

SA3

2

VERBAL I. Q. = 133

SZONDI

| EWS | Info. | Comp. | Digit | Arith. | Sim. |
|-----|-------|-------|-------|--------|------|
| 18 | 25 | 20 | | (14) | 23-24 |
| 17 | 24 | 19 | 17 | 13 | 21-22 |
| 16 | 23 | 18 | 16 | 12 | 20 |
| 15 | (21-22) | 17 | | 11 | 19 |
| 14 | 20 | 16 | (15) | | 7-18 |
| 13 | 18-19 | (15) | 14 | 10 | (16) |
| 12 | 17 | 14 | | 9 | 15 |

| SEXUAL | | PAROXYSMAL | | EGO | | CONTACT | |
|--------|---|------------|----|-----|---|---------|---|
| h | s | e | hy | k | p | d | m |
| | | X | | | | | |
| X | X | X | X | | | | X |
| X | X | X | X | X | X | | X |
| X | | X | X | X | | X | X |
| X | | | X | X | | X | |
| | | | | | | X | |
| | | | | | | X | |

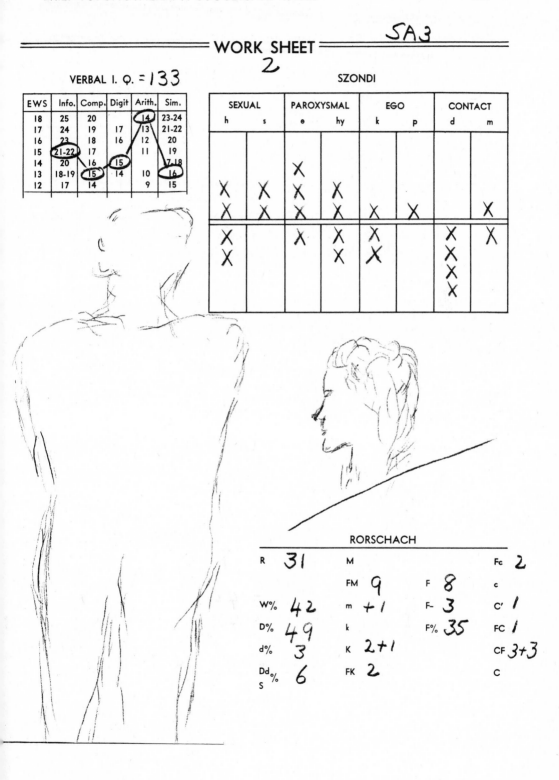

## RORSCHACH

| | | | | | |
|---|---|---|---|---|---|
| R | 31 | M | | Fc | 2 |
| | | FM | 9 | F | 8 | c | |
| W% | 42 | m | +1 | F- | 3 | C' | 1 |
| D% | 49 | k | | F% | 35 | FC | 1 |
| d% | 3 | K | 2+1 | | | CF | 3+3 |
| Dd% | 6 | FK | 2 | | | c | |
| S | | | | | | |

# SUMMARY OF TEST FINDINGS   SA 3

## MANNER DURING TEST

| (1) Overly distressed | (2) Tense | (3) Indifferent | (4) Appropriate | (5) Relaxed and actively interested |
|---|---|---|---|---|
| (1) Hostile | (2) *Uneasy* | | | |

## I.Q. (Bellevue-Wechsler)

| (1) Below average | (2) Average | (3) High average | (4) Superior | (5) *Very superior* |
|---|---|---|---|---|

## PRODUCTIVITY (Rorschach)

| (1) Impoverished | (2) Reduced output | (3) *Adequate* | (4) Better than average | (5) Rich and well-ordered |
|---|---|---|---|---|
| | (2) Compulsive productivity | | | |

## RELATION TO REALITY (Rorschach, Bellevue-Wechsler, Drawings)

| (1) Loose | (2) Lapses—together with good form | (3) *Not noticeably disturbed* | (4) Essentially firm | (5) Firm and good |
|---|---|---|---|---|

## USUAL-UNUSUAL THOUGHT CONTENT (Rorschach, Unpleasant Concept)

| (1) Bizarre | (2) Tendency toward the bizarre | (3) *Adequate* | (4) Original trends | (5) Outstandingly original |
|---|---|---|---|---|
| (1) Stereotyped | (2) Tendency toward stereotypy | | | |

## CONSTRUCTIVE FANTASY (Rorschach)

| (1) *Absent* | (2) Barely accessible | (3) Accessible | (4) Readily accessible | (5) Active but not hampering |
|---|---|---|---|---|
| (1) Withdrawal into fantasy | | | | |

## DRIVE (Rorschach, Szondi, Unpleasant Concept)

| (1) Overpowering aggression | (2) Over-aggressive | (3) *Adequate* | (4) Clearly sufficient | (5) Sufficient—exceptionally well-directed |
|---|---|---|---|---|
| (1) Hampering passivity | (2) Insufficient drive | | | |

## EMOTIONAL TONE (Rorschach, Szondi)

| (1) Explosive emotions | (2) Getting out of hand | (3) *Trend toward emotional expression* | (4) Warmth available | (5) Warm, readily available |
|---|---|---|---|---|
| (1) Lacking | (2) Indicated but repressed emotions | | | |

## SOCIAL ATTITUDE (T. A. T.)

| (1) Uncontrolled | (2) *Constricted or neglected* | (3) Adequate | (4) Well-regulated | (5) Free and flexible |
|---|---|---|---|---|

## ANXIETY

| (1) Disintegrating | (2) Marked | (3) *Moderate* | (4) Not marked | (5) Lack of evidence of anxiety |
|---|---|---|---|---|

## OVER-ALL EVALUATION

| (1) Markedly disturbed personality | (2) Less than adequate personality with some psychological problems | (3) *Adequate personality* | (4) Better than average functioning personality | (5) Exceptionally well-integrated personality with excellent potential |
|---|---|---|---|---|

## SUMMARY OF THERAPIST'S FINDINGS    SA 3

### ESTIMATED INTELLIGENCE LEVEL

| (1) Below average | (2) Average | (3) High average | (4) Superior | (5) Very superior |
|---|---|---|---|---|

### FLOW OF ASSOCIATIVE MATERIAL

| (1) Impoverished | (2) Reduced output | (3) Adequate | (4) Better than average | (5) Rich and well-ordered |
|---|---|---|---|---|
| | (2) Compulsive productivity | | | |

### RELATION TO REALITY

| (1) Loose | (2) Lapses—together with good form | (3) Not noticeably disturbed | (4) Essentially firm | (5) Firm and good |
|---|---|---|---|---|

### USUAL-UNUSUAL THOUGHT CONTENT

| (1) Bizarre | (2) Tendency toward the bizarre | (3) Adequate | (4) Original trends | (5) Outstandingly original |
|---|---|---|---|---|
| (1) Stereotyped | (2) Tendency toward stereotypy | | | |

### CONSTRUCTIVE FANTASY

| (1) Absent | (2) Barely accessible | (3) Accessible | (4) Readily accessible | (5) Active but not hampering |
|---|---|---|---|---|
| (1) Withdrawal into fantasy | | | | |

### DRIVE

| (1) Overpowering aggression | (2) Over-aggressive | (3) Adequate | (4) Clearly sufficient | (5) Sufficient—exceptionally well-directed |
|---|---|---|---|---|
| (1) Hampering passivity | (2) Insufficient drive | | | |

### EMOTIONAL TONE

| (1) Explosive emotions | (2) Getting out of hand | (3) Trend toward emotional expression | (4) Warmth available | (5) Warm, readily available |
|---|---|---|---|---|
| (1) Lacking | (2) Indicated but re-pressed emotions | | | |

### SOCIAL ATTITUDE

| (1) Uncontrolled | (2) Constricted or neglected | (3) Adequate | (4) Well-regulated | (5) Free and flexible |
|---|---|---|---|---|

### ANXIETY

| (1) Disintegrating | (2) Marked | (3) Moderate | (4) Not marked | (5) Lack of evidence of anxiety |
|---|---|---|---|---|

### OVER-ALL EVALUATION

| (1) Markedly disturbed personality | (2) Less than adequate personality with some psychological problems | (3) Adequate personality | (4) Better than average functioning personality | (5) Exceptionally well-integrated personality with excellent potential |
|---|---|---|---|---|

SA4 was in his twenties and unmarried at the time of testing and at the time of follow-up four years later. The therapist's rating on the OVER-ALL EVALUATION scale was 2 at the start of therapy, 3 at the time of retesting, with this latter level being retained four years later.

As can be seen on the Work Sheet, the Bellevue-Wechsler gives scores of uniform excellence, a slight change in the retest reflecting a gain of four points on the Information.

The Szondi shows a marked change in the ego vector, which parallels the clinical observations made at the same time that retesting took place. One of the problems, behaviorally, of SA4 was the fact that he was held in the grip of strong repressive forces which inhibited activity in several directions. The second Szondi reflects the fact that a freer, more extensive and constructive type of action has now become possible. (The loaded –k now becomes open k, and the p becomes positive.) Also important on the Szondi is the reversal of the –m to +m, essentially a constructive sign. The bisexuality indicated in Record 1 becomes clearer in Record 2. Perhaps one may say this individual has become increasingly aware of his difficulties. Clinically, he is reported as grappling with them.

A comparison of the formal Rorschach scores indicates a slight change for the better. We would rate as the most important change the differing ratio between the F and F– responses. In record 1 there is a precarious balance between the four F– and the six F+ responses. In Record 2, with the addition of many good F responses this relationship has changed. As has been stated previously, we discount the mere addition of responses so that the increase to 37 responses from 20 is not such an important factor. Two additional M responses have been added, and the good, superficial adjustment as reflected in the six FC responses has been retained.

The Drawings remain in the same class; neither one appears superior to the other.

In terms of the OVER-ALL EVALUATION this individual starts from a position of 29 and ends with a score of 32, an increase of 3 points.

(Records for SA4 will be found on pages 246-249, for SA5 on pages 250-253.)

The therapist's first evaluation of patient SA5, who was in his late twenties when he entered therapy, was at the level of 2. He was assessed as having reached the level of *Adequate personality* at the time of re-testing, and to have progressed beyond this to the level of 4 at the time of the follow-up, four years after the termination of treatment. Although one of the presenting symptoms remained unchanged it was felt clinically that in terms of total capacity to function, improved interpersonal re-lationships and increased satisfaction in, and capacity to, work, the over-all improvement was marked.

Turning to a comparison of the Work Sheets, one finds identical Wechslers in the first and second testing. There is a specific and notable change in the Figure Drawings. During the first procedure the patient was unable to follow the instructions to draw a male and female person, but produced sexless "persons" in response to both instructions. At the time of the second testing this had become modified, and male and female drawings resulted.

Apart from this, which we would consider a positive change, there is little else of note; in fact, there is even the loss of a few points in the OVER-ALL EVALUATION. The Rorschach, for instance, reflects a slight rise in the F– per cent, a loss of the much needed additional FC re-sponse, and a reduction in the number of M's and FM's. At the time of retesting, this individual appears to be in flux but only one of the prob-lems which brought him into therapy, namely, a problem in psychosexual orientation, may be said to be on the move toward a healthier or more mature direction. The test findings in this instance do not parallel the clinical assessment.

# WORK SHEET

**SA 4**

1

## VERBAL I. Q. = 139

| EWS | Info. | Comp. | Digit | Arith. | Sim. |
|---|---|---|---|---|---|
| 18 | 25 | 20 |  | 14 | 23-24 |
| 17 | 24 | 19 | 17 | 13 | 21-22 |
| 16 | 23 | 18 | (16) | (12) | 20 |
| 15 | (21-22) | (17) |  | 11 | (19) |
| 14 | 20 | 16 | 15 |  | 17-18 |
| 13 | 18-19 | 15 | 14 | 10 | 16 |
| 12 | 17 | 14 |  | 9 | 15 |

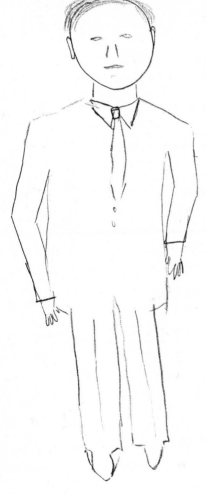

## SZONDI

| SEXUAL | | PAROXYSMAL | | EGO | | CONTACT | |
|---|---|---|---|---|---|---|---|
| h | s | e | hy | k | p | d | m |
|  |  |  |  |  |  | X |  |
| X | X |  | X |  | X | X |  |
| X | X | X | X |  | X | X | X |
| X | X |  | X | X | X |  | X |
|  |  |  | X | X |  |  | X |
|  |  |  |  | X |  |  |  |
|  |  |  |  | X |  |  |  |
|  |  |  |  | X |  |  |  |
|  |  |  |  | X |  |  |  |

## OVER-ALL EVALUATION = 29

| | | | | | |
|---|---|---|---|---|---|
| OVER-ALL RATING | 1 | 2 | 3 | 4 | 5 |
| PRODUCTIVITY | 1 | 2 | ③ | 4 | 5 |
| RELATION TO REALITY | 1 | 2 | ③ | 4 | 5 |
| THOUGHT CONTENT | 1 | 2 | ③ | 4 | 5 |
| CONSTRUCTIVE FANTASY | 1 | ② | 3 | 4 | 5 |
| DRIVE | 1 | 2 | ③ | 4 | 5 |
| EMOTIONAL TONE | 1 | 2 | 3 | ④ | 5 |
| SOCIAL ATTITUDE | 1 | 2 | ③ | 4 | 5 |
| ANXIETY | 1 | 2 | ③ | 4 | 5 |
| I. Q. RATING  139 | 1 | 2 | 3 | 4 | ⑤ |

## RORSCHACH

| | | | | | |
|---|---|---|---|---|---|
| R 20 | M 2 | | | | Fc |
| | FM 2 | | F 6 | | c |
| W% 25 | m | | F- 4 | | C' |
| D% 60 | k | | F% 50 | | FC 6+ |
| d% 5 | K | | | | CF |
| Dd% 10 | FK | | | | C |
| S | | | | | |

## WORK SHEET  SA 4

2

### VERBAL I. Q. = 144

| EWS | Info. | Comp. | Digit | Arith. | Sim. |
|-----|-------|-------|-------|--------|------|
| 18 | 25 | 20 | | 14 | 23-24 |
| 17 | 24 | 19 | 17 | 13 | 21-22 |
| 16 | 23 | 18 | 16 | 12 | 20 |
| 15 | 21-22 | 17 | | 11 | 19 |
| 14 | 20 | 16 | 15 | | 17-18 |
| 13 | 18-19 | 15 | 14 | 10 | 16 |
| 12 | 17 | 14 | | 9 | 15 |
| | | | | | |
| 11 | 15-16 | 12-13 | 13 | | 13-14 |
| 10 | 13-14 | 11 | 12 | 8 | 12 |
| 9 | 12 | 10 | 11 | 7 | 11 |
| 8 | 10-11 | 9 | | | 9-10 |
| 7 | 9 | 8 | 10 | 6 | 8 |
| 6 | 7-8 | 7 | 9 | 5 | 7 |

### SZONDI

| | SEXUAL | | PAROXYSMAL | | EGO | | CONTACT | |
|---|---|---|---|---|---|---|---|---|
| | h | s | e | hy | k | p | d | m |
| | | | | | | X | | |
| | | | | | | X | | |
| | | | | | | X | | X |
| | X | X | X | | X | X | | X |
| | X | X | | | | X | | |
| | X | X | | X | X | X | X | X |
| | X | X | | X | | | | |
| | | | | X | | | | |
| | | | | X | | | | |
| | | | | X | | | | |

### OVER-ALL EVALUATION = 32

| | | | | | |
|---|---|---|---|---|---|
| OVER-ALL RATING | 1 | 2 | 3 | 4 | 5 |
| PRODUCTIVITY | 1 | 2 | ③ | 4 | 5 |
| RELATION TO REALITY | 1 | 2 | ③ | 4 | 5 |
| THOUGHT CONTENT | 1 | 2 | 3 | ④ | 5 |
| CONSTRUCTIVE FANTASY | 1 | 2 | ③ | 4 | 5 |
| DRIVE | 1 | 2 | ③ | 4 | 5 |
| EMOTIONAL TONE | 1 | 2 | 3 | ④ | 5 |
| SOCIAL ATTITUDE | 1 | 2 | 3 | ④ | 5 |
| ANXIETY | 1 | 2 | ③ | 4 | 5 |
| I. Q. RATING  = 144 | 1 | 2 | 3 | 4 | ⑤ |

### RORSCHACH

| R 37 | M 4 | | Fc 1 |
|------|-----|-----|------|
| | FM 2 | F 19 | c 1 |
| W% 19 | m | F- 4 | C' |
| D% 53 | k | F% 62 | FC 6 |
| d% 14 | K | | CF |
| Dd% 14 S | FK | | C |

# SUMMARY OF TEST FINDINGS   *SA 4*

### MANNER DURING TEST

| (1) Overly distressed | (2) Tense | (3) Indifferent | (4) Appropriate | (5) Relaxed and actively interested |
|---|---|---|---|---|
| (1) Hostile | (2) Uneasy ⟲ | | | |

### I.Q. (Bellevue-Wechsler)

| (1) Below average | (2) Average | (3) High average | (4) Superior | (5) Very superior ⟲ |
|---|---|---|---|---|

### PRODUCTIVITY (Rorschach)

| (1) Impoverished | (2) Reduced output | (3) Adequate ⟲ | (4) Better than average | (5) Rich and well-ordered |
|---|---|---|---|---|
| | (2) Compulsive productivity | 20 → 37 | | |

### RELATION TO REALITY (Rorschach, Bellevue-Wechsler, Drawings)

| (1) Loose | (2) Lapses—together with good form | (3) Not noticeably disturbed ⟲ | (4) Essentially firm | (5) Firm and good |
|---|---|---|---|---|

### USUAL-UNUSUAL THOUGHT CONTENT (Rorschach, Unpleasant Concept)

| (1) Bizarre | (2) Tendency toward the bizarre | (3) Adequate ⟲ | (4) Original trends | (5) Outstandingly original |
|---|---|---|---|---|
| (1) Stereotyped | (2) Tendency toward stereotypy | | | |

### CONSTRUCTIVE FANTASY (Rorschach)

| (1) Absent | (2) Barely accessible ⟲ | (3) Accessible | (4) Readily accessible | (5) Active but not hampering |
|---|---|---|---|---|
| (1) Withdrawal into fantasy | | | | |

### DRIVE (Rorschach, Szondi, Unpleasant Concept)

| (1) Overpowering aggression | (2) Over-aggressive | (3) Adequate ⟲ | (4) Clearly sufficient | (5) Sufficient—exceptionally well-directed |
|---|---|---|---|---|
| (1) Hampering passivity | (2) Insufficient drive | | | |

### EMOTIONAL TONE (Rorschach, Szondi)

| (1) Explosive emotions | (2) Getting out of hand | (3) Trend toward emotional expression | (4) Warmth available ⟲ | (5) Warm, readily available |
|---|---|---|---|---|
| (1) Lacking | (2) Indicated but repressed emotions | | | |

### SOCIAL ATTITUDE (T. A. T.)

| (1) Uncontrolled | (2) Constricted or neglected | (3) Adequate ⟲ | (4) Well-regulated | (5) Free and flexible |
|---|---|---|---|---|

### ANXIETY

| (1) Disintegrating | (2) Marked | (3) Moderate ⟲ | (4) Not marked | (5) Lack of evidence of anxiety |
|---|---|---|---|---|

### OVER-ALL EVALUATION

| (1) Markedly disturbed personality | (2) Less than adequate personality with some psychological problems | (3) Adequate personality ⟲ | (4) Better than average functioning personality | (5) Exceptionally well-integrated personality with excellent potential |
|---|---|---|---|---|

## SUMMARY OF THERAPIST'S FINDINGS   *SA 4*

### ESTIMATED INTELLIGENCE LEVEL

| (1) Below average | (2) Average | (3) High average | (4) Superior | (5) (Very superior) |
|---|---|---|---|---|

### FLOW OF ASSOCIATIVE MATERIAL

| (1) Impoverished | (2) (Reduced output) / (2) Compulsive productivity | (3) Adequate | (4) Better than average | (5) Rich and well-ordered |
|---|---|---|---|---|

### RELATION TO REALITY

| (1) Loose | (2) (Lapses—together with good form) | (3) Not noticeably disturbed | (4) Essentially firm | (5) Firm and good |
|---|---|---|---|---|

### USUAL-UNUSUAL THOUGHT CONTENT

| (1) Bizarre | (2) Tendency toward the bizarre | (3) Adequate | (4) Original trends | (5) Outstandingly original |
|---|---|---|---|---|
| (1) Stereotyped | (2) (Tendency toward stereotypy) | | | |

### CONSTRUCTIVE FANTASY

| (1) Absent | (2) Barely accessible | (3) (Accessible) | (4) Readily accessible | (5) Active but not hampering |
|---|---|---|---|---|
| (1) Withdrawal into fantasy | | | | |

### DRIVE

| (1) Overpowering aggression | (2) Over-aggressive | (3) (Adequate) | (4) Clearly sufficient | (5) Sufficient—exceptionally well-directed |
|---|---|---|---|---|
| (1) Hampering passivity | (2) Insufficient drive | | | |

### EMOTIONAL TONE

| (1) Explosive emotions | (2) Getting out of hand | (3) Trend toward emotional expression | (4) Warmth available | (5) Warm, readily available |
|---|---|---|---|---|
| (1) Lacking | (2) (Indicated but re-pressed emotions) | | | |

### SOCIAL ATTITUDE

| (1) Uncontrolled | (2) (Constricted or neglected) | (3) Adequate | (4) Well-regulated | (5) Free and flexible |
|---|---|---|---|---|

### ANXIETY

| (1) Disintegrating | (2) (Marked) | (3) Moderate | (4) Not marked | (5) Lack of evidence of anxiety |
|---|---|---|---|---|

### OVER-ALL EVALUATION

| (1) Markedly disturbed personality | (2) (Less than adequate personality with some psychological problems) | (3) Adequate personality | (4) Better than average functioning personality | (5) Exceptionally well-integrated personality with excellent potential |
|---|---|---|---|---|

# WORK SHEET — SA5

## VERBAL I. Q. = 130

| EWS | Info. | Comp. | Digit | Arith. | Sim. |
|-----|-------|-------|-------|--------|------|
| 18 | 25 | 20 | | 14 | 23-24 |
| 17 | 24 | 19 | 17 | 13 | 21-22 |
| 16 | 23 | 18 | 16 | 12 | 20 |
| 15 | 21-22 | 17 | | 11 | 19 |
| 14 | 20 | 16 | 15 | | 17-18 |
| 13 | 18-19 | 15 | 14 | 10 | 16 |
| 12 | 17 | 14 | | 9 | 15 |
| | | | | | |
| 11 | 15-16 | 12-13 | 13 | | 13-14 |
| 10 | 13-14 | 11 | 12 | 8 | 12 |
| 9 | 12 | 10 | 11 | 7 | 11 |
| 8 | 10-11 | 9 | | | 9-10 |
| 7 | 9 | 8 | 10 | 6 | 8 |
| 6 | 7-8 | 7 | 9 | 5 | 7 |
| | | | | | |
| 5 | 6 | 5-6 | | | 5-6 |
| 4 | 4-5 | 4 | 8 | 4 | 4 |
| 3 | 2-3 | 3 | 7 | 3 | 3 |
| 2 | 1 | 2 | 6 | | 1-2 |
| 1 | 0 | 1 | | 2 | 0 |
| 0 | | 0 | 5 | 1 | |

## SZONDI

| SEXUAL | | PAROXYSMAL | | EGO | | CONTACT | |
|---|---|---|---|---|---|---|---|
| h | s | e | hy | k | p | d | m |

### OVER-ALL EVALUATION = 27

| | | | | | |
|---|---|---|---|---|---|
| OVER-ALL RATING | 1 | 2 | 3 | 4 | 5 |
| PRODUCTIVITY | 1 | ②　 | 3 | 4 | 5 |
| RELATION TO REALITY | 1 | 2 | ③ | 4 | 5 |
| THOUGHT CONTENT | 1 | 2 | ③ | 4 | 5 |
| CONSTRUCTIVE FANTASY | 1 | 2 | 3 | ④ | 5 |
| DRIVE | 1 | 2 | ③ | 4 | 5 |
| EMOTIONAL TONE | 1 | ② | 3 | 4 | 5 |
| SOCIAL ATTITUDE | 1 | ② | 3 | 4 | 5 |
| ANXIETY | 1 | 2 | ③ | 4 | 5 |
| I. Q. RATING  130 | 1 | 2 | 3 | 4 | ⑤ |

### RORSCHACH

| R 17 | M 6 | | Fc |
|------|-----|---|-----|
| | FM 6 | F 2 | c |
| W% 35 | m +1 | F- 2 | C' + |
| D% 65 | k | F% 24 | FC + |
| d% | K | | CF / |
| Dd% | FK | | c + |
| S | | | |

# WORK SHEET ===== *SA5*

**2**

## VERBAL I. Q. = *131*

| EWS | Info. | Comp. | Digit | Arith. | Sim. |
|-----|-------|-------|-------|--------|------|
| 18 | 25 | 20 | | 14 | 23-24 |
| 17 | 24 | 19 | 17 | 13 | 21-22 |
| 16 | 23 | 18 | 16 | 12 | 20 |
| 15 | 21-22 | 17 | | 11 | 19 |
| 14 | 20 | 16 | 15 | | 17-18 |
| 13 | 18-19 | 15 | 14 | 10 | 16 |
| 12 | 17 | 14 | | 9 | 15 |
| | | | | | |
| 11 | 15-16 | 12-13 | 13 | | 13-14 |
| 10 | 13-14 | 11 | 12 | 8 | 12 |
| 9 | 12 | 10 | 11 | 7 | 11 |
| 8 | 10-11 | 9 | | | 9-10 |
| 7 | 9 | 8 | 10 | 6 | 8 |
| 6 | 7-8 | 7 | 9 | 5 | 7 |
| | | | | | |
| 5 | 6 | 5-6 | | | 5-6 |
| 4 | 4-5 | 4 | 8 | 4 | 4 |
| 3 | 2-3 | 3 | 7 | 3 | 3 |
| 2 | 1 | 2 | 6 | | 1-2 |
| 1 | 0 | 1 | | 2 | 0 |
| 0 | | 0 | 5 | 1 | |

(circled: Info. 21-22, Comp. 15, Digit 16, Arith. 11, Sim. 17-18)

## SZONDI

| SEXUAL | | PAROXYSMAL | | EGO | | CONTACT | |
|--------|--------|------------|--------|--------|--------|--------|--------|
| h | s | e | hy | k | p | d | m |

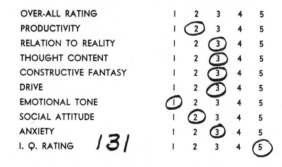

## OVER-ALL EVALUATION = *25*

| | 1 | 2 | 3 | 4 | 5 |
|--|---|---|---|---|---|
| OVER-ALL RATING | 1 | 2 | 3 | 4 | 5 |
| PRODUCTIVITY | 1 | (2) | 3 | 4 | 5 |
| RELATION TO REALITY | 1 | 2 | (3) | 4 | 5 |
| THOUGHT CONTENT | 1 | 2 | (3) | 4 | 5 |
| CONSTRUCTIVE FANTASY | 1 | 2 | (3) | 4 | 5 |
| DRIVE | 1 | 2 | (3) | 4 | 5 |
| EMOTIONAL TONE | (1) | 2 | 3 | 4 | 5 |
| SOCIAL ATTITUDE | 1 | (2) | 3 | 4 | 5 |
| ANXIETY | 1 | 2 | (3) | 4 | 5 |
| I. Q. RATING  *131* | 1 | 2 | 3 | 4 | (5) |

## RORSCHACH

| R | *15* | M | *4* | | | Fc | |
| | | FM | *4* | F | *3* | c | |
| W% | *40* | m | | F- | *4* | c' | *+1* |
| D% | *53* | k | | F% | *47* | FC | |
| d% | *7* | K | | | | CF | |
| Dd% | | FK | | | | c | *+1* |
| S | | | | | | | |

# SUMMARY OF TEST FINDINGS   SA 5

### MANNER DURING TEST

| (1) Overly distressed | (2) Tense | (3) Indifferent | (4) Appropriate | (5) Relaxed and actively interested |
|---|---|---|---|---|
| (1) Hostile | (2) Uneasy | | | |

### I.Q. (Bellevue-Wechsler)

| (1) Below average | (2) Average | (3) High average | (4) Superior | (5) Very superior |
|---|---|---|---|---|

### PRODUCTIVITY (Rorschach)

| (1) Impoverished | (2) Reduced output | (3) Adequate | (4) Better than average | (5) Rich and well-ordered |
|---|---|---|---|---|
| | (2) Compulsive productivity | | | |

### RELATION TO REALITY (Rorschach, Bellevue-Wechsler, Drawings)

| (1) Loose | (2) Lapses—together with good form | (3) Not noticeably disturbed | (4) Essentially firm | (5) Firm and good |
|---|---|---|---|---|

### USUAL-UNUSUAL THOUGHT CONTENT (Rorschach, Unpleasant Concept)

| (1) Bizarre | (2) Tendency toward the bizarre | (3) Adequate | (4) Original trends | (5) Outstandingly original |
|---|---|---|---|---|
| (1) Stereotyped | (2) Tendency toward stereotypy | | | |

### CONSTRUCTIVE FANTASY (Rorschach)

| (1) Absent | (2) Barely accessible | (3) Accessible | (4) Readily accessible | (5) Active but not hampering |
|---|---|---|---|---|
| (1) Withdrawal into fantasy | | | | |

### DRIVE (Rorschach, Szondi, Unpleasant Concept)

| (1) Overpowering aggression | (2) Over-aggressive | (3) Adequate | (4) Clearly sufficient | (5) Sufficient—exceptionally well-directed |
|---|---|---|---|---|
| (1) Hampering passivity | (2) Insufficient drive | | | |

### EMOTIONAL TONE (Rorschach, Szondi)

| (1) Explosive emotions | (2) Getting out of hand | (3) Trend toward emotional expression | (4) Warmth available | (5) Warm, readily available |
|---|---|---|---|---|
| (1) Lacking | (2) Indicated but repressed emotions | | | |

### SOCIAL ATTITUDE (T. A. T.)

| (1) Uncontrolled | (2) Constricted or neglected | (3) Adequate | (4) Well-regulated | (5) Free and flexible |
|---|---|---|---|---|

### ANXIETY

| (1) Disintegrating | (2) Marked | (3) Moderate | (4) Not marked | (5) Lack of evidence of anxiety |
|---|---|---|---|---|

### OVER-ALL EVALUATION

| (1) Markedly disturbed personality | (2) Less than adequate personality with some psychological problems | (3) Adequate personality | (4) Better than average functioning personality | (5) Exceptionally well-integrated personality with excellent potential |
|---|---|---|---|---|

## SUMMARY OF THERAPIST'S FINDINGS _SA S_

### ESTIMATED INTELLIGENCE LEVEL

| (1) Below average | (2) Average | (3) High average | (4) (Superior) | (5) Very superior |
|---|---|---|---|---|

### FLOW OF ASSOCIATIVE MATERIAL

| (1) Impoverished | (2) Reduced output | (3) (Adequate) | (4) Better than average | (5) Rich and well-ordered |
|---|---|---|---|---|
| | (2) Compulsive productivity | | | |

### RELATION TO REALITY

| (1) Loose | (2) Lapses—together with good form | (3) (Not noticeably disturbed) | (4) Essentially firm | (5) Firm and good |
|---|---|---|---|---|

### USUAL-UNUSUAL THOUGHT CONTENT

| (1) Bizarre | (2) Tendency toward the bizarre | (3) (Adequate) | (4) Original trends | (5) Outstandingly original |
|---|---|---|---|---|
| (1) Stereotyped | (2) Tendency toward stereotypy | | | |

### CONSTRUCTIVE FANTASY

| (1) Absent | (2) (Barely accessible) | (3) Accessible | (4) Readily accessible | (5) Active but not hampering |
|---|---|---|---|---|
| (1) Withdrawal into fantasy | | | | |

### DRIVE

| (1) Overpowering aggression | (2) Over-aggressive | (3) (Adequate) | (4) Clearly sufficient | (5) Sufficient—exceptionally well-directed |
|---|---|---|---|---|
| (1) Hampering passivity | (2) Insufficient drive | | | |

### EMOTIONAL TONE

| (1) Explosive emotions | (2) Getting out of hand | (3) (Trend toward emotional expression) | (4) Warmth available | (5) Warm, readily available |
|---|---|---|---|---|
| (1) Lacking | (2) Indicated but repressed emotions | | | |

### SOCIAL ATTITUDE

| (1) Uncontrolled | (2) Constricted or neglected | (3) (Adequate) | (4) Well-regulated | (5) Free and flexible |
|---|---|---|---|---|

### ANXIETY

| (1) Disintegrating | (2) (Marked) | (3) Moderate | (4) Not marked | (5) Lack of evidence of anxiety |
|---|---|---|---|---|

### OVER-ALL EVALUATION

| (1) Markedly disturbed personality | (2) (Less than adequate personality with some psychological problems) | (3) Adequate personality | (4) Better than average functioning personality | (5) Exceptionally well-integrated personality with excellent potential |
|---|---|---|---|---|

The therapist's estimate of SA6 was at the highly disturbed level at the start of her treatment. The estimate at the time of retesting was described as 3+, with improvement in varying degree in all the presenting problems and symptoms. At the time of a five-year follow-up, this improvement had been maintained, clinically. The patient had married in the interim.

A comparison of the subtests on the Bellevue-Wechsler reveals a noticeable difference in the verbal I.Q. and in the scattergram. The Comprehension, Reasoning and Judgment which, at first, had been completely invaded by this individual's conflicts and disturbances increases six points on the weighted scale at the retesting. There is improvement also in the abstract thinking, and the Digit Memory can be handled in a satisfactory manner.

The Szondi cannot be said to represent a stabilized picture at the time of the second testing. It is necessary for this individual to repress aggression to the point where inertia and inability to function may well be expected. At the same time, the pressures within the ego toward expansion, perhaps on an unrealistic basis, have become greater. However, interestingly enough, in terms of this patient's specific problems, this pattern probably resulted in better adjustment at the behavioral level at the time of retesting.

In the Rorschach the human movement responses have doubled and have become more realistic, indicative of better human identification. On the other hand, a rise in the F− responses from two to eight unquestionably offsets the gain achieved through the increase in human movement. On the color side, despite the loss of one FC response, the picture remains essentially unchanged, as do the F per cent and the characteristic mental approach.

The Figure Drawings reflect this individual's changing self-concept, from her need for activity to an awareness of a more passive feminine role.

On the OVER-ALL EVALUATION this individual starts with a sum total of 26 points and achieves 32 on the retest.

In our opinion, genuine change has occurred only in the decrease of highly personalized and rather bizarre answers on the Comprehension, Reasoning and Judgment. However, this change, which is rare, seems to carry with it a very marked increase in the capacity to function more adequately.

(Records for SA6 will be found on pages 256-259, for SA7 on pages 260-263.)

SA7, married and in his mid-forties, was estimated clinically as between the second and third level on the over-all scale when he first consulted the therapist. He progressed, after brief psychotherapy, to between the level of 3 and 4.

At the time when the second psychological evaluation was made, SA7 had reached a point where, according to his therapist, there had been "a manifest reduction in tension, the absence of depression, and greater ease in handling his anxiety."

A comparison of the subtest scores reveals a clear-cut change of pattern on the Wechsler scattergram. By and large, it has been our finding that the scattergram does not change in its gestalt quality subsequent to successful therapy. SA7, however, is an exception.

The change here seems to parallel the clinical observations rather closely. There is indication of a capacity to work better in a pressureful, anxiety-producing situation. The arithmetical problems are now done in accordance with this individual's basic capacity rather than reflecting the kind of emotional tailspin which he went into in pressureful situations. There has also been a significant rise in the Similarities scores, reflecting a lessening of the highly personalized orientation originally noted.

The initial Figure Drawing was of a head so large that it took up the whole page. In accordance with other indications of less grandiose behavior, the second drawing portrays the individual in a less space-occupying way.

On the Rorschach, four of the six F− responses have been dropped. Characteristic of the record is a retrenchment rather than an expansion, a more careful approach to the task in hand. This has resulted in the loss of the impulsive CF and also of one form-color answer.

On the OVER-ALL EVALUATION, this individual netted a 25 score at the starting point and terminated with 27. Changes are indicated in both directions, suggesting that despite some improvement, there is still considerable flux and that a stabilized position has not yet been reached.*

---

*SA7 has since re-entered psychotherapy for more prolonged treatment.

===== **WORK SHEET** =====   *SA 6*

1

### VERBAL I. Q. = *104*

| EWS | Info. | Comp. | Digit | Arith. | Sim. |
|-----|-------|-------|-------|--------|------|
| 18 | 25 | 20 | | 14 | 23-24 |
| 17 | 24 | 19 | 17 | 13 | 21-22 |
| 16 | 23 | 18 | 16 | 12 | 20 |
| 15 | 21-22 | 17 | | 11 | 19 |
| 14 | (20) | 16 | 15 | | 17-18 |
| 13 | 18-19 | 15 | 14 | 10 | 16 |
| 12 | 17 | 14 | | 9 | 15 |
| 11 | 15-16 | 12-13 | (13) | | (13-14) |
| 10 | 13-14 | 11 | 12 | 8 | 12 |
| 9 | 12 | 10 | 11 | (7) | 11 |
| 8 | 10-11 | 9 | | | 9-10 |
| 7 | 9 | 8 | 10 | 6 | 8 |
| 6 | 7-8 | 7 | 9 | 5 | 7 |
| 5 | 6 | (5-6) | | | 5-6 |
| 4 | 4-5 | 4 | 8 | 4 | 4 |
| 3 | 2-3 | 3 | 7 | 3 | 3 |
| 2 | 1 | 2 | 6 | | 1-2 |
| 1 | 0 | 1 | | 2 | 0 |
| 0 | | 0 | 5 | 1 | |

### SZONDI

| SEXUAL | | PAROXYSMAL | | EGO | | CONTACT | |
|--------|---|------------|----|-----|---|---------|---|
| h | s | e | hy | k | p | d | m |
| | | | | | X | | |
| | | | | | X | X | X |
| | | | | X | X | X | XX |
| | | | | X | X | X | X |
| X | X | X | X | | | | X |
| X | X | X | X | | | | |
| X | X | X | | | | | |

### OVER-ALL EVALUATION = *26*

| | | | | | |
|---|---|---|---|---|---|
| OVER-ALL RATING | 1 | 2 | 3 | 4 | 5 |
| PRODUCTIVITY | 1 | 2 | 3 | (4) | 5 |
| RELATION TO REALITY | 1 | (2) | 3 | 4 | 5 |
| THOUGHT CONTENT | 1 | 2 | 3 | (4) | 5 |
| CONSTRUCTIVE FANTASY | 1 | 2 | (3) | 4 | 5 |
| DRIVE | 1 | 2 | (3) | 4 | 5 |
| EMOTIONAL TONE | 1 | 2 | (3) | 4 | 5 |
| SOCIAL ATTITUDE | 1 | 2 | (3) | 4 | 5 |
| ANXIETY | 1 | (2) | 3 | 4 | 5 |
| I. Q. RATING *104* | 1 | (2) | 3 | 4 | 5 |

### RORSCHACH

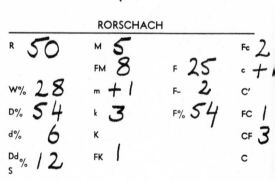

| R *50* | M *5* | | Fc *2* |
|--------|-------|------|--------|
| | FM *8* | F *25* | c *+* |
| W% *28* | m *+1* | F- *2* | C' |
| D% *54* | k *3* | F% *54* | FC *1* |
| d% *6* | K | | CF *3* |
| Dd% S *12* | FK *1* | | C |

## WORK SHEET

SA 6

2

### VERBAL I. Q. = 127

| EWS | Info. | Comp. | Digit | Arith. | Sim. |
|---|---|---|---|---|---|
| 18 | 25 | 20 | | 14 | 23-24 |
| 17 | 24 | 19 | 17 | 13 | 21-22 |
| 16 | (23) | 18 | 16 | 12 | 20 |
| 15 | 21-22 | 17 | | 11 | 19 |
| 14 | 20 | 16 | 15 | | (17-18) |
| 13 | 18-19 | 15 | 14 | 10 | 16 |
| 12 | 17 | 14 | | (9) | 15 |
| 11 | 15-16 | (12-13) | 13 | | 13-14 |
| 10 | 13-14 | 11 | 12 | 8 | 12 |
| 9 | 12 | 10 | 11 | 7 | 11 |
| 8 | 10-11 | 9 | | | 9-10 |
| 7 | 9 | 8 | 10 | 6 | 8 |
| 6 | 7-8 | 7 | 9 | 5 | 7 |
| 5 | 6 | 5-6 | | | 5-6 |
| 4 | 4-5 | 4 | 8 | 4 | 4 |
| 3 | 2-3 | 3 | 7 | 3 | 3 |
| 2 | 1 | 2 | 6 | | 1-2 |
| 1 | 0 | 1 | | 2 | 0 |
| 0 | | 0 | 5 | 1 | |

### SZONDI

| SEXUAL | | PAROXYSMAL | | EGO | | CONTACT | |
|---|---|---|---|---|---|---|---|
| h | s | e | hy | k | p | d | m |
| | | | | | X | | |
| | | | | | X | | |
| | | | X | | X | | |
| | | | X | | X | | X |
| | | | | | X | | X |
| | | X | X | | X | X | X |
| X | X | X | X | X | X | | X |
| | X | X | | X | | | |
| | X | | | | | | |
| | X | | | | | | |
| | X | | | | | | |

### OVER-ALL EVALUATION = 32

| | 1 | 2 | 3 | 4 | 5 |
|---|---|---|---|---|---|
| OVER-ALL RATING | 1 | 2 | 3 | 4 | 5 |
| PRODUCTIVITY | 1 | 2 | 3 | 4 | (5) |
| RELATION TO REALITY | 1 | 2 | (3) | 4 | 5 |
| THOUGHT CONTENT | 1 | 2 | 3 | (4) | 5 |
| CONSTRUCTIVE FANTASY | 1 | 2 | 3 | 4 | (5) |
| DRIVE | 1 | (2) | 3 | 4 | 5 |
| EMOTIONAL TONE | 1 | 2 | (3) | 4 | 5 |
| SOCIAL ATTITUDE | 1 | 2 | (3) | 4 | 5 |
| ANXIETY | 1 | 2 | (3) | 4 | 5 |
| I. Q. RATING  127 | 1 | 2 | 3 | (4) | 5 |

### RORSCHACH

R 62    M 10      Fc 2

FM 8    F 28    c +1

W% 24    m +3    F- 8    C' 1

D% 44    k 2    F% 58    FC

d% 8    K 1      CF 2+1

Dd% 24    FK +1      C
S

# SUMMARY OF TEST FINDINGS          *SA 6*

## MANNER DURING TEST

| (1) Overly distressed | (2) Tense | (3) Indifferent | (4) Appropriate | (5) Relaxed and actively interested |
|---|---|---|---|---|
| (1) Hostile | (2) *Uneasy* | | | |

## I.Q. (Bellevue-Wechsler)

| (1) Below average | (2) *Average* | (3) High average | (4) Superior | (5) Very superior |
|---|---|---|---|---|

## PRODUCTIVITY (Rorschach)

| (1) Impoverished | (2) Reduced output | (3) Adequate | (4) *Better than average* | (5) Rich and well-ordered |
|---|---|---|---|---|
| | (2) Compulsive productivity | | | |

## RELATION TO REALITY (Rorschach, Bellevue-Wechsler, Drawings)

| (1) Loose | (2) *Lapses—together with good form* | (3) Not noticeably disturbed | (4) Essentially firm | (5) Firm and good |
|---|---|---|---|---|

## USUAL-UNUSUAL THOUGHT CONTENT (Rorschach, Unpleasant Concept)

| (1) Bizarre | (2) Tendency toward the bizarre | (3) Adequate | (4) *Original trends* | (5) Outstandingly original |
|---|---|---|---|---|
| (1) Stereotyped | (2) Tendency toward stereotypy | | | |

## CONSTRUCTIVE FANTASY (Rorschach)

| (1) Absent | (2) Barely accessible | (3) *Accessible* | (4) Readily accessible | (5) Active but not hampering |
|---|---|---|---|---|
| (1) Withdrawal into fantasy | | | | |

## DRIVE (Rorschach, Szondi, Unpleasant Concept)

| (1) Overpowering aggression | (2) Over-aggressive | (3) *Adequate* | (4) Clearly sufficient | (5) Sufficient— exceptionally well-directed |
|---|---|---|---|---|
| (1) Hampering passivity | (2) Insufficient drive | | | |

## EMOTIONAL TONE (Rorschach, Szondi)

| (1) Explosive emotions | (2) Getting out of hand | (3) *Trend toward emotional expression* | (4) Warmth available | (5) Warm, readily available |
|---|---|---|---|---|
| (1) Lacking | (2) Indicated but repressed emotions | | | |

## SOCIAL ATTITUDE (T. A. T.)

| (1) Uncontrolled | (2) Constricted or neglected | (3) *Adequate* | (4) Well-regulated | (5) Free and flexible |
|---|---|---|---|---|

## ANXIETY

| (1) Disintegrating | (2) *Marked* | (3) Moderate | (4) Not marked | (5) Lack of evidence of anxiety |
|---|---|---|---|---|

## OVER-ALL EVALUATION

| (1) Markedly disturbed personality | (2) *Less than adequate personality with some psychological problems* | (3) Adequate personality | (4) Better than average functioning personality | (5) Exceptionally well-integrated personality with excellent potential |
|---|---|---|---|---|

## SUMMARY OF THERAPIST'S FINDINGS  *SA 6*

### ESTIMATED INTELLIGENCE LEVEL

| (1) Below average | (2) Average | (3) High average | (4) Superior | (5) Very superior |
|---|---|---|---|---|

### FLOW OF ASSOCIATIVE MATERIAL

| (1) Impoverished | (2) Reduced output | (3) Adequate | (4) Better than average | (5) Rich and well-ordered |
|---|---|---|---|---|
| | (2) Compulsive productivity | | | |

### RELATION TO REALITY

| (1) Loose | (2) Lapses—together with good form | (3) Not noticeably disturbed | (4) Essentially firm | (5) Firm and good |
|---|---|---|---|---|

### USUAL-UNUSUAL THOUGHT CONTENT

| (1) Bizarre | (2) Tendency toward the bizarre | (3) Adequate | (4) Original trends | (5) Outstandingly original |
|---|---|---|---|---|
| (1) Stereotyped | (2) Tendency toward stereotypy | | | |

### CONSTRUCTIVE FANTASY

| (1) Absent | (2) Barely accessible | (3) Accessible | (4) Readily accessible | (5) Active but not hampering |
|---|---|---|---|---|
| (1) Withdrawal into fantasy | | | | |

### DRIVE

| (1) Overpowering aggression | (2) Over-aggressive | (3) Adequate | (4) Clearly sufficient | (5) Sufficient—exceptionally well-directed |
|---|---|---|---|---|
| (1) Hampering passivity | (2) Insufficient drive | | | |

### EMOTIONAL TONE

| (1) Explosive emotions | (2) Getting out of hand | (3) Trend toward emotional expression | (4) Warmth available | (5) Warm, readily available |
|---|---|---|---|---|
| (1) Lacking | (2) Indicated but repressed emotions | | | |

### SOCIAL ATTITUDE

| (1) Uncontrolled | (2) Constricted or neglected | (3) Adequate | (4) Well-regulated | (5) Free and flexible |
|---|---|---|---|---|

### ANXIETY

| (1) Disintegrating | (2) Marked | (3) Moderate | (4) Not marked | (5) Lack of evidence of anxiety |
|---|---|---|---|---|

### OVER-ALL EVALUATION

| (1) Markedly disturbed personality | (2) Less than adequate personality with some psychological problems | (3) Adequate personality | (4) Better than average functioning personality | (5) Exceptionally well-integrated personality with excellent potential |
|---|---|---|---|---|

# WORK SHEET —— *SA 7*

*1*

## VERBAL I. Q. = *114*

| EWS | Info. | Comp. | Digit | Arith. | Sim. |
|-----|-------|-------|-------|--------|------|
| 18 | 25 | 20 |  | 14 | 23-24 |
| 17 | 24 | 19 | 17 | 13 | 21-22 |
| 16 | 23 | 18 | 16 | 12 | 20 |
| 15 | 21-22 | 17 |  | 11 | 19 |
| 14 | 20 | 16 | 15 |  | 17-18 |
| 13 | 18-19 | 15 | 14 | 10 | 16 |
| 12 | 17 | 14 |  | 9 | 15 |
|  |  |  |  |  |  |
| 11 | 15-16 | 12-13 | 13 |  | 13-14 |
| 10 | 13-14 | 11 | 12 | 8 | 12 |
| 9 | 12 | 10 | 11 | 7 | 11 |
| 8 | 10-11 | 9 |  |  | 9-10 |
| 7 | 9 | 8 | 10 | 6 | 8 |
| 6 | 7-8 | 7 | 9 | 5 | 7 |
|  |  |  |  |  |  |
| 5 | 6 | 5-6 |  |  | 5-6 |
| 4 | 4-5 | 4 | 8 | 4 | 4 |
| 3 | 2-3 | 3 | 7 | 3 | 3 |
| 2 | 1 | 2 | 6 |  | 1-2 |
| 1 | 0 | 1 |  | 2 | 0 |
| 0 |  | 0 | 5 | 1 |  |

## SZONDI

| SEXUAL | | PAROXYSMAL | | EGO | | CONTACT | |
|--------|--------|--------|--------|--------|--------|--------|--------|
| h | s | e | hy | k | p | d | m |
|  |  |  |  |  |  |  | X |
|  |  |  |  |  |  |  | X |
|  |  |  |  |  |  |  | X |
|  |  | X |  |  |  |  | X |
| X | X |  | X | X | X | X | X |
| X | X | X | X | X |  |  |  |
| X | X |  | X | X |  |  |  |
| X |  |  | X |  |  |  |  |
|  |  |  | X |  |  |  |  |

## OVER-ALL EVALUATION = *25*

|  | | | | | |
|---|---|---|---|---|---|
| OVER-ALL RATING | 1 | 2 | 3 | 4 | 5 |
| PRODUCTIVITY | 1 | 2 | ③ | 4 | 5 |
| RELATION TO REALITY | 1 | ② | 3 | 4 | 5 |
| THOUGHT CONTENT | 1 | 2 | ③ | 4 | 5 |
| CONSTRUCTIVE FANTASY | 1 | 2 | ③ | 4 | 5 |
| DRIVE | 1 | 2 | ③ | 4 | 5 |
| EMOTIONAL TONE | 1 | 2 | ③ | 4 | 5 |
| SOCIAL ATTITUDE | 1 | 2 | ③ | 4 | 5 |
| ANXIETY | 1 | ② | 3 | 4 | 5 |
| I. Q. RATING  *114* | 1 | 2 | ③ | 4 | 5 |

## RORSCHACH

| | | | | | |
|---|---|---|---|---|---|
| R *36* | M *3* | | | Fc *3* |
| | FM *2* | F *16* | | c *2* |
| W% *25* | m *+1* | F- *6* | | C' |
| D% *56* | k | F% *61* | | FC *2* |
| d% *6* | K *1* | | | CF *1* |
| Dd% *13*  S | FK | | | C |

# WORK SHEET     *SA 7*

*2*

## VERBAL I. Q. = *130*

| EWS | Info. | Comp. | Digit | Arith. | Sim. |
|---|---|---|---|---|---|
| 18 | 25 | 20 | | 14 | 23-24 |
| 17 | 24 | 19 | 17 | 13 | 21-22 |
| 16 | 23 | 18 | 16 | 12 | 20 |
| 15 | 21-22 | 17 | | 11 | 19 |
| 14 | 20 | 16 | 15 | | 17-18 |
| 13 | 18-19 | 15 | 14 | 10 | 16 |
| 12 | 17 | 14 | | 9 | 15 |
| | | | | | |
| 11 | 15-16 | 12-13 | 13 | | 13-14 |
| 10 | 13-14 | 11 | 12 | 8 | 12 |
| 9 | 12 | 10 | 11 | 7 | 11 |
| 8 | 10-11 | 9 | | | 9-10 |
| 7 | 9 | 8 | 10 | 6 | 8 |
| 6 | 7-8 | 7 | 9 | 5 | 7 |
| | | | | | |
| 5 | 6 | 5-6 | | | 5-6 |
| 4 | 4-5 | 4 | 8 | 4 | 4 |
| 3 | 2-3 | 3 | 7 | 3 | 3 |
| 2 | 1 | 2 | 6 | | 1-2 |
| 1 | 0 | 1 | | 2 | 0 |
| 0 | | 0 | 5 | 1 | |

## SZONDI

| SEXUAL | | PAROXYSMAL | | EGO | | CONTACT | |
|---|---|---|---|---|---|---|---|
| h | s | e | hy | k | p | d | m |
| | | | | | X | | X |
| | | | | | | | X |
| | | X | | | X | | X |
| X | X | X | X | | X | X | X |
| | X | | X | X | X | X | |
| | X | | X | X | X | X | |
| | | | X | X | | | |

OVER-ALL EVALUATION = *27*

| | | | | | |
|---|---|---|---|---|---|
| OVER-ALL RATING | 1 | 2 | 3 | 4 | 5 |
| PRODUCTIVITY | 1 | 2 | ③ | 4 | 5 |
| RELATION TO REALITY | 1 | 2 | ③ | 4 | 5 |
| THOUGHT CONTENT | 1 | 2 | ③ | 4 | 5 |
| CONSTRUCTIVE FANTASY | 1 | ② | 3 | 4 | 5 |
| DRIVE | 1 | 2 | ③ | 4 | 5 |
| EMOTIONAL TONE | 1 | ② | 3 | 4 | 5 |
| SOCIAL ATTITUDE | 1 | 2 | ③ | 4 | 5 |
| ANXIETY | 1 | 2 | ③ | 4 | 5 |
| I. Q. RATING *130* | 1 | 2 | 3 | 4 | ⑤ |

## RORSCHACH

| | | | | | | |
|---|---|---|---|---|---|---|
| R | 29 | M | 2 | | Fc | 1 |
| | | FM | 4 | F *15* | c | 2 |
| W% | 28 | m | +1 | F- 2 | C' | |
| D% | 59 | k | | F% 59 | FC | 1 |
| d% | 3 | K | 1 | | CF | |
| Dd% | 10 | FK | 1 | | C | |
| S | | | | | | |

## SUMMARY OF TEST FINDINGS  *SA 7*

### MANNER DURING TEST

| (1) Overly distressed | (2) Tense | (3) Indifferent | (4) Appropriate | (5) Relaxed and actively interested |
|---|---|---|---|---|
| (1) Hostile | (2) Uneasy | | | |

### I.Q. (Bellevue-Wechsler)

| (1) Below average | (2) Average | (3) High average | (4) Superior | (5) Very superior |
|---|---|---|---|---|

### PRODUCTIVITY (Rorschach)

| (1) Impoverished | (2) Reduced output | (3) Adequate | (4) Better than average | (5) Rich and well-ordered |
|---|---|---|---|---|
| | (2) Compulsive productivity | | | |

### RELATION TO REALITY (Rorschach, Bellevue-Wechsler, Drawings)

| (1) Loose | (2) Lapses—together with good form | (3) Not noticeably disturbed | (4) Essentially firm | (5) Firm and good |
|---|---|---|---|---|

### USUAL-UNUSUAL THOUGHT CONTENT (Rorschach, Unpleasant Concept)

| (1) Bizarre | (2) Tendency toward the bizarre | (3) Adequate | (4) Original trends | (5) Outstandingly original |
|---|---|---|---|---|
| (1) Stereotyped | (2) Tendency toward stereotypy | | | |

### CONSTRUCTIVE FANTASY (Rorschach)

| (1) Absent | (2) Barely accessible | (3) Accessible | (4) Readily accessible | (5) Active but not hampering |
|---|---|---|---|---|
| (1) Withdrawal into fantasy | | | | |

### DRIVE (Rorschach, Szondi, Unpleasant Concept)

| (1) Overpowering aggression | (2) Over-aggressive | (3) Adequate | (4) Clearly sufficient | (5) Sufficient—exceptionally well-directed |
|---|---|---|---|---|
| (1) Hampering passivity | (2) Insufficient drive | | | |

### EMOTIONAL TONE (Rorschach, Szondi)

| (1) Explosive emotions | (2) Getting out of hand | (3) Trend toward emotional expression | (4) Warmth available | (5) Warm, readily available |
|---|---|---|---|---|
| (1) Lacking | (2) Indicated but repressed emotions | | | |

### SOCIAL ATTITUDE (T. A. T.)

| (1) Uncontrolled | (2) Constricted or neglected | (3) Adequate | (4) Well-regulated | (5) Free and flexible |
|---|---|---|---|---|

### ANXIETY

| (1) Disintegrating | (2) Marked | (3) Moderate | (4) Not marked | (5) Lack of evidence of anxiety |
|---|---|---|---|---|

### OVER-ALL EVALUATION

| (1) Markedly disturbed personality | (2) Less than adequate personality with some psychological problems | (3) Adequate personality | (4) Better than average functioning personality | (5) Exceptionally well-integrated personality with excellent potential |
|---|---|---|---|---|

## SUMMARY OF THERAPIST'S FINDINGS   SA 7

### ESTIMATED INTELLIGENCE LEVEL

| (1) Below average | (2) Average | (3) High average | (4) *Superior* | (5) Very superior |
|---|---|---|---|---|

### FLOW OF ASSOCIATIVE MATERIAL

| (1) Impoverished | (2) Reduced output | (3) *Adequate* | (4) Better than average | (5) Rich and well-ordered |
|---|---|---|---|---|
| | (2) Compulsive productivity | | | |

### RELATION TO REALITY

| (1) Loose | (2) Lapses—together with good form | (3) *Not noticeably disturbed* | (4) Essentially firm | (5) Firm and good |
|---|---|---|---|---|

### USUAL-UNUSUAL THOUGHT CONTENT

| (1) Bizarre | (2) Tendency toward the bizarre | (3) Adequate | (4) *Original trends* | (5) Outstandingly original |
|---|---|---|---|---|
| (1) Stereotyped | (2) Tendency toward stereotypy | | | |

### CONSTRUCTIVE FANTASY

| (1) Absent | (2) Barely accessible | (3) *Accessible* | (4) Readily accessible | (5) Active but not hampering |
|---|---|---|---|---|
| (1) Withdrawal into fantasy | | | | |

### DRIVE

| (1) Overpowering aggression | (2) Over-aggressive | (3) Adequate | (4) *Clearly sufficient* | (5) Sufficient—exceptionally well-directed |
|---|---|---|---|---|
| (1) Hampering passivity | (2) Insufficient drive | | | |

### EMOTIONAL TONE

| (1) Explosive emotions | (2) Getting out of hand | (3) Trend toward emotional expression | (4) *Warmth available* | (5) Warm, readily available |
|---|---|---|---|---|
| (1) Lacking | (2) Indicated but repressed emotions | | | |

### SOCIAL ATTITUDE

| (1) Uncontrolled | (2) Constricted or neglected | (3) *Adequate* | (4) Well-regulated | (5) Free and flexible |
|---|---|---|---|---|

### ANXIETY

| (1) Disintegrating | (2) Marked | (3) *Moderate* | (4) Not marked | (5) Lack of evidence of anxiety |
|---|---|---|---|---|

### OVER-ALL EVALUATION

| (1) Markedly disturbed personality | (2) Less than adequate personality with some psychological problems | (3) *Adequate personality* | (4) Better than average functioning personality | (5) Exceptionally well-integrated personality with excellent potential |
|---|---|---|---|---|

SA8 was rated by his therapist as at the level of 2 on the OVER-ALL EVALUATION at the time of first seeking help and to have improved to a 3+ level at the termination of this phase of therapy. Follow-up after several years reveals that he has retained the gains described by his therapist and reflected in the performance at the time of the second testing.

Comparison of the subtests in the Bellevue-Wechsler reveals little change either in the level or pattern of the scattergram. SA8 fell into the *Very Superior Group* of the total population at the start of treatment and remained in this category. The rise of two points in the Similarities is consistent with the total gain shown elsewhere but cannot be considered significant in its own right.

At the time of retesting, virtually no change had occurred in the Szondi, only one vector showing a different distribution.

The Rorschach indicated, however, a rather marked expansion of personality, particularly in the emergence of the all-important FC responses totally absent in Record 1. In Record 2 there are five strong animal movement responses, a mode of expression which had been completely denied before. Human movement responses have risen from one to three and are of an acceptable, realistic variety. The undifferentiated whole responses, which were characteristic of Record 1 and which netted this individual a 91 per cent W, have been diluted on the later testing by more adequate perception of detail. The peculiar personal problem, epitomized in the drawings in Record 1, has ceased to intrude in Record 2, although the rigid and unbending concept of the female is still portrayed.

On the OVER-ALL EVALUATION SA8, who started with a score of 26, progresses to 34 at the time of retesting.

(The records of SA8 will be found on pages 266-269.)

The findings here would seem to suggest that retesting immediately on termination of brief psychotherapy results, on occasion, in second test profiles which have much in common with those of patients tested in "mid-stream" during long-term therapy. The clinical improvement at the termination of brief psychotherapy of the SA group (SA 1-8) can be vouched for by this examiner as well as the therapist. Yet, we cannot help feeling that the impact made on the second tests is a weak one. Improvement on the tests is not as marked as that found subsequent to long-term psychotherapy, and it does not match in dramaticness or impact the actual behavioral changes and loss of symptoms.

Our feeling is that *time* is necessary for changes to become sufficiently a part of the personality so that they register through the medium of the test material. We have had an opportunity to test this hypothesis by the retesting, after a ten-year period, of two individuals treated by brief psychotherapy whose records at the termination of treatment did not carry the full impact of the clinical improvement. After the ten-year interval, the projective material was found to mirror the change which had taken place behaviorally (see Chapter XIV).

# WORK SHEET

*SA 8*

## VERBAL I. Q.

| EWS | Info. | Comp. | Digit | Arith. | Sim. |
|-----|-------|-------|-------|--------|------|
| 18 | 25 | 20 | | 14 | 23-24 |
| 17 | 24 | 19 | 17 | 13 | 21-22 |
| 16 | 23 | 18 | 16 | 12 | 20 |
| 15 | 21-22 | 17 | | 11 | 19 |
| 14 | 20 | 16 | 15 | | 17-18 |
| 13 | 18-19 | 15 | 14 | 10 | 16 |
| 12 | 17 | 14 | | 9 | 15 |
| | | | | | |
| 11 | 15-16 | 12-13 | 13 | | 13-14 |
| 10 | 13-14 | 11 | 12 | 8 | 12 |
| 9 | 12 | 10 | 11 | 7 | 11 |
| 8 | 10-11 | 9 | | | 9-10 |
| 7 | 9 | 8 | 10 | 6 | 8 |
| 6 | 7-8 | 7 | 9 | 5 | 7 |
| | | | | | |
| 5 | 6 | 5-6 | | | 5-6 |
| 4 | 4-5 | 4 | 8 | 4 | 4 |
| 3 | 2-3 | 3 | 7 | 3 | 3 |
| 2 | 1 | 2 | 6 | | 1-2 |
| 1 | 0 | 1 | | 2 | 0 |
| 0 | | 0 | 5 | 1 | |

## SZONDI

| SEXUAL | | PAROXYSMAL | | EGO | | CONTACT | |
|--------|---|------------|----|-----|---|---------|---|
| h | s | e | hy | k | p | d | m |

## RORSCHACH

| R | 11 | M | 1 | | | Fc | |
|---|----|---|---|---|---|----|---|
| | | FM | | F | 5 | c | 1 |
| W% | 91 | m | | F- | 2 | C' | |
| D% | 9 | k | 1 | F% | 64 | FC | |
| d% | | K | | | | CF | 1- |
| Dd% | | FK | | | | C | |
| S | | | | | | | |

# WORK SHEET
## -2-

SA 8

## VERBAL I. Q.

| EWS | Info. | Comp. | Digit | Arith. | Sim. |
|---|---|---|---|---|---|
| 18 | 25 | 20 | | 14 | 23-24 |
| 17 | 24 | 19 | 17 | 13 | 21-22 |
| 16 | 23 | 18 | 16 | 12 | 20 |
| 15 | 21-22 | 17 | | 11 | 19 |
| 14 | 20 | 16 | 15 | | 17-18 |
| 13 | 18-19 | 15 | 14 | 10 | 16 |
| 12 | 17 | 14 | | 9 | 15 |
| | | | | | |
| 11 | 15-16 | 12-13 | 13 | | 13-14 |
| 10 | 13-14 | 11 | 12 | 8 | 12 |
| 9 | 12 | 10 | 11 | 7 | 11 |
| 8 | 10-11 | 9 | | | 9-10 |
| 7 | 9 | 8 | 10 | 6 | 8 |
| 6 | 7-8 | 7 | 9 | 5 | 7 |
| | | | | | |
| 5 | 6 | 5-6 | | | 5-6 |
| 4 | 4-5 | 4 | 8 | 4 | 4 |
| 3 | 2-3 | 3 | 7 | 3 | 3 |
| 2 | 1 | 2 | 6 | | 1-2 |
| 1 | 0 | 1 | | 2 | 0 |
| 0 | | 0 | 5 | 1 | |

## SZONDI

| SEXUAL | | PAROXYSMAL | | EGO | | CONTACT | |
|---|---|---|---|---|---|---|---|
| h | s | e | hy | k | p | d | m |
| | X | | | | | | X |
| | X | | | | | | X |
| | X | X | | | | | X |
| X | X | X | | X | | | X |
| | X | | X | X | X | X | X |
| | X | | X | X | | | |
| | | | X | X | | | |
| | | | | X | | | |

## RORSCHACH

| R | 31 | M | 3 | | | Fc | 1 |
|---|---|---|---|---|---|---|---|
| | | FM | 5 | F | 13 | c | |
| W% | 55 | m | +1 | F- | 1 | C' | |
| D% | 45 | k | | F% | 45 | FC | 6 |
| d% | | K | | | | CF | 1 |
| Dd% | | FK | | | | C | 1 |
| S | | | | | | | |

## SUMMARY OF TEST FINDINGS  *SA 8*

### MANNER DURING TEST

| (1) Overly distressed | (2) Tense | (3) Indifferent | (4) Appropriate | (5) Relaxed and actively interested |
|---|---|---|---|---|
| (1) ~~Hostile~~ | (2) Uneasy | | | |

### I.Q. (Bellevue-Wechsler)

| (1) Below average | (2) Average | (3) High average | (4) Superior | (5) Very superior |
|---|---|---|---|---|

### PRODUCTIVITY (Rorschach)

| (1) Impoverished | (2) Reduced output | (3) Adequate | (4) Better than average | (5) Rich and well-ordered |
|---|---|---|---|---|
| | (2) Compulsive productivity | | | |

### RELATION TO REALITY (Rorschach, Bellevue-Wechsler, Drawings)

| (1) Loose | (2) Lapses—together with good form | (3) Not noticeably disturbed | (4) Essentially firm | (5) Firm and good |
|---|---|---|---|---|

### USUAL-UNUSUAL THOUGHT CONTENT (Rorschach, Unpleasant Concept)

| (1) Bizarre | (2) Tendency toward the bizarre | (3) Adequate | (4) Original trends | (5) Outstandingly original |
|---|---|---|---|---|
| (1) Stereotyped | (2) Tendency toward stereotypy | | | |

### CONSTRUCTIVE FANTASY (Rorschach)

| (1) Absent | (2) Barely accessible | (3) Accessible | (4) Readily accessible | (5) Active but not hampering |
|---|---|---|---|---|
| (1) Withdrawal into fantasy | | | | |

### DRIVE (Rorschach, Szondi, Unpleasant Concept)

| (1) Overpowering aggression | (2) Over-aggressive | (3) Adequate | (4) Clearly sufficient | (5) Sufficient—exceptionally well-directed |
|---|---|---|---|---|
| (1) Hampering passivity | (2) Insufficient drive | | | |

### EMOTIONAL TONE (Rorschach, Szondi)

| (1) Explosive emotions | (2) Getting out of hand | (3) Trend toward emotional expression | (4) Warmth available | (5) Warm, readily available |
|---|---|---|---|---|
| (1) Lacking | (2) Indicated but repressed emotions | | | |

### SOCIAL ATTITUDE (T. A. T.)

| (1) Uncontrolled | (2) Constricted or neglected | (3) Adequate | (4) Well-regulated | (5) Free and flexible |
|---|---|---|---|---|

### ANXIETY

| (1) Disintegrating | (2) Marked | (3) Moderate | (4) Not marked | (5) Lack of evidence of anxiety |
|---|---|---|---|---|

### OVER-ALL EVALUATION

| (1) Markedly disturbed personality | (2) Less than adequate personality with some psychological problems | (3) Adequate personality | (4) Better than average functioning personality | (5) Exceptionally well-integrated personality with excellent potential |
|---|---|---|---|---|

## SUMMARY OF THERAPIST'S FINDINGS     *SA8*

### ESTIMATED INTELLIGENCE LEVEL

| (1) Below average | (2) Average | (3) High average | (4) Superior | (5) Very superior |
|---|---|---|---|---|

### FLOW OF ASSOCIATIVE MATERIAL

| (1) Impoverished | (2) Reduced output | (3) Adequate | (4) Better than average | (5) Rich and well-ordered |
|---|---|---|---|---|
| | (2) Compulsive productivity | | | |

### RELATION TO REALITY

| (1) Loose | (2) Lapses—together with good form | (3) Not noticeably disturbed | (4) Essentially firm | (5) Firm and good |
|---|---|---|---|---|

### USUAL-UNUSUAL THOUGHT CONTENT

| (1) Bizarre | (2) Tendency toward the bizarre | (3) Adequate | (4) Original trends | (5) Outstandingly original |
|---|---|---|---|---|
| (1) Stereotyped | (2) Tendency toward stereotypy | | | |

### CONSTRUCTIVE FANTASY

| (1) Absent | (2) Barely accessible | (3) Accessible | (4) Readily accessible | (5) Active but not hampering |
|---|---|---|---|---|
| (1) Withdrawal into fantasy | | | | |

### DRIVE

| (1) Overpowering aggression | (2) Over-aggressive | (3) Adequate | (4) Clearly sufficient | (5) Sufficient—exceptionally well-directed |
|---|---|---|---|---|
| (1) Hampering passivity | (2) Insufficient drive | | | |

### EMOTIONAL TONE

| (1) Explosive emotions | (2) Getting out of hand | (3) Trend toward emotional expression | (4) Warmth available | (5) Warm, readily available |
|---|---|---|---|---|
| (1) Lacking | (2) Indicated but repressed emotions | | | |

### SOCIAL ATTITUDE

| (1) Uncontrolled | (2) Constricted or neglected | (3) Adequate | (4) Well-regulated | (5) Free and flexible |
|---|---|---|---|---|

### ANXIETY

| (1) Disintegrating | (2) Marked | (3) Moderate | (4) Not marked | (5) Lack of evidence of anxiety |
|---|---|---|---|---|

### OVER-ALL EVALUATION

| (1) Markedly disturbed personality | (2) Less than adequate personality with some psychological problems | (3) Adequate personality | (4) Better than average functioning personality | (5) Exceptionally well-integrated personality with excellent potential |
|---|---|---|---|---|

## XIII. Retesting following brief psychotherapy.
## Unsuccessful cases.

SA10 was in his middle forties and unmarried at the time of the first testing when he entered psychotherapy. He had married at the time of the follow-up four years later.

This patient was rated by his therapist as between 1 and 2 on the OVER-ALL EVALUATION scale in terms of the acuteness of his disturbance at the start of therapy, and was again so rated at the end of the therapeutic period. Moreover, no further progress in terms of alleviation of the presenting symptoms could be found at the time of the four-year follow-up.

A comparison of the subtests on the Bellevue-Wechsler reveals improvement in the Comprehension scores. The near-bizarre responses have dropped out of the second testing. The change on the Szondi is in the direction of less repression within the ego. On the other hand, this particular constellation of +h, –s, and loaded +p is an unfavorable one in some male subjects.

Although the total R on the Rorschach has risen somewhat in the second record, the essential pattern of the psychogram remains the same. The Drawings are at an equally anxiety-ridden and immature level. There is nothing in the Sentence Completion to confirm the change in the Comprehension, so that in essence the total test picture remains unaltered.

The OVER-ALL EVALUATION on the quantitative scale for this individual shows 19 on both the first and second testing.

(The records of SA10 will be found on pages 272-275, of SA11 on pages 276-279.)

SA11 was between the ages of 25 and 30 at the start of his treatment, and was rated by the therapist at this time as profoundly disturbed. His condition was considered unchanged at the time of retesting, and the diagnosis was equally serious at the time of the four-year follow-up.

Comparison of the subtests on the verbal Bellevue-Wechsler shows a marked scatter on both the test and retest scores. Very slight improvement is indicated in the Similarities on the second record, but the essential quality of unevenness of performance still remains.

The total R on the Rorschach has more than doubled in the second testing, so that SA11 gains a point in regard to this in the OVER-ALL

EVALUATION quantitative scale. There is also a dropping out of two CF responses and a gain of one FC, which would be considered as movement in the right direction. On the other hand, two bizarre F– answers have crept in, so that improvement in this test is questionable.

Although he is now able to portray the total human figure, in contrast to the heads in Record 1, the primitive quality of the drawing is obvious; the juxtaposition of the naked breasts and the sacklike garment bespeaks the lack of realistic handling. The quantitative scores are 23 and 24—an insignificant change.

# WORK SHEET — SA10

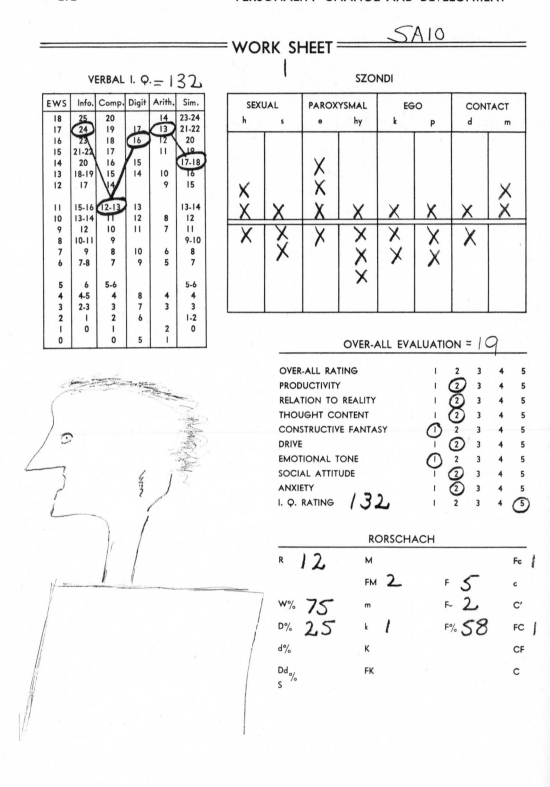

VERBAL I. Q. = 132

| EWS | Info. | Comp. | Digit | Arith. | Sim. |
|---|---|---|---|---|---|
| 18 | 25 | 20 | | 14 | 23-24 |
| 17 | 24 | 19 | 17 | 13 | 21-22 |
| 16 | 23 | 18 | 16 | 12 | 20 |
| 15 | 21-22 | 17 | | 11 | 19 |
| 14 | 20 | 16 | 15 | | 17-18 |
| 13 | 18-19 | 15 | 14 | 10 | 16 |
| 12 | 17 | 14 | | 9 | 15 |
| 11 | 15-16 | 12-13 | 13 | | 13-14 |
| 10 | 13-14 | 11 | 12 | 8 | 12 |
| 9 | 12 | 10 | 11 | 7 | 11 |
| 8 | 10-11 | 9 | | | 9-10 |
| 7 | 9 | 8 | 10 | 6 | 8 |
| 6 | 7-8 | 7 | 9 | 5 | 7 |
| 5 | 6 | 5-6 | | | 5-6 |
| 4 | 4-5 | 4 | 8 | 4 | 4 |
| 3 | 2-3 | 3 | 7 | 3 | 3 |
| 2 | 1 | 2 | 6 | | 1-2 |
| 1 | 0 | 1 | | 2 | 0 |
| 0 | | 0 | 5 | 1 | |

## SZONDI

| SEXUAL | | PAROXYSMAL | | EGO | | CONTACT | |
|---|---|---|---|---|---|---|---|
| h | s | e | hy | k | p | d | m |

## OVER-ALL EVALUATION = 19

| | 1 | 2 | 3 | 4 | 5 |
|---|---|---|---|---|---|
| OVER-ALL RATING | 1 | 2 | 3 | 4 | 5 |
| PRODUCTIVITY | 1 | (2) | 3 | 4 | 5 |
| RELATION TO REALITY | 1 | (2) | 3 | 4 | 5 |
| THOUGHT CONTENT | 1 | (2) | 3 | 4 | 5 |
| CONSTRUCTIVE FANTASY | (1) | 2 | 3 | 4 | 5 |
| DRIVE | 1 | (2) | 3 | 4 | 5 |
| EMOTIONAL TONE | (1) | 2 | 3 | 4 | 5 |
| SOCIAL ATTITUDE | 1 | (2) | 3 | 4 | 5 |
| ANXIETY | 1 | (2) | 3 | 4 | 5 |
| I. Q. RATING  132 | 1 | 2 | 3 | 4 | (5) |

## RORSCHACH

| | | | | | |
|---|---|---|---|---|---|
| R | 12 | M | | Fc | 1 |
| | | FM | 2 | F | 5 | c | |
| W% | 75 | m | | F- | 2 | C' | |
| D% | 25 | k | 1 | F% | 58 | FC | 1 |
| d% | | K | | | | CF | |
| Dd% | | FK | | | | C | |
| S | | | | | | |

## WORK SHEET *SA10*

## 2

### VERBAL I. Q. = 141

| EWS | Info. | Comp. | Digit | Arith. | Sim. |
|-----|-------|-------|-------|--------|------|
| 18 | 25 | 20 | | (14) | 23-24 |
| 17 | (24) | 19 | 17 | 13 | 21-22 |
| 16 | 23 | 18 | (16) | 12 | (20) |
| 15 | 21-22 | (17) | | 11 | 19 |
| 14 | 20 | 16 | 15 | | 17-18 |
| 13 | 18-19 | 15 | 14 | 10 | 16 |
| 12 | 17 | 14 | | 9 | 15 |
| | | | | | |
| 11 | 15-16 | 12-13 | 13 | | 13-14 |
| 10 | 13-14 | 11 | 12 | 8 | 12 |
| 9 | 12 | 10 | 11 | 7 | 11 |
| 8 | 10-11 | 9 | | | 9-10 |
| 7 | 9 | 8 | 10 | 6 | 8 |
| 6 | 7-8 | 7 | 9 | 5 | 7 |
| | | | | | |
| 5 | 6 | 5-6 | | | 5-6 |
| 4 | 4-5 | 4 | 8 | 4 | 4 |
| 3 | 2-3 | 3 | 7 | 3 | 3 |
| 2 | 1 | 2 | 6 | | 1-2 |
| 1 | 0 | 1 | | 2 | 0 |
| 0 | | 0 | 5 | 1 | |

### SZONDI

| SEXUAL | | PAROXYSMAL | | EGO | | CONTACT | |
|--------|--------|------------|--------|--------|--------|--------|--------|
| h | s | e | hy | k | p | d | m |
| | | | | | X | | |
| | | | | | X | | |
| | | | | | X | | X |
| X | | | | | X | | |
| X | | | | | X | | |
| X | | X | | X | X | X | X |
| X | X | X | X | X | X | X | |
| | X | | X | X | | | |
| | | | X | X | | | |

### OVER-ALL EVALUATION = 19

| | | | | | |
|---|---|---|---|---|---|
| OVER-ALL RATING | 1 | (2) | 3 | 4 | 5 |
| PRODUCTIVITY | 1 | (2) | 3 | 4 | 5 |
| RELATION TO REALITY | 1 | (2) | 3 | 4 | 5 |
| THOUGHT CONTENT | 1 | (2) | 3 | 4 | 5 |
| CONSTRUCTIVE FANTASY | (1) | 2 | 3 | 4 | 5 |
| DRIVE | 1 | (2) | 3 | 4 | 5 |
| EMOTIONAL TONE | (1) | 2 | 3 | 4 | 5 |
| SOCIAL ATTITUDE | 1 | (2) | 3 | 4 | 5 |
| ANXIETY | 1 | (2) | 3 | 4 | 5 |
| I. Q. RATING *141* | 1 | 2 | 3 | 4 | (5) |

### RORSCHACH

| | | | | | |
|---|---|---|---|---|---|
| R *20* | M | | | Fc | |
| | FM *5* | F | *10* | c | *2* |
| W% *60* | m | F- | *3* | C' | |
| D% *40* | k | F% | *65* | FC | |
| d% | K | | | CF | |
| Dd% | FK | | | C | |
| S % | | | | | |

# SUMMARY OF TEST FINDINGS    SA 10

## MANNER DURING TEST

| (1) Overly distressed | (2) Tense | (3) Indifferent | (4) Appropriate | (5) Relaxed and actively interested |
|---|---|---|---|---|
| (1) Hostile | (2) **(Uneasy)** | | | |

## I.Q. (Bellevue-Wechsler)

| (1) Below average | (2) Average | (3) High average | (4) Superior | (5) **(Very superior)** |
|---|---|---|---|---|

## PRODUCTIVITY (Rorschach)

| (1) Impoverished | (2) **(Reduced output)** | (3) Adequate | (4) Better than average | (5) Rich and well-ordered |
|---|---|---|---|---|
| | (2) Compulsive productivity | | | |

## RELATION TO REALITY (Rorschach, Bellevue-Wechsler, Drawings)

| (1) Loose | (2) **(Lapses—together with good form)** | (3) Not noticeably disturbed | (4) Essentially firm | (5) Firm and good |
|---|---|---|---|---|

## USUAL-UNUSUAL THOUGHT CONTENT (Rorschach, Unpleasant Concept)

| (1) Bizarre | (2) Tendency toward the bizarre | (3) Adequate | (4) Original trends | (5) Outstandingly original |
|---|---|---|---|---|
| (1) Stereotyped | (2) **(Tendency toward stereotypy)** | | | |

## CONSTRUCTIVE FANTASY (Rorschach)

| (1) **(Absent)** | (2) Barely accessible | (3) Accessible | (4) Readily accessible | (5) Active but not hampering |
|---|---|---|---|---|
| (1) Withdrawal into fantasy | | | | |

## DRIVE (Rorschach, Szondi, Unpleasant Concept)

| (1) Overpowering aggression | (2) Over-aggressive | (3) Adequate | (4) Clearly sufficient | (5) Sufficient—exceptionally well-directed |
|---|---|---|---|---|
| (1) Hampering passivity | (2) **(Insufficient drive)** | | | |

## EMOTIONAL TONE (Rorschach, Szondi)

| (1) Explosive emotions | (2) Getting out of hand | (3) Trend toward emotional expression | (4) Warmth available | (5) Warm, readily available |
|---|---|---|---|---|
| (1) **(Lacking)** | (2) Indicated but repressed emotions | | | |

## SOCIAL ATTITUDE (T. A. T.)

| (1) Uncontrolled | (2) **(Constricted or neglected)** | (3) Adequate | (4) Well-regulated | (5) Free and flexible |
|---|---|---|---|---|

## ANXIETY

| (1) Disintegrating | (2) **(Marked)** | (3) Moderate | (4) Not marked | (5) Lack of evidence of anxiety |
|---|---|---|---|---|

## OVER-ALL EVALUATION

| (1) Markedly disturbed personality | (2) **(Less than adequate personality with some psychological problems)** | (3) Adequate personality | (4) Better than average functioning personality | (5) Exceptionally well-integrated personality with excellent potential |
|---|---|---|---|---|

## SUMMARY OF THERAPIST'S FINDINGS  *SA 10*

### ESTIMATED INTELLIGENCE LEVEL

| (1) Below average | (2) Average | (3) High average ⟨circled⟩ | (4) Superior | (5) Very superior |
|---|---|---|---|---|

### FLOW OF ASSOCIATIVE MATERIAL

| (1) Impoverished | (2) Reduced output | (3) Adequate ⟨circled⟩ | (4) Better than average | (5) Rich and well-ordered |
|---|---|---|---|---|
| | (2) Compulsive productivity | | | |

### RELATION TO REALITY

| (1) Loose | (2) Lapses—together with good form | (3) Not noticeably disturbed ⟨circled⟩ | (4) Essentially firm | (5) Firm and good |
|---|---|---|---|---|

### USUAL-UNUSUAL THOUGHT CONTENT

| (1) Bizarre | (2) Tendency toward the bizarre | (3) Adequate ⟨circled⟩ | (4) Original trends | (5) Outstandingly original |
|---|---|---|---|---|
| (1) Stereotyped | (2) Tendency toward stereotypy | | | |

### CONSTRUCTIVE FANTASY

| (1) Absent | (2) Barely accessible ⟨circled⟩ | (3) Accessible | (4) Readily accessible | (5) Active but not hampering |
|---|---|---|---|---|
| (1) Withdrawal into fantasy | | | | |

### DRIVE

| (1) Overpowering aggression | (2) Over-aggressive | (3) Adequate ⟨circled⟩ | (4) Clearly sufficient | (5) Sufficient—exceptionally well-directed |
|---|---|---|---|---|
| (1) Hampering passivity | (2) Insufficient drive | | | |

### EMOTIONAL TONE

| (1) Explosive emotions | (2) Getting out of hand | (3) Trend toward emotional expression | (4) Warmth available | (5) Warm, readily available |
|---|---|---|---|---|
| (1) Lacking | (2) Indicated but repressed emotions ⟨circled⟩ | | | |

### SOCIAL ATTITUDE

| (1) Uncontrolled | (2) Constricted or neglected ⟨circled⟩ | (3) Adequate | (4) Well-regulated | (5) Free and flexible |
|---|---|---|---|---|

### ANXIETY

| (1) Disintegrating | (2) Marked | (3) Moderate ⟨circled⟩ | (4) Not marked | (5) Lack of evidence of anxiety |
|---|---|---|---|---|

### OVER-ALL EVALUATION

| (1) Markedly disturbed personality | (2) Less than adequate personality with some psychological problems ⟨circled⟩ | (3) Adequate personality | (4) Better than average functioning personality | (5) Exceptionally well-integrated personality with excellent potential |
|---|---|---|---|---|

## WORK SHEET — _SA 11_

### VERBAL I. Q. = _124_

| EWS | Info. | Comp. | Digit | Arith. | Sim. |
|-----|-------|-------|-------|--------|------|
| 18 | 25 | 20 |  | 14 | 23-24 |
| 17 | 24 | 19 | 17 | 13 | 21-22 |
| 16 | 23 | 18 | 16 | 12 | 20 |
| 15 | 21-22 | 17 |  | 11 | 19 |
| 14 | 20 | 16 | 15 |  | 17-18 |
| 13 | 18-19 | 15 | 14 | 10 | 16 |
| 12 | 17 | 14 |  | 9 | 15 |
|  |  |  |  |  |  |
| 11 | 15-16 | 12-13 | 13 |  | 13-14 |
| 10 | 13-14 | 11 | 12 | 8 | 12 |
| 9 | 12 | 10 | 11 | 7 | 11 |
| 8 | 10-11 | 9 |  |  | 9-10 |
| 7 | 9 | 8 | 10 | 6 | 8 |
| 6 | 7-8 | 7 | 9 | 5 | 7 |
|  |  |  |  |  |  |
| 5 | 6 | 5-6 |  |  | 5-6 |
| 4 | 4-5 | 4 | 8 | 4 | 4 |
| 3 | 2-3 | 3 | 7 | 3 | 3 |
| 2 | 1 | 2 | 6 |  | 1-2 |
| 1 | 0 | 1 |  | 2 | 0 |
| 0 |  | 0 | 5 | 1 |  |

### SZONDI

| SEXUAL | | PAROXYSMAL | | EGO | | CONTACT | |
|--------|--|-----------|--|-----|--|--------|--|
| h | s | e | hy | k | p | d | m |

(markings as shown on chart)

### OVER-ALL EVALUATION = _23_

| | 1 | 2 | 3 | 4 | 5 |
|---|---|---|---|---|---|
| OVER-ALL RATING | 1 | 2 | 3 | 4 | 5 |
| PRODUCTIVITY | 1 | (2) | 3 | 4 | 5 |
| RELATION TO REALITY | 1 | 2 | (3) | 4 | 5 |
| THOUGHT CONTENT | 1 | (2) | 3 | 4 | 5 |
| CONSTRUCTIVE FANTASY | 1 | (2) | 3 | 4 | 5 |
| DRIVE | 1 | 2 | (3) | 4 | 5 |
| EMOTIONAL TONE | 1 | (2) | 3 | 4 | 5 |
| SOCIAL ATTITUDE | 1 | (2) | 3 | 4 | 5 |
| ANXIETY | 1 | 2 | (3) | 4 | 5 |
| I. Q. RATING = _124_ | 1 | 2 | 3 | (4) | 5 |

### RORSCHACH

R _10_     M _2_                   Fc _1_

           FM _2_     F _1_         c

W% _100_     m       F−            C'

D%          k _1_     F% _10_     FC _1_

d%          K                CF _2_

Dd%       FK                C
S

## WORK SHEET — *SA II*

2

### VERBAL I. Q.

| EWS | Info. | Comp. | Digit | Arith. | Sim. |
|-----|-------|-------|-------|--------|------|
| 18 | 25 | 20 | | 14 | 23-24 |
| 17 | 24 | 19 | 17 | 13 | 21-22 |
| 16 | 23 | 18 | 16 | 12 | 20 |
| 15 | 21-22 | 17 | | 11 | 19 |
| 14 | 20 | 16 | 15 | | 17-18 |
| 13 | 18-19 | 15 | 14 | 10 | 16 |
| 12 | 17 | 14 | | 9 | 15 |
| | | | | | |
| 11 | 15-16 | 12-13 | 13 | | 13-14 |
| 10 | 13-14 | 11 | 12 | 8 | 12 |
| 9 | 12 | 10 | 11 | 7 | 11 |
| 8 | 10-11 | 9 | | | 9-10 |
| 7 | 9 | 8 | 10 | 6 | 8 |
| 6 | 7-8 | 7 | 9 | 5 | 7 |
| | | | | | |
| 5 | 6 | 5-6 | | | 5-6 |
| 4 | 4-5 | 4 | 8 | 4 | 4 |
| 3 | 2-3 | 3 | 7 | 3 | 3 |
| 2 | 1 | 2 | 6 | | 1-2 |
| 1 | 0 | 1 | | 2 | 0 |
| 0 | | 0 | 5 | 1 | |

### SZONDI

| SEXUAL | | PAROXYSMAL | | EGO | | CONTACT | |
|---|---|---|---|---|---|---|---|
| h | s | e | hy | k | p | d | m |

OVER-ALL EVALUATION = **24**

| | | | | | |
|---|---|---|---|---|---|
| OVER-ALL RATING | 1 | 2 | 3 | 4 | 5 |
| PRODUCTIVITY | 1 | 2 | (3) | 4 | 5 |
| RELATION TO REALITY | 1 | (2) | 3 | 4 | 5 |
| THOUGHT CONTENT | 1 | (2) | 3 | 4 | 5 |
| CONSTRUCTIVE FANTASY | 1 | (2) | 3 | 4 | 5 |
| DRIVE | 1 | 2 | (3) | 4 | 5 |
| EMOTIONAL TONE | 1 | (2) | 3 | 4 | 5 |
| SOCIAL ATTITUDE | 1 | (2) | 3 | 4 | 5 |
| ANXIETY | 1 | 2 | (3) | 4 | 5 |
| I. Q. RATING = *132* | 1 | 2 | 3 | 4 | (5) |

### RORSCHACH

| R 23 | M 2 | | Fc 2 |
|---|---|---|---|
| | FM 4 | F 10 | c |
| W% 48 | m | F- 2 | C' 1 |
| D% 52 | k | F% 52 | FC 2 |
| d% | K | | CF |
| Dd% | FK | | C |
| S | | | |

# SUMMARY OF TEST FINDINGS  *SA 11*

## MANNER DURING TEST

| (1) Overly distressed | (2) Tense | (3) Indifferent | (4) Appropriate | (5) Relaxed and actively interested |
|---|---|---|---|---|
| (1) Hostile | (2) Uneasy | | | |

## I.Q. (Bellevue-Wechsler)

| (1) Below average | (2) Average | (3) High average | (4) Superior | (5) Very superior |
|---|---|---|---|---|

## PRODUCTIVITY (Rorschach)

| (1) Impoverished | (2) Reduced output | (3) Adequate | (4) Better than average | (5) Rich and well-ordered |
|---|---|---|---|---|
| | (2) Compulsive productivity | | | |

## RELATION TO REALITY (Rorschach, Bellevue-Wechsler, Drawings)

| (1) Loose | (2) Lapses—together with good form | (3) Not noticeably disturbed | (4) Essentially firm | (5) Firm and good |
|---|---|---|---|---|

## USUAL-UNUSUAL THOUGHT CONTENT (Rorschach, Unpleasant Concept)

| (1) Bizarre | (2) Tendency toward the bizarre | (3) Adequate | (4) Original trends | (5) Outstandingly original |
|---|---|---|---|---|
| (1) Stereotyped | (2) Tendency toward stereotypy | | | |

## CONSTRUCTIVE FANTASY (Rorschach)

| (1) Absent | (2) Barely accessible | (3) Accessible | (4) Readily accessible | (5) Active but not hampering |
|---|---|---|---|---|
| (1) Withdrawal into fantasy | | | | |

## DRIVE (Rorschach, Szondi, Unpleasant Concept)

| (1) Overpowering aggression | (2) Over-aggressive | (3) Adequate | (4) Clearly sufficient | (5) Sufficient—exceptionally well-directed |
|---|---|---|---|---|
| (1) Hampering passivity | (2) Insufficient drive | | | |

## EMOTIONAL TONE (Rorschach, Szondi)

| (1) Explosive emotions | (2) Getting out of hand | (3) Trend toward emotional expression | (4) Warmth available | (5) Warm, readily available |
|---|---|---|---|---|
| (1) Lacking | (2) Indicated but repressed emotions | | | |

## SOCIAL ATTITUDE (T. A. T.)

| (1) Uncontrolled | (2) Constricted or neglected | (3) Adequate | (4) Well-regulated | (5) Free and flexible |
|---|---|---|---|---|

## ANXIETY

| (1) Disintegrating | (2) Marked | (3) Moderate | (4) Not marked | (5) Lack of evidence of anxiety |
|---|---|---|---|---|

## OVER-ALL EVALUATION

| (1) Markedly disturbed personality | (2) Less than adequate personality with some psychological problems | (3) Adequate personality | (4) Better than average functioning personality | (5) Exceptionally well-integrated personality with excellent potential |
|---|---|---|---|---|

## SUMMARY OF THERAPIST'S FINDINGS  SA II

---

### ESTIMATED INTELLIGENCE LEVEL

| (1) Below average | (2) Average | (3) High average | (4) Superior | (5) Very superior |
|---|---|---|---|---|

### FLOW OF ASSOCIATIVE MATERIAL

| (1) Impoverished | (2) Reduced output | (3) Adequate | (4) Better than average | (5) Rich and well-ordered |
|---|---|---|---|---|
|  | (2) Compulsive productivity |  |  |  |

### RELATION TO REALITY

| (1) Loose | (2) Lapses—together with good form | (3) Not noticeably disturbed | (4) Essentially firm | (5) Firm and good |
|---|---|---|---|---|

### USUAL-UNUSUAL THOUGHT CONTENT

| (1) Bizarre | (2) Tendency toward the bizarre | (3) Adequate | (4) Original trends | (5) Outstandingly original |
|---|---|---|---|---|
| (1) Stereotyped | (2) Tendency toward stereotypy |  |  |  |

### CONSTRUCTIVE FANTASY

| (1) Absent | (2) Barely accessible | (3) Accessible | (4) Readily accessible | (5) Active but not hampering |
|---|---|---|---|---|
| (1) Withdrawal into fantasy |  |  |  |  |

### DRIVE

| (1) Overpowering aggression | (2) Over-aggressive | (3) Adequate | (4) Clearly sufficient | (5) Sufficient—exceptionally well-directed |
|---|---|---|---|---|
| (1) Hampering passivity | (2) Insufficient drive |  |  |  |

### EMOTIONAL TONE

| (1) Explosive emotions | (2) Getting out of hand | (3) Trend toward emotional expression | (4) Warmth available | (5) Warm, readily available |
|---|---|---|---|---|
| (1) Lacking | (2) Indicated but re-pressed emotions |  |  |  |

### SOCIAL ATTITUDE

| (1) Uncontrolled | (2) Constricted or neglected | (3) Adequate | (4) Well-regulated | (5) Free and flexible |
|---|---|---|---|---|

### ANXIETY

| (1) Disintegrating | (2) Marked | (3) Moderate | (4) Not marked | (5) Lack of evidence of anxiety |
|---|---|---|---|---|

### OVER-ALL EVALUATION

| (1) Markedly dis-turbed personality | (2) Less than adequate personality with some psycholog-ical problems | (3) Adequate personality | (4) Better than average function-ing personality | (5) Exceptionally well-integrated person-ality with excellent potential |
|---|---|---|---|---|

SA12 was in his early twenties and unmarried when first tested. He was evaluated by the therapist as profoundly disturbed, rating a 1 on the 5-point over-all scale. At the time of retesting, which took place at the termination of therapy, and at the time of the follow-up study five years later, at which time a lobotomy was performed, the clinical evaluation remained unchanged.

The general level of the Wechsler scattergram is lower in this case, and remains lower on the second testing, than for the majority of patients we have considered here. The pattern is essentially similar in the interrelation of the subtests on the two occasions.

The Szondi reveals some slight change in the ego vector, suggesting less repression. The Figure Drawings present virtually identical attempts on the first and second testing; in each case they are small heads set in the middle of the page. The Rorschach also remains virtually identical, with an alteration of one or two responses at most. It is recorded here in full.

| RORSCHACH 1 | RORSCHACH 2 |
|---|---|
| *Card I* | *Card I* |
| 1. A bat. | This won't mean anything to me. |
| | 1. Like a bat or something. |
| *Card II* | *Card II* |
| 1. Two men fighting | 1. Could be two people holding hands together. |
| *Card III* | *Card III* |
| 1. Also two men. | Are you supposed to see people? |
| | 1. Just ink to me. |
| | 2. Might be a group of islands. |
| *Card IV* | *Card IV* |
| 1. Some kind of vegetation reflected in water. | 1. Like a leaf, half-rotten. |
| *Card V* | *Card V* |
| 1. Like a fur collar. | 1. Call this a fur collar and let it go at that. |
| *Card VI* | *Card VI* |
| I give up. | ——— |
| *Card VII* | *Card VII* |
| 1. These look like scotty dogs. | 1. These look like scotty dogs. |

<table>
<tr><td colspan="2" align="center">RORSCHACH 1</td><td colspan="2" align="center">RORSCHACH 2</td></tr>
</table>

| RORSCHACH 1 | RORSCHACH 2 |
|---|---|
| *Card VIII* | *Card VIII* |
| 1. This is an animal looking in water. | 1. Like some animal looking in water. |
| *Card IX* | *Card IX* |
| 1. Like a tree. | Still trying to find something. |
| *Card X* | *Card X* |
| 1. This is Spring. | 1. Spring. |

The quantitative score on the OVER-ALL EVALUATION scale remains unchanged. There would appear to be almost complete agreement between the therapeutic and test findings in this instance.

SA12's records follow, pages 282-285.

## WORK SHEET   *SA 12*

### VERBAL I. Q. = *96*

| EWS | Info. | Comp. | Digit | Arith. | Sim. |
|---|---|---|---|---|---|
| 18 | 25 | 20 |  | 14 | 23-24 |
| 17 | 24 | 19 | 17 | 13 | 21-22 |
| 16 | 23 | 18 | 16 | 12 | 20 |
| 15 | 21-22 | 17 |  | 11 | 19 |
| 14 | 20 | 16 | 15 |  | 17-18 |
| 13 | 18-19 | 15 | 14 | 10 | 16 |
| 12 | (17) | 14 |  | 9 | 15 |
| 11 | 15-16 | 12-13 | 13 |  | 13-14 |
| 10 | 13-14 | 11 | 12 | 8 | 12 |
| 9 | 12 | 10 | 11 | 7 | 11 |
| 8 | 10-11 |  |  |  | 9-10 |
| 7 | 9 | 8 | 10 | 6 | 8 |
| 6 | 7-8 | 7 | 9 | 5 | 7 |
| 5 | 6 | 5-6 |  |  | 5-6 |
| 4 | 4-5 | 4 | 8 | 4 | 4 |
| 3 | 2-3 | 3 | 7 | 3 | 3 |
| 2 | 1 | 2 | 6 |  | 1-2 |
| 1 | 0 | 1 |  | 2 | 0 |
| 0 |  | 0 | 5 | 1 |  |

### SZONDI

| SEXUAL | | PAROXYSMAL | | EGO | | CONTACT | |
|---|---|---|---|---|---|---|---|
| h | s | e | hy | k | p | d | m |
|  |  |  |  |  |  |  |  |
|  |  | X |  |  |  |  |  |
|  |  | X | X |  |  |  | X |
|  |  | X | X |  |  |  | X |
| X | X | X | X | X | X | X | X |
| X | X | X |  | X | X | X |  |
| X | X |  |  | X |  | X |  |
| X |  |  |  | X |  |  |  |

### OVER-ALL EVALUATION = *18*

| | 1 | 2 | 3 | 4 | 5 |
|---|---|---|---|---|---|
| OVER-ALL RATING | 1 | 2 | 3 | 4 | 5 |
| PRODUCTIVITY | (1) | 2 | 3 | 4 | 5 |
| RELATION TO REALITY | 1 | 2 | (3) | 4 | 5 |
| THOUGHT CONTENT | 1 | (2) | 3 | 4 | 5 |
| CONSTRUCTIVE FANTASY | 1 | (2) | 3 | 4 | 5 |
| DRIVE | 1 | (2) | 3 | 4 | 5 |
| EMOTIONAL TONE | 1 | (2) | 3 | 4 | 5 |
| SOCIAL ATTITUDE | 1 | (2) | 3 | 4 | 5 |
| ANXIETY | 1 | (2) | 3 | 4 | 5 |
| I. Q. RATING   *96* | 1 | (2) | 3 | 4 | 5 |

### RORSCHACH

| | | | | | |
|---|---|---|---|---|---|
| R *9* | M *2* | | | | Fc |
| | FM *2* | | F *1* | | c *2* |
| W% *78* | m | | F- | | C' |
| D% *22* | k | | F% *11* | | FC |
| d% | K | | | | CF *1-* |
| Dd% | FK | | | | c |
| S | | | | | C SYM *1* |

## WORK SHEET  SA 12
### 2

### VERBAL I. Q. = 101

| EWS | Info. | Comp. | Digit | Arith. | Sim. |
|-----|-------|-------|-------|--------|------|
| 18 | 25 | 20 |  | 14 | 23-24 |
| 17 | 24 | 19 | 17 | 13 | 21-22 |
| 16 | 23 | 18 | 16 | 12 | 20 |
| 15 | 21-22 | 17 |  | 11 | 19 |
| 14 | 20 | 16 | 15 |  | 17-18 |
| 13 | 18-19 | 15 | 14 | 10 | 16 |
| 12 | 17 | 14 |  | 9 | 15 |
| 11 | ⟨15-16⟩ | 12-13 | 13 |  | ⟨13-14⟩ |
| 10 | 13-14 | 11 | ⟨12⟩ | 8 | 12 |
| 9 | 12 | ⟨10⟩ | 11 | ⟨7⟩ | 11 |
| 8 | 10-11 | ⟨9⟩ |  |  | 9-10 |
| 7 | 9 | 8 | 10 | 6 | 8 |
| 6 | 7-8 | 7 | 9 | 5 | 7 |
| 5 | 6 | 5-6 |  |  | 5-6 |
| 4 | 4-5 | 4 | 8 | 4 | 4 |
| 3 | 2-3 | 3 | 7 | 3 | 3 |
| 2 | 1 | 2 | 6 |  | 1-2 |
| 1 | 0 | 1 |  | 2 | 0 |
| 0 |  | 0 | 5 | 1 |  |

### SZONDI

| SEXUAL | | PAROXYSMAL | | EGO | | CONTACT | |
|--------|--------|------------|--------|--------|--------|--------|--------|
| h | s | e | hy | k | p | d | m |
|  |  | X |  | X | X |  |  |
|  |  | X |  | X | X |  |  |
|  | X | X | X | X | X |  | X |
| X | X |  | X | X |  | X | X |
| X | X |  | X |  |  |  |  |
| X | X |  |  |  |  |  |  |
| X |  |  |  |  |  |  |  |

### OVER-ALL EVALUATION  18

| | 1 | 2 | 3 | 4 | 5 |
|---|---|---|---|---|---|
| OVER-ALL RATING | ① | 2 | 3 | 4 | 5 |
| PRODUCTIVITY | ① | 2 | ③ | 4 | 5 |
| RELATION TO REALITY | 1 | 2 | ③ | 4 | 5 |
| THOUGHT CONTENT | 1 | ② | 3 | 4 | 5 |
| CONSTRUCTIVE FANTASY | 1 | ② | 3 | 4 | 5 |
| DRIVE | 1 | ② | 3 | 4 | 5 |
| EMOTIONAL TONE | 1 | ② | 3 | 4 | 5 |
| SOCIAL ATTITUDE | 1 | ② | 3 | 4 | 5 |
| ANXIETY | 1 | ② | 3 | 4 | 5 |
| I. Q. RATING  101 | 1 | ② | 3 | 4 | 5 |

### RORSCHACH

| R 9 | M 1 | | Fc |
|-----|-----|-----|-----|
|  | FM 2 | F 1 | c 2 |
| W% 78 | m | F- 1 | C' |
| D% 22 | k | F% 22 | FC |
| d% |  |  | CF |
| Dd% | FK |  | c 1 |
| S |  |  | CSYM 1 |

# SUMMARY OF TEST FINDINGS    *SA 12*

## MANNER DURING TEST

| (1) Overly distressed | (2) Tense | (3) Indifferent | (4) Appropriate | (5) Relaxed and actively interested |
|---|---|---|---|---|
| (1) Hostile | (2) ~~Uneasy~~ | | | |

## I.Q. (Bellevue-Wechsler)

| (1) Below average | (2) ~~Average~~ | (3) High average | (4) Superior | (5) Very superior |
|---|---|---|---|---|

## PRODUCTIVITY (Rorschach)

| (1) ~~Impoverished~~ | (2) Reduced output | (3) Adequate | (4) Better than average | (5) Rich and well-ordered |
|---|---|---|---|---|
| | (2) Compulsive productivity | | | |

## RELATION TO REALITY (Rorschach, Bellevue-Wechsler, Drawings)

| (1) Loose | (2) Lapses—together with good form | (3) ~~Not noticeably disturbed~~ | (4) Essentially firm | (5) Firm and good |
|---|---|---|---|---|

## USUAL-UNUSUAL THOUGHT CONTENT (Rorschach, Unpleasant Concept)

| (1) Bizarre | (2) Tendency toward the bizarre | (3) Adequate | (4) Original trends | (5) Outstandingly original |
|---|---|---|---|---|
| (1) Stereotyped | (2) ~~Tendency toward stereotypy~~ | | | |

## CONSTRUCTIVE FANTASY (Rorschach)

| (1) Absent | (2) ~~Barely accessible~~ | (3) Accessible | (4) Readily accessible | (5) Active but not hampering |
|---|---|---|---|---|
| (1) Withdrawal into fantasy | | | | |

## DRIVE (Rorschach, Szondi, Unpleasant Concept)

| (1) Overpowering aggression | (2) Over-aggressive | (3) Adequate | (4) Clearly sufficient | (5) Sufficient— exceptionally well-directed |
|---|---|---|---|---|
| (1) Hampering passivity | (2) ~~Insufficient drive~~ | | | |

## EMOTIONAL TONE (Rorschach, Szondi)

| (1) Explosive emotions | (2) Getting out of hand | (3) Trend toward emotional expression | (4) Warmth available | (5) Warm, readily available |
|---|---|---|---|---|
| (1) Lacking | (2) ~~Indicated but repressed emotions~~ | | | |

## SOCIAL ATTITUDE (T. A. T.)

| (1) Uncontrolled | (2) ~~Constricted or neglected~~ | (3) Adequate | (4) Well-regulated | (5) Free and flexible |
|---|---|---|---|---|

## ANXIETY

| (1) Disintegrating | (2) ~~Marked~~ | (3) Moderate | (4) Not marked | (5) Lack of evidence of anxiety |
|---|---|---|---|---|

## OVER-ALL EVALUATION

| (1) Markedly disturbed personality | (2) ~~Less than adequate personality with some psychological problems~~ | (3) Adequate personality | (4) Better than average functioning personality | (5) Exceptionally well-integrated personality with excellent potential |
|---|---|---|---|---|

## SUMMARY OF THERAPIST'S FINDINGS  *SA 12*

### ESTIMATED INTELLIGENCE LEVEL

| (1) Below average | (2) (Average) | (3) High average | (4) Superior | (5) Very superior |
|---|---|---|---|---|

### FLOW OF ASSOCIATIVE MATERIAL

| (1) (Impoverished) | (2) Reduced output | (3) Adequate | (4) Better than average | (5) Rich and well-ordered |
|---|---|---|---|---|
| | (2) Compulsive productivity | | | |

### RELATION TO REALITY

| (1) (Loose) | (2) Lapses—together with good form | (3) Not noticeably disturbed | (4) Essentially firm | (5) Firm and good |
|---|---|---|---|---|

### USUAL-UNUSUAL THOUGHT CONTENT

| (1) Bizarre | (2) (Tendency toward the bizarre) | (3) Adequate | (4) Original trends | (5) Outstandingly original |
|---|---|---|---|---|
| (1) Stereotyped | (2) Tendency toward stereotypy | | | |

### CONSTRUCTIVE FANTASY

| (1) (Absent) | (2) Barely accessible | (3) Accessible | (4) Readily accessible | (5) Active but not hampering |
|---|---|---|---|---|
| (1) Withdrawal into fantasy | | | | |

### DRIVE

| (1) Overpowering aggression | (2) Over-aggressive | (3) Adequate | (4) Clearly sufficient | (5) Sufficient— exceptionally well-directed |
|---|---|---|---|---|
| (1) (Hampering passivity) | (2) Insufficient drive | | | |

### EMOTIONAL TONE

| (1) Explosive emotions | (2) Getting out of hand | (3) Trend toward emotional expression | (4) Warmth available | (5) Warm, readily available |
|---|---|---|---|---|
| (1) (Lacking) | (2) Indicated but re-pressed emotions | | | |

### SOCIAL ATTITUDE

| (1) Uncontrolled | (2) (Constricted or neglected) | (3) Adequate | (4) Well-regulated | (5) Free and flexible |
|---|---|---|---|---|

### ANXIETY

| (1) Disintegrating | (2) Marked | (3) (Moderate) | (4) Not marked | (5) Lack of evidence of anxiety |
|---|---|---|---|---|

### OVER-ALL EVALUATION

| (1) (Markedly dis-turbed personality) | (2) Less than adequate personality with some psycholog-ical problems | (3) Adequate personality | (4) Better than average function-ing personality | (5) Exceptionally well-integrated person-ality with excellent potential |
|---|---|---|---|---|

SA13 was in her early forties and married at the time of seeking treatment. This patient was estimated by the therapist as at the level of 1 at the time of the initial contact and to have remained unimproved after treatment.

A comparison of the two Bellevue-Wechsler scores indicates, in this instance, a rise from 104 to 121. This improvement is carried by the Comprehension scores (five points on the weighted scale) and by a comparable "jump" in the Similarities. The Information also has increased three points.

On the Szondi, the strong repression in the realm of ideas and feelings, indicated by the –hy, –k, remains unchanged. As a matter of fact, the hy is even more strongly loaded on the second testing. There would seem to be more experienced anxiety in the loaded +m in the second record.

Essentially the same features are reflected in each of the Figure Drawings. A slight degree of improvement might perhaps be attributed to the second but it is not sufficient to change its basic classification.

The Rorschach, despite the few extra answers, hardly deviates either in structural components or in content. The color responses, in particular the –CF and the pure C's, together with the high number of F– responses, give a bizarre quality to the record which remains unchanged. Some of the more disturbed answers are recorded here to indicate the flavor.

|  |  |
|---|---|
| RORSCHACH 1 | RORSCHACH 2 |
| *Card II* | *Card II* |
| 1. Blood—menstruation. | 1. Blood. |
| 2. Some one's insides. | 2. Women's female organs, vagina. |
| 3. A lung. | 3. Dogs. |
| 4. The bottom of somebody. |  |
| *Card IV* | *Card IV* |
| 1. All like an x-ray picture. | 1. Dog's ears. |
| 2. Rats—bats, they're unpleasant to me. | 2. Vagina. |
| 3. A woman, too. | 3. Insides. |
| *Card VII* | *Card VII* |
| 1. Reminds me of the body—vagina. | 1. Blobs. |
|  | 2. Vagina. |
|  | 3. Clouds. |

|  |  |
|---|---|
| RORSCHACH 1 | RORSCHACH 2 |

*Card VIII*

1. Colors.
2. Rats. Doesn't mean very much.

*Card VIII*

1. Colors.
2. Insides.
3. Two animals at the sides—may be rats without tails.
4. X-ray.

SA13's records follow, pages 288-291.

# WORK SHEET — *SA 13*

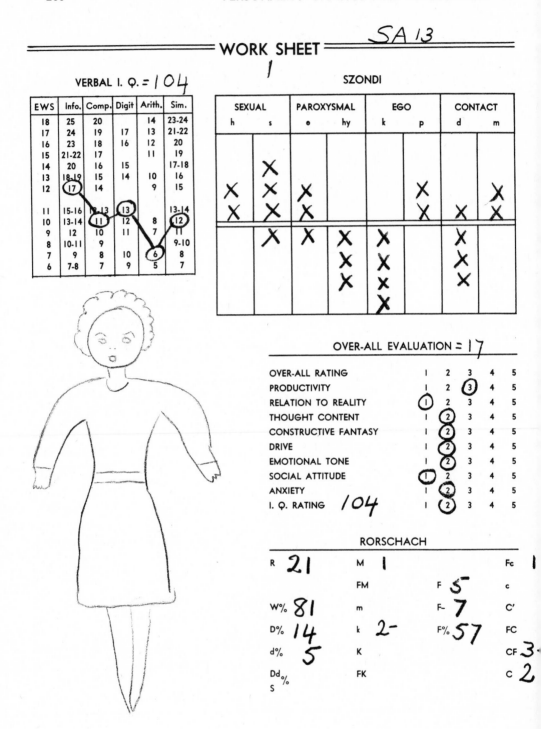

**VERBAL I. Q. = 104**

| EWS | Info. | Comp. | Digit | Arith. | Sim. |
|-----|-------|-------|-------|--------|------|
| 18 | 25 | 20 | | 14 | 23-24 |
| 17 | 24 | 19 | 17 | 13 | 21-22 |
| 16 | 23 | 18 | 16 | 12 | 20 |
| 15 | 21-22 | 17 | | 11 | 19 |
| 14 | 20 | 16 | 15 | | 17-18 |
| 13 | 18-19 | 15 | 14 | 10 | 16 |
| 12 | (17) | 14 | | 9 | 15 |
| 11 | 15-16 | 12-13 | (13) | | 13-14 |
| 10 | 13-14 | (11) | 12 | 8 | (12) |
| 9 | 12 | 10 | 11 | 7 | 11 |
| 8 | 10-11 | 9 | | | 9-10 |
| 7 | 9 | 8 | 10 | (6) | 8 |
| 6 | 7-8 | 7 | 9 | 5 | 7 |

## SZONDI

| | SEXUAL | | PAROXYSMAL | | EGO | | CONTACT | |
|---|--------|---|------------|---|-----|---|---------|---|
| | h | s | e | hy | k | p | d | m |

OVER-ALL EVALUATION = 17

| | 1 | 2 | 3 | 4 | 5 |
|---|---|---|---|---|---|
| OVER-ALL RATING | 1 | 2 | 3 | 4 | 5 |
| PRODUCTIVITY | 1 | 2 | ③ | 4 | 5 |
| RELATION TO REALITY | ① | 2 | 3 | 4 | 5 |
| THOUGHT CONTENT | 1 | ② | 3 | 4 | 5 |
| CONSTRUCTIVE FANTASY | 1 | ② | 3 | 4 | 5 |
| DRIVE | 1 | ② | 3 | 4 | 5 |
| EMOTIONAL TONE | 1 | ② | 3 | 4 | 5 |
| SOCIAL ATTITUDE | ① | 2 | 3 | 4 | 5 |
| ANXIETY | 1 | ② | 3 | 4 | 5 |
| I. Q. RATING  104 | 1 | ② | 3 | 4 | 5 |

## RORSCHACH

| R 21 | M 1 | | Fc 1 |
|------|-----|---|------|
| | FM | F 5 | c |
| W% 81 | m | F- 7 | C' |
| D% 14 | k 2- | F% 57 | FC |
| d% 5 | K | | CF 3 |
| Dd% | FK | | c 2 |
| S | | | |

# WORK SHEET — SA 13

2)

## VERBAL I. Q. = 121

| EWS | Info. | Comp. | Digit | Arith. | Sim. |
|---|---|---|---|---|---|
| 18 | 25 | 20 | | 14 | 23-24 |
| 17 | 24 | 19 | 17 | 13 | 21-22 |
| 16 | 23 | 18 | 16 | 12 | 20 |
| 15 | 21-22 | 17 | | 11 | 19 |
| 14 | 20 | 16 | 15 | | 17-18 |
| 13 | 18-19 | 15 | 14 | 10 | 16 |
| 12 | 17 | 14 | | 9 | 15 |
| | | | | | |
| 11 | 15-16 | 12-13 | 13 | | 13-14 |
| 10 | 13-14 | 11 | 12 | 8 | 12 |
| 9 | 12 | 10 | 11 | 7 | 11 |
| 8 | 10-11 | 9 | | | 9-10 |
| 7 | 9 | 8 | 10 | 6 | 8 |
| 6 | 7-8 | 7 | 9 | 5 | 7 |

## SZONDI

| SEXUAL | | PAROXYSMAL | | EGO | | CONTACT | |
|---|---|---|---|---|---|---|---|
| h | s | e | hy | k | p | d | m |

## OVER-ALL EVALUATION = 19

| | | | | | |
|---|---|---|---|---|---|
| OVER-ALL RATING | 1 | 2 | 3 | 4 | 5 |
| PRODUCTIVITY | 1 | 2 | (3) | 4 | 5 |
| RELATION TO REALITY | (1) | 2 | 3 | 4 | 5 |
| THOUGHT CONTENT | 1 | (2) | 3 | 4 | 5 |
| CONSTRUCTIVE FANTASY | 1 | (2) | 3 | 4 | 5 |
| DRIVE | 1 | (2) | 3 | 4 | 5 |
| EMOTIONAL TONE | 1 | (2) | 3 | 4 | 5 |
| SOCIAL ATTITUDE | (1) | 2 | 3 | 4 | 5 |
| ANXIETY | 1 | (2) | 3 | 4 | 5 |
| I. Q. RATING  121 | 1 | 2 | 3 | (4) | 5 |

## RORSCHACH

| | | | |
|---|---|---|---|
| R 28 | M 1 | | Fc |
| | FM | F 8 | c 1 |
| W% 71 | m | F- 9 | C' |
| D% 18 | k 3- | F% 61 | FC |
| d% | K 1 | | CF 3- |
| Dd% 11 | FK | | c 2 |
| S | | | |

## SUMMARY OF TEST FINDINGS  *SA 13*

### MANNER DURING TEST

| (1) Overly distressed | (2) Tense | (3) Indifferent | (4) Appropriate | (5) Relaxed and actively interested |
|---|---|---|---|---|
| (1) Hostile | (2) Uneasy | | | |

### I.Q. (Bellevue-Wechsler)

| (1) Below average | (2) Average | (3) High average | (4) Superior | (5) Very superior |
|---|---|---|---|---|

### PRODUCTIVITY (Rorschach)

| (1) Impoverished | (2) Reduced output | (3) Adequate | (4) Better than average | (5) Rich and well-ordered |
|---|---|---|---|---|
| | (2) Compulsive productivity | | | |

### RELATION TO REALITY (Rorschach, Bellevue-Wechsler, Drawings)

| (1) Loose | (2) Lapses—together with good form | (3) Not noticeably disturbed | (4) Essentially firm | (5) Firm and good |
|---|---|---|---|---|

### USUAL-UNUSUAL THOUGHT CONTENT (Rorschach, Unpleasant Concept)

| (1) Bizarre | (2) Tendency toward the bizarre | (3) Adequate | (4) Original trends | (5) Outstandingly original |
|---|---|---|---|---|
| (1) Stereotyped | (2) Tendency toward stereotypy | | | |

### CONSTRUCTIVE FANTASY (Rorschach)

| (1) Absent | (2) Barely accessible | (3) Accessible | (4) Readily accessible | (5) Active but not hampering |
|---|---|---|---|---|
| (1) Withdrawal into fantasy | | | | |

### DRIVE (Rorschach, Szondi, Unpleasant Concept)

| (1) Overpowering aggression | (2) Over-aggressive | (3) Adequate | (4) Clearly sufficient | (5) Sufficient—exceptionally well-directed |
|---|---|---|---|---|
| (1) Hampering passivity | (2) Insufficient drive | | | |

### EMOTIONAL TONE (Rorschach, Szondi)

| (1) Explosive emotions | (2) Getting out of hand | (3) Trend toward emotional expression | (4) Warmth available | (5) Warm, readily available |
|---|---|---|---|---|
| (1) Lacking | (2) Indicated but repressed emotions | | | |

### SOCIAL ATTITUDE (T. A. T.)

| (1) Uncontrolled | (2) Constricted or neglected | (3) Adequate | (4) Well-regulated | (5) Free and flexible |
|---|---|---|---|---|

### ANXIETY

| (1) Disintegrating | (2) Marked | (3) Moderate | (4) Not marked | (5) Lack of evidence of anxiety |
|---|---|---|---|---|

### OVER-ALL EVALUATION

| (1) Markedly disturbed personality | (2) Less than adequate personality with some psychological problems | (3) Adequate personality | (4) Better than average functioning personality | (5) Exceptionally well-integrated personality with excellent potential |
|---|---|---|---|---|

## SUMMARY OF THERAPIST'S FINDINGS  *SA 13*

### ESTIMATED INTELLIGENCE LEVEL

| (1) Below average | (2) Average | (3) High average | (4) Superior | (5) Very superior |
|---|---|---|---|---|

### FLOW OF ASSOCIATIVE MATERIAL

| (1) Impoverished | (2) Reduced output | (3) Adequate | (4) Better than average | (5) Rich and well-ordered |
|---|---|---|---|---|
| | (2) Compulsive productivity | | | |

### RELATION TO REALITY

| (1) Loose | (2) Lapses—together with good form | (3) Not noticeably disturbed | (4) Essentially firm | (5) Firm and good |
|---|---|---|---|---|

### USUAL-UNUSUAL THOUGHT CONTENT

| (1) Bizarre | (2) Tendency toward the bizarre | (3) Adequate | (4) Original trends | (5) Outstandingly original |
|---|---|---|---|---|
| (1) Stereotyped | (2) Tendency toward stereotypy | | | |

### CONSTRUCTIVE FANTASY

| (1) Absent | (2) Barely accessible | (3) Accessible | (4) Readily accessible | (5) Active but not hampering |
|---|---|---|---|---|
| (1) Withdrawal into fantasy | | | | |

### DRIVE

| (1) Overpowering aggression | (2) Over-aggressive | (3) Adequate | (4) Clearly sufficient | (5) Sufficient—exceptionally well-directed |
|---|---|---|---|---|
| (1) Hampering passivity | (2) Insufficient drive | | | |

### EMOTIONAL TONE

| (1) Explosive emotions | (2) Getting out of hand | (3) Trend toward emotional expression | (4) Warmth available | (5) Warm, readily available |
|---|---|---|---|---|
| (1) Lacking | (2) Indicated but re-pressed emotions | | | |

### SOCIAL ATTITUDE

| (1) Uncontrolled | (2) Constricted or neglected | (3) Adequate | (4) Well-regulated | (5) Free and flexible |
|---|---|---|---|---|

### ANXIETY

| (1) Disintegrating | (2) Marked | (3) Moderate | (4) Not marked | (5) Lack of evidence of anxiety |
|---|---|---|---|---|

### OVER-ALL EVALUATION

| (1) Markedly disturbed personality | (2) Less than adequate personality with some psychological problems | (3) Adequate personality | (4) Better than average functioning personality | (5) Exceptionally well-integrated personality with excellent potential |
|---|---|---|---|---|

SA14 was unmarried and in her mid-thirties when she first went for treatment. She was estimated by the therapist as markedly disturbed at that time, and was considered unimproved when she came for the second psychological assessment and again at the end of the four-year follow-up.

On the Bellevue-Wechsler, the scattergram is identical in the two tests, netting this individual a score in the *Very Superior* adult range.

The $+m$, which was a hopeful feature in the first Szondi record, has become a $-m$ on the second; this, together with the increased pressure in the s factor, suggests a more restless and unhappy picture.

The Figure Drawings have changed only in the direction of further withdrawal. The scant facial features originally portrayed have now disappeared. Even the hat, which gives the shattered male figure at least some social status, has been removed.

The Rorschach records are virtually identical, the same features of withdrawal being apparent in the second record as well as in the first. There is also a loss of a CF response, which in this particular constellation, so overweighted on the introversial side, was a constructive ingredient.

The OVER-ALL EVALUATION score was 24 at the first testing and 23 at the second.

(The records of SA14 will be found on pages 294-297, of SA15 on pages 298-301.)

SA15, married and in her early thirties, was assessed by the therapist as between 1 and 2 on the OVER-ALL EVALUATION scale and to have remained without improvement both at the time of retesting after brief psychotherapy and at the four-year follow-up.

A comparison of the subtests on the Wechsler scores reveals an important increase in the quality of abstract thinking, with a gain of five points on the weighted scale at the time of the second testing. This and other minor changes bring the verbal I.Q. up from 109 to 116, so that this individual passes from the *Average Group* to the *High Average* rating.

Minor changes are reflected in the Szondi. The $+p$, for example, would suggest some capacity within the ego to strive for self-determined goals.

The Rorschach still remains that of a clearly disturbed individual, for while the F– responses have dropped from 10 to 7 and there is a gain of one FC response, the essential characteristics both structurally and in terms of content remain the same. The characteristic of both psychograms is the high F per cent, together with the indication of tension and anxiety reflected in the m, k, K and FK responses. There is considerable perseveration throughout both records. Oral and anal characteristics are somewhat grotesquely expressed through obsessional reiteration of "buttocks" and "teeth." There is a bizarre quality to much of the thought content.

The quantitative assessement on the first test is a score of 20; on the second, 23.

## WORK SHEET — SA 14

### VERBAL I. Q. = 133

| EWS | Info. | Comp. | Digit | Arith. | Sim. |
|-----|-------|-------|-------|--------|------|
| 18 | 25 | 20 | | 14 | 23-24 |
| 17 | 24 | 19 | 17 | 13 | 21-22 |
| 16 | 23 | 18 | 16 | 12 | 20 |
| 15 | 21-22 | 17 | | 11 | 19 |
| 14 | 20 | 16 | 15 | | 17-18 |
| 13 | 18-19 | 15 | 14 | 10 | 16 |
| 12 | 17 | 14 | | 9 | 15 |
| 11 | 15-16 | 12-13 | 13 | | 13-14 |
| 10 | 13-14 | 11 | 12 | 8 | 12 |
| 9 | 12 | 10 | 11 | 7 | 11 |
| 8 | 10-11 | 9 | | | 9-10 |
| 7 | 9 | 8 | 10 | 6 | 8 |
| 6 | 7-8 | 7 | 9 | 5 | 7 |
| 5 | 6 | 5-6 | | | 5-6 |
| 4 | 4-5 | 4 | 8 | 4 | 4 |
| 3 | 2-3 | 3 | 7 | 3 | 3 |
| 2 | 1 | 2 | 6 | | 1-2 |
| 1 | 0 | 1 | | 2 | 0 |
| 0 | | 0 | 5 | 1 | |

### SZONDI

| SEXUAL | | PAROXYSMAL | | EGO | | CONTACT | |
|---|---|---|---|---|---|---|---|
| h | s | e | hy | k | p | d | m |

(test markings as plotted)

### RORSCHACH

| | | | | | |
|---|---|---|---|---|---|
| R **34** | M **10** | | | Fc | |
| | FM **1** | F **19** | | c | |
| W% **6** | m **+1** | F- **1** | | C' **+1** | |
| D% **58** | k **1** | F% **59** | | FC **1** | |
| d% **12** | K | | | CF **1** | |
| Dd% S **24** | FK | | | c | |

## WORK SHEET  *SA 14*

2

### VERBAL I. Q. = 133

| EWS | Info. | Comp. | Digit | Arith. | Sim. |
|-----|-------|-------|-------|--------|------|
| 18 | 25 | 20 | | 14 | 23-24 |
| 17 | 24 | 19 | 17 | 13 | 21-22 |
| 16 | 23 | 18 | 16 | 12 | 20 |
| 15 | 21-22 | 17 | | 11 | 19 |
| 14 | 20 | 16 | 15 | | 17-18 |
| 13 | 18-19 | 15 | 14 | 10 | 16 |
| 12 | 17 | 14 | | 9 | 15 |
| | | | | | |
| 11 | 15-16 | 12-13 | 13 | | 13-14 |
| 10 | 13-14 | 11 | 12 | 8 | 12 |
| 9 | 12 | 10 | 11 | 7 | 11 |
| 8 | 10-11 | 9 | | | 9-10 |
| 7 | 9 | 8 | 10 | 6 | 8 |
| 6 | 7-8 | 7 | 9 | 5 | 7 |
| | | | | | |
| 5 | 6 | 5-6 | | | 5-6 |
| 4 | 4-5 | 4 | 8 | 4 | 4 |
| 3 | 2-3 | 3 | 7 | 3 | 3 |
| 2 | 1 | 2 | 6 | | 1-2 |
| 1 | 0 | 1 | | 2 | 0 |
| 0 | | 0 | 5 | 1 | |

### SZONDI

| SEXUAL | | PAROXYSMAL | | EGO | | CONTACT | |
|--------|---|-----------|----|-----|---|---------|---|
| h | s | e | hy | k | p | d | m |
| X | X | | | | | X | |
| X | X | | | | | X | |
| X | X | X | | | X | X | X |
| X | X | X | X | X | X | X | X |
| X | | | | | | X | X | X |

### RORSCHACH

| | | | | | |
|---|---|---|---|---|---|
| R | 32 | M | 9 | | Fc |
| | | FM | 3 | F | 16 | c |
| W% | 9 | m | | F- | 3 | C' |
| D% | 69 | k | | F% | 59 | FC  1 |
| d% | 13 | K | | | | CF |
| Dd% | 9 | FK | | | | c |
| S | | | | | | |

## SUMMARY OF TEST FINDINGS    SA 14

### MANNER DURING TEST

| (1) Overly distressed | (2) Tense | (3) (Indifferent) | (4) Appropriate | (5) Relaxed and actively interested |
|---|---|---|---|---|
| (1) Hostile | (2) Uneasy | | | |

### I.Q. (Bellevue-Wechsler)

| (1) Below average | (2) Average | (3) High average | (4) Superior | (5) (Very superior) |
|---|---|---|---|---|

### PRODUCTIVITY (Rorschach)

| (1) Impoverished | (2) Reduced output | (3) (Adequate) | (4) Better than average | (5) Rich and well-ordered |
|---|---|---|---|---|
| | (2) Compulsive productivity | | | |

### RELATION TO REALITY (Rorschach, Bellevue-Wechsler, Drawings)

| (1) Loose | (2) Lapses—together with good form | (3) (Not noticeably disturbed) | (4) Essentially firm | (5) Firm and good |
|---|---|---|---|---|

### USUAL-UNUSUAL THOUGHT CONTENT (Rorschach, Unpleasant Concept)

| (1) Bizarre | (2) Tendency toward the bizarre | (3) (Adequate) | (4) Original trends | (5) Outstandingly original |
|---|---|---|---|---|
| (1) Stereotyped | (2) Tendency toward stereotypy | | | |

### CONSTRUCTIVE FANTASY (Rorschach)

| (1) Absent | (2) Barely accessible | (3) Accessible | (4) Readily accessible | (5) Active but not hampering |
|---|---|---|---|---|
| (1) (Withdrawal into fantasy) | | | | |

### DRIVE (Rorschach, Szondi, Unpleasant Concept)

| (1) Overpowering aggression | (2) Over-aggressive | (3) Adequate | (4) Clearly sufficient | (5) Sufficient—exceptionally well-directed |
|---|---|---|---|---|
| (1) Hampering passivity | (2) (Insufficient drive) | | | |

### EMOTIONAL TONE (Rorschach, Szondi)

| (1) Explosive emotions | (2) Getting out of hand | (3) Trend toward emotional expression | (4) Warmth available | (5) Warm, readily available |
|---|---|---|---|---|
| (1) Lacking | (2) (Indicated but repressed emotions) | | | |

### SOCIAL ATTITUDE (T. A. T.)

| (1) Uncontrolled | (2) (Constricted or neglected) | (3) Adequate | (4) Well-regulated | (5) Free and flexible |
|---|---|---|---|---|

### ANXIETY

| (1) Disintegrating | (2) Marked | (3) (Moderate) | (4) Not marked | (5) Lack of evidence of anxiety |
|---|---|---|---|---|

### OVER-ALL EVALUATION

| (1) Markedly disturbed personality | (2) (Less than adequate personality with some psychological problems) | (3) Adequate personality | (4) Better than average functioning personality | (5) Exceptionally well-integrated personality with excellent potential |
|---|---|---|---|---|

## SUMMARY OF THERAPIST'S FINDINGS   *SA 14*

### ESTIMATED INTELLIGENCE LEVEL

| (1) Below average | (2) Average | (3) ~~High average~~ | (4) Superior | (5) Very superior |
|---|---|---|---|---|

### FLOW OF ASSOCIATIVE MATERIAL

| (1) Impoverished | (2) Reduced output | (3) ~~Adequate~~ | (4) Better than average | (5) Rich and well-ordered |
|---|---|---|---|---|
| | (2) Compulsive productivity | | | |

### RELATION TO REALITY

| (1) ~~Loose~~ | (2) Lapses—together with good form | (3) Not noticeably disturbed | (4) Essentially firm | (5) Firm and good |
|---|---|---|---|---|

### USUAL-UNUSUAL THOUGHT CONTENT

| (1) ~~Bizarre~~ | (2) Tendency toward the bizarre | (3) Adequate | (4) Original trends | (5) Outstandingly original |
|---|---|---|---|---|
| (1) Stereotyped | (2) Tendency toward stereotypy | | | |

### CONSTRUCTIVE FANTASY

| (1) Absent | (2) ~~Barely accessible~~ | (3) Accessible | (4) Readily accessible | (5) Active but not hampering |
|---|---|---|---|---|
| (1) Withdrawal into fantasy | | | | |

### DRIVE

| (1) Overpowering aggression | (2) ~~Over-aggressive~~ | (3) Adequate | (4) Clearly sufficient | (5) Sufficient—exceptionally well-directed |
|---|---|---|---|---|
| (1) Hampering passivity | (2) ~~Insufficient drive~~ | | | |

### EMOTIONAL TONE

| (1) Explosive emotions | (2) ~~Getting out of hand~~ | (3) Trend toward emotional expression | (4) Warmth available | (5) Warm, readily available |
|---|---|---|---|---|
| (1) Lacking | (2) Indicated but re-pressed emotions | | | |

### SOCIAL ATTITUDE

| (1) Uncontrolled | (2) ~~Constricted or neglected~~ | (3) Adequate | (4) Well-regulated | (5) Free and flexible |
|---|---|---|---|---|

### ANXIETY

| (1) Disintegrating | (2) ~~Marked~~ | (3) Moderate | (4) Not marked | (5) Lack of evidence of anxiety |
|---|---|---|---|---|

### OVER-ALL EVALUATION

| (1) ~~Markedly disturbed personality~~ | (2) Less than adequate personality with some psychological problems | (3) Adequate personality | (4) Better than average functioning personality | (5) Exceptionally well-integrated personality with excellent potential |
|---|---|---|---|---|

## WORK SHEET    *SA 15*

### VERBAL I. Q. = *109*

| EWS | Info. | Comp. | Digit | Arith. | Sim. |
|-----|-------|-------|-------|--------|------|
| 18 | 25 | 20 | | 14 | 23-24 |
| 17 | 24 | 19 | 17 | 13 | 21-22 |
| 16 | 23 | 18 | 16 | 12 | 20 |
| 15 | 21-22 | 17 | | 11 | 19 |
| 14 | 20 | 16 | 15 | | 17-18 |
| 13 | 18-19 | 15 | 14 | *10* | 16 |
| 12 | 17 | 14 | | 9 | 15 |
| | | | | | |
| 11 | *15-16* | 12-13 | 13 | | 13-14 |
| 10 | *13-14* | *11* | 12 | 8 | 12 |
| 9 | 12 | 10 | 11 | 7 | 11 |
| 8 | 10-11 | 9 | | | *9-10* |
| 7 | 9 | 8 | *10* | 6 | 8 |

### SZONDI

| SEXUAL | | PAROXYSMAL | | EGO | | CONTACT | |
|--------|---|------------|----|-----|---|---------|---|
| h | s | e | hy | k | p | d | m |
| | | | | | | | X |
| X | | | | | | | X |
| X | X | X | | | | | X |
| X | X | X | | | X | | X |
| X | | X | X | | | X | X |
| | | X | X | | | X | X |
| | | X | X | | | X | |
| | | X | X | | | | |

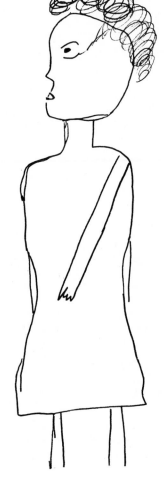

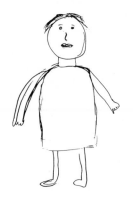

### RORSCHACH

| R | *47* | M | *1* | | | Fc | *1* |
|---|------|----|------|---|------|----|-----|
| | | FM | *3* | F | *24* | c | *1* |
| W% | *21* | m | *+1* | F- | *10* | C' | |
| D% | *47* | k | *2* | F% | *72* | FC | *1* |
| d% | *17* | K | *+2* | | | CF | *1* |
| Dd% / S% | *15* | FK | *1* | | | C | *2* |

## WORK SHEET 2

SA 15

### VERBAL I. Q. = 116

| EWS | Info. | Comp. | Digit | Arith. | Sim. |
|---|---|---|---|---|---|
| 18 | 25 | 20 | | 14 | 23-24 |
| 17 | 24 | 19 | 17 | 13 | 21-22 |
| 16 | 23 | 18 | 16 | 12 | 20 |
| 15 | 21-22 | 17 | | 11 | 19 |
| 14 | 20 | 16 | 15 | | 17-18 |
| 13 | 18-19 | 15 | 14 | (10) | (16) |
| 12 | (17) | 14 | | 9 | 15 |
| 11 | 15-16 | (12-13) | (13) | | 13-14 |
| 10 | 13-14 | 11 | 12 | 8 | 12 |
| 9 | 12 | 10 | 11 | 7 | 11 |
| 8 | 10-11 | 9 | | | 9-10 |
| 7 | 9 | 8 | 10 | 6 | 8 |
| 6 | 7-8 | 7 | 9 | 5 | 7 |
| 5 | 6 | 5-6 | | | 5-6 |
| 4 | 4-5 | 4 | 8 | 4 | 4 |
| 3 | 2-3 | 3 | 7 | 3 | 3 |

### SZONDI

| SEXUAL | | PAROXYSMAL | | EGO | | CONTACT | |
|---|---|---|---|---|---|---|---|
| h | s | e | hy | k | p | d | m |
| X | | | | | X | | X |
| X | X | | | | X | | X X |
| X | X | | X | | X | | X |
| X | X | X | X | X | X | X | X |
| | | | X | X | | | |
| | | | | X | | | |
| | | | | X | | | |

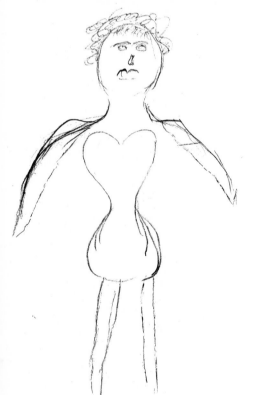

### RORSCHACH

| | | | | | |
|---|---|---|---|---|---|
| R | 62 | M | 2 | Fc | 1 |
| | | FM | 8 | F 34 | c 2 |
| W% | 11 | m | +1 | F- 7 | C' |
| D% | 53 | k | 1 | F% 66 | FC 2 |
| d% | 21 | K | 1+1 | | CF 1+1 |
| Dd% S | 15 | FK | 1 | | C 2 |

# SUMMARY OF TEST FINDINGS    SA 15

### MANNER DURING TEST

| (1) Overly distressed | (2) Tense | (3) Indifferent | (4) Appropriate | (5) Relaxed and actively interested |
|---|---|---|---|---|
| (1) Hostile | (2) (Uneasy) | | | |

### I.Q. (Bellevue-Wechsler)

| (1) Below average | (2) (Average) → | (3) High average | (4) Superior | (5) Very superior |
|---|---|---|---|---|

### PRODUCTIVITY (Rorschach)

| (1) Impoverished | (2) Reduced output | (3) Adequate | (4) Better than average | (5) Rich and well-ordered |
|---|---|---|---|---|
| | (2) (Compulsive productivity) | | | |

### RELATION TO REALITY (Rorschach, Bellevue-Wechsler, Drawings)

| (1) Loose | (2) (Lapses—together with good form) | (3) Not noticeably disturbed | (4) Essentially firm | (5) Firm and good |
|---|---|---|---|---|

### USUAL-UNUSUAL THOUGHT CONTENT (Rorschach, Unpleasant Concept)

| (1) Bizarre | (2) Tendency toward the bizarre | (3) Adequate | (4) Original trends | (5) Outstandingly original |
|---|---|---|---|---|
| (1) Stereotyped | (2) (Tendency toward stereotypy) → | | | |

### CONSTRUCTIVE FANTASY (Rorschach)

| (1) Absent | (2) (Barely accessible) | (3) Accessible | (4) Readily accessible | (5) Active but not hampering |
|---|---|---|---|---|
| (1) Withdrawal into fantasy | | | | |

### DRIVE (Rorschach, Szondi, Unpleasant Concept)

| (1) Overpowering aggression | (2) Over-aggressive | (3) (Adequate) | (4) Clearly sufficient | (5) Sufficient—exceptionally well-directed |
|---|---|---|---|---|
| (1) Hampering passivity | (2) Insufficient drive | | | |

### EMOTIONAL TONE (Rorschach, Szondi)

| (1) Explosive emotions | (2) (Getting out of hand) | (3) Trend toward emotional expression | (4) Warmth available | (5) Warm, readily available |
|---|---|---|---|---|
| (1) Lacking | (2) Indicated but re-pressed emotions | | | |

### SOCIAL ATTITUDE (T. A. T.)

| (1) Uncontrolled | (2) (Constricted or neglected) → | (3) Adequate | (4) Well-regulated | (5) Free and flexible |
|---|---|---|---|---|

### ANXIETY

| (1) Disintegrating | (2) Marked | (3) (Moderate) | (4) Not marked | (5) Lack of evidence of anxiety |
|---|---|---|---|---|

### OVER-ALL EVALUATION

| (1) Markedly dis-turbed personality | (2) (Less than adequate personality with some psycholog-ical problems) | (3) Adequate personality | (4) Better than average function-ing personality | (5) Exceptionally well-integrated person-ality with excellent potential |
|---|---|---|---|---|

## SUMMARY OF THERAPIST'S FINDINGS  SA 15

### ESTIMATED INTELLIGENCE LEVEL

| (1) Below average | (2) Average | (3) High average | (4) Superior | (5) Very superior |
|---|---|---|---|---|

### FLOW OF ASSOCIATIVE MATERIAL

| (1) Impoverished | (2) Reduced output | (3) Adequate | (4) Better than average | (5) Rich and well-ordered |
|---|---|---|---|---|
| | (2) Compulsive productivity | | | |

### RELATION TO REALITY

| (1) Loose | (2) Lapses—together with good form | (3) Not noticeably disturbed | (4) Essentially firm | (5) Firm and good |
|---|---|---|---|---|

### USUAL-UNUSUAL THOUGHT CONTENT

| (1) Bizarre | (2) Tendency toward the bizarre | (3) Adequate | (4) Original trends | (5) Outstandingly original |
|---|---|---|---|---|
| (1) Stereotyped | (2) Tendency toward stereotypy | | | |

### CONSTRUCTIVE FANTASY

| (1) Absent | (2) Barely accessible | (3) Accessible | (4) Readily accessible | (5) Active but not hampering |
|---|---|---|---|---|
| (1) Withdrawal into fantasy | | | | |

### DRIVE

| (1) Overpowering aggression | (2) Over-aggressive | (3) Adequate | (4) Clearly sufficient | (5) Sufficient—exceptionally well-directed |
|---|---|---|---|---|
| (1) Hampering passivity | (2) Insufficient drive | | | |

### EMOTIONAL TONE

| (1) Explosive emotions | (2) Getting out of hand | (3) Trend toward emotional expression | (4) Warmth available | (5) Warm, readily available |
|---|---|---|---|---|
| (1) Lacking | (2) Indicated but repressed emotions | | | |

### SOCIAL ATTITUDE

| (1) Uncontrolled | (2) Constricted or neglected | (3) Adequate | (4) Well-regulated | (5) Free and flexible |
|---|---|---|---|---|

### ANXIETY

| (1) Disintegrating | (2) Marked | (3) Moderate | (4) Not marked | (5) Lack of evidence of anxiety |
|---|---|---|---|---|

### OVER-ALL EVALUATION

| (1) Markedly disturbed personality | (2) Less than adequate personality with some psychological problems | (3) Adequate personality | (4) Better than average functioning personality | (5) Exceptionally well-integrated personality with excellent potential |
|---|---|---|---|---|

SA16, in her mid-twenties, was rated by her therapist between 1 and 2 on the OVER-ALL EVALUATION scale at the commencement of therapy and was considered to be unimproved at its termination. A five-year follow-up indicated some change for the better in her condition clinically, subsequent to the use of tranquilizing drugs while under the care of another therapist.

This is one of the few instances where the initial I.Q., 120, is higher than that obtained on the retest, 113. SA16 was able to score initially in the *Superior* range of the total population chiefly as the result of a perfect score on the Arithmetic subtest. At the time of the re-examination, she was acutely anxious, and this anxiety was reflected in her inability to handle the problems she had taken in stride before. Thus, the scattergram assumes a very different distribution on the two occasions.

Little can be said in terms of a contrast on the Szondi. True, the shift from a +m, −d to an open m and more loaded −d is an unfavorable one, but the changes elsewhere are too slight for comment.

The Figure Drawings are virtually identical. They bear a personalized stamp and are clearly recognizable as the work of the same individual. The concept of the woman has not changed — the need for a glamorous approach, the wasp waist and the evening dress. Concern with her own death continues to be a preoccupation in the Sentence Completion and in the Most Unpleasant Concept tests.

The Rorschach, both structurally and in terms of content, is extremely similar both times. The psychogram is characterized by the high F per cent and virtual absence of responses on the extroversial side. If anything, the second record indicates greater disturbance, for the human movement responses are more bizarre and the one color response available in the first record has dropped out. The mental approach remains unchanged.

The quantitative score for the first test is 28; for the second, 23.

(The records of SA16 will be found on pages 304-307, of SA17 on pages 308-311.)

SA17 was in his early twenties and unmarried when first seen for diagnostic testing. The therapist estimated him as a markedly disturbed personality when he entered treatment and considered his condition virtually unchanged at its termination. There was, however, a brief period of greater control and less destructive aggression, this occurring at the time the second testing took place. When a follow-up study was made five years later, SA17 was found to be hospitalized, the records showing that he had become dangerously assaultive on several occasions.

Comparison of the Wechsler-Bellevue for the two testings reveals a highly disturbed pattern, with completely bizarre responses accounting for the low Comprehension scores. Only two responses in the entire performance differ in the first and second tests. The Szondi also remained essentially unchanged.

Little comment is required concerning the Figure Drawings.* The reduction in size on the second attempt and the appearance of some neck structure was felt to indicate a little less grandiose and unrealistic self-concept and some increase in control.

The structural aspects of the Rorschach convey its thoroughly pathologic quality. Some slight improvement is indicated in the second record in that the flagrant CF responses were reduced from eleven to seven and the two pure C answers dropped out entirely. The F− responses were also reduced from fifteen to eight. This parallels the temporary improvement seen clinically, which, however, was not maintained over more than a few weeks.

The clinical and psychological assessment here is almost identical. Quantitatively, SA17 received a score of 16 on the first test and 17 on the second.

* The picture of the man on Work Sheet 1 was reduced before reproduction to approximately half its size; that on Work Sheet 2 is reproduced from the original.

===== WORK SHEET =====  SA16

1

## VERBAL I. Q. = 120

| EWS | Info. | Comp. | Digit | Arith. | Sim. |
|-----|-------|-------|-------|--------|------|
| 18 | 25 | 20 | | (14) | 23-24 |
| 17 | 24 | 19 | 17 | 13 | 21-22 |
| 16 | 23 | 18 | 16 | 12 | 20 |
| 15 | 21-22 | 17 | | 11 | 19 |
| 14 | 20 | 16 | 15 | | (17-18) |
| 13 | 18-19 | 15 | 14 | 10 | 16 |
| 12 | 17 | 14 | | 9 | 15 |
| 11 | (15-16) | 12-13 | (13) | | 13-14 |
| 10 | 13-14 | (11) | 12 | 8 | 12 |
| 9 | 12 | 10 | 11 | 7 | 11 |
| 8 | 10-11 | 9 | | | 9-10 |
| 7 | 9 | 8 | 10 | 6 | 8 |
| 6 | 7-8 | 7 | 9 | 5 | 7 |

## SZONDI

| SEXUAL | | PAROXYSMAL | | EGO | | CONTACT | |
|---|---|---|---|---|---|---|---|
| h | s | e | hy | k | p | d | m |
| | X | | | | | | |
| X | X | X | | | | | X |
| X | X | X | | X | X | X | X |
| X | | X | X | X | X | X | X |
| | | | X | X | X | X | |
| | | | | | | X | |

## RORSCHACH

| | | | | |
|---|---|---|---|---|
| R **39** | M **6(1-)** | | | Fc **2** |
| | FM **1** | | F **27** | c **+** |
| W% **15** | m | | F- **1** | C' |
| D% **59** | k **1** | | F% **72** | FC |
| d% **13** | K | | | CF |
| Dd% **13** | FK | | | C |
| S | | | | |

## WORK SHEET SA16

2

### VERBAL I. Q. = 113

| EWS | Info. | Comp. | Digit | Arith. | Sim. |
|---|---|---|---|---|---|
| 18 | 25 | 20 | | 14 | 23-24 |
| 17 | 24 | 19 | 17 | 13 | 21-22 |
| 16 | 23 | 18 | 16 | 12 | 20 |
| 15 | 21-22 | 17 | | 11 | 19 |
| 14 | 20 | 16 | 15 | | (17-18) |
| 13 | 18-19 | 15 | (14) | 10 | 16 |
| 12 | 17 | 14 | | 9 | 15 |
| 11 | (15-16) | (12-17) | 13 | | 13-14 |
| 10 | 13-14 | (11) | 12 | (8) | 12 |
| 9 | 12 | 10 | 11 | 7 | 11 |
| 8 | 10-11 | 9 | | | 9-10 |
| 7 | 9 | 8 | 10 | 6 | 8 |
| 6 | 7-8 | 7 | 9 | 5 | 7 |

### SZONDI

| SEXUAL | | PAROXYSMAL | | EGO | | CONTACT | |
|---|---|---|---|---|---|---|---|
| h | s | e | hy | k | p | d | m |
| X | X | | | | | | |
| X | X | X | | | | | |
| X | X | X | X | X | | X | X |
| X | | X | X | X | X | X | |
| | | X | X | X | | X | |
| | | X | X | X | | X | |
| | | | | | | X | |
| | | | | | | X | |

### RORSCHACH

| | | | | | |
|---|---|---|---|---|---|
| R | 33 | M | 6(3-) | Fc | 2 |
| | | FM | | F | 24 | c | |
| W% | 15 | m | | F- | 1 | C' | |
| D% | 55 | k | | F% | 76 | FC | |
| d% | 15 | K | | | | CF | |
| Dd% | 15 | FK | | | | C | |
| S | | | | | | | |

## SUMMARY OF TEST FINDINGS     *SA 16*

### MANNER DURING TEST

| (1) Overly distressed | (2) Tense | (3) Indifferent | (4) Appropriate | (5) Relaxed and actively interested |
|---|---|---|---|---|
| (1) Hostile | (2) Uneasy | | | |

### I.Q. (Bellevue-Wechsler)

| (1) Below average | (2) Average | (3) High average | (4) Superior | (5) Very superior |
|---|---|---|---|---|

### PRODUCTIVITY (Rorschach)

| (1) Impoverished | (2) Reduced output | (3) Adequate | (4) Better than average | (5) Rich and well-ordered |
|---|---|---|---|---|
| | (2) Compulsive productivity | | | |

### RELATION TO REALITY (Rorschach, Bellevue-Wechsler, Drawings)

| (1) Loose | (2) Lapses—together with good form | (3) Not noticeably disturbed | (4) Essentially firm | (5) Firm and good |
|---|---|---|---|---|

### USUAL-UNUSUAL THOUGHT CONTENT (Rorschach, Unpleasant Concept)

| (1) Bizarre | (2) Tendency toward the bizarre | (3) Adequate | (4) Original trends | (5) Outstandingly original |
|---|---|---|---|---|
| (1) Stereotyped | (2) Tendency toward stereotypy | | | |

### CONSTRUCTIVE FANTASY (Rorschach)

| (1) Absent | (2) Barely accessible | (3) Accessible | (4) Readily accessible | (5) Active but not hampering |
|---|---|---|---|---|
| (1) Withdrawal into fantasy | | | | |

### DRIVE (Rorschach, Szondi, Unpleasant Concept)

| (1) Overpowering aggression | (2) Over-aggressive | (3) Adequate | (4) Clearly sufficient | (5) Sufficient—exceptionally well-directed |
|---|---|---|---|---|
| (1) Hampering passivity | (2) Insufficient drive | | | |

### EMOTIONAL TONE (Rorschach, Szondi)

| (1) Explosive emotions | (2) Getting out of hand | (3) Trend toward emotional expression | (4) Warmth available | (5) Warm, readily available |
|---|---|---|---|---|
| (1) Lacking | (2) Indicated but repressed emotions | | | |

### SOCIAL ATTITUDE (T. A. T.)

| (1) Uncontrolled | (2) Constricted or neglected | (3) Adequate | (4) Well-regulated | (5) Free and flexible |
|---|---|---|---|---|

### ANXIETY

| (1) Disintegrating | (2) Marked | (3) Moderate | (4) Not marked | (5) Lack of evidence of anxiety |
|---|---|---|---|---|

### OVER-ALL EVALUATION

| (1) Markedly disturbed personality | (2) Less than adequate personality with some psychological problems | (3) Adequate personality | (4) Better than average functioning personality | (5) Exceptionally well-integrated personality with excellent potential |
|---|---|---|---|---|

## SUMMARY OF THERAPIST'S FINDINGS          *SA 16*

### ESTIMATED INTELLIGENCE LEVEL

| (1) Below average | (2) ~~Average~~ (circled) | (3) High average | (4) Superior | (5) Very superior |
|---|---|---|---|---|

### FLOW OF ASSOCIATIVE MATERIAL

| (1) Impoverished | (2) ~~Reduced output~~ (circled) | (3) Adequate | (4) Better than average | (5) Rich and well-ordered |
|---|---|---|---|---|
| | (2) Compulsive productivity | | | |

### RELATION TO REALITY

| (1) Loose | (2) Lapses—together with good form | (3) ~~Not noticeably disturbed~~ (circled) | (4) Essentially firm | (5) Firm and good |
|---|---|---|---|---|

### USUAL-UNUSUAL THOUGHT CONTENT

| (1) Bizarre | (2) Tendency toward the bizarre | (3) ~~Adequate~~ (circled) | (4) Original trends | (5) Outstandingly original |
|---|---|---|---|---|
| (1) Stereotyped | (2) Tendency toward stereotypy | | | |

### CONSTRUCTIVE FANTASY

| (1) Absent | (2) ~~Barely accessible~~ (circled) | (3) Accessible | (4) Readily accessible | (5) Active but not hampering |
|---|---|---|---|---|
| (1) Withdrawal into fantasy | | | | |

### DRIVE

| (1) Overpowering aggression | (2) Over-aggressive | (3) Adequate | (4) Clearly sufficient | (5) Sufficient—exceptionally well-directed |
|---|---|---|---|---|
| (1) Hampering passivity | (2) ~~Insufficient drive~~ (circled) | | | |

### EMOTIONAL TONE

| (1) Explosive emotions | (2) Getting out of hand | (3) Trend toward emotional expression | (4) Warmth available | (5) Warm, readily available |
|---|---|---|---|---|
| (1) Lacking | (2) Indicated but repressed emotions | | | |

### SOCIAL ATTITUDE

| (1) Uncontrolled | (2) ~~Constricted or neglected~~ (circled) | (3) Adequate | (4) Well-regulated | (5) Free and flexible |
|---|---|---|---|---|

### ANXIETY

| (1) Disintegrating | (2) ~~Marked~~ (circled) | (3) Moderate | (4) Not marked | (5) Lack of evidence of anxiety |
|---|---|---|---|---|

### OVER-ALL EVALUATION

| (1) Markedly disturbed personality | (2) ~~Less than adequate personality with some psychological problems~~ (circled) | (3) Adequate personality | (4) Better than average functioning personality | (5) Exceptionally well-integrated personality with excellent potential |
|---|---|---|---|---|

## WORK SHEET    SA17

I

VERBAL I. Q. *114*

| EWS | Info. | Comp. | Digit | Arith. | Sim. |
|-----|-------|-------|-------|--------|------|
| 18 | 25 | 20 | | 14 | 23-24 |
| 17 | 24 | 19 | 17 | 13 | 21-22 |
| 16 | 23 | 18 | 16 | 12 | ⟨20⟩ |
| 15 | 21-22 | 17 | | 11 | 19 |
| 14 | ⟨20⟩ | 16 | 15 | | 17-18 |
| 13 | 18-19 | 15 | 14 | ⟨10⟩ | 16 |
| 12 | 17 | 14 | | 9 | 15 |
| | | | | | |
| 11 | 15-16 | 12-13 | 13 | | 13-14 |
| 10 | 13-14 | 11 | ⟨12⟩ | 8 | 12 |
| 9 | 12 | 10 | 11 | 7 | 11 |
| 8 | 10-11 | 9 | | | 9-10 |
| 7 | 9 | 8 | 10 | 6 | 8 |
| 6 | 7-8 | ⟨7⟩ | 9 | 5 | 7 |
| | | | | | |
| 5 | 6 | 5-6 | | | 5-6 |
| 4 | 4-5 | 4 | 8 | 4 | 4 |
| 3 | 2-3 | 3 | 7 | 3 | 3 |
| 2 | 1 | 2 | 6 | | 1-2 |
| 1 | 0 | 1 | | 2 | 0 |
| 0 | | 0 | 5 | 1 | |

### SZONDI

| SEXUAL | | PAROXYSMAL | | EGO | | CONTACT | |
|--------|--------|------------|--------|--------|--------|--------|--------|
| h | s | e | hy | k | p | d | m |

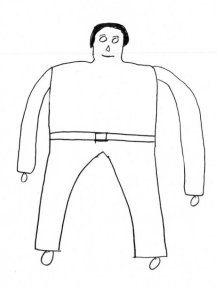

### RORSCHACH

| | | | | |
|---|---|---|---|---|
| R | 51 | M | 1 | Fc |
| | | FM | 3 | F 12 | c +3 |
| W% | 29 | m | 1 | F- 15 | C' 1 |
| D% | 61 | k | | F% 53 | FC 1 |
| d% | 8 | K | 3 | | CF 11 |
| Dd% | 2 | FK | 1 | | c 2 |
| S | | | | |

# WORK SHEET

SA 17

2

## VERBAL I. Q. = 113

| EWS | Info. | Comp. | Digit | Arith. | Sim. |
|---|---|---|---|---|---|
| 18 | 25 | 20 | | 14 | 23-24 |
| 17 | 24 | 19 | 17 | 13 | 21-22 |
| 16 | 23 | 18 | 16 | 12 | 20 |
| 15 | 21-22 | 17 | | 11 | (19) |
| 14 | (20) | 16 | 15 | | 17-18 |
| 13 | 18-19 | 15 | 14 | (10) | 16 |
| 12 | 17 | 14 | | 9 | 15 |
| 11 | 15-16 | 12-13 | (13) | | 13-14 |
| 10 | 13-14 | 11 | 12 | 8 | 12 |
| 9 | 12 | 0 | 11 | 7 | 11 |
| 8 | 10-11 | 9 | | | 9-10 |
| 7 | 9 | | 10 | 6 | 8 |
| 6 | 7-8 | (7) | 9 | 5 | 7 |
| 5 | 6 | 5-6 | | | 5-6 |
| 4 | 4-5 | 4 | 8 | 4 | 4 |
| 3 | 2-3 | 3 | 7 | 3 | 3 |
| 2 | 1 | 2 | 6 | | 1-2 |
| 1 | 0 | 1 | | 2 | 0 |
| 0 | | 0 | 5 | 1 | |

## SZONDI

| SEXUAL | | PAROXYSMAL | | EGO | | CONTACT | |
|---|---|---|---|---|---|---|---|
| h | s | e | hy | k | p | d | m |
| | | | | | X | | |
| | X | | | | X | | |
| | X | | | | X | | X |
| X | X | X | X | | X | | X |
| X | X | X | X | X | | X | X |
| X | | X | X | X | | | X |

## RORSCHACH

| R | 52 | M | 2 | | | Fc | |
|---|---|---|---|---|---|---|---|
| | | FM | 6 | F | 24 | c | |
| W% | 25 | m | +3 | F- | 8 | C' | |
| D% | 54 | k | | F% | 62 | FC | |
| d% | 15 | K | 3 | | | CF | 7 |
| Dd% | 6 | FK | 2 | | | C | |
| S | | | | | | | |

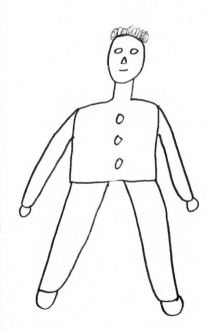

# SUMMARY OF TEST FINDINGS   *SA 17*

## MANNER DURING TEST

| (1) Overly distressed | (2) Tense | (3) Indifferent | (4) Appropriate | (5) Relaxed and actively interested |
|---|---|---|---|---|
| (1) Hostile | (2) Uneasy | | | |

## I.Q. (Bellevue-Wechsler)

| (1) Below average | (2) Average | (3) High average | (4) Superior | (5) Very superior |
|---|---|---|---|---|

## PRODUCTIVITY (Rorschach)

| (1) Impoverished | (2) Reduced output | (3) Adequate | (4) Better than average | (5) Rich and well-ordered |
|---|---|---|---|---|
| | (2) Compulsive productivity | | | |

## RELATION TO REALITY (Rorschach, Bellevue-Wechsler, Drawings)

| (1) Loose | (2) Lapses—together with good form | (3) Not noticeably disturbed | (4) Essentially firm | (5) Firm and good |
|---|---|---|---|---|

## USUAL-UNUSUAL THOUGHT CONTENT (Rorschach, Unpleasant Concept)

| (1) Bizarre | (2) Tendency toward the bizarre | (3) Adequate | (4) Original trends | (5) Outstandingly original |
|---|---|---|---|---|
| (1) Stereotyped | (2) Tendency toward stereotypy | | | |

## CONSTRUCTIVE FANTASY (Rorschach)

| (1) Absent | (2) Barely accessible | (3) Accessible | (4) Readily accessible | (5) Active but not hampering |
|---|---|---|---|---|
| (1) Withdrawal into fantasy | | | | |

## DRIVE (Rorschach, Szondi, Unpleasant Concept)

| (1) Overpowering aggression | (2) Over-aggressive | (3) Adequate | (4) Clearly sufficient | (5) Sufficient—exceptionally well-directed |
|---|---|---|---|---|
| (1) Hampering passivity | (2) Insufficient drive | | | |

## EMOTIONAL TONE (Rorschach, Szondi)

| (1) Explosive emotions | (2) Getting out of hand | (3) Trend toward emotional expression | (4) Warmth available | (5) Warm, readily available |
|---|---|---|---|---|
| (1) Lacking | (2) Indicated but repressed emotions | | | |

## SOCIAL ATTITUDE (T. A. T.)

| (1) Uncontrolled | (2) Constricted or neglected | (3) Adequate | (4) Well-regulated | (5) Free and flexible |
|---|---|---|---|---|

## ANXIETY

| (1) Disintegrating | (2) Marked | (3) Moderate | (4) Not marked | (5) Lack of evidence of anxiety |
|---|---|---|---|---|

## OVER-ALL EVALUATION

| (1) Markedly disturbed personality | (2) Less than adequate personality with some psychological problems | (3) Adequate personality | (4) Better than average functioning personality | (5) Exceptionally well-integrated personality with excellent potential |
|---|---|---|---|---|

## SUMMARY OF THERAPIST'S FINDINGS    *SA 17*

### ESTIMATED INTELLIGENCE LEVEL

| (1) Below average | (2) Average | (3) High average | (4) Superior | (5) Very superior |
|---|---|---|---|---|

### FLOW OF ASSOCIATIVE MATERIAL

| (1) Impoverished | (2) Reduced output | (3) Adequate | (4) Better than average | (5) Rich and well-ordered |
|---|---|---|---|---|
| | (2) Compulsive productivity | | | |

### RELATION TO REALITY

| (1) Loose | (2) Lapses—together with good form | (3) Not noticeably disturbed | (4) Essentially firm | (5) Firm and good |
|---|---|---|---|---|

### USUAL-UNUSUAL THOUGHT CONTENT

| (1) Bizarre | (2) Tendency toward the bizarre | (3) Adequate | (4) Original trends | (5) Outstandingly original |
|---|---|---|---|---|
| (1) Stereotyped | (2) Tendency toward stereotypy | | | |

### CONSTRUCTIVE FANTASY

| (1) Absent | (2) Barely accessible | (3) Accessible | (4) Readily accessible | (5) Active but not hampering |
|---|---|---|---|---|
| (1) Withdrawal into fantasy | | | | |

### DRIVE

| (1) Overpowering aggression | (2) Over-aggressive | (3) Adequate | (4) Clearly sufficient | (5) Sufficient—exceptionally well-directed |
|---|---|---|---|---|
| (1) Hampering passivity | (2) Insufficient drive | | | |

### EMOTIONAL TONE

| (1) Explosive emotions | (2) Getting out of hand | (3) Trend toward emotional expression | (4) Warmth available | (5) Warm, readily available |
|---|---|---|---|---|
| (1) Lacking | (2) Indicated but repressed emotions | | | |

### SOCIAL ATTITUDE

| (1) Uncontrolled | (2) Constricted or neglected | (3) Adequate | (4) Well-regulated | (5) Free and flexible |
|---|---|---|---|---|

### ANXIETY

| (1) Disintegrating | (2) Marked | (3) Moderate | (4) Not marked | (5) Lack of evidence of anxiety |
|---|---|---|---|---|

### OVER-ALL EVALUATION

| (1) Markedly disturbed personality | (2) Less than adequate personality with some psychological problems | (3) Adequate personality | (4) Better than average functioning personality | (5) Exceptionally well-integrated personality with excellent potential |
|---|---|---|---|---|

## XIV. Retesting following psychotherapy and again ten years later.

TY1, TY2 and TY3 are representative of a group of twelve individuals who were tested for the third time after a ten-year interval, the first retesting having occurred subsequent to the termination of brief or long-term psychotherapy. These cases have been selected primarily because they are known intimately to the particular therapists, who have been in close touch with them over the intervening years. The work record of each is also known to the examiner, thus making their achievements easily verifiable.

These cases are good examples of the fact that changes in behavior and behavioral adjustment take place prior to the appearance of indication of these changes in the projective techniques, and also of the fact that the magnitude of behavioral change is rarely, if ever, as dramatically indicated in the test material as in the individual's life. But they also show that changes *do* register after a time interval, changes which have not been "caught" in too-precipitous retesting.

Retested after brief psychotherapy (less than a year after the initial testing) TY1, a woman in her forties, does not show a markedly different picture on the psychological tests from that which had been given at the time of the pretherapy evaluation. Yet, it was clear clinically that important changes were already evident in adjustment, work satisfaction and loss of symptoms.

The appraisal of the therapist in regard to TY1 was as follows:

"At the start of therapy TY1 was almost entirely a captive of early childhood emotional goals. Most conspicuous emotional behavior was the explosion of violent rages. This patient had good intellectual capacity and good and useful social and personal goals, but was unable to achieve the latter nor to use the former for her own benefit to any marked degree. TY1 hated women, was able to hold fast to only a few relationships, male or female, but did have two strong ones. Some warmth was present, and she desperately wanted to use it but rarely could. She held jobs only for short periods. She aroused in those around her a constant fear of offending her or of stirring up smoldering resentment or rage.

"She has become a warm, giving, companionable person, comfortable and easy to be with. Rage is not seen at all. Her life has financial troubles in it but outside evidences of frustration are lacking. She is a clear, objective thinker, unhampered by the old shackles. She feels like a newly created person."

TY1 gives a somewhat comparable account of her own progress:

312

"I don't know how best to phrase it, but as a result of therapy I seemed to begin to learn how to live. Most important of all is the fact that I have a feeling of kinship with human beings which I never had before. I also feel I have learned a startling thing—that I have a choice of behavior. I no longer have to act in certain ways. I feel I can accept myself, and I can accept myself in relation to other people. Ninety-five per cent of the time, I would say, I can think what I'm doing. Only very few things can ever trigger off the old rages."

On a 5-point scale this patient places herself initially as having been at 2, quite seriously disturbed; she now places herself on the same scale at 4.

In the course of conversation at the time of the ten-year retesting, this patient commented on some of the things which had previously been baffling but into which, subsequent to therapy, she had acquired growing insight. For example, the Most Unpleasant Concept she had originally drawn was "discordant noise." In the retest, ten years after, she drew this noise (discordant musical notes) coming out of the mouth of a female: "I realize now that all this time my hatred of noise was that of my mother's harsh and angry voice many years ago."

Turning now to the test material, one finds little difference between Work Sheets 1 and 2, the quantitative scores in both instances being 20. To conserve space, Work Sheet 2 is not included here but there is essentially the same "level" of drawing (graded at level 2) and little change in the Rorschach either in its formal properties or in terms of the somewhat stereotyped responses given. The Most Unpleasant Concept remained discordant noise, neither explained nor understood.

On Work Sheet 3, a considerable change has taken place, the most startling being in the formal properties and the content of the Rorschach record. Although the number of responses has not changed spectacularly, the quality and the distribution of the determinants have been altered beyond recognition. Particularly striking are the five good FC responses, with an additional two which now appear. The warmth spoken of by the therapist is now definitely available. Four rather vivid human movement responses are given; the three F− responses have dropped out; d and dds responses have found their way into the record, and there is much less indication of the striving for W responses, the over-reaching intellectually to compensate for the many feelings of personal inadequacy that characterized Record 1.

The drawings are now rated as 3 instead of 2; the female figure reproduced on page 25 (central figure) as an example of the third level of Figure Drawing, is now drawn full-length, whereas previously it was only a somewhat distorted head. Contrasting the drawings of the male on Work Sheets 1 and 3, a different concept of the human being will be

## WORK SHEET

_Tyi_

### VERBAL I. Q. = 112

| EWS | Info. | Comp. | Digit | Arith. | Sim. |
|---|---|---|---|---|---|
| 18 | 25 | 20 |  | 14 | 23-24 |
| 17 | 24 | 19 | 17 | 13 | 21-22 |
| 16 | 23 | 18 | 16 | 12 | 20 |
| 15 | 21-22 | 17 |  | 11 | 19 |
| 14 | 20 | 16 | 15 |  | 17-18 |
| 13 | 18-19 | 15 | 14 | 10 | 16 |
| 12 | 17 | 14 |  | 9 | 15 |
|  |  |  |  |  |  |
| 11 | 15-16 | 12-13 | 13 |  | 13-14 |
| 10 | 13-14 | 11 | 12 | 8 | 12 |
| 9 | 12 | 10 | 11 | 7 | 11 |
| 8 | 10-11 | 9 |  |  | 9-10 |
| 7 | 9 | 8 | 10 | 6 | 8 |
| 6 | 7-8 | 7 | 9 | 5 | 7 |
|  |  |  |  |  |  |
| 5 | 6 | 5-6 |  |  | 5-6 |
| 4 | 4-5 | 4 | 8 | 4 | 4 |
| 3 | 2-3 | 3 | 7 | 3 | 3 |
| 2 | 1 | 2 | 6 |  | 1-2 |
| 1 | 0 | 1 |  | 2 | 0 |
| 0 |  | 0 | 5 | 1 |  |

### SZONDI

| SEXUAL | | PAROXYSMAL | | EGO | | CONTACT | |
|---|---|---|---|---|---|---|---|
| h | s | e | hy | k | p | d | m |
|  |  |  |  |  | X |  | X |
|  |  |  |  |  | X |  | X |
|  |  |  |  |  | X |  | X |
| X | X | X |  |  | X | X | X |
| X | X | X | X | X | X | X | X |
|  |  |  | X | X | X | X | X |
|  |  |  |  | X |  |  |  |

### RORSCHACH

| R | 13 | M | 2 | | | Fc | 2 |
|---|---|---|---|---|---|---|---|
|  |  | FM | 3 | F | 4 | c | 1 |
| W% | 61 | m |  | F- |  | C' |  |
| D% | 39 | k |  | F% | 31 | FC |  |
| d% |  | K |  |  |  | CF |  |
| Dd% |  | FK |  |  |  | C |  |
| S |  |  |  |  |  |  |  |

## WORK SHEET

*Ty 1*

3

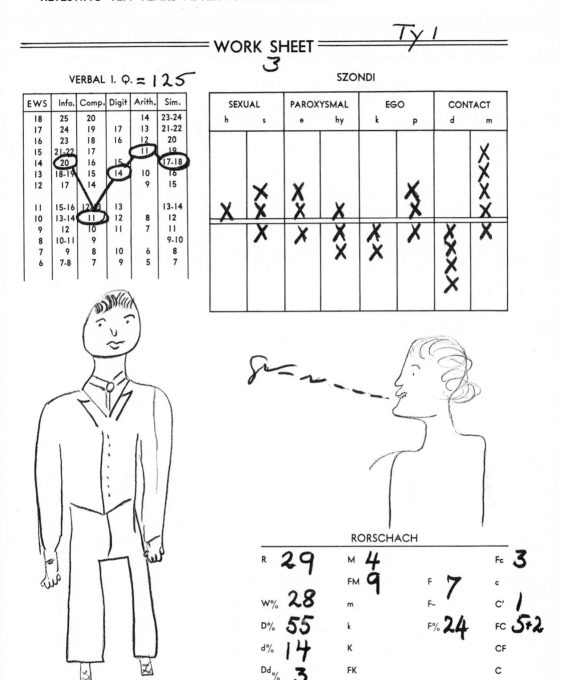

VERBAL I. Q. = 125

| EWS | Info. | Comp. | Digit | Arith. | Sim. |
|-----|-------|-------|-------|--------|------|
| 18 | 25 | 20 | | 14 | 23-24 |
| 17 | 24 | 19 | 17 | 13 | 21-22 |
| 16 | 23 | 18 | 16 | 12 | 20 |
| 15 | 21-22 | 17 | | 11 | 19 |
| 14 | 20 | 16 | 15 | | 17-18 |
| 13 | 18-19 | 15 | 14 | 10 | 16 |
| 12 | 17 | 14 | | 9 | 15 |
| 11 | 15-16 | 12-13 | 13 | | 13-14 |
| 10 | 13-14 | 11 | 12 | 8 | 12 |
| 9 | 12 | 10 | 11 | 7 | 11 |
| 8 | 10-11 | 9 | | | 9-10 |
| 7 | 9 | 8 | 10 | 6 | 8 |
| 6 | 7-8 | 7 | 9 | 5 | 7 |

SZONDI

| SEXUAL | | PAROXYSMAL | | EGO | | CONTACT | |
|--------|---|------------|----|-----|---|---------|---|
| h | s | e | hy | k | p | d | m |

RORSCHACH

R 29    M 4    Fc 3
        FM 9   F 7    c
W% 28   m      F-     C' 1
D% 55   k      F% 24  FC 5+2
d% 14   K             CF
Dd% 3   FK            c
S

*1 AND 3*     # SUMMARY OF TEST FINDINGS     *Ty 1*

## MANNER DURING TEST

| (1) Overly distressed | (2) Tense | (3) Indifferent | (4) Appropriate | (5) Relaxed and actively interested |
|---|---|---|---|---|
| (1) **Hostile** | (2) Uneasy | | | |

## I.Q. (Bellevue-Wechsler)

| (1) Below average | (2) Average | (3) **High average** | (4) Superior | (5) Very superior |
|---|---|---|---|---|

## PRODUCTIVITY (Rorschach)

| (1) Impoverished | (2) **Reduced output** | (3) Adequate | (4) Better than average | (5) Rich and well-ordered |
|---|---|---|---|---|
| | (2) Compulsive productivity | | | |

## RELATION TO REALITY (Rorschach, Bellevue-Wechsler, Drawings)

| (1) Loose | (2) **Lapses—together with good form** | (3) Not noticeably disturbed | (4) Essentially firm | (5) Firm and good |
|---|---|---|---|---|

## USUAL-UNUSUAL THOUGHT CONTENT (Rorschach, Unpleasant Concept)

| (1) Bizarre | (2) Tendency toward the bizarre | (3) Adequate | (4) Original trends | (5) Outstandingly original |
|---|---|---|---|---|
| (1) Stereotyped | (2) **Tendency toward stereotypy** | | | |

## CONSTRUCTIVE FANTASY (Rorschach)

| (1) Absent | (2) **Barely accessible** | (3) Accessible | (4) Readily accessible | (5) Active but not hampering |
|---|---|---|---|---|
| (1) Withdrawal into fantasy | | | | |

## DRIVE (Rorschach, Szondi, Unpleasant Concept)

| (1) Overpowering aggression | (2) Over-aggressive | (3) **Adequate** | (4) Clearly sufficient | (5) Sufficient—exceptionally well-directed |
|---|---|---|---|---|
| (1) Hampering passivity | (2) Insufficient drive | | | |

## EMOTIONAL TONE (Rorschach, Szondi)

| (1) Explosive emotions | (2) Getting out of hand | (3) Trend toward emotional expression | (4) Warmth available | (5) Warm, readily available |
|---|---|---|---|---|
| (1) **Lacking** | (2) Indicated but repressed emotions | | | |

## SOCIAL ATTITUDE (T. A. T.)

| (1) Uncontrolled | (2) **Constricted or neglected** | (3) Adequate | (4) Well-regulated | (5) Free and flexible |
|---|---|---|---|---|

## ANXIETY

| (1) Disintegrating | (2) Marked | (3) **Moderate** | (4) Not marked | (5) Lack of evidence of anxiety |
|---|---|---|---|---|

## OVER-ALL EVALUATION

| (1) Markedly disturbed personality | (2) **Less than adequate personality with some psychological problems** | (3) Adequate personality | (4) Better than average functioning personality | (5) Exceptionally well-integrated personality with excellent potential |
|---|---|---|---|---|

## SUMMARY OF THERAPIST'S FINDINGS  *Tyl*

### ESTIMATED INTELLIGENCE LEVEL

| (1) Below average | (2) Average | (3) High average | (4) Superior | (5) Very superior |
|---|---|---|---|---|

### FLOW OF ASSOCIATIVE MATERIAL

| (1) Impoverished | (2) Reduced output | (3) Adequate | (4) Better than average | (5) Rich and well-ordered |
|---|---|---|---|---|
| | (2) Compulsive productivity | | | |

### RELATION TO REALITY

| (1) Loose | (2) Lapses—together with good form | (3) Not noticeably disturbed | (4) Essentially firm | (5) Firm and good |
|---|---|---|---|---|

### USUAL-UNUSUAL THOUGHT CONTENT

| (1) Bizarre | (2) Tendency toward the bizarre | (3) Adequate | (4) Original trends | (5) Outstandingly original |
|---|---|---|---|---|
| (1) Stereotyped | (2) Tendency toward stereotypy | | | |

### CONSTRUCTIVE FANTASY

| (1) Absent | (2) Barely accessible | (3) Accessible | (4) Readily accessible | (5) Active but not hampering |
|---|---|---|---|---|
| (1) Withdrawal into fantasy | | | | |

### DRIVE

| (1) Overpowering aggression | (2) Over-aggressive | (3) Adequate | (4) Clearly sufficient | (5) Sufficient—exceptionally well-directed |
|---|---|---|---|---|
| (1) Hampering passivity | (2) Insufficient drive | | | |

### EMOTIONAL TONE

| (1) Explosive emotions | (2) Getting out of hand | (3) Trend toward emotional expression | (4) Warmth available | (5) Warm, readily available |
|---|---|---|---|---|
| (1) Lacking | (2) Indicated but repressed emotions | | | |

### SOCIAL ATTITUDE

| (1) Uncontrolled | (2) Constricted or neglected | (3) Adequate | (4) Well-regulated | (5) Free and flexible |
|---|---|---|---|---|

### ANXIETY

| (1) Disintegrating | (2) Marked | (3) Moderate | (4) Not marked | (5) Lack of evidence of anxiety |
|---|---|---|---|---|

### OVER-ALL EVALUATION

| (1) Markedly disturbed personality | (2) Less than adequate personality with some psychological problems | (3) Adequate personality | (4) Better than average functioning personality | (5) Exceptionally well-integrated personality with excellent potential |
|---|---|---|---|---|

clearly recognized. The arms belong; there is hair on the head; and the figure is not split into two halves as was the case originally.

To illustrate the changing qualitative aspects of the Rorschach, a few answers may be given. On Card V, for instance, in the first two tests she gave simply the response, "A butterfly." The third record includes, in addition to this: "Here are the silhouettes of two children; their arms are folded, they are lying down against a central figure. In the center there is someone in an old hat. It is rather like the wimples worn by women in the Middle Ages. The children are very distinct." In the initial two records, Card II elicited the following responses: "A formal garden. A butterfly. Two baby elephants." The spontaneous responses on Record 3 are as follows: "A couple of bears juggling something on their noses. Now these things could be colored shrimp. Two children playing pat-a-cake. In the red at the bottom there is a vulva. These little spiny things are like delicate seashells" (a response involving both texture and color).

The quantitative score on Work Sheet 3 is now 31, having been 19 on the first and second testings.

Concerning TY2 the therapist writes:

"Perhaps the main changes are in his relationships to others and in his creative work. Originally he was unable to maintain easy give-and-take relations even with those with whom it should have been possible. He could not maintain his marriage; there was too much anxiety, rage and tension with his wife. Difficulty arose in other relations as well at a superficial level, again mainly due to anxiety to please or to rage. His creative work was attempted only infrequently and with great reluctance. Although full of fine social ideas, he was quite a liar and faker even in important matters.

"Now this patient has maintained a satisfactory marriage over a five-year period. He has a warm and fine relationship with his child. He writes creatively a great deal and is extremely successful financially with it. He has insight into his rage, tension and anxiety. He enjoys people thoroughly and is truly beloved. Socially he lives more in accord with his own basic standards than before."

From Work Sheet 1, it will become evident that despite his difficulties TY2 was, and is, highly gifted. The formal scores on the Rorschach bear witness to much that was said by his therapist to characterize him. The great preponderance of CF and C over FC reflects the explosive rages. The tension can be seen in the $9 + 9$ m. That this is an exceptional record, however, goes without saying, as witnessed by the high productivity and the high M score, to mention only the most obvious features.

Years later, the personal signature of the record is still there almost in its entirety, but various important relationships have changed. As we notice many times, the rise in FC responses correlates more than any one item with reliably reported changes in better adjustment. Greater productivity and an even higher number of good M responses are found in this brilliant production. There is greater concern with small, original details than ten years previously.

There is a rise in the I.Q. and a general upward shift in the scattergram. This, however, the individual himself somewhat discredits, feeling that he may have become more test-wise during the interval.

The Szondi is remarkably similar in six of the eight factors. The change from + to –e may be seen as possibly indicating less inhibiting control, greater freedom for expression of his obvious creativity. The change from + to open m would not be one that we would expect necessarily, but it appears less important in the light of the obvious increased social adjustment reflected in the Rorschach color scores.

The initial Figure Drawings were essentially caricatures, although cleverly executed. TY2 originally feels his inadequacy but laughs it off by poking fun at man in general. The woman is a witchlike shrew, and the exaggerated hairdo and prominently spiked nose bear witness to the concept of the thoroughly aggressive female which characterized TY2's outlook at that time.

The drawings after the ten-year interval are handled seriously and straightforwardly. They are real people, with their inadequacies and failings, but they are not scoffed at.

The Summary of Test Findings, although it shows marked improvement over the ten years, must be considered as a conservative rating when compared with those of the therapist. Yet, the therapist has recorded accurately the changes in terms of outer adjustment and subjective satisfaction. We are not suggesting that the behavioral or clinical ratings are exaggerated but rather that for every increment in behavioral change, a much smaller difference is reflected in the projective tests.

TY2's records are shown on the next four pages.

# WORK SHEET

Ty 2

1

## VERBAL I. Q. = 133

| EWS | Info. | Comp. | Digit | Arith. | Sim. |
|-----|-------|-------|-------|--------|------|
| 18 | 25 | 20 | | 14 | 23-24 |
| 17 | 24 | 19 | 17 | 13 | 21-22 |
| 16 | (23) | (18) | 16 | 12 | 20 |
| 15 | 21-22 | 17 | | (11) | 19 |
| 14 | 20 | 16 | (15) | | (17-18) |
| 13 | 18-19 | 15 | 14 | 10 | 16 |
| 12 | 17 | 14 | | 9 | 15 |

## SZONDI

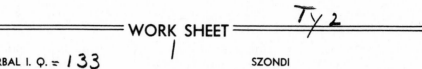

| SEXUAL | | PAROXYSMAL | | EGO | | CONTACT | |
|---|---|---|---|---|---|---|---|
| h | s | e | hy | k | p | d | m |
| | | | | | | | X |
| X | | X | | X | X | | X |
| X | X | X | | X | X | | X |
| | | X | X | X | | X | X |
| | | X | X | X | | X | |
| | | X | | X | | X | |
| | | | | | | X | |

## RORSCHACH

| | | | | |
|---|---|---|---|---|
| R 84 | M 14 | | | Fc 5 |
| | FM 10 | F 32 | | c +1 |
| W% 25 | m 9+9 | F- 3 | | C' 1+1 |
| D% 46 | k | F% 42 | | FC 1 |
| d% 12 | K 2+6 | | | CF 4 |
| Dd% / S 17 | FK | | | c 3 |

Ty2

# WORK SHEET

3

## VERBAL I. Q. = 145

| EWS | Info. | Comp. | Digit | Arith. | Sim. |
|-----|-------|-------|-------|--------|------|
| 18 | 25 | 20 | | 14 | 23-24 |
| 17 | 24 | 19 | 17 | 13 | 21-22 |
| 16 | 23 | 18 | 16 | 12 | 20 |
| 15 | 21-22 | 17 | | 11 | 19 |
| 14 | 20 | 16 | 15 | | 17-18 |
| 13 | 18-19 | 15 | 14 | 10 | 16 |
| 12 | 17 | 14 | | 9 | 15 |

## SZONDI

| SEXUAL | | PAROXYSMAL | | EGO | | CONTACT | |
|--------|--------|--------|--------|--------|--------|--------|--------|
| h | s | e | hy | k | p | d | m |
| X | | | | X | | | |
| X | | | | X | X | | |
| X | X | X | X | X | X | | X |
| | X | X | X | X | | X | |
| | X | X | X | | | X | |
| | X | X | | | | | |
| | X | | | | | | |

## RORSCHACH

| R 119 | M 18 | | Fc 6 |
|-------|------|-----|------|
| | FM 10 | F 57 | c 3+2 |
| W% 12 | m 9+12 | F- 3 | C' 1+1 |
| D% 42 | k | F% 50 | FC 4+3 |
| d% 14 | K 1+5 | | CF 3+3 |
| Dd% 32 | FK | | c 3+3 |
| S | | | F/C 1 |

# SUMMARY OF TEST FINDINGS    TY 2

## MANNER DURING TEST

| (1) Overly distressed | (2) Tense | (3) Indifferent | (4) Appropriate | (5) Relaxed and actively interested |
|---|---|---|---|---|
| (1) Hostile | (2) Uneasy | | | |

## I.Q. (Bellevue-Wechsler)

| (1) Below average | (2) Average | (3) High average | (4) Superior | (5) Very superior |
|---|---|---|---|---|

## PRODUCTIVITY (Rorschach)

| (1) Impoverished | (2) Reduced output | (3) Adequate | (4) Better than average | (5) Rich and well-ordered |
|---|---|---|---|---|
| | (2) Compulsive productivity | | | |

## RELATION TO REALITY (Rorschach, Bellevue-Wechsler, Drawings)

| (1) Loose | (2) Lapses—together with good form | (3) Not noticeably disturbed | (4) Essentially firm | (5) Firm and good |
|---|---|---|---|---|

## USUAL-UNUSUAL THOUGHT CONTENT (Rorschach, Unpleasant Concept)

| (1) Bizarre | (2) Tendency toward the bizarre | (3) Adequate | (4) Original trends | (5) Outstandingly original |
|---|---|---|---|---|
| (1) Stereotyped | (2) Tendency toward stereotypy | | | |

## CONSTRUCTIVE FANTASY (Rorschach)

| (1) Absent | (2) Barely accessible | (3) Accessible | (4) Readily accessible | (5) Active but not hampering |
|---|---|---|---|---|
| (1) Withdrawal into fantasy | | | | |

## DRIVE (Rorschach, Szondi, Unpleasant Concept)

| (1) Overpowering aggression | (2) Over-aggressive | (3) Adequate | (4) Clearly sufficient | (5) Sufficient—exceptionally well-directed |
|---|---|---|---|---|
| (1) Hampering passivity | (2) Insufficient drive | | | |

## EMOTIONAL TONE (Rorschach, Szondi)

| (1) Explosive emotions | (2) Getting out of hand | (3) Trend toward emotional expression | (4) Warmth available | (5) Warm, readily available |
|---|---|---|---|---|
| (1) Lacking | (2) Indicated but repressed emotions | | | |

## SOCIAL ATTITUDE (T. A. T.)

| (1) Uncontrolled | (2) Constricted or neglected | (3) Adequate | (4) Well-regulated | (5) Free and flexible |
|---|---|---|---|---|

## ANXIETY

| (1) Disintegrating | (2) Marked | (3) Moderate | (4) Not marked | (5) Lack of evidence of anxiety |
|---|---|---|---|---|

## OVER-ALL EVALUATION

| (1) Markedly disturbed personality | (2) Less than adequate personality with some psychological problems | (3) Adequate personality | (4) Better than average functioning personality | (5) Exceptionally well-integrated personality with excellent potential |
|---|---|---|---|---|

## SUMMARY OF THERAPIST'S FINDINGS     _TY 2_

### ESTIMATED INTELLIGENCE LEVEL

| (1) Below average | (2) Average | (3) High average | (4) Superior | **(5)** Very superior |
|---|---|---|---|---|

### FLOW OF ASSOCIATIVE MATERIAL

| (1) Impoverished | (2) Reduced output | (3) Adequate | **(4)** Better than average | (5) Rich and well-ordered |
|---|---|---|---|---|
| | (2) Compulsive productivity | | | |

### RELATION TO REALITY

| (1) Loose | (2) Lapses—together with good form | **(3)** Not noticeably disturbed | (4) Essentially firm | (5) Firm and good |
|---|---|---|---|---|

### USUAL-UNUSUAL THOUGHT CONTENT

| (1) Bizarre | (2) Tendency toward the bizarre | **(3)** Adequate | (4) Original trends | (5) Outstandingly original |
|---|---|---|---|---|
| (1) Stereotyped | (2) Tendency toward stereotypy | | | |

### CONSTRUCTIVE FANTASY

| (1) Absent | (2) Barely accessible | **(3)** Accessible | (4) Readily accessible | (5) Active but not hampering |
|---|---|---|---|---|
| (1) Withdrawal into fantasy | | | | |

### DRIVE

| (1) Overpowering aggression | **(2)** Over-aggressive _mixed_ | (3) Adequate | (4) Clearly sufficient | (5) Sufficient—exceptionally well-directed |
|---|---|---|---|---|
| (1) Hampering passivity | **(2)** Insufficient drive | | | |

### EMOTIONAL TONE

| (1) Explosive emotions | (2) Getting out of hand | **(3)** Trend toward emotional expression | (4) Warmth available | (5) Warm, readily available |
|---|---|---|---|---|
| (1) Lacking | (2) Indicated but repressed emotions | | | |

### SOCIAL ATTITUDE

| (1) Uncontrolled | (2) Constricted or neglected | **(3)** Adequate | (4) Well-regulated | **(5)** Free and flexible |
|---|---|---|---|---|

### ANXIETY

| (1) Disintegrating | (2) Marked | **(3)** Moderate | **(4)** Not marked | (5) Lack of evidence of anxiety |
|---|---|---|---|---|

### OVER-ALL EVALUATION

| (1) Markedly disturbed personality | (2) Less than adequate personality with some psychological problems | **(3)** Adequate personality | (4) Better than average functioning personality | (5) Exceptionally well-integrated personality with excellent potential |
|---|---|---|---|---|

The therapist reported that TY3 presented quite a disturbed picture on first entering therapy ten years previously. Although still in her early twenties at that time, she had been involved in two disastrous marriages, with strangely similar patterns, resulting from her masochistic needs and strong self-destructive tendencies. Her willingness to accept physical hardship and punishment from the hands of two successive, pathologic mates had reached the point where her health and morale were endangered. While subjecting herself to these hardships, she had somehow retained a genuine devotion to her mates, although this was based on a blind and unrealistic orientation. She had even remained in seclusion for several years, living out the disturbed fantasies of one of her husbands.

After two years of intensive psychotherapy she had improved to the point where she had completely rehabilitated herself socially, creatively in her profession, and in terms of interpersonal relationships. The therapist now reports that she has been successfully married for over six years, has several children, and plays an important part in community affairs. She has remained in close touch with the therapist on a friendly basis.

The first set of projective tests gave evidence of ego strength that seemed at variance with the bizarre clinical picture. Despite the low Similarities and Comprehension, and the three F– responses, the total picture did not actually appear to be as disturbed as might have been expected.

The second testing, which was carried out immediately after termination of psychotherapy, showed a one point rise on the quantitative scale due to an increase in the I.Q. score. This is hardly significant. However, on the third testing, which took place eight years later, striking changes may be seen to have occurred. There is, for instance, the rise in the Similarities score, where too-personalized answers have dropped out in favor of a more realistic approach. There is now considerably more warmth available, as seen in the color scores on the Rorschach, and the poor-form answers have disappeared from the record. The handless, static, and somewhat ethereal drawing of the woman has been replaced by an active participant in everyday affairs. The expression is more lively; there is a look of activity about the figure.

It must be admitted, however, that, impressive as these changes are, they do not seem to be of the same order of magnitude as the changes observed clinically. There is a close parallelism here between this case and that of SA2 where it seemed as if nothing in the test findings quite measured up to the dramatic changes in adjustment and subsequent work achievements. There seems to be, in life situations, an opportunity for cumulative and progressive adjustment to manifest itself in increasingly apparent ways, while the tests still remain a static, cross-sectional picture which cannot quite carry the total change.

TY3's records are reproduced on the next four pages.

# WORK SHEET *Ty.3*

*1*

## VERBAL I. Q. = *115*

| EWS | Info. | Comp. | Digit | Arith. | Sim. |
|-----|-------|-------|-------|--------|------|
| 18 | 25 | 20 | | 14 | 23-24 |
| 17 | 24 | 19 | 17 | 13 | 21-22 |
| 16 | 23 | 18 | 16 | 12 | 20 |
| 15 | 21-22 | 17 | | (11) | 19 |
| 14 | 20 | 16 | 15 | | 17-18 |
| 13 | 18-19 | 15 | (14) | 10 | 16 |
| 12 | 17 | 14 | | 9 | 15 |
| 11 | (15-16) | (12-13) | 13 | | (13-14) |
| 10 | 13-14 | 11 | 12 | 8 | 12 |
| 9 | 12 | 10 | 11 | 7 | 11 |
| 8 | 10-11 | 9 | | | 9-10 |
| 7 | 9 | 8 | 10 | 6 | 8 |

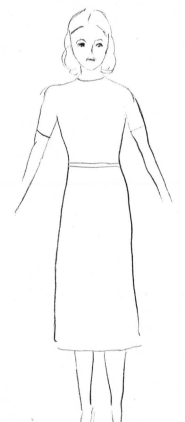

## SZONDI

| SEXUAL | | PAROXYSMAL | | EGO | | CONTACT | |
|--------|---|-----------|----|-----|---|---------|---|
| h | s | e | hy | k | p | d | m |

(X marks as plotted)

## OVER-ALL EVALUATION = *26*

| | | | | | |
|---|---|---|---|---|---|
| OVER-ALL RATING | 1 | 2 | 3 | 4 | 5 |
| PRODUCTIVITY | 1 | 2 | ③ | 4 | 5 |
| RELATION TO REALITY | 1 | 2 | ③ | 4 | 5 |
| THOUGHT CONTENT | 1 | 2 | ③ | 4 | 5 |
| CONSTRUCTIVE FANTASY | 1 | 2 | ③ | 4 | 5 |
| DRIVE | 1 | 2 | ③ | 4 | 5 |
| EMOTIONAL TONE | 1 | ② | 3 | 4 | 5 |
| SOCIAL ATTITUDE | 1 | ② | 3 | 4 | 5 |
| ANXIETY | 1 | 2 | 3 | ④ | 5 |
| I. Q. RATING | 1 | 2 | ③ | 4 | 5 |

## RORSCHACH

| | | | | | |
|---|---|---|---|---|---|
| R | *23* | M | *4* | | Fc |
| | | FM | *4* | F *10* | c |
| W% | *61* | m | | F- *3* | C' |
| D% | *39* | k | | F% *57* | FC *1+1* |
| d% | | K | | | CF *1* |
| Dd% | | FK | | | C |
| S | | | | | |

TY3

# WORK SHEET
## 3

VERBAL I. Q. = 139

| EWS | Info. | Comp. | Digit | Arith. | Sim. |
|-----|-------|-------|-------|--------|------|
| 18 | 25 | 20 | | 14 | 23-24 |
| 17 | 24 | 19 | 17 | 13 | 21-22 |
| 16 | 23 | 18 | 16 | 12 | 20 |
| 15 | 21-22 | 17 | | 11 | 19 |
| 14 | 20 | 16 | 15 | | 17-18 |
| 13 | 18-19 | 15 | 14 | 10 | 16 |
| 12 | 17 | 14 | | 9 | 15 |

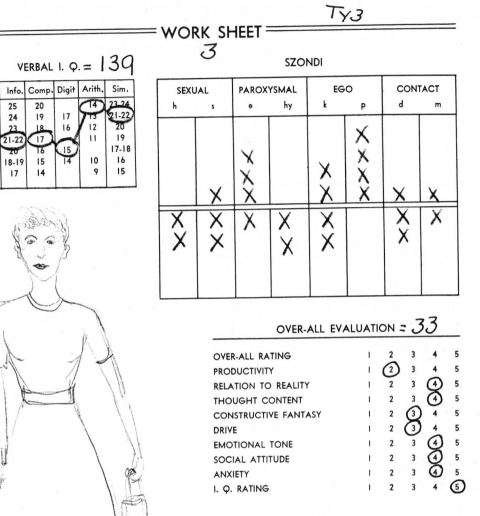

## SZONDI

| SEXUAL | | PAROXYSMAL | | EGO | | CONTACT | |
|--------|---|-----------|----|-----|---|---------|---|
| h | s | e | hy | k | p | d | m |

## OVER-ALL EVALUATION = 33

| | | | | | |
|---|---|---|---|---|---|
| OVER-ALL RATING | 1 | 2 | 3 | 4 | 5 |
| PRODUCTIVITY | 1 | ②| 3 | 4 | 5 |
| RELATION TO REALITY | 1 | 2 | 3 | ④ | 5 |
| THOUGHT CONTENT | 1 | 2 | 3 | ④ | 5 |
| CONSTRUCTIVE FANTASY | 1 | 2 | ③ | 4 | 5 |
| DRIVE | 1 | 2 | ③ | 4 | 5 |
| EMOTIONAL TONE | 1 | 2 | 3 | ④ | 5 |
| SOCIAL ATTITUDE | 1 | 2 | 3 | ④ | 5 |
| ANXIETY | 1 | 2 | 3 | ④ | 5 |
| I. Q. RATING | 1 | 2 | 3 | 4 | ⑤ |

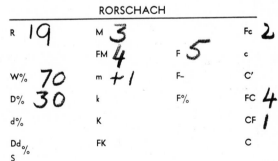

## RORSCHACH

| R 19 | M 3 | | Fc 2 |
|------|------|------|------|
| | FM 4 | F 5 | c |
| W% 70 | m +1 | F- | C' |
| D% 30 | k | F% | FC 4 |
| d% | K | | CF 1 |
| Dd% | FK | | C |
| S | | | |

# SUMMARY OF TEST FINDINGS   *Ty 3*

## MANNER DURING TEST

| (1) Overly distressed | (2) Tense | (3) Indifferent | (4) **Appropriate** | (5) Relaxed and actively interested |
|---|---|---|---|---|
| (1) Hostile | (2) Uneasy | | | |

## I.Q. (Bellevue-Wechsler)

| (1) Below average | (2) Average | (3) **High average** | (4) Superior | (5) Very superior |
|---|---|---|---|---|

## PRODUCTIVITY (Rorschach)

| (1) Impoverished | (2) Reduced output | (3) **Adequate** | (4) Better than average | (5) Rich and well-ordered |
|---|---|---|---|---|
| | (2) Compulsive productivity | | | |

## RELATION TO REALITY (Rorschach, Bellevue-Wechsler, Drawings)

| (1) Loose | (2) Lapses—together with good form | (3) **Not noticeably disturbed** | (4) Essentially firm | (5) Firm and good |
|---|---|---|---|---|

## USUAL-UNUSUAL THOUGHT CONTENT (Rorschach, Unpleasant Concept)

| (1) Bizarre | (2) Tendency toward the bizarre | (3) **Adequate** | (4) Original trends | (5) Outstandingly original |
|---|---|---|---|---|
| (1) Stereotyped | (2) Tendency toward stereotypy | | | |

## CONSTRUCTIVE FANTASY (Rorschach)

| (1) Absent | (2) Barely accessible | (3) **Accessible** | (4) Readily accessible | (5) Active but not hampering |
|---|---|---|---|---|
| (1) Withdrawal into fantasy | | | | |

## DRIVE (Rorschach, Szondi, Unpleasant Concept)

| (1) Overpowering aggression | (2) Over-aggressive | (3) **Adequate** | (4) Clearly sufficient | (5) Sufficient— exceptionally well-directed |
|---|---|---|---|---|
| (1) Hampering passivity | (2) Insufficient drive | | | |

## EMOTIONAL TONE (Rorschach, Szondi)

| (1) Explosive emotions | (2) Getting out of hand | (3) Trend toward emotional expression | (4) Warmth available | (5) Warm, readily available |
|---|---|---|---|---|
| (1) Lacking | (2) **Indicated but repressed emotions** | | | |

## SOCIAL ATTITUDE (T. A. T.)

| (1) Uncontrolled | (2) **Constricted or neglected** | (3) Adequate | (4) Well-regulated | (5) Free and flexible |
|---|---|---|---|---|

## ANXIETY

| (1) Disintegrating | (2) Marked | (3) Moderate | (4) **Not marked** | (5) Lack of evidence of anxiety |
|---|---|---|---|---|

## OVER-ALL EVALUATION

| (1) Markedly disturbed personality | (2) Less than adequate personality with some psychological problems | (3) **Adequate personality** | (4) Better than average functioning personality | (5) Exceptionally well-integrated personality with excellent potential |
|---|---|---|---|---|

# SUMMARY OF THERAPIST'S FINDINGS     TY 3

## ESTIMATED INTELLIGENCE LEVEL

| (1) Below average | (2) Average | (3) High average | (4) Superior | (5) Very superior |
|---|---|---|---|---|

## FLOW OF ASSOCIATIVE MATERIAL

| (1) Impoverished | (2) Reduced output | (3) Adequate | (4) Better than average | (5) Rich and well-ordered |
|---|---|---|---|---|
| | (2) Compulsive productivity | | | |

## RELATION TO REALITY

| (1) Loose | (2) Lapses—together with good form | (3) Not noticeably disturbed | (4) Essentially firm | (5) Firm and good |
|---|---|---|---|---|

## USUAL-UNUSUAL THOUGHT CONTENT

| (1) Bizarre | (2) Tendency toward the bizarre | (3) Adequate | (4) Original trends | (5) Outstandingly original |
|---|---|---|---|---|
| (1) Stereotyped | (2) Tendency toward stereotypy | | | |

## CONSTRUCTIVE FANTASY

| (1) Absent | (2) Barely accessible | (3) Accessible | (4) Readily accessible | (5) Active but not hampering |
|---|---|---|---|---|
| (1) Withdrawal into fantasy | | | | |

## DRIVE

| (1) Overpowering aggression | (2) Over-aggressive | (3) Adequate | (4) Clearly sufficient | (5) Sufficient—exceptionally well-directed |
|---|---|---|---|---|
| (1) Hampering passivity | (2) Insufficient drive | | | |

## EMOTIONAL TONE

| (1) Explosive emotions | (2) Getting out of hand | (3) Trend toward emotional expression | (4) Warmth available | (5) Warm, readily available |
|---|---|---|---|---|
| (1) Lacking | (2) Indicated but repressed emotions | | | |

## SOCIAL ATTITUDE

| (1) Uncontrolled | (2) Constricted or neglected | (3) Adequate | (4) Well-regulated | (5) Free and flexible |
|---|---|---|---|---|

## ANXIETY

| (1) Disintegrating | (2) Marked | (3) Moderate | (4) Not marked | (5) Lack of evidence of anxiety |
|---|---|---|---|---|

## OVER-ALL EVALUATION

| (1) Markedly disturbed personality | (2) Less than adequate personality with some psychological problems | (3) Adequate personality | (4) Better than average functioning personality | (5) Exceptionally well-integrated personality with excellent potential |
|---|---|---|---|---|

## XV. Retesting during relapse and improvement.
## Cases followed over an eleven-year period.

The case of IR1 has been selected because it exemplifies a history of improvement and relapse, of a return to therapy following a revival of the original symptoms after a long period of clinical remission and marked improvement in general adjustment.

IR1's therapist has made available an account of her symptoms and of her progress:

"IR1 came for treatment in 1948 at the age of eleven and was seen up to the end of the year 1950. She was not seen again until 1955 in the late spring. She returned at this time because she felt so much had been accomplished in her early treatment that she wanted to be prepared to go to college. She returned for *continuous* treatment in November 1955 after she had found she could not remain in college because of her excessive anxiety and return of symptoms.

"The symptoms at the beginning of treatment, age eleven, were almost exactly those present again when she returned in '55. One of these was a fear she would die in the night. This occurred during her first camp experience so that she had had to be removed from camp at that time. The chief symptom during her early college experience was that she could not sleep because she was afraid that she would die; she had to feel her pulse and watch the veins in her wrist constantly. Another symptom, which occurred a month before she went to camp, age eleven, was her fear that she would die if she had a tooth pulled. At the time of her return to therapy, she was still overly concerned about going to the dentist.

"An additional symptom, nausea, expressed itself in early childhood in the form of, 'I can't swallow' (age three). An actual experience at two-and-a-half, when she swallowed a life-saver, seemed to have precipitated this. Nausea as a present-day symptom is linked with the feeling that she cannot breathe and with a fear that she will be poisoned by medication. This latter fear she had as a child and again on being given tranquilizing medication by the college physician.

"The hysterical nausea and her inability to eat have been successfully analyzed in the past month, leading to marked improvement in these symptoms; what appeared like schizophrenic symptoms in childhood can now be seen as hysterical anxiety. IR1 came to her therapeutic hour during lunchtime, and frequently brought her lunch to eat. Then she herself related the nausea to the eating and has discontinued this practice. The relation of oral and anal activity was revealed in that she was frequently compelled to move her bowels during the hour.

"Another symptom, fear of the father's dying or committing suicide, which she had at age eleven, was again present on her return in 1955. At eleven she thought of this because of LaGuardia's death; later, because of the death of the father of one of her friends in school.

"In 1948 excitability was an outstanding symptom. As a child she appeared to be a behavior problem. She bumped into people; she teased and hit other children; she fought constantly with her mother, her brother and her friends.

Excessive irritability still characterizes her behavior, especially before her menstrual period. She glares at people when she bumps into them in the street as if they were to blame, and she feels herself entirely justified in doing this.

"The most recent symptom, appearing within the last month, has been trembling and shaking of her hands a week prior to menstruation. She has a feeling that her symptoms and distress in general are more intense at this time but also that she has periods of complete freedom from symptoms never experienced before, periods when she feels better than she ever has in her life and really recognizes what a healthy response feels like.

"The basic claustrophobic symptom, which concealed itself behind all other symptoms originally, emerged in the form of fear of riding in the subway, going home in the train alone, staying at home on weekends, being afraid to stay at home alone at night, a sudden incapacity to remain in class when the class lasted two hours so that at times she had to get up and leave at the beginning of the second hour. Recently the analysis of a pregnancy dream has led to the recall of the birth of her brother, five years younger than she. She was in a crib and the mother was waiting for the grandmother to take over before going to the hospital. She had already begun nursery school but thinks that she was absent from school while the mother was in the hospital. After analysis of this dream, claustrophobic symptoms were markedly reduced. She has now mastered her desire to run out of class; she has no anxiety about going home on the train alone, nor has she called her mother on the telephone for reassurance as she did previously.

"The treatment throughout was basically psychoanalytic, with educational help during periods when she was in resistance or when her blocked fantasy was such that she could give no free association. No modification of any environmental factor has been introduced, although the girl slept in the same room with her brother, a room adjacent to the living room where her parents slept. Any attempt on the part of the therapist to relieve this situation was immediately thwarted by the mother. Only after the child terminated treatment did the family move into a bigger apartment where she had a room to herself. Shortly, the family will move again, and for the first time the parents will have their own bedroom.

"IR1 has had no insight until recently into her problem. She projected the conflict on to her mother. She was never able to recall the situation which created the first intense quarrel with her mother. She had previously no desire for cure because she considered the fault lay entirely with the parents, and, realistically, she was often justified. She had, originally, complete inability to control her responses of irritability. Strangely enough, however, in school she was always a quiet and compliant child. Her quarrels with girls of her own age and her inability to make friends or keep friends were the conspicuous trouble. Her acting-out of any behavior, her aggression, her irritability and hostility gave the general impression of a girl with limited, restricted or borderline intelligence, and with a possible schizoid diagnosis. However, the intensity of the anxiety symptoms perhaps militated against this diagnosis.

"At the present time, since masturbatory conflicts, fantasies and behavior have been freely confessed to and dealt with, since her guilt is reduced, and since she is free of claustrophobic symptoms, the hysterical nature of her bodily symptoms has become clear. It is hoped that if she continues as at present, the blocked intelligence will prove to have been the form her symptoms took and

## WORK SHEET

1

IR 1

### SZONDI

| SEXUAL | | PAROXYSMAL | | EGO | | CONTACT | |
|---|---|---|---|---|---|---|---|
| h | s | e | hy | k | p | d | m |
| X | X |  |  |  |  |  |  |
| X | X |  |  |  |  |  |  |
| X | X | X |  |  |  |  |  |
| X | X | X | X |  | X |  |  |
| X |  |  | X | X | X | X | X |
|  |  |  | X |  | X | X | X |
|  |  |  | X |  |  | X |  |

OVER-ALL EVALUATION = $15^x$

### RORSCHACH

| R 9 | M 1 | | Fc |
|---|---|---|---|
| | FM 3 | F 2 | c |
| W% 56 | m | F– | C' |
| D% 44 | k | F% 22 | FC 1 |
| d% | K 1 | | CF 1 |
| Dd% | FK | | C |
| S | | | |

# WORK SHEET

2

IR1

## VERBAL I. Q.

| EWS | Info. | Comp. | Digit | Arith. | Sim. |
|-----|-------|-------|-------|--------|------|
| 18 | 25 | 20 | | 14 | 23-24 |
| 17 | 24 | 19 | 17 | 13 | 21-22 |
| 16 | 23 | 18 | 16 | 12 | 20 |
| 15 | 21-22 | 17 | | 11 | 19 |
| 14 | 20 | 16 | 15 | | 17-18 |
| 13 | 18-19 | 15 | 14 | 10 | 16 |
| 12 | 17 | 14 | | 9 | 15 |
| 11 | 15-16 | 12-13 | 13 | | 13-14 |
| 10 | 13-14 | 11 | 12 | 8 | 12 |
| 9 | 12 | 10 | 11 | 7 | 11 |
| 8 | 10-11 | 9 | | | 9-10 |
| 7 | 9 | 8 | 10 | 6 | 8 |
| 6 | 7-8 | 7 | 9 | 5 | 7 |

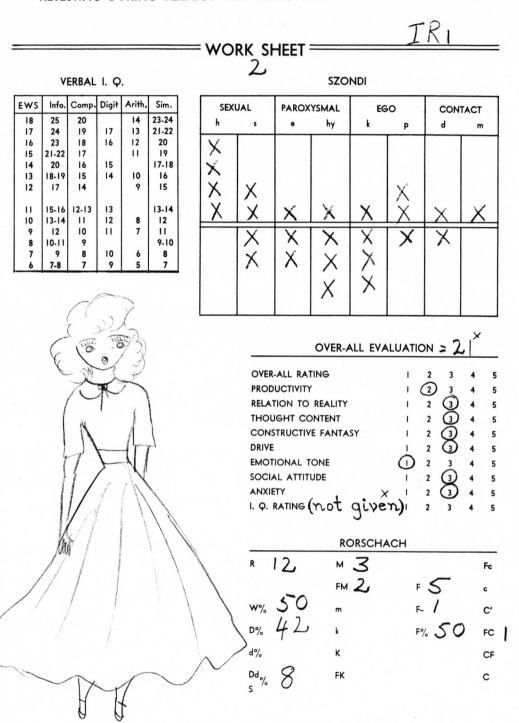

## SZONDI

| SEXUAL | | PAROXYSMAL | | EGO | | CONTACT | |
|--------|---|-----------|----|-----|---|---------|---|
| h | s | e | hy | k | p | d | m |

## OVER-ALL EVALUATION = 2|ˣ

| | 1 | 2 | 3 | 4 | 5 |
|---|---|---|---|---|---|
| OVER-ALL RATING | 1 | 2 | 3 | 4 | 5 |
| PRODUCTIVITY | 1 | (2) | 3 | 4 | 5 |
| RELATION TO REALITY | 1 | 2 | (3) | 4 | 5 |
| THOUGHT CONTENT | 1 | 2 | (3) | 4 | 5 |
| CONSTRUCTIVE FANTASY | 1 | 2 | (3) | 4 | 5 |
| DRIVE | 1 | 2 | (3) | 4 | 5 |
| EMOTIONAL TONE | (1) | 2 | 3 | 4 | 5 |
| SOCIAL ATTITUDE | 1 | 2 | (3) | 4 | 5 |
| ANXIETY | 1 | 2 | (3) | 4 | 5 |
| I. Q. RATING (not given) | 1 | 2 | 3 | 4 | 5 |

## RORSCHACH

| | | | | | |
|---|---|---|---|---|---|
| R | 12 | M | 3 | | Fc |
| | | FM | 2 | F 5 | c |
| W% | 50 | m | | F- 1 | C' |
| D% | 42 | k | | F% 50 | FC 1 |
| d% | | K | | | CF |
| Dd% S% | 8 | FK | | | c |

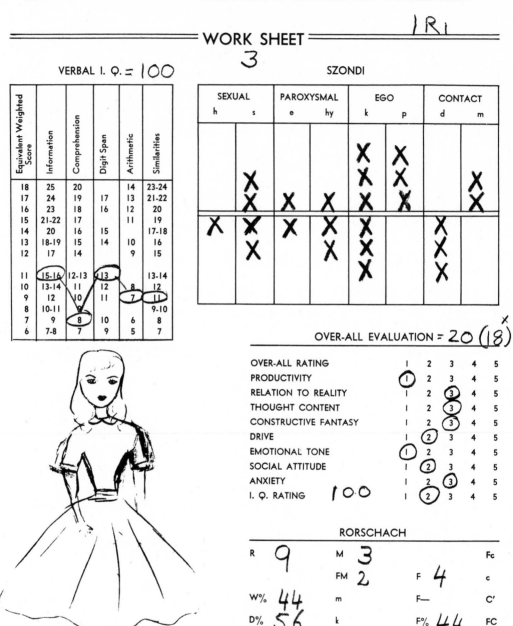

WORK SHEET

3

| R |

### VERBAL I. Q. = 100

| Equivalent Weighted Score | Information | Comprehension | Digit Span | Arithmetic | Similarities |
|---|---|---|---|---|---|
| 18 | 25 | 20 | | 14 | 23-24 |
| 17 | 24 | 19 | 17 | 13 | 21-22 |
| 16 | 23 | 18 | 16 | 12 | 20 |
| 15 | 21-22 | 17 | | 11 | 19 |
| 14 | 20 | 16 | 15 | | 17-18 |
| 13 | 18-19 | 15 | 14 | 10 | 16 |
| 12 | 17 | 14 | | 9 | 15 |
| 11 | 15-16 | 12-13 | 13 | | 13-14 |
| 10 | 13-14 | 11 | 12 | 8 | 12 |
| 9 | 12 | 10 | 11 | 7 | 11 |
| 8 | 10-11 | 9 | | | 9-10 |
| 7 | 9 | 8 | 10 | 6 | 8 |
| 6 | 7-8 | 7 | 9 | 5 | 7 |

### SZONDI

| SEXUAL | | PAROXYSMAL | | EGO | | CONTACT | |
|---|---|---|---|---|---|---|---|
| h | s | e | hy | k | p | d | m |

OVER-ALL EVALUATION = 20 (18)

| | 1 | 2 | 3 | 4 | 5 |
|---|---|---|---|---|---|
| OVER-ALL RATING | 1 | 2 | 3 | 4 | 5 |
| PRODUCTIVITY | (1) | 2 | 3 | 4 | 5 |
| RELATION TO REALITY | 1 | 2 | (3) | 4 | 5 |
| THOUGHT CONTENT | 1 | 2 | (3) | 4 | 5 |
| CONSTRUCTIVE FANTASY | 1 | 2 | (3) | 4 | 5 |
| DRIVE | 1 | (2) | 3 | 4 | 5 |
| EMOTIONAL TONE | (1) | 2 | 3 | 4 | 5 |
| SOCIAL ATTITUDE | 1 | (2) | 3 | 4 | 5 |
| ANXIETY | 1 | 2 | (3) | 4 | 5 |
| I. Q. RATING  100 | 1 | (2) | 3 | 4 | 5 |

### RORSCHACH

| | | | |
|---|---|---|---|
| R 9 | M 3 | | Fc |
| | FM 2 | F 4 | c |
| W% 44 | m | F— | C' |
| D% 56 | k | F% 44 | FC |
| d% | K | | CF |
| Dd% | FK | | C |
| S | | | |

## WORK SHEET IR1

4

### VERBAL I. Q. = 123

| EWS | Info. | Comp. | Digit | Arith. | Sim. |
|-----|-------|-------|-------|--------|------|
| 18 | 25 | 20 | | 14 | 23-24 |
| 17 | 24 | 19 | 17 | 13 | 21-22 |
| 16 | 23 | 18 | 16 | 12 | 20 |
| 15 | 21-22 | 17 | | 11 | 19 |
| 14 | 20 | 16 | 15 | | 17-18 |
| 13 | 18-19 | 15 | 14 | 10 | 16 |
| 12 | 17 | 14 | | 9 | 15 |
| | | | | | |
| 11 | 15-16 | 12-13 | 13 | | 13-14 |
| 10 | 13-14 | 11 | 12 | 8 | 12 |
| 9 | 12 | 10 | 11 | 7 | 11 |
| 8 | 10-11 | 9 | | | 9-10 |
| 7 | 9 | 8 | 10 | 6 | 8 |
| 6 | 7-8 | 7 | 9 | 5 | 7 |
| | | | | | |
| 5 | 6 | 5-6 | | | 5-6 |
| 4 | 4-5 | 4 | 8 | 4 | 4 |
| 3 | 2-3 | 3 | 7 | 3 | 3 |
| 2 | 1 | 2 | 6 | | 1-2 |
| 1 | 0 | 1 | | 2 | 0 |
| 0 | | 0 | 5 | 1 | |

### SZONDI

| SEXUAL | | PAROXYSMAL | | EGO | | CONTACT | |
|--------|---|------------|----|-----|---|---------|---|
| h | s | e | hy | k | p | d | m |

### OVER-ALL EVALUATION = 27

| | | | | | |
|---|---|---|---|---|---|
| OVER-ALL RATING | 1 | 2 | 3 | 4 | 5 |
| PRODUCTIVITY | 1 | ② | 3 | 4 | 5 |
| RELATION TO REALITY | 1 | 2 | ③ | 4 | 5 |
| THOUGHT CONTENT | 1 | 2 | ③ | 4 | 5 |
| CONSTRUCTIVE FANTASY | 1 | 2 | ③ | 4 | 5 |
| DRIVE | 1 | ② | 3 | 4 | 5 |
| EMOTIONAL TONE | 1 | 2 | ③ | 4 | 5 |
| SOCIAL ATTITUDE | 1 | 2 | ③ | 4 | 5 |
| ANXIETY | 1 | 2 | 3 | ④ | 5 |
| I. Q. RATING 123 | 1 | 2 | 3 | ④ | 5 |

### RORSCHACH

| | | | | | |
|---|---|---|---|---|---|
| R 15 | M 4 | | | Fc | |
| | FM 2 | F 5 | | c | |
| W% 47 | m | F- | | C' | |
| D% 53 | k | F% 33 | | FC 1 |
| d% | K | | | CF 2 |
| Dd% | FK | | | c 1 |
| S | | | | | |

TESTS 1 AND 4    **SUMMARY OF TEST FINDINGS**    IR 1

## MANNER DURING TEST

| (1) Overly distressed | (2) Tense | (3) Indifferent | (4) (Appropriate) | (5) Relaxed and actively interested |
|---|---|---|---|---|
| (1) Hostile | (2) Uneasy | | | |

## I.Q. (Bellevue-Wechsler)

| (1) Below average | (2) (Average) | (3) High average | (4) Superior | (5) Very superior |
|---|---|---|---|---|

## PRODUCTIVITY (Rorschach)

| (1) (Impoverished) | (2) Reduced output | (3) Adequate | (4) Better than average | (5) Rich and well-ordered |
|---|---|---|---|---|
| | (2) Compulsive productivity | | | |

## RELATION TO REALITY (Rorschach, Bellevue-Wechsler, Drawings)

| (1) Loose | (2) (Lapses—together with good form) | (3) Not noticeably disturbed | (4) Essentially firm | (5) Firm and good |
|---|---|---|---|---|

## USUAL-UNUSUAL THOUGHT CONTENT (Rorschach, Unpleasant Concept)

| (1) Bizarre | (2) Tendency toward the bizarre | (3) Adequate | (4) Original trends | (5) Outstandingly original |
|---|---|---|---|---|
| (1) Stereotyped | (2) (Tendency toward stereotypy) | | | |

## CONSTRUCTIVE FANTASY (Rorschach)

| (1) Absent | (2) (Barely accessible) | (3) Accessible | (4) Readily accessible | (5) Active but not hampering |
|---|---|---|---|---|
| (1) Withdrawal into fantasy | | | | |

## DRIVE (Rorschach, Szondi, Unpleasant Concept)

| (1) Overpowering aggression | (2) (Over-aggressive) | (3) Adequate | (4) Clearly sufficient | (5) Sufficient—exceptionally well-directed |
|---|---|---|---|---|
| (1) Hampering passivity | (2) Insufficient drive | | | |

## EMOTIONAL TONE (Rorschach, Szondi)

| (1) Explosive emotions | (2) Getting out of hand | (3) Trend toward emotional expression | (4) Warmth available | (5) Warm, readily available |
|---|---|---|---|---|
| (1) Lacking | (2) (Indicated but re-pressed emotions) | | | |

## SOCIAL ATTITUDE (T. A. T.)

| (1) Uncontrolled | (2) (Constricted or neglected) | (3) Adequate | (4) Well-regulated | (5) Free and flexible |
|---|---|---|---|---|

## ANXIETY

| (1) Disintegrating | (2) (Marked) | (3) Moderate | (4) Not marked | (5) Lack of evidence of anxiety |
|---|---|---|---|---|

## OVER-ALL EVALUATION

| (1) Markedly disturbed personality | (2) (Less than adequate personality with some psychological problems) | (3) Adequate personality | (4) Better than average functioning personality | (5) Exceptionally well-integrated personality with excellent potential |
|---|---|---|---|---|

## 1—4   SUMMARY OF THERAPIST'S FINDINGS   *IR 1*

### ESTIMATED INTELLIGENCE LEVEL

| (1) Below average | (2) Average | (3) High average | (4) Superior | (5) Very superior |
|---|---|---|---|---|

### FLOW OF ASSOCIATIVE MATERIAL

| (1) Impoverished | (2) Reduced output | (3) Adequate | (4) Better than average | (5) Rich and well-ordered |
|---|---|---|---|---|
| | (2) Compulsive productivity | | | |

### RELATION TO REALITY

| (1) Loose | (2) Lapses—together with good form | (3) Not noticeably disturbed | (4) Essentially firm | (5) Firm and good |
|---|---|---|---|---|

### USUAL-UNUSUAL THOUGHT CONTENT

| (1) Bizarre | (2) Tendency toward the bizarre | (3) Adequate | (4) Original trends | (5) Outstandingly original |
|---|---|---|---|---|
| (1) Stereotyped | (2) Tendency toward stereotypy | | | |

### CONSTRUCTIVE FANTASY

| (1) Absent | (2) Barely accessible | (3) Accessible | (4) Readily accessible | (5) Active but not hampering |
|---|---|---|---|---|
| (1) Withdrawal into fantasy | | | | |

### DRIVE

| (1) Overpowering aggression | (2) Over-aggressive | (3) Adequate | (4) Clearly sufficient | (5) Sufficient—exceptionally well-directed |
|---|---|---|---|---|
| (1) Hampering passivity | (2) Insufficient drive | | | |

### EMOTIONAL TONE

| (1) Explosive emotions | (2) Getting out of hand | (3) Trend toward emotional expression | (4) Warmth available | (5) Warm, readily available |
|---|---|---|---|---|
| (1) Lacking | (2) Indicated but repressed emotions | | | |

### SOCIAL ATTITUDE

| (1) Uncontrolled | (2) Constricted or neglected | (3) Adequate | (4) Well-regulated | (5) Free and flexible |
|---|---|---|---|---|

### ANXIETY

| (1) Disintegrating | (2) Marked | (3) Moderate | (4) Not marked | (5) Lack of evidence of anxiety |
|---|---|---|---|---|

### OVER-ALL EVALUATION

| (1) Markedly disturbed personality | (2) Less than adequate personality with some psychological problems | (3) Adequate personality | (4) Better than average functioning personality | (5) Exceptionally well-integrated personality with excellent potential |
|---|---|---|---|---|

that, therefore, her prognosis, on the basis of an anxiety neurosis, is better than it might otherwise have been.

"At the present time, in the transference relationship she is warmer, suggestible, compliant and finally shows a more positive attitude toward her mother and toward her friends. Her facial expression and the nature of her speech are calm and have changed markedly; they give an impression of normality."[*]

Turning now to the psychological tests, there are only two Bellevue-Wechsler scores, those of the third and fourth testing, since at the two initial examinations the parents refused to have this child's intelligence assessed. Between the third and fourth testings, there is a dramatic improvement, with a rise in I.Q. from 100 to 123. Particularly outstanding is the change in the Comprehension score from 7 to 15 on the weighted scale, reflecting a marked change in maturity and social adjustment.

Comparisons can be made between the first and fourth testings in terms of the Szondi, the Figure Drawings, the Most Unpleasant Concept and the Rorschach. On the Most Unpleasant Concept, at the age of eleven, IR1 gave the unusual response of concern over the possibility of finding herself in a mental hospital. She draws herself lying on a bed by the side of the hospital structure. Eleven years later, the drawing of the telephone, with the statement, "No ring," reflects a much more natural apprehension, namely, that her date might not call her.

The Szondi, with the strong +h and +s and −m, shows a frustrated, unfulfilled and unhappy picture at the early age, which is modified in terms of successful sublimation and decrease in subjectively experienced tension on the final testing.

The four Rorschach records can be considered an expansion and enrichment of the original core personality. In the final testing, both the M responses and the color answers have increased but the core personality has not changed essentially. *All* answers originally given reappear eleven years later! The mental approach also scarcely varies.

The handling of the eyes in the initial drawing gives the female figure a somewhat bizarre look. Although the eyes receive special attention throughout all subsequent drawings, in the later ones they are drawn in a more usual fashion.

The improvement shown in the tests, while in the same direction as that found clinically, is less marked. Slight fluctuations, however, *do parallel* the clinical improvement and relapse. Record 3, with the loss of color answers, indicates a regression from the slightly more advantageous position achieved in Record 2. Record 2, in its turn, is a slight improve-

---

[*] As this book goes to press, the reports on IR1 are even more encouraging. Her scholastic record is now so good that she has been able to make up the additional six months' work necessary in order to graduate from college with her class.

ment over Record 1. As might be expected, the maximum amount of change on the tests is found when the first and final performances are compared.

The quantitative scores in this instance rise from 15 at the first testing to 27 eleven years later. The second evaluation, with its score of 21, does not include a score for the I.Q. since the test was not given. If this score is also omitted from the third evaluation, one finds a drop from 21 to 18 points at the time when symptoms recurred. The therapist's scores are 9 at the first assessment and 31 at the final appraisal.

During the eleven years which elapsed between the first and third testings of IR2 (in his late fifties when first seen), he may be said to have passed from a period of compulsive productivity through a profound depression, for which he was hospitalized and received shock treatment, to achievement of a plateau of stable adjustment.

Detailed clinical evaluation from a therapist is available only for the second, most disturbed period, although the initial referral for psychological testing was the result of IR2 having sought psychiatric help at that time also. He was not in therapy at the time of the final testing, having reached a comfortable and sufficiently productive state of being.

It is felt that a slightly different method of presenting the material is in order here. One of the most striking findings on the test is the drastic curtailment of productivity and originality on the second Rorschach test, the perseveration, and the poor-form responses which crept into it. Total R dropped from 71 to 50, and outstanding changes occurred in the psychogram. We have attempted to illustrate this by use of an abbreviated content graph, a method described elsewhere,[11] whereby the change in the key determinants together with the content itself can be seen. The bottom half of the graph represents the answers given by IR2 during the first testing. The upper graph shows his production during the deep depression for which shock therapy was given. The graph is abbreviated in that the F column, which changed least and afforded no sharp contrast, has been omitted.

As can be seen from the two graphs, the FM responses dropped from nine to one, and where active and varied movements occurred before, "animals lying" is the only response of this kind in Record 2. The k responses show the perseverative trend in Record 2, where eight answers in terms of "relief map" are given with monotonous repetition. F− responses were absent during the first testing but occur in the second. Undifferentiated c responses are prominent in the second record, while minimal in number in the first. The FC responses drop from seven to two; there is a decrease also in the stronger color answers.

| M | FM | k | F- | c | FC | CF | C+Csym. |
|---|---|---|---|---|---|---|---|
| Devils tongues sticking out | Animal lying | Relief map | Canyon in desert | Rocks | Caterpillars | Dissected body | |
| Grotesque figure dancing | | Relief map | Animal with feather, wings | Rags | Wings of yellow butterfly | | |
| Two dancers | | Relief map | Reptile with short paws | Folded material | | | |
| | | Relief map | Skull | Skin | | | |
| | | Relief map | Trunk of tree | Skin | | | |
| | | Relief map | Anus and testicles | | | | |
| | | Relief map | | | | | |
| | | Relief map | | | | | |

| M | FM | k | F- | c | FC | CF | C+Csym. |
|---|---|---|---|---|---|---|---|
| Fantastic man | Lion crouched | Relief map | | Skin | Green insect | Mineral specimen | Blood |
| Savage figure | Bird-devil flying | | | | Yellow flower | Chart with blood vessels | |
| Man flying, with wings | Greyhound leaping | | | | Flowers and leaves | | |
| Men with baskets | Gopher walking | | | | A costume (colored) | | |
| Female in military coat | Goose flying | | | | Indian pipe plant | | |
| Nude female | Bird sitting up | | | | Butterfly | | |
| Figure with raised hands | Birds flying | | | | A red turban | | |
| | Two young bears | | | | | | |
| | Dogs pointing noses | | | | | | |

## #3

VERBAL I. Q. = 138

| EWS | Info. | Comp. | Digit | Arith. | Sim. |
|---|---|---|---|---|---|
| 18 | **25** | 20 | | **14** | 23-24 |
| 17 | 24 | 19 | 17 | 3 | **21-22** |
| 16 | 23 | 18 | 16 | 12 | 20 |
| 15 | 21-22 | **16** | 15 | 11 | 19 |
| 14 | 20 | 15 | 14 | 10 | 17-18 |
| 13 | 18-19 | 14 | **13** | 9 | 15 |
| 12 | 17 | | 12 | | |
| 11 | 15-16 | 12-13 | 11 | 8 | 13-14 |
| 10 | 13-14 | 11 | | 7 | 12 |
| 9 | 12 | 10 | | | 11 |
| 8 | 10-11 | 9 | 10 | 6 | 9-10 |
| 7 | | | 9 | 5 | 8 |
| 6 | 7-8 | 7 | | | 7 |

## #2

VERBAL I. Q. = 140

| EWS | Info. | Comp. | Digit | Arith. | Sim. |
|---|---|---|---|---|---|
| 18 | 25 | 20 | | 14 | **23-24** |
| 17 | **24** | 19 | 17 | 13 | 21-22 |
| 16 | 23 | **18** | 16 | 12 | 20 |
| 15 | 21-22 | 17 | **15** | **11** | 19 |
| 14 | 20 | 16 | 14 | 10 | 17-18 |
| 13 | 18-19 | 15 | 13 | 9 | 15 |
| 12 | 17 | 14 | 12 | | |
| 11 | 15-16 | 12-13 | 11 | 8 | 13-14 |
| 10 | 13-14 | 11 | 10 | 7 | 12 |
| 9 | 12 | 10 | | | 11 |
| 8 | 10-11 | 9 | 9 | 6 | 9-10 |
| 7 | 9 | 8 | | 5 | 8 |
| 6 | 7-8 | 7 | | | 7 |

## #1

VERBAL I. Q. = 142

| EWS | Info. | Comp. | Digit | Arith. | Sim. |
|---|---|---|---|---|---|
| 18 | 25 | 20 | | 14 | **23-24** |
| 17 | **24** | 19 | 17 | 13 | 21-22 |
| 16 | 23 | **18** | **16** | 12 | 20 |
| 15 | 21-22 | 17 | 15 | **11** | 19 |
| 14 | 20 | 16 | 14 | 10 | 17-18 |
| 13 | 18-19 | 15 | 13 | | 15 |
| 12 | 17 | 14 | 12 | 9 | |
| 11 | 15-16 | 12-13 | | 8 | 13-14 |
| 10 | 13-14 | 11 | 11 | 7 | 12 |
| 9 | 12 | 10 | | | 11 |
| 8 | 10-11 | 9 | 10 | 6 | 9-10 |
| 7 | 9 | 8 | 9 | 5 | 8 |
| 6 | 7-8 | 7 | | | 7 |

## *1R2*   SUMMARY OF TEST FINDINGS   *1 AND 2*

### MANNER DURING TEST

| (1) Overly distressed | (2) Tense | (3) Indifferent | (4) Appropriate | (5) Relaxed and actively interested |
|---|---|---|---|---|
| (1) Hostile | (2) Uneasy | | | |

### I.Q. (Bellevue-Wechsler)

| (1) Below average | (2) Average | (3) High average | (4) Superior | (5) Very superior |
|---|---|---|---|---|

### PRODUCTIVITY (Rorschach)

| (1) Impoverished | (2) Reduced output | (3) Adequate | (4) Better than average | (5) Rich and well-ordered |
|---|---|---|---|---|
| | (2) Compulsive productivity | | | |

### RELATION TO REALITY (Rorschach, Bellevue-Wechsler, Drawings)

| (1) Loose | (2) Lapses—together with good form | (3) Not noticeably disturbed | (4) Essentially firm | (5) Firm and good |
|---|---|---|---|---|

### USUAL-UNUSUAL THOUGHT CONTENT (Rorschach, Unpleasant Concept)

| (1) Bizarre | (2) Tendency toward the bizarre | (3) Adequate | (4) Original trends | (5) Outstandingly original |
|---|---|---|---|---|
| (1) Stereotyped | (2) Tendency toward stereotypy | | | |

### CONSTRUCTIVE FANTASY (Rorschach)

| (1) Absent | (2) Barely accessible | (3) Accessible | (4) Readily accessible | (5) Active but not hampering |
|---|---|---|---|---|
| (1) Withdrawal into fantasy | | | | |

### DRIVE (Rorschach, Szondi, Unpleasant Concept)

| (1) Overpowering aggression | (2) Over-aggressive | (3) Adequate | (4) Clearly sufficient | (5) Sufficient—exceptionally well-directed |
|---|---|---|---|---|
| (1) Hampering passivity | (2) Insufficient drive | | | |

### EMOTIONAL TONE (Rorschach, Szondi)

| (1) Explosive emotions | (2) Getting out of hand | (3) Trend toward emotional expression | (4) Warmth available | (5) Warm, readily available |
|---|---|---|---|---|
| (1) Lacking | (2) Indicated but repressed emotions | | | |

### SOCIAL ATTITUDE (T. A. T.)

| (1) Uncontrolled | (2) Constricted or neglected | (3) Adequate | (4) Well-regulated | (5) Free and flexible |
|---|---|---|---|---|

### ANXIETY

| (1) Disintegrating | (2) Marked | (3) Moderate | (4) Not marked | (5) Lack of evidence of anxiety |
|---|---|---|---|---|

### OVER-ALL EVALUATION

| (1) Markedly disturbed personality | (2) Less than adequate personality with some psychological problems | (3) Adequate personality | (4) Better than average functioning personality | (5) Exceptionally well-integrated personality with excellent potential |
|---|---|---|---|---|

IR2  SUMMARY OF TEST FINDINGS  *TESTS 2 → 3*

### MANNER DURING TEST

| (1) Overly distressed | (2) Tense | (3) Indifferent | (4) Appropriate | (5) Relaxed and actively interested |
|---|---|---|---|---|
| (1) Hostile | (2) Uneasy | | | |

### I.Q. (Bellevue-Wechsler)

| (1) Below average | (2) Average | (3) High average | (4) Superior | (5) Very superior |
|---|---|---|---|---|

### PRODUCTIVITY (Rorschach)

| (1) Impoverished | (2) Reduced output | (3) Adequate | (4) Better than average | (5) Rich and well-ordered |
|---|---|---|---|---|
| | (2) Compulsive productivity | | | |

### RELATION TO REALITY (Rorschach, Bellevue-Wechsler, Drawings)

| (1) Loose | (2) Lapses—together with good form | (3) Not noticeably disturbed | (4) Essentially firm | (5) Firm and good |
|---|---|---|---|---|

### USUAL-UNUSUAL THOUGHT CONTENT (Rorschach, Unpleasant Concept)

| (1) Bizarre | (2) Tendency toward the bizarre | (3) Adequate | (4) Original trends | (5) Outstandingly original |
|---|---|---|---|---|
| (1) Stereotyped | (2) Tendency toward stereotypy | | | |

### CONSTRUCTIVE FANTASY (Rorschach)

| (1) Absent | (2) Barely accessible | (3) Accessible | (4) Readily accessible | (5) Active but not hampering |
|---|---|---|---|---|
| (1) Withdrawal into fantasy | | | | |

### DRIVE (Rorschach, Szondi, Unpleasant Concept)

| (1) Overpowering aggression | (2) Over-aggressive | (3) Adequate | (4) Clearly sufficient | (5) Sufficient—exceptionally well-directed |
|---|---|---|---|---|
| (1) Hampering passivity | (2) Insufficient drive | | | |

### EMOTIONAL TONE (Rorschach, Szondi)

| (1) Explosive emotions | (2) Getting out of hand | (3) Trend toward emotional expression | (4) Warmth available | (5) Warm, readily available |
|---|---|---|---|---|
| (1) Lacking | (2) Indicated but repressed emotions | | | |

### SOCIAL ATTITUDE (T. A. T.)

| (1) Uncontrolled | (2) Constricted or neglected | (3) Adequate | (4) Well-regulated | (5) Free and flexible |
|---|---|---|---|---|

### ANXIETY

| (1) Disintegrating | (2) Marked | (3) Moderate | (4) Not marked | (5) Lack of evidence of anxiety |
|---|---|---|---|---|

### OVER-ALL EVALUATION

| (1) Markedly disturbed personality | (2) Less than adequate personality with some psychological problems | (3) Adequate personality | (4) Better than average functioning personality | (5) Exceptionally well-integrated personality with excellent potential |
|---|---|---|---|---|

## SUMMARY OF THERAPIST'S FINDINGS          IR 2

### ESTIMATED INTELLIGENCE LEVEL

| (1) Below average | (2) Average | (3) High average | (4) Superior | (5) Very superior |
|---|---|---|---|---|

### FLOW OF ASSOCIATIVE MATERIAL

| (1) Impoverished | (2) Reduced output / (2) Compulsive productivity | (3) Adequate | (4) Better than average | (5) Rich and well-ordered |
|---|---|---|---|---|

### RELATION TO REALITY

| (1) Loose | (2) Lapses—together with good form | (3) Not noticeably disturbed | (4) Essentially firm | (5) Firm and good |
|---|---|---|---|---|

### USUAL-UNUSUAL THOUGHT CONTENT

| (1) Bizarre / (1) Stereotyped | (2) Tendency toward the bizarre / (2) Tendency toward stereotypy | (3) Adequate | (4) Original trends | (5) Outstandingly original |
|---|---|---|---|---|

### CONSTRUCTIVE FANTASY

| (1) Absent / (1) Withdrawal into fantasy | (2) Barely accessible | (3) Accessible ? | (4) Readily accessible | (5) Active but not hampering |
|---|---|---|---|---|

### DRIVE

| (1) Overpowering aggression / (1) Hampering passivity | (2) Over-aggressive / (2) Insufficient drive | (3) Adequate | (4) Clearly sufficient | (5) Sufficient—exceptionally well-directed |
|---|---|---|---|---|

### EMOTIONAL TONE

| (1) Explosive emotions / (1) Lacking | (2) Getting out of hand / (2) Indicated but re-pressed emotions | (3) Trend toward emotional expression | (4) Warmth available | (5) Warm, readily available |
|---|---|---|---|---|

### SOCIAL ATTITUDE

| (1) Uncontrolled | (2) Constricted or neglected | (3) Adequate | (4) Well-regulated | (5) Free and flexible |
|---|---|---|---|---|

### ANXIETY

| (1) Disintegrating | (2) Marked | (3) Moderate | (4) Not marked | (5) Lack of evidence of anxiety |
|---|---|---|---|---|

### OVER-ALL EVALUATION

| (1) Markedly disturbed personality | (2) Less than adequate personality with some psychological problems | (3) Adequate personality | (4) Better than average functioning personality | (5) Exceptionally well-integrated personality with excellent potential |
|---|---|---|---|---|

The Rorschach record at the time of the third testing bears no similarity whatsoever to that obtained during the disturbed and depressed period. However, it does have a close resemblance to the initial record, with the important exception that the CF and pure C responses are now missing. Five of the original seven FC responses are found again. The perseverative responses and F− responses are eliminated, and the total R has dropped to 44.

Although on the third testing the Bellevue-Wechsler scores show greater scatter, the I.Q. remains at all times at the *Very Superior* level, and while the Digit Memory scores are poorer, the Arithmetic for the first time is handled with poise and ease.

The Figure Drawings in the first and third testing are full figures, those during the depressed period, large, rather vacuous and space-filling heads.

M AND COLOR RESPONSES DURING PERIODS OF IMPROVEMENT AND RELAPSE, IR3

| Condition when Tested | M Responses | FC Responses | C Responses |
|---|---|---|---|
| 1. *Pre-overt disturbance.* Roommates sense student having difficulties and report to college authorities. | Monks holding their arms out. Two people rowing a boat. People praying. Two convicts. Two hooded figures. Two hooded monks praying. Two men carrying a large mat. Santa Clauses. | A chandelier made of blue glass. | Dead animals smoldering in the fire. Yellow lights, smoldering fire. Blood. Blood. Bleeding bodies. |
| 2. *Acute onset.* Patient referred for treatment. Therapist reports: "Prognosis is only poor to fair, even after long-term treatment." | Figures groping in a cloud. A clown. Two persons standing up. Two people waving goodbye. Someone with hands outstretched. Two people standing holding on to something. Two nuns. Two girls dancing. Two people putting something into the fire. Two people dancing. Two devils glaring at each other. Two people laughing with their mouths wide open. A person standing. People with arms outstretched. | None. | Blood. A clash, the red means fighting. |
| 3. *Remission.* Therapist reports: "We no longer take such a gloomy view of the future. Prognosis now appears better than it did before . . . We are tentatively heartened by the fact that patient seems to be developing positive feelings of trust and confidence which may lay the foundation upon which therapeutic achievement may be built." | Two women. Two men lying down. Some one running. A little boy. Two people roasting at a barbecue. Two people looking up. Two women waving goodbye. A baby with its mouth open. Two men. Two nuns praying. Two girls bending over, dancing. Two Negro boys. Two women washing something. Two women talking to each other and then waving goodbye. Two women floating. | Flowers appear here. This is foliage and plants. | None. |
| 4. *Renewed onset of symptoms.* Therapist recommends further treatment. | Two men shooting. Figures in a KKK. Two people waving goodbye. Policeman standing. Two nuns praying. Two figures touching a bull's head. Two figures. Two figures. Two men in hooded robes. | None. | Blood. Blood. |
| 5. *Remission, increased stability and adjustment.* Psychologist in role of counselor records considerable clinical improvement which is confirmed from environmental sources. | A woman sitting down. Two human figures talking to each other, their hands together. Two human figures with skulls in their hands. Human figures bending over. Nuns putting out their hands toward Mecca. Two men looking, talking to each other. Two figures with hands outstretched. Two women waving goodbye. Two human figures turning a skewer. A maid cleaning house, bending down. Two little elves dancing around a wood with flowers. Two men or women eating something. Two human figures looking down. | Red shoes. Dental plate, teeth and gums. A jacket, soft pink color. Flowers. Blue birds. | None. |

For various reasons detailed presentation of the raw data of IR3's test material has not been possible. Mention of it in some form is merited, however, since five test protocols have been obtained over an eleven-year period, and their acquisition has coincided with marked fluctuations in the clinical picture.

The first record was a Rorschach taken when IR3, as a college student in his first year, took part in some experiments as a control subject. Although there was no overt disturbance at this time, IR3's roommates sensed the fact that he was having difficulties, and reports on erratic and disturbed behavior trickled in to the college authorities.

The second record, a full battery, was obtained at the time of the first onset of acute symptoms, when IR3 was referred for diagnostic examination and shortly thereafter went into treatment.

The third test protocol was obtained one year later. This was the first retesting with the full battery. It was given during a period of clinical remission, at a time when the therapist was able to give an unexpectedly hopeful account of the patient.

Four years later, the patient was no longer in therapy but there was a renewed onset of symptoms and he came spontaneously for an additional psychological assessment. Subsequent to this, he went back into therapeutic treatment (see page 348).

The final record was taken subsequent to several years of psychotherapy and at a time when the psychologist was able to make an assessment of the clinical condition from the vantage point of a friend and counselor.

The material on the opposite page illustrates one important finding from the Rorschach record, namely, that *during periods of remission the CF responses and pure C responses drop out and FC responses appear. Conversely, during the periods of acute disturbance, FC responses disappear and flagrant pure C responses are found.*

What we have called the pre-overt disturbance record contains both types of color response, the most blatant pure C's together with a single FC response. We might envisage the patient at this time as building up toward an explosive and uncontrolled period, yet, while still able to handle his classwork, reflecting in the Rorschach at least one good, controlled color response.

The M responses during both the acutely disturbed period and the periods of social adjustment and increased stability do not deviate so markedly. All records are what we have described elsewhere as "M-dominated" records.

The I.Q. did not vary more than a few points in the five examinations. This boy remained at all times in the *Very Superior Group* of the total population.

## TESTS 3 and 4　SUMMARY OF TEST FINDINGS　　I R 3

### MANNER DURING TEST

| (1) Overly distressed | (2) Tense | (3) Indifferent | (4) Appropriate | (5) Relaxed and actively interested |
| (1) Hostile | (2) Uneasy | | | |

### I.Q. (Bellevue-Wechsler)

| (1) Below average | (2) Average | (3) High average | (4) Superior | (5) Very superior |

### PRODUCTIVITY (Rorschach)

| (1) Impoverished | (2) Reduced output | (3) Adequate | (4) Better than average | (5) Rich and well-ordered |
| | (2) Compulsive productivity | | | |

### RELATION TO REALITY (Rorschach, Bellevue-Wechsler, Drawings)

| (1) Loose | (2) Lapses—together with good form | (3) Not noticeably disturbed | (4) Essentially firm | (5) Firm and good |

### USUAL-UNUSUAL THOUGHT CONTENT (Rorschach, Unpleasant Concept)

| (1) Bizarre | (2) Tendency toward the bizarre | (3) Adequate | (4) Original trends | (5) Outstandingly original |
| (1) Stereotyped | (2) Tendency toward stereotypy | | | |

### CONSTRUCTIVE FANTASY (Rorschach)

| (1) Absent | (2) Barely accessible | (3) Accessible | (4) Readily accessible | (5) Active but not hampering |
| (1) Withdrawal into fantasy | | | | |

### DRIVE (Rorschach, Szondi, Unpleasant Concept)

| (1) Overpowering aggression | (2) Over-aggressive | (3) Adequate | (4) Clearly sufficient | (5) Sufficient—exceptionally well-directed |
| (1) Hampering passivity | (2) Insufficient drive | | | |

### EMOTIONAL TONE (Rorschach, Szondi)

| (1) Explosive emotions | (2) Getting out of hand | (3) Trend toward emotional expression | (4) Warmth available | (5) Warm, readily available |
| (1) Lacking | (2) Indicated but repressed emotions | | | |

### SOCIAL ATTITUDE (T. A. T.)

| (1) Uncontrolled | (2) Constricted or neglected | (3) Adequate | (4) Well-regulated | (5) Free and flexible |

### ANXIETY

| (1) Disintegrating | (2) Marked | (3) Moderate | (4) Not marked | (5) Lack of evidence of anxiety |

### OVER-ALL EVALUATION

| (1) Markedly disturbed personality | (2) Less than adequate personality with some psychological problems | (3) Adequate personality ? | (4) Better than average functioning personality | (5) Exceptionally well-integrated personality with excellent potential |

## XVI. The therapeutic effect of change in environmental conditions.

The case of EN1 has been reported twice before. The change in the clinical and behavioral picture after four years of treatment seemed striking enough to his physician to warrant publication,[6] while the case of twin boys, one with epilepsy, was of interest from the psychologist's standpoint also.[11]

EN1 was first seen, along with his twin brother as a control subject, at the age of eleven. At this time he was living under a constant fear of epileptic attacks. When the psychological evaluation was made, the vicious cycle whereby fear of an attack would precipitate further attacks was noted, and suggestions were made for relieving his feelings of inferiority engendered by his contrast to his more outgoing and aggressive brother.

The following account sets the stage for a comparison of the two psychological test records on EN1. As this clinical report shows, there was indisputable behavioral and scholastic improvement. The test findings mirror this improvement very closely. EN1's case offers a good example of the fact that control of a patient's seizures, combined with a strenuous effort to ameliorate the conditions under which he lives, that is, to alter his psychological environment, can result in measurable growth, both intellectual and emotional.

"EN1 was one of a pair of identical twins. His brother was born first, with a vertex presentation, the patient nine minutes later, by breech presentation. There was a single placenta. The father and the mother's sister had experienced convulsions in childhood. Three brothers were not remarkable.

"At one and a half years of age, the patient fell down eight steps, striking his head against a stone. Immediately thereafter, he seemed sleepy and was not acting just right. One and one-half hours later he had a generalized convulsive seizure. During the next week, whenever this infant would strike his head against the rail of the crib, he would have an attack. This occurred seven times.

"At nine and a half years of age, he was struck by his father's car, but not injured. EN1 describes this incident as follows: 'I was coming back from Mass when my father backed the automobile out of the driveway. He turned a way I did not expect and the front bumper hooked me and threw me against the front of the car. I was not hurt but badly scared. Father bawled me out, shouting at me.' One hour later there was a major seizure.

"Three months later, after a frightening motion picture, there was a second attack. Again, a seizure occurred following a prolonged period in crowded traffic during which the family temper was lost. Another time, an attack followed a tooth extraction. The general frequency was one attack every two or three months.

## WORK SHEET

*E N I*

I

### VERBAL I. Q. 119

| EWS | Info. | Comp. | Digit | Arith. | Sim. |
|-----|-------|-------|-------|--------|------|
| 18 | 25 | 20 | | 14 | 23-24 |
| 17 | 24 | 19 | 17 | 13 | 21-22 |
| 16 | 23 | 18 | 16 | 12 | 20 |
| 15 | 21-22 | 17 | | 11 | 19 |
| 14 | 20 | 16 | 15 | | 17-18 |
| 13 | 18-19 | 15 | 14 | 10 | 16 |
| 12 | 17 | 14 | | 9 | 15 |
| 11 | 15-16 | 12-13 | (13) | | 13-14 |
| 10 | 13-14 | 11 | 12 | 8 | 12 |
| 9 | 12 | 10 | 11 | (7) | (11) |
| 8 | (10-11) | 9 | | | 9-10 |
| 7 | 9 | (8) | 10 | 6 | 8 |
| 6 | 7-8 | 7 | 9 | 5 | 7 |
| 5 | 6 | 5-6 | | | 5-6 |
| 4 | 4-5 | 4 | 8 | 4 | 4 |
| 3 | 2-3 | 3 | 7 | 3 | 3 |
| 2 | 1 | 2 | 6 | | 1-2 |
| 1 | 0 | 1 | | 2 | 0 |
| 0 | | 0 | 5 | 1 | |

### SZONDI

| SEXUAL | | PAROXYSMAL | | EGO | | CONTACT | |
|--------|--------|------------|--------|--------|--------|--------|--------|
| h | s | e | hy | k | p | d | m |
| X | | | | | | | |
| X | | | | | | | |
| X | | | | | | | |
| X | X | | | | | | |
| X | X | X | X | X | X | X | |
| | X | X | X | X | X | X | X |
| | | | X | | | X | X |
| | | | | | | X | X |

### OVER-ALL EVALUATION = 18

| | 1 | 2 | 3 | 4 | 5 |
|---|---|---|---|---|---|
| OVER-ALL RATING | 1 | 2 | 3 | 4 | 5 |
| PRODUCTIVITY | (1) | 2 | 3 | 4 | 5 |
| RELATION TO REALITY | 1 | 2 | (3) | 4 | 5 |
| THOUGHT CONTENT | 1 | (2) | 3 | 4 | 5 |
| CONSTRUCTIVE FANTASY | 1 | 2 | (3) | 4 | 5 |
| DRIVE | (1) | 2 | 3 | 4 | 5 |
| EMOTIONAL TONE | (1) | 2 | 3 | 4 | 5 |
| SOCIAL ATTITUDE | 1 | (2) | 3 | 4 | 5 |
| ANXIETY | 1 | (2) | 3 | 4 | 5 |
| I. Q. RATING | 1 | 2 | (3) | 4 | 5 |

### RORSCHACH

| R 8 | M 3 | | Fc |
|-----|------|------|-----|
| | FM 1 | F 3 | c |
| W% 88 | m | F- 1 | C' |
| D% 12 | k | F% 50 | FC |
| d% | K | | CF |
| Dd% | FK | | C |
| S | | | |

# WORK SHEET

ENI

2

## VERBAL I. Q. = 130

| EWS | Info. | Comp. | Digit | Arith. | Sim. |
|-----|-------|-------|-------|--------|------|
| 18 | 25 | 20 | | 14 | 23-24 |
| 17 | 24 | 19 | 17 | 13 | 21-22 |
| 16 | 23 | 18 | 16 | 12 | 20 |
| 15 | 21-22 | 17 | | (11) | 19 |
| 14 | 20 | 16 | 15 | | (17-18) |
| 13 | 18-19 | 15 | 14 | 10 | 16 |
| 12 | (17) | (14) | | 9 | 15 |
| 11 | 15-16 | 12-13 | 13 | | 13-14 |
| 10 | 13-14 | 11 | 12 | 8 | 12 |
| 9 | 12 | 10 | 11 | 7 | 11 |
| 8 | 10-11 | 9 | | | 9-10 |
| 7 | 9 | 8 | 10 | 6 | 8 |
| 6 | 7-8 | 7 | 9 | 5 | 7 |
| 5 | 6 | 5-6 | | | 5-6 |
| 4 | 4-5 | 4 | 8 | 4 | 4 |
| 3 | 2-3 | 3 | 7 | 3 | 3 |
| 2 | 1 | 2 | 6 | | 1-2 |
| 1 | 0 | 1 | | 2 | 0 |
| 0 | | 0 | 5 | 1 | |

## SZONDI

| SEXUAL | | PAROXYSMAL | | EGO | | CONTACT | |
|--------|--------|--------|--------|--------|--------|--------|--------|
| h | s | e | hy | k | p | d | m |
| | | | | | X | | |
| | | X | | | X | | X |
| X | | X | | | X | | |
| X | X | X | | X | X | | X |
| X | X | X | X | X | X | X X | X |
| | X | | | X | | X X | |
| | X X | | | | | | |
| | X | | | | | | |

## OVER-ALL EVALUATION = 31

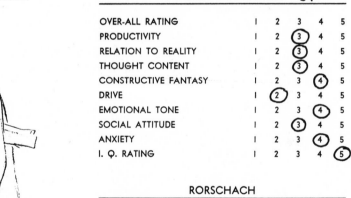

| | 1 | 2 | 3 | 4 | 5 |
|---|---|---|---|---|---|
| OVER-ALL RATING | 1 | 2 | 3 | 4 | 5 |
| PRODUCTIVITY | 1 | 2 | (3) | 4 | 5 |
| RELATION TO REALITY | 1 | 2 | (3) | 4 | 5 |
| THOUGHT CONTENT | 1 | 2 | (3) | 4 | 5 |
| CONSTRUCTIVE FANTASY | 1 | 2 | 3 | (4) | 5 |
| DRIVE | 1 | (2) | 3 | 4 | 5 |
| EMOTIONAL TONE | 1 | 2 | 3 | (4) | 5 |
| SOCIAL ATTITUDE | 1 | 2 | (3) | 4 | 5 |
| ANXIETY | 1 | 2 | 3 | (4) | 5 |
| I. Q. RATING | 1 | 2 | 3 | 4 | (5) |

## RORSCHACH

| | | | | | |
|---|---|---|---|---|---|
| R 34 | M 8 | | | Fc 2 | |
| | FM 2 | | F 15 | c | |
| W% 15 | m +1 | | F- 2 | C' | |
| D% 67 | k | | F% 50 | FC 4 | |
| d% 18 | K 1 | | | CF | |
| Dd% | FK | | | c | |
| S | | | | | |

"When first seen at the Neurological Institute of New York, in February 1950, at age 11, EN1 had had 12 major seizures in the previous 19 months. In these attacks, he had no subjective warning; there was only a sudden loss of consciousness. *Objectively,* the patient emitted a stuttering sound, his eyes rolled back, he became rigid and then shook. No focal aspect was noted. Neurologic examination revealed no significant abnormality. Electroencephalography showed generalized high amplitude rhythmic slow waves during hyperventilation. His twin brother showed a similar record to a less marked degree, and little significance was attached to this.

"In the 19 months during which he had repeated seizures, the patient did poorly in school and received lower grades than his twin brother. His father described him as introspective, his mother as being subdued. She adds that during one examination in the fifth grade, EN1, who was indecisive about his answers, remained in school all afternoon. His writing was poor. In contrast to his twin, he always hung back at school entertainments.

"The management in this case included the establishment of a better understanding by the parents, reassuring and encouraging the patient, separation of the twins at school, and the control of the attacks by effective anticonvulsant medication. Since the initial examinations there has been but one seizure—in early 1951.

"In re-evaluating this case four years later, in March 1954, the following progress was noted: In the new school, although nervous at first EN1 improved scholastically and in his general performance. Both boys did exceptionally well during seventh and eighth grades. Each in his respective school last year received the medal of excellence for the best over-all scholastic average. They are now in high school. The twin brother is vice-president of his class and EN1 is secretary of his fraternal order. In the summer they both work and participate in community affairs. The mother states there is little difference in the two boys, EN1 having perhaps become a little more certain of his knowledge and more outgoing in his play and work activity even than his brother.

"In discussing the former period during which he was having seizures, EN1 states: 'At first, that is, with the first attack or two, I thought, This is something that happens once in a lifetime. Then when it was repeated several times, I didn't know. I got nervous, I did not do well in school, particularly in the sixth grade. My mathematics was bad. My writing was bad. I was not scared, but I was not relaxed. I was more careful. I was less sure of myself. In the seventh and eighth grades and now in high school, my math is much better and my writing has improved.'

"*Comment.* In this case, the evidence would indicate that heredity played a small part and brain trauma a considerable part in establishing the recurrent seizures. Emotional factors were influential in precipitating at least three and probably more of the childhood attacks. *Of most importance, however, was the stress, evoked by the recurrent seizures, that interfered with academic performance and interpersonal relations. With medical control and better understanding on the part of the patient and his parents, the stress was alleviated and the emotional problems resolved.*"[6]

Turning to a comparison of the Work Sheets, we find that the I.Q. jumped from 119 to 130 and that there was little scatter on the second performance. The Rorschach expanded both in quality and in quantity of responses. The second record is well within normal limits, with good color responses and rich human-movement answers.

The important changes in the Szondi are away from the loaded +h and −m responses, a classically unfavorable picture in which insatiable demands for love run parallel to basic oral frustration. A more structured ego picture has also replaced the amorphous one shown in the first testing. EN1's over-dependency on his mother, seen in the Figure Drawing, where the female figure was five or six times as large as the male, and in the Sentence Completion, is no longer evidenced in Record 2. His drawing of the man has "grown" to normal size and the female, if anything, is slightly smaller. On the Sentence Completion, a repetitious harping on oral needs has vanished.

This case meets our criteria that the same basic trend should be shown from the four possible sources of information. In this instance, EN1, his parents, his physician, and the test findings all agree. EN1 when first tested was a restricted and unhappy child; four years later he could be assessed as well within normal limits and, in many respects, superior to the average boy of his age.


EN2 was an acute behavior problem at the time her parents sought psychological assistance in evaluating the situation. Wild outbursts of temper at the most trivial provocation and a fierce antagonism to her mother made her almost unmanageable.

The initial psychological picture was anything but favorable. The Szondi at this time, as will be seen from Work Sheet 1, reflects her experienced frustration and insatiable needs for affection (loaded +h, −m). The aggressive outbursts (+s, open e) are also indicated.

The Rorschach record was that of an acutely disturbed child. The five pure C responses and the four bizarre F− answers suggested serious psychopathology. The drawings were also unusually primitive for the eleven-year-old level. Fear of failure, and herself as ostracized, was portrayed as the Most Unpleasant Concept.

The parents, on advice, sought psychiatric assistance *but the therapist never saw or worked with EN2 herself.* Suggestions were given as to her management and the mother alerted to some of their interpersonal difficulties. A complete change of environment occurred when the family moved to a different part of the country. EN2 attended a different school and made new friends. Almost immediately, marked improvement was noted by the parents, and on retesting two years later, a much more mature and balanced psychological picture was found.

It will be noted that the pure C and F− answers have dropped out

EN 2

## = WORK SHEET =

1

### SZONDI

| SEXUAL | | PAROXYSMAL | | EGO | | CONTACT | |
|---|---|---|---|---|---|---|---|
| h | s | e | hy | k | p | d | m |
| X | | | | | | | |
| X | X | | | | X | X | |
| X | X | | | | X | X | |
| X | X | X | | | | X | |
| X | X | X | X | X | X | X | X |
| | | | X | | X | | X |
| | | | | | | | X |
| | | | | | | | X |
| | | | | | | | X |

### OVER-ALL EVALUATION = 15

| | 1 | 2 | 3 | 4 | 5 |
|---|---|---|---|---|---|
| OVER-ALL RATING | 1 | 2 | 3 | 4 | 5 |
| PRODUCTIVITY | 1 | 2 | ③ | 4 | 5 |
| RELATION TO REALITY | 1 | ② | 3 | 4 | 5 |
| THOUGHT CONTENT | ① | 2 | 3 | 4 | 5 |
| CONSTRUCTIVE FANTASY | 1 | ② | 3 | 4 | 5 |
| DRIVE | 1 | ② | 3 | 4 | 5 |
| EMOTIONAL TONE | ① | 2 | 3 | 4 | 5 |
| SOCIAL ATTITUDE | 1 | ② | 3 | 4 | 5 |
| ANXIETY | 1 | ② | 3 | 4 | 5 |
| I. Q. RATING NOT GIVEN | 1 | 2 | 3 | 4 | 5 |

### RORSCHACH

| R 29 | M 3 (1-) | | Fc |
|---|---|---|---|
| | FM | F 14 | c |
| W% 41 | m | F- 4 | C' |
| D% 34 | k | F% 62 | FC 2 |
| d% 3 | K | | CF 1 |
| Dd% 22 | FK | | c 5 |
| S | | | |

## WORK SHEET

EN2

2

### SZONDI

| SEXUAL | | PAROXYSMAL | | EGO | | CONTACT | |
|---|---|---|---|---|---|---|---|
| h | s | e | hy | k | p | d | m |
| X<br>X | X | X | X<br>X | X<br>X | X<br>X | | X<br>X |
| X | X | X<br>X<br>X<br>X | X<br>X | | X<br>X | X | X |

### OVER-ALL EVALUATION = 26

| | | | | | |
|---|---|---|---|---|---|
| OVER-ALL RATING | I | 2 | 3 | 4 | 5 |
| PRODUCTIVITY | I | 2 | ③ | 4 | 5 |
| RELATION TO REALITY | I | 2 | 3 | ④ | 5 |
| THOUGHT CONTENT | I | 2 | ③ | 4 | 5 |
| CONSTRUCTIVE FANTASY | I | 2 | ③ | 4 | 5 |
| DRIVE | I | 2 | ③ | 4 | 5 |
| EMOTIONAL TONE | I | 2 | ③ | 4 | 5 |
| SOCIAL ATTITUDE | I | 2 | 3 | ④ | 5 |
| ANXIETY | I | 2 | ③ | 4 | 5 |
| I. Q. RATING NOT GIVEN | I | 2 | 3 | 4 | 5 |

### RORSCHACH

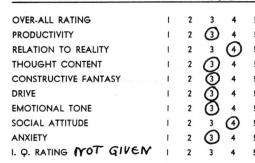

| | | | | | | |
|---|---|---|---|---|---|---|
| R 20 | M 4 | | | | Fc | |
| | FM 2 | | F 8 | | c 1 | |
| W% 40 | m | | F- | | C' | |
| D% 45 | k | | F% 40 | | FC 1 | |
| d% 5 | K 1 | | | | CF 2 | |
| Dd% 10<br>S | FK 1 | | | | C | |

*PARENTS*

# SUMMARY OF ~~THERAPIST'S~~ FINDINGS    *EN 2*

## ESTIMATED INTELLIGENCE LEVEL

| (1) Below average | (2) Average | (3) High average | (4) Superior | (5) Very superior |
|---|---|---|---|---|

## FLOW OF ASSOCIATIVE MATERIAL

| (1) Impoverished | (2) Reduced output | (3) Adequate | (4) Better than average | (5) Rich and well-ordered |
|---|---|---|---|---|
| | (2) Compulsive productivity | | | |

## RELATION TO REALITY

| (1) (Loose) | (2) Lapses—together ~~with good form~~ | (3) Not noticeably ~~disturbed~~ | (4) Essentially firm | (5) Firm and good |
|---|---|---|---|---|

## USUAL-UNUSUAL THOUGHT CONTENT

| (1) Bizarre | (2) Tendency toward the bizarre | (3) Adequate | (4) Original trends | (5) Outstandingly original |
|---|---|---|---|---|
| (1) Stereotyped | (2) Tendency toward stereotypy | | | |

## CONSTRUCTIVE FANTASY

| (1) Absent | (2) Barely accessible | (3) Accessible | (4) Readily accessible | (5) Active but not hampering |
|---|---|---|---|---|
| (1) Withdrawal into fantasy | | | | |

## DRIVE

| (1) (Overpowering aggression) | (2) Over-aggressive | (3) Adequate | (4) Clearly sufficient | (5) Sufficient—exceptionally well-directed |
|---|---|---|---|---|
| (1) Hampering passivity | (2) Insufficient drive | | | |

## EMOTIONAL TONE

| (1) (Explosive emotions) | (2) Getting out of ~~hand~~ | (3) Trend toward ~~emotional~~ expression | (4) Warmth available | (5) Warm, readily available |
|---|---|---|---|---|
| (1) Lacking | (2) Indicated but repressed emotions | | | |

## SOCIAL ATTITUDE

| (1) (Uncontrolled) | (2) Constricted or ~~neglected~~ | (3) Adequate | (4) Well-regulated | (5) Free and flexible |
|---|---|---|---|---|

## ANXIETY

| (1) Disintegrating | (2) (Marked) | (3) Moderate | (4) Not marked | (5) Lack of evidence of anxiety |
|---|---|---|---|---|

## OVER-ALL EVALUATION

| (1) Markedly disturbed personality | (2) Less than adequate personality with some psychological problems | (3) Adequate personality | (4) Better than average functioning personality | (5) Exceptionally well-integrated personality with excellent potential |
|---|---|---|---|---|

from the Rorschach record, and a much more benign structure is present.

Two years have made an enormous difference in her concept of the human person; the glamorous girl attending the party replaces the homely little waif which was originally drawn. An even more marked change has come about in terms of the concept of the man; the thoroughly grotesque figure of Work Sheet 1 has been replaced by a realistic and energetic looking figure.

The frustrated picture of the first Szondi is replaced by a much more balanced one.

In this instance, the parents utilized a modified Summary Chart to assess those aspects of their daughter's behavior which they felt had changed dramatically during the two years. The quantitative assessment from the tests is 15 for the first protocol and 26 for the second.

EN3 was first tested at the age of 15, with the second psychological battery being given ten years later. At the time of the first referral, her parents felt that her work did not measure up to her capacity and that she was emotionally incapable of making close, individualized attachments either with youngsters of her own age or with adults. The parents also described periodic, recurrent bouts of profound moodiness and depression which apparently interfered with her work and relationships.

Since the parents were unwilling for EN3 to enter therapy, a simple environmental change was suggested. It had been reported that EN3 disliked the school she attended, and it was therefore suggested that a different school might be advisable. This was done, and it later transpired that EN3 had been much happier in the new environment, that she had gone on to college and to appreciable success in her chosen career.

If one contrasts the changes that have been reflected over a ten-year interval in the cases we have seen, some of which are contained in this volume, we find three groups: First, there are those who have retained over the years an essentially similar personality structure which is recognizable at each of the testing points as that of the same individual. G2 is a good example of this type of growth. Secondly, there are cases which show abrupt changes of pattern, intervening tests being not recognizable as the product of the same individual who gave the test results obtained at the beginning and end of the ten-year period. The records of G1 and IR2 illustrate this, G1 showing emergence from an acute adolescent turmoil and IR2 showing recovery subsequent to a profound depression. A third type of case would be that illustrated by IR3 for whom, during the ten-year period, there is oscillation between levels of disturbance.

The pattern portrayed by EN3 can best be described as yet another

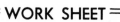

## WORK SHEET    *EN3*

*1*

### VERBAL I. Q. = *104*

| EWS | Info. | Comp. | Digit | Arith. | Sim. |
|-----|-------|-------|-------|--------|------|
| 18 | 25 | 20 | | 14 | 23-24 |
| 17 | 24 | 19 | 17 | 13 | 21-22 |
| 16 | 23 | 18 | 16 | 12 | 20 |
| 15 | 21-22 | 17 | | 11 | 19 |
| 14 | 20 | 16 | 15 | | 17-18 |
| 13 | 18-19 | 15 | 14 | 10 | 16 |
| 12 | 17 | 14 | | 9 | 15 |
| | | | | | |
| 11 | 15-16 | 12-13 | 13 | | 13-14 |
| 10 | (13-14) | (11) | (12) | (8) | 12 |
| 9 | 12 | 10 | 11 | 7 | 11 |
| 8 | 10-11 | 9 | | | (9-10) |
| 7 | 9 | 8 | 10 | 6 | 8 |
| 6 | 7-8 | 7 | 9 | 5 | 7 |
| | | | | | |
| 5 | 6 | 5-6 | | | 5-6 |
| 4 | 4-5 | 4 | 8 | 4 | 4 |
| 3 | 2-3 | 3 | 7 | 3 | 3 |
| 2 | 1 | 2 | 6 | | 1-2 |
| 1 | 0 | 1 | | 2 | 0 |
| 0 | | 0 | 5 | 1 | |

### SZONDI

| SEXUAL | | PAROXYSMAL | | EGO | | CONTACT | |
|--------|---|------------|----|-----|---|---------|---|
| h | s | e | hy | k | p | d | m |
| | | | | | | | X |
| | | X | | X | | | X X |
| | | X | | X | | | X X |
| | X | X | | X | X | | X X |
| X | X | X | X | X | X | X | |
| | X | X | X | | | | |
| | X | | X | | | | |

---

### OVER-ALL EVALUATION = *21*

| | | | | | |
|---|---|---|---|---|---|
| OVER-ALL RATING | 1 | 2 | 3 | 4 | 5 |
| PRODUCTIVITY | 1 | (2) | 3 | 4 | 5 |
| RELATION TO REALITY | 1 | 2 | (3) | 4 | 5 |
| THOUGHT CONTENT | 1 | 2 | (3) | 4 | 5 |
| CONSTRUCTIVE FANTASY | 1 | 2 | (3) | 4 | 5 |
| DRIVE | 1 | 2 | (3) | 4 | 5 |
| EMOTIONAL TONE | (1) | 2 | 3 | 4 | 5 |
| SOCIAL ATTITUDE | 1 | (2) | 3 | 4 | 5 |
| ANXIETY | 1 | (2) | 3 | 4 | 5 |
| I. Q. RATING | 1 | (2) | 3 | 4 | 5 |

### RORSCHACH

| | | | | | |
|---|---|---|---|---|---|
| R | *17* | M | *4* | | Fc |
| | | FM | *4* | F *6* | c |
| W% | *41* | m | | F- *2* | C' |
| D% | *59* | k | | F% *47* | FC |
| d% | | K | *1* | | CF |
| Dd% | | FK | | | c |
| S | | | | | |

# WORK SHEET

EN3

2

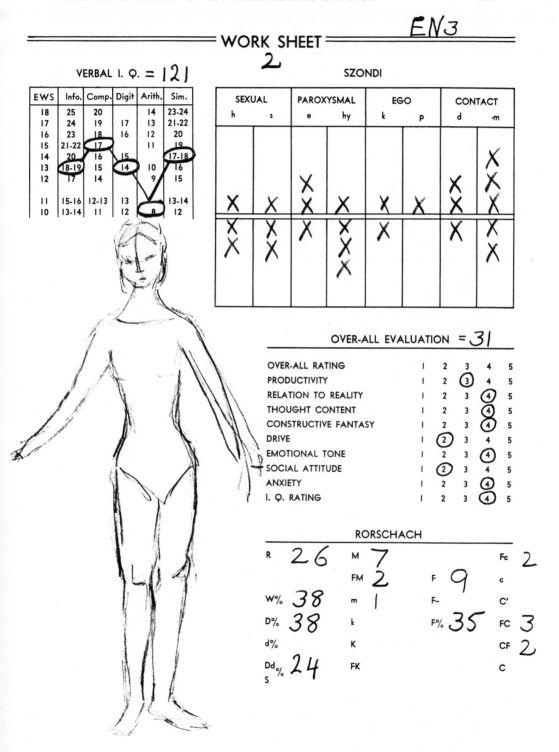

**VERBAL I. Q. = 121**

| EWS | Info. | Comp. | Digit | Arith. | Sim. |
|-----|-------|-------|-------|--------|------|
| 18 | 25 | 20 | | 14 | 23-24 |
| 17 | 24 | 19 | 17 | 13 | 21-22 |
| 16 | 23 | 18 | 16 | 12 | 20 |
| 15 | 21-22 | 17 | | 11 | 19 |
| 14 | 20 | 16 | 15 | | 17-18 |
| 13 | 18-19 | 15 | 14 | 10 | 16 |
| 12 | 17 | 14 | | 9 | 15 |
| 11 | 15-16 | 12-13 | 13 | | 13-14 |
| 10 | 13-14 | 11 | 12 | 8 | 12 |

## SZONDI

| SEXUAL | | PAROXYSMAL | | EGO | | CONTACT | |
|--------|--|------------|--|-----|--|---------|--|
| h | s | e | hy | k | p | d | ·m |

## OVER-ALL EVALUATION = 31

| | 1 | 2 | 3 | 4 | 5 |
|--|--|--|--|--|--|
| OVER-ALL RATING | 1 | 2 | 3 | 4 | 5 |
| PRODUCTIVITY | 1 | 2 | ③ | 4 | 5 |
| RELATION TO REALITY | 1 | 2 | 3 | ④ | 5 |
| THOUGHT CONTENT | 1 | 2 | 3 | ④ | 5 |
| CONSTRUCTIVE FANTASY | 1 | 2 | 3 | ④ | 5 |
| DRIVE | 1 | ② | 3 | 4 | 5 |
| EMOTIONAL TONE | 1 | 2 | 3 | ④ | 5 |
| SOCIAL ATTITUDE | 1 | ② | 3 | 4 | 5 |
| ANXIETY | 1 | 2 | 3 | ④ | 5 |
| I. Q. RATING | 1 | 2 | 3 | ④ | 5 |

## RORSCHACH

| | | | | | |
|--|--|--|--|--|--|
| R | 26 | M | 7 | Fc | 2 |
| | | FM | 2 | F | 9 | c | |
| W% | 38 | m | 1 | F- | | C' | |
| D% | 38 | k | | F% | 35 | FC | 3 |
| d% | | K | | | | CF | 2 |
| Dd% S | 24 | FK | | | | c | |

pattern of growth, namely, as steady improvement, as *amplification of the core personality* to a point where growth and change have been achieved.

Comparison of the Work Sheets of EN3 shows that the change in I.Q. status is considerable. From an original score of 104, which placed her in the *Average Group* of the total population, she moves into the *Superior Group* ten years later with a score of 121. If the two Scattergrams are compared, it will be seen that improvement occurred in all tests but the Arithmetic. EN3 reacts in this particular test with an essentially emotional, rather than logical, approach. She belongs to that group of individuals for whom it is somehow a foregone conclusion that arithmetical problems, short of the very easy ones, cannot be answered, and, in essence, she refuses to become involved in anything which will bring in its wake failure and embarrassment.

On the Information subtest the rise of three points on the weighted scale is the result of answering easy questions on which she had failed before. She had, for instance, claimed there were 16 pints in a quart, failed on the capital of Japan, and so on.

The Comprehension, Reasoning and Judgment shows the most marked and significant change. In the earlier testing, personal problems broke through to a rather marked degree, while later a much more realistic, commonsense approach appears.

The Similarities shows a comparable rise and the dropping out of the less appropriate or somewhat personalized answers. Insofar as there is a problem today, it links up with the sexual squeamishness reflected in the projectives; thus, the egg and the seed cannot be assessed as the beginning of life but are described as "nucleus, beginnings, essence."

At first sight the scattergram of the second testing appears to be much less uniform than that of the original record. However, had the Arithmetic score improved as much as the others, or, let us say, were this area still not performed at the immature level, there would be very little deviation between the subtests.

EN3's productiveness, as reflected in the flow of associative material in the Rorschach, has changed so that it now appears in the category of *Adequate* rather than *Reduced output*. It is not only the increase in the total number of responses that is important but the fact that these responses are given in an even and uninhibited manner and that there are no areas of blocking or undue delay. The initial record showed failures on Card I (too difficult to get going on a new task), on Card VI (with its sexual symbolism) and on Card IX (which virtually demands some type of emotional responsiveness).

There is no essential difference in the test findings in regard to EN3's RELATION TO REALITY. Although a good index to some of her personal problems, both now and previously, the drawings can by no means be considered to reflect any bizarre distortions. There has been a slight change, in a positive direction, in the dropping out of the two somewhat poor-form answers which occurred in Record 1.

The THOUGHT CONTENT, in terms of its unusualness, originality or bizarre quality, remains in both records at the *Adequate* level. While there are slight indications of greater originality in the later record than in Record 1, they are not quite pronounced enough to justify a quantitative change from a 3 to a 4 rating.

Assessing CONSTRUCTIVE FANTASY is more difficult to do on a simplified scheme such as this Summary Sheet. During the first test, although M responses numbered only four (which placed her in the *Accessible* category), because of the total absence of any emotional liveliness to offset this trend there was a tendency toward a withdrawal into fantasy life. At the present time, the number of human responses has risen to seven, yet the indication of withdrawal is lessened.

Concerning the category of DRIVE, although infinitely freer and less inhibited than in Record 1, this patient would still seem to lack a completely desirable degree of freedom and she is still hampered to some extent by repressive forces.

A marked change occurs in those aspects of the test findings which reflect freedom of emotionality. The early record showed an absence of emotional liveliness and the capacity to respond freely emotionally. The spontaneous use of color at the present time, the quality of the color answers, and the absence of completely blocked or inhibited areas reflect a very real increase in emotional maturity.

SOCIAL ATTITUDE, as reflected by the Sentence Completion and the TAT, may also be said to have improved but not sufficiently to take her out of the previously established category. At the present time, the problems reflected here might be subsumed under the heading of defining her feminine role to herself and thus developing her attitude vis-a-vis others. The fantasies involving man and woman, male and female, show a trend, also seen in the drawings, to minimize the sex differences and, in the TAT, to equate sexuality with brutal assault, shame and remorse: "A man has just killed his lover . . . . he made love to her and then killed her, both actions the result of sudden passion. He dressed himself before the killing and now, overcome by his act, is momentarily stunned but trying to decide whether to run away and hide or to give himself up. He will eventually give himself up."

There is a strong element of self-punishment in EN3. She envisages herself as "forgiving and tender though terribly hurt," and she struggles with sadomasochistic feelings, seeing herself again in another fantasy: "A menacing, angry touch to her gesture of holding the figure but she will overcome this through love and wisdom. She realizes the other person's helplessness and will help him, though not without an inner struggle first."

In the first record, considerably more anxiety was manifest than at the present time. It is obvious, of course, that sexual problems loom up now — the Most Unpleasant Concept is that of a needle or syringe with its obvious symbolic concomitants — yet, in terms of her total capacity to function, the increased spontaneity and emotional freedom, ANXIETY would be assessed as diminished to a point on the scale somewhere between *Moderate* and *Not marked*.

A statement from the original referring physician reiterates the fact that there has been no treatment beyond the change of schools, which resulted in her working well and happily. The statement ends: "The changes which are recognizable in the tests are especially interesting and important as a control on changes which occur under treatment."

It should not be assumed, however, that the passage of time alone will necessarily relieve tensions or allay anxieties sufficiently to allow for "normal" growth to take place. The case of EN4, an astonishingly gifted yet clearly disturbed ten-year-old at the time of the first testing, exemplifies this.

When first referred for diagnostic testing, EN4 was described by the referring physician in the following way:

"He is an extraordinarily good student, highly gifted in certain areas, adept and aggressive in sports, well liked by his contemporaries. In all these respects the youngster seems like a well-adjusted child. However, at the same time he lives in a tense emotional world, with a great deal of fantasy, some of which will need investigation. . . . To his mother he has described certain sensations which he localizes in his forehead, in his chest, and sometimes in his stomach. The sensation is of two wheels revolving in the opposite direction, one rapidly and one slowly. He has a panicky feeling that they must not touch each other because if they did, something terrible would happen. Perhaps something would go up in flames. When these feelings are intense, he may get prickly sensations in his hands and feet. To me [the referring physician] he described these experiences rather differently. He said that whenever he is bored, whenever he has work to do in which he is not interested, unpleasant, frightening, nightmarish, uneasy feelings arise. They begin with a rather obsessional fantasy that he must take a ship and go to some place, to some distant continent, usually South America. He is a stowaway. There are wings on the ship and an outboard motor, and sails go up. The ship acquires momentum and goes 'too fast for our own good.' Then it gets too close to the rocks; there almost is a crack-up, saved by a margin of half an inch. The wheels sensation which is described to his mother occurs in association with these fantasies, and he points out that like the ship and the rocks, the wheels never quite touch each other, although they 'nearly collide.'" The physician continues: "He has been a dawdler all his life. In earlier years he was afraid of the dark and he still has to keep the door open at night. For many years he had been afraid of strange visitors, particularly men."

Despite strong recommendation for therapeutic intervention, no professional help was utilized for EN4, with the result that at the end of five years, and at the time of the second testing, a more disturbed, clearly inhibited and disappointing personality picture was presented through the test material. Commenting on this, his physician stated to the parents that this was the best the boy could achieve "under the inhibiting influence of his several phobias and interfering emotional processes. Unfortunately, in spite of his high native endowments many of his emotions, both conscious and unconscious, block his utilization of his own talents."

Comparing Work Sheets 1 and 2, we find the I.Q. has dropped from 130 to 109. Five years have passed but the scattergrams have remained almost identical. It is as if, despite the passage of the years, he has been at a standstill. Moreover, the bizarre answers which color the abstract thinking (Similarities scores in both tests, 11 on the weighted scale) are identical and the grandiose, unrealistic ideas which account for his low scores on the Comprehension, while admittedly not too startling in a ten-year old, are features which alert the examiner to consider more serious trouble when they continue to be present at fifteen years of age.

In the second testing, EN4 refused to attempt drawing anything more of a person than the head. Drawing what he finally decided was the male character, he spoke of it as "it" and would assign no sex to it. He mentioned repeatedly the importance of the cleft in the hat, and at the same time, when drawing the woman, was concerned with giving her "a little peak on the tip of her head," suggesting the symbolic reversal of male and female characteristics.

Peculiarly striking in the Rorschach was the appearance of nearly 50 per cent poor form and rather bizarre answers, the loss of the M and FM responses, and the flattening out of the affect. Throughout the Rorschach test he made repetitive statements concerning the "need to fill up each hole" and "to cut off each jutting area."

The first quantitative score achieved by EN4 was 25, while at the time of the obvious "slump" he totaled a score of 14. Interestingly enough, five years later EN4, now in his twenties, sought psychotherapeutic assistance on his own initiative.

## WORK SHEET    EN 4

### VERBAL I. Q. = 130

| EWS | Info. | Comp. | Digit | Arith. | Sim. |
|-----|-------|-------|-------|--------|------|
| 18 | 25 | 20 | | 14 | 23-24 |
| 17 | 24 | 19 | 17 | 13 | 21-22 |
| 16 | 23 | 18 | 16 | 12 | 20 |
| 15 | 21-22 | 17 | | 11 | 19 |
| 14 | 20 | 16 | 15 | | 17-18 |
| 13 | 18-19 | 15 | 14 | 10 | 16 |
| 12 | 17 | 14 | | 9 | 15 |
| 11 | 15-16 | 12-13 | 13 | | 13-14 |
| 10 | 13-14 | 11 | 12 | 8 | 12 |
| 9 | 12 | 10 | 11 | 7 | 11 |
| 8 | 10-11 | 9 | | | 9-10 |
| 7 | 9 | 8 | 10 | 6 | 8 |
| 6 | 7-8 | 7 | 9 | 5 | 7 |
| 5 | 6 | 5-6 | | | 5-6 |

### SZONDI

| SEXUAL | | PAROXYSMAL | | EGO | | CONTACT | |
|--------|---|-----------|----|-----|---|---------|---|
| h | s | e | hy | k | p | d | m |
| X | | | | | | | |
| X | | | | | X | | |
| X | | | | | X X | | |
| X | X | | | | X X | | |
| X | X | | | | | | |
| X | | X | X | X | X | | X |
| | | X | X | X | | | |
| | | | | X | | | |
| | | | | X | | | |

### OVER-ALL EVALUATION = 25

| | 1 | 2 | 3 | 4 | 5 |
|---|---|---|---|---|---|
| OVER-ALL RATING | 1 | 2 | 3 | 4 | 5 |
| PRODUCTIVITY | 1 | 2 | (3) | 4 | 5 |
| RELATION TO REALITY | 1 | (2) | 3 | 4 | 5 |
| THOUGHT CONTENT | 1 | 2 | (3) | 4 | 5 |
| CONSTRUCTIVE FANTASY | 1 | (2) | 3 | 4 | 5 |
| DRIVE | 1 | (2) | 3 | 4 | 5 |
| EMOTIONAL TONE | 1 | 2 | (3) | 4 | 5 |
| SOCIAL ATTITUDE | 1 | (2) | 3 | 4 | 5 |
| ANXIETY | 1 | 2 | (3) | 4 | 5 |
| I. Q. RATING  130 | 1 | 2 | 3 | 4 | (5) |

### RORSCHACH

| R | 21 | M | 2 | | | Fc | |
|---|----|----|----|----|----|----|---|
| | | FM | 1 | F | 10 | c | |
| W% | 39 | m | 2 | F- | 2 | C' | |
| D% | 57 | k | | F% | | FC | 1 |
| d% | | K | 1 | | | CF | 1 |
| Dd% S | 4 | FK | | | | c | 1 |

## WORK SHEET

2

EN4

### VERBAL I. Q. = 109

| EWS | Info. | Comp. | Digit | Arith. | Sim. |
|-----|-------|-------|-------|--------|------|
| 18 | 25 | 20 | | 14 | 23-24 |
| 17 | 24 | 19 | 17 | 13 | 21-22 |
| 16 | 23 | 18 | 16 | 12 | 20 |
| 15 | 21-22 | 17 | | 11 | 19 |
| 14 | 20 | 16 | 15 | | 17-18 |
| 13 | 18-19 | 15 | 14 | 10 | 16 |
| 12 | 17 | 14 | | 9 | 15 |
| | | | | | |
| 11 | 15-16 | 12-13 | 13 | | 13-14 |
| 10 | 13-14 | 11 | 12 | 8 | 12 |
| 9 | 12 | 10 | 11 | 7 | 11 |
| 8 | 10-11 | 9 | | | 9-10 |
| 7 | 9 | 8 | 10 | 6 | 8 |
| 6 | 7-8 | 7 | 9 | 5 | 7 |
| | | | | | |
| 5 | 6 | 5-6 | | | 5-6 |
| 4 | 4-5 | 4 | 8 | 4 | 4 |
| 3 | 2-3 | 3 | 7 | 3 | 3 |
| 2 | 1 | 2 | 6 | | 1-2 |
| 1 | 0 | 1 | | 2 | 0 |
| 0 | | 0 | 5 | 1 | |

### SZONDI

| SEXUAL | | PAROXYSMAL | | EGO | | CONTACT | |
|--------|---|------------|----|-----|---|---------|---|
| h | s | e | hy | k | p | d | m |

(Szondi chart with X markings)

### OVER-ALL EVALUATION = 14

| | | | | | |
|---|---|---|---|---|---|
| OVER-ALL RATING | 1 | 2 | 3 | 4 | 5 |
| PRODUCTIVITY | 1 | (2) | 3 | 4 | 5 |
| RELATION TO REALITY | (1) | 2 | 3 | 4 | 5 |
| THOUGHT CONTENT | 1 | (2) | 3 | 4 | 5 |
| CONSTRUCTIVE FANTASY | (1) | 2 | 3 | 4 | 5 |
| DRIVE | (1) | 2 | 3 | 4 | 5 |
| EMOTIONAL TONE | (1) | 2 | 3 | 4 | 5 |
| SOCIAL ATTITUDE | 1 | (2) | 3 | 4 | 5 |
| ANXIETY | 1 | (2) | 3 | 4 | 5 |
| I. Q. RATING   109 | 1 | (2) | 3 | 4 | 5 |

### RORSCHACH

| R | 11 | M | | Fc | |
|---|----|----|----|----|----|
| | | FM | F 5 | c | |
| W% | 45 | m | F- 5 | C' | |
| D% | 55 | k | F% | FC | 1 |
| d% | | K | | CF | |
| Dd% | | FK | | C | |
| S | | | | | |

# XVII. Discussion of the over-all characteristics
## of retest findings

In this chapter we have attempted to pull together for assessment and discussion the findings from the quantitative evaluations made by the therapists and the psychologist. These quantitative scores, we are well aware, are an arbitrary device but they do provide a consistent framework whereby the amount of "movement," either forward or backward, can be charted for each individual and for various groups of patients.

Table VI records the quantitative evaluation scores of eight subjects retested with a full battery of projective tests after a thirty-day interval. The Work Sheets of six of these subjects appear in Chapter V and quantitative scores for two others of the twenty who were so tested and retested have been added to keep the sample as equal for each Table as possible. Minimal or no environmental change had occurred for these subjects during the time interval of thirty days. There can, of course, be no therapists' evaluations since none were involved. It will be noted that repetition of the tests after thirty days brought about an average loss in evaluation scores of 1.1 for this group as a whole.

Table VII lists the quantitative evaluation scores of subjects retested after one year. No marked environmental change or therapeutic intervention had occurred in the intervening year. The findings are for Subjects Y1 through Y6 who have been considered in detail in Chapter VI, and for G2 who appeared in Chapter VII. For G2, the scores achieved on the second and third testings have been used since the time interval between them was one year.

The chief finding here is the fact that, other things being equal, it would seem that the passage of a year's time *may* result in gains of as much as 5 points on the quantitative scale. The average gain for this group was 3.5.

Table VIII records the scores of individuals who, through amelioration of environmental conditions, have progressed without the intervention of any form of psychotherapeutic help. The time interval between tests in the majority of cases was five years; in one case, ten years elapsed; in another, only three. These individuals were retested at a time when they felt themselves to be, or were reliably reported by others to be, happier and better adjusted.

It will be seen that the average gain for this group is 10.1 points. In this instance we have no reports from therapists, but for EN2 an assessment from the parents is included showing a gain of 14 points.

TABLE VI.    EVALUATION SCORES OF EIGHT CONTROL SUBJECTS RETESTED AFTER A THIRTY-DAY INTERVAL.

| Code # | Test 1 | Test 2 | Gain or Loss | Time between tests (days) |
|---|---|---|---|---|
| 307 | 25 | 24 | −1 | 30 |
| 306 | 21 | 19 | −2 | 30 |
| 303 | 27 | 25 | −2 | 30 |
| 302 | 19 | 17 | −2 | 30 |
| 301 | 25 | 25 | 0 | 30 |
| 305 | 37 | 33 | −4 | 30 |
| 3010 * | 20 | 22 | +2 | 30 |
| 3013 * | 29 | 29 | 0 | 30 |
| Total | 203 | 194 | −9 | |
| Average | 25.4 | 24.3 | −1.1 | |

* Rorschach scores for 3010 and 3013 will be found in Table 4, Chapter V. Their I.Q.'s did not change. Drawings and Szondis did not result in altered quantitative scores. The additional two points achieved by 3010 resulted from his greater productivity (one point) and the emergence of one color response (one point).

TABLE VII.    EVALUATION SCORES OF SUBJECTS RETESTED AFTER ONE YEAR. NO MARKED ENVIRONMENTAL CHANGE OR THERAPEUTIC INTERVENTION IN THE INTERVAL.

| Code # | Test 1 | Test 2 | Gain or Loss | Time between tests (years) |
|---|---|---|---|---|
| Y1 | 25 | 29 | +4 | 1 |
| Y2 | 31 | 35 | +4 | 1 |
| Y3 | 28 | 31 | +3 | 1 |
| Y4 | 28 | 30 | +2 | 1 |
| Y5 | 30 | 32 | +2 | 1 |
| Y6 | 26 | 31 | +5 | 1 |
| G2 (2-3) | 25 | 30 | +5 | 1 |
| Total | 193 | 218 | +25 | |
| Average | 27.5 | 31.1 | +3.5 | |

TABLE VIII.    EVALUATION SCORES OF SUBJECTS RETESTED FOLLOWING POSITIVE ENVIRONMENTAL CHANGE.

| Code # | Test 1 | Test 2 | Gain or Loss | Time between tests (years) |
|---|---|---|---|---|
| L1 | 23 | 34 | +11 | 5 |
| AB1 | 24 | 33 | +9 | 5 |
| AB2 | 23 | 30 | +7 | 5 |
| AB3 | 25 | 35 | +10 | 5 |
| AB4 | 28 | 38 | +10 | 5 |
| EN1 | 18 | 31 | +13 | 5 |
| EN2 | 15 | 26 | +11 | 3 |
| EN3 | 21 | 31 | +10 | 10 |
| Total | 177 | 258 | +81 | |
| Average | 22.1 | 32.2 | +10.1 | |

TABLE IX.    EVALUATION SCORES OF SUBJECTS RETESTED AT TIME OF WORSENING OF CLINICAL CONDITION.

| Code # | Test 1 | Test 2 | Gain or Loss | Time between tests (years) |
|---|---|---|---|---|
| G1 | 30 | 20 | −10 | 5 |
| IR1 * | 21 | 18 | −3 | 5 |
| IR2 | 37 | 26 | −11 | 5 |
| IR3 † | 27 | 21 | −6 | 1 |
| EN4 | 25 | 14 | −11 | 5 |
| A9 | 27 | 23 | −4 | 9 |
| PT6 | 20 | 18 | −2 | 5 |
| A10 | 28 | 26 | −2 | 6 |
| Total | 215 | 166 | −49 | |
| Average | 26.9 | 20.8 | −6.1 | |

* Comparison between second and third tests.
† Comparison between third and fourth tests.

For these three groups of control subjects, the Tables show there to be a steady increase in the average gain. There is nothing in these findings to contradict our essential hypothesis that an enriching of personality may occur when life conditions are ameliorated and psychological stress reduced.

The subjects in Tables VI, VII and VIII are all individuals whose growth has not been aided or reinforced by psychotherapy. In the remaining five Tables, we shall consider, in contrast, patients who have received some form of therapy.

Table IX groups together all those patients who were tested for the second time when they were showing an increase in symptoms, an unexpected "slump" or reversal in normal behavior, an acute depression, or a flare-up of symptoms in a fluctuating picture of improvement and re-

TABLE X.    Evaluation Scores of Patients Who Received Brief Psychotherapy; Clinical Condition Unchanged; Same Therapist.

| Code # | Test 1 | Test 2 | Gain or Loss | Therapist 1 | Therapist 2 | Gain or Loss | Time between tests (mos., approx.) |
|---|---|---|---|---|---|---|---|
| SA10 | 19 | 19 | 0 | 24 | 25 | +1 | 6 |
| SA11 | 23 | 24 | +1 | 19 | 19 | 0 | 6 |
| SA12 | 18 | 18 | 0 | 12 | 12 | 0 | 6 |
| SA13 | 17 | 19 | +2 | 23 | 24 | +1 | 6 |
| SA14 | 24 | 23 | −1 | 18 | 18 | 0 | 6 |
| SA15 | 20 | 23 | +3 | 20 | 22 | +2 | 6 |
| SA16 | 28 | 23 | −5 | 20 | 22 | +2 | 6 |
| SA17 | 16 | 17 | +1 | 13 | 13 | 0 | 6 |
| Total | 165 | 166 | +1 | 149 | 155 | +6 | |
| Average | 20.6 | 20.7 | +0.1 | 18.6 | 19.4 | +0.8 | |

TABLE XI.   Evaluation Scores of Patients Who Received Brief Psychotherapy; Clinical Gains Reported; Same Therapist.

| Code # | Test 1 | Test 2 | Gain or Loss | Therapist 1 | Therapist 2 | Gain or Loss | Time between tests (mos., approx.) |
|---|---|---|---|---|---|---|---|
| SA1 | 28 | 31 | +3 | 21 | 24 | +3 | 6 |
| SA2 | 30 | 36 | +6 | 27 | 36 | +9 | 6 |
| SA3 | 26 | 26 | 0 | 30 | 34 | +4 | 6 |
| SA4 | 29 | 32 | +3 | 23 | 30 | +7 | 6 |
| SA5 | 27 | 25 | −2 | 26 | 34 | +8 | 6 |
| SA6 | 26 | 32 | +6 | 20 | 27 | +7 | 6 |
| SA7 | 25 | 27 | +2 | 31 | 36 | +5 | 6 |
| SA8 | 26 | 34 | +8 | 22 | 30 | +8 | 6 |
| Total | 217 | 243 | +26 | 200 | 251 | +51 | |
| Average | 27.1 | 30.3 | +3.2 | 25 | 31.4 | +6.4 | |

lapse. We have also, in A9 and PT6, patients who have regressed despite strenuous psychotherapeutic efforts, even when these were continued over a considerable length of time. Included, too, is EN4 whose condition worsened subsequent to failure to follow the strong recommendations for psychotherapeutic treatment.

As will be seen, the average *loss* here was 6.1, a figure quite striking when contrasted with the gains achieved, for instance, by the average individual over one uneventful year.

Tables X and XI contrast the evaluation scores of patients who did not respond to brief psychotherapy (Table X) with the scores of patients treated by the same therapist who showed considerable amelioration of their symptoms (Table XI). The average for the first group is an 0.1 "gain," for the second group, an average 3.2 is recorded. The time interval involved here between tests is in every instance approximately six months.

Tables X and XI include the therapist's assessment of these patients. The therapist reports virtually no gain, as might well be expected, for those in whom general clinical improvement was not evidenced. The assessment by the therapist of those who were considered improved averaged out to a gain of 6.4, as opposed to assessment by the tests of 3.2.

TABLE XII. EVALUATION SCORES OF PATIENTS WHO RECEIVED LONG-TERM PSYCHOTHERAPY; CLINICAL GAINS REPORTED; DIFFERENT THERAPISTS.

| Code # | Test 1 | Test 2 | Gain or Loss | Therapist 1 | Therapist 2 | Gain or Loss | Time between tests (years) |
|---|---|---|---|---|---|---|---|
| PT1 | 13 | 16 | +3 | 15 | 24 | +9 | 3 |
| PT2 | 19 | 28 | +9 | 19 | 28 | +9 | 2 |
| PT3 | 17 | 31 | +14 | 26 | 32 | +6 | 2 |
| PT4 | 18 | 29 | +11 | 17 | 30 | +13 | 8 |
| PT5 | 22 | 32 | +10 | 23 | 33 | +10 | 1 |
| TY1 | 20 | 31 | +11 | 18 | 32 | +14 | 10 |
| TY2 | 34 | 40 | +6 | 29 | 43 | +14 | 10 |
| TY3 | 26 | 33 | +7 | 25 | 36 | +11 | 10 |
| Total | 169 | 240 | +71 | 172 | 258 | +86 | |
| Average | 21.1 | 30.0 | +8.9 | 21.5 | 32.2 | +10.7 | |

TABLE XIII. EVALUATION SCORES OF PATIENTS WHO RECEIVED LONG-TERM ANALYTIC THERAPY; CLINICAL GAINS REPORTED; DIFFERENT THERAPISTS.

| Code # | Test 1 | Test 2 | Gain or Loss | Therapist 1 | Therapist 2 | Gain or Loss | Time between tests (years) |
|---|---|---|---|---|---|---|---|
| A1 | 21 | 30 | +9 | 14 | 37 | +23 | 7 |
| A2 | 22 | 32 | +10 | 26 | 28 | +2 | 10 |
| A3 | 22 | 37 | +15 | 19 | 32 | +13 | 8 |
| A4 | 28 | 36 | +8 | 31 | 40 | +9 | 7 |
| A5 | 21 | 35 | +14 | 22 | 34 | +12 | 5 |
| A6 | 25 | 31 | +6 | 19 | 22 | +3 | 5 |
| A7 | 30 | 36 | +6 | 21 | 28 | +7 | 10 |
| A8 | 20 | 29 | +9 | 22 | 36 | +14 | 10 |
| Total | 189 | 266 | +77 | 174 | 257 | +83 | |
| Average | 23.6 | 33.2 | +9.6 | 21.7 | 32.1 | +10.4 | |

As discussed earlier, it has been our feeling that this discrepancy rests *not on the fact that the therapist is over-optimistic* but that very brief time intervals do not permit a comparable gain to register in the test findings.

Tables XII and XIII deal with patients who have received long-term therapy, a differentiation being made between orthodox analytic treatment and various forms of psychotherapy. The gains in each instance are of the same order of magnitude: 8.9 in Table XII, 9.6 in Table XIII. Similarly, the therapists' assessments are virtually identical, 10.7 and 10.4. It is of interest to note that there is far less discrepancy between the therapists' estimates and those from the tests in these long-term cases. Also included in Table XII are TY1 and TY2 whose initial treatment belonged more in the category of brief and intensive psychotherapy but who were retested ten years later, thus allowing an interval of time for the changes induced by therapy to become consolidated.

Some aspects of the findings from Tables VI through XIII are recapitulated in Table XIV, which groups the average gains or losses according to where they appear on a spectrum of improvement. We would place at a point in the spectrum labeled *Marked loss* the −6.1 average of those individuals retested at a time when their clinical condition had

TABLE XIV

| Marked Loss | Average Loss or Gain |
|---|---|
| Retest at "Worsening"............................................. | −6.1 |
| **Insignificant Gain**<br>**or loss** | |
| 30-Day Retest ............................................. | −1.1 |
| Brief Therapy, Unimproved............................... | +0.1 |
| **Moderate Gains** | |
| One-Year Interval ....................................... | +3.5 |
| Brief Therapy, Improved................................. | +3.2 |
| **Marked Gains** | |
| Long-Term Psychotherapy ................................ | +8.9 |
| Analytic Therapy ....................................... | +9.6 |
| "Positive" Environmental Change....................... | +10.1 |

worsened. *Insignificant loss or gain* seems to characterize the individuals retested after thirty days and those retested after six months of treatment which produced, clinically, no signs of improvement. We might consider as *Moderate gains* the average of those individuals who showed marked improvement clinically after brief, intensive psychotherapy and the average of those individuals retested after one year of "'normal," uneventful growth. Finally, *Marked gains* categorizes the scores resulting from successful long-term psychotherapy, from long-term analytic treatment, and from marked changes in life conditions.

In the Introduction, three general questions were formulated, curiosity concerning which led to the undertaking of this work: First, to what extent do the projective techniques mirror changes (for better or for worse) which have been recorded clinically or for which other reliable, objective evidence can be found? Second, when growth and maturation (or deterioration) occur in the clinical picture, in what way are such changes demonstrated in the tests? Third, are there any specific changes in test materials which pertain to therapeutic intervention alone or can the passage of time and/or improved environmental conditions also bring about all the test evidence of maturation?

Concerning the first question, our findings may be briefly enumerated as follows:

1) When improvement in general adjustment and freedom from symptoms are reported clinically, some measure of positive change is invariably shown on the projective tests.

2) In general, it can be said that clinical improvement is assessed as more marked than the improvement which is reflected in the test material, or, stated differently, for any recognizable change in behavior a smaller increment may be expected to have appeared in the tests. Quantitatively, there is a very close correlation between the therapist's estimate and the test estimate after long-term therapy, and a greater discrepancy between

the improvement noted clinically after short-term therapy and the test counterpart.

3) When changes in the direction of increased disturbance occur clinically, these are also mirrored in the projectives by increased evidence of emotional disintegration.

4) When no progress is reported clinically, a difference between the first and second testing is also nonexistent.

5) In general, our cases seem to support the hypothesis that the "better" the initial test picture, the greater the subsequent improvement will be regardless of the type of therapy employed. This will be dealt with at greater length and subjected to much closer scrutiny in a subsequent publication.

6) Lack of agreement between therapist and the projective techniques, as in the case of A10, may be the result of special conditions pertaining during the retesting period, conditions which can account for the temporary worsening of the test picture.

Concerning our second question, we may state that the changes in the test findings which parallel *clinical improvement* may be listed as follows:

1) A general rise in the total I.Q. (PT1, PT3, A8, and others).

2) A rise in the Comprehension or Similarities scores, or both, showing lessening of intrusive personal preoccupation (A1, TY3, PT4, and others).

3) A dropping out of pure C responses (IR3 during remission).

4) A dropping out of F– responses (SA1, SA7).

5) A dropping out of bizarre answers on the Rorschach (A3).

6) A change from a Szondi profile in which one area was conspicuously loaded to a more balanced one.*

7) A change of level in the Figure Drawings (PT3, TY1, A1).

8) The appearance of FC responses (IR3 during remission, TY1, PT5, and others).

9) The enriching of TAT stories and the reflection in the Sentence Completion of a more mature social attitude (A3, A6).

10) The general enriching and amplification of Rorschach records (A5, and others).

11) The appearance of M responses (A1, A2, A5).

12) The enriching and maturing of the self-concept as reflected in the qualitative aspects of the M responses (A3).

---

* Although no striking illustration of this appears in the cases in this volume, it has been our experience that this may occur.

As characteristic of test changes indicating *increased disturbance,* the following may be cited:

1) The appearance of perseveration and increased stereotypy in the Rorschach record (IR2).

2) A rise in pure C and CF responses (A9).

3) A dropping out of FC responses (IR3).

4) A general impoverishment in both quality and quantity of Rorschach responses (G1, EN4).

5) A loss of originality in the Rorschach record (G1, EN4).

6) The introduction of specific problems in the Figure Drawings (G1, EN4).

7) The lowering of the Figure Drawing level (IR2).

8) The loading of the Sentence Completion with current antagonisms or immediate personal pressures (G1).

So much for the answer to our second question. The third, which grows out of it, relates to whether or not these changes are peculiar to the effect of psychotherapy.

In our opinion, the changes which can come about even though there has been no psychotherapeutic intervention do not differ markedly, if at all, from those mentioned above. We find, for instance, examples of the following:

1) General enrichment of the Rorschach record (EN1 and L1).

2) A rise in FC responses (AB1, AB3, AB4, EN3).

3) The dropping out of pure C and F− responses (EN2).

4) A rise in I.Q. (EN1, EN3).

There may well be more of a trend for F− responses to drop out in the group that has successfully undergone psychotherapy than in the group that received no treatment. However, it cannot be stated with certainty whether this is the result of the specific effects of psychotherapy or the fact that those entering therapy are more apt to show F− responses in their initial record.

Although the average quantitative scores based on the tests and on the therapists' appraisals are approximately equal in the instance of the patients who received long-term therapy, we nevertheless feel that behaviorial changes are apt to be more spectacular and noted sooner clinically than on the tests. We have the impression that several months must elapse before changes can successfully "register" in the tests. Patients SA1 through SA8, for example, were genuinely improved at the termination of psychotherapy, meeting certain objective criteria established by the therapist for assessing improvement. When such criteria were not met, the therapist without hesitation classified his patients as unimproved (the SA10 through SA17 group). Yet, the immediate post-therapeutic tests records of SA1 through SA8 are by no means as impressive as might be expected in the light of the behavioral changes.

There is one important difference which must be borne in mind relative to this apparent discrepancy and that is the fact that the observation of behavior is continuous whereas a retest takes place at a single point in time. Moreover, behavior must be thought of as "projection" on a much larger scale than is the projection that is possible through the test media. Let us assume, for the sake of argument, that therapy has brought about the complete alleviation of a panic state of anxiety that was sufficiently crippling to block the patient from all normal social contact and keep him self-imprisoned. Once the block is removed, once the patient starts to go out and make contact again, a whole chain reaction of "can-now-do" activities will develop. Each of these "can-now-do" activities, when observed from the outside, will look like new achievements and will reinforce, quite legitimately, the clinical picture of improvement. All the ramifications of this removal of the inhibiting influence may not show in the test findings in the same way, however. The fact that the patient is less panicky on the second testing may be carried by one or two scores, and the test situation will not necessarily provide him with the same opportunity to express his rehabilitation, time and time again, as does his normal or work-a-day environment. It would seem, then, that we would have to be satisfied to accept small changes in the projectives as significant and be willing to amplify them considerably if we expect to predict their actual behavioral counterpart.

This, however, is not completely satisfactory since we meet up now with the question of fluctuations on a day-to-day retesting basis. There are still unsolved problems here of such a kind as to restrain us from making too many categorical assumptions. Too sanguine interpretation of every small change in the test material has its dangers. In Figure 10, for instance, we have a drawing made by a patient while in analytic therapy. It took several years of intensive treatment before the figure "turned around" and finally faced the world. Therapist and psychologist were, one would think, more than entitled to the assumption that this portrayed this patient's newly gained capacity to face life and its problems. Yet, the drawings in Figure 5 (Chapter IV) are those of a control subject who on two successive days, and for no apparently good reason, reversed the figure originally drawn with his back to the world and presented it full-face!

Or take the sudden emergence of M responses in a few of the 93 control cases retested after a few days (Table I): code number 1, for instance, whose M's rise from 5 to 18, or number 8 whose M responses rise from 3 to 10 (see Table II). One could hardly refrain from assuming,

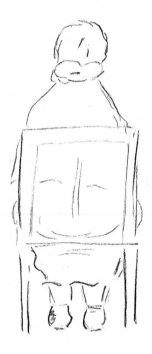

FIG. 10. FIGURE DRAWN WITH "BACK TO AUDIENCE."

were such changes found after several years of treatment, that they reflected growth in inner life in the range of human identification and in richer psychic experiences arising, presumably, out of the resolution of inhibiting anxieties and energy-consuming conflicts. Yet, sufficiently often to give us pause, a control subject will produce a wealth of M responses differing both in quality and quantity from his production of the day before. Granted that some, unknown to us, special circumstances may have inhibited the production of this material in our control subject on, say, Monday which are not present on Tuesday, even so, how can we guarantee that patient "x" tested prior to treatment may not also be experiencing one of these transiently inhibiting set of conditions during the first test?

Consider code numbers 9 and 89 (Table I). In the first case we find a rise in FC from 1 to 8; in the second, a sudden appearance of 5 CF responses in the second testing. The very fact that such changes occur, even if very infrequently, should be a constant reminder of some of the unexplored territory in this field.

The foregoing examples are admittedly exceptions and may be treated as such and seen in perspective. To gloss them over or to deny their existence, however, contributes little to the most meaningful and relevant use of the test instruments. More often than not, the projective tests, if used carefully, can catch much of the full impact and import of established changes in behavior and subjective experience. Occasionally, they may be even more telling than the accumulation of material from clinical sessions. For example, PT5's graphic portrayal in Test 1 of the man as a snowman and the woman as a paper doll strikingly revealed the extent to which she was forced to deny her own humanity and that of others in order to protect herself from what she felt to be the dangers to which a sentient person is vulnerable. This patient, in a post-therapeutic discussion of her test findings, freely spoke of the fear that had persisted since childhood that it was not safe to give or receive love.

Describing her own assessment of "change" experienced subjectively, this patient stated, "I have not changed but I'm able to act differently." Effective psychotherapy, she felt, had made satisfactory behavioral adjustments possible. It had also brought about subjective comfort, freedom from panic, depression and anxiety. PT5, it will be remembered, on the quantitative scale gained a total of 10 points as assessed both by the tests and her therapist. In the light of Schafer's concept of ego mastery, the two protocols of PT5 are an excellent example of change along these lines. We have a richness in the Rorschach and a capacity to portray conflict in both the Rorschach and the Sentence Completion. A genuine relationship and kinship with other human beings has been established and is reflected in the dramatic shift in the concept of the person. The former traumatic experiences of depression and panic are now held at a distance and are dealt with with humor. PT5 has achieved a controlling distance between herself and overpowering feelings. Even the still vividly remembered experience epitomized in the first Most Unpleasant Concept drawing is no longer overwhelming. The patient decides, so to speak, what is to be done with it.

Such examples are reassuring, for, despite some unexplained discrepancies between clinical observations and test productions and despite the gaps in our knowledge that still exist as to what the tests actually measure, such a projective battery as we have used over these years appears to offer a reasonably reliable means of assessing some aspects of personality changes.

# REFERENCES

1. Allen, R. M.: A note on persistent responses in longitudinal Rorschach protocols. J. Proj. Tech. 21:362, 1957.
2. Anderson, H. H., and Anderson, G. L.: An Introduction to Projective Techniques. New York, Prentice-Hall, 1951.
3. Berle, B. B., and Javert, C. T.: Stress and habitual abortion: their relationship and the effect of therapy. Obst. & Gynec. 3:298, 1954.
4. Buhler, C., Buhler, K., and Lefever, D. W.: Development of the Basic Rorschach Score, with Manual of Directions. Los Angeles, Rorschach Standardization Studies, No. 1, 1948.
5. Carr, A. C.: An evaluation of nine non-directive psychotherapy cases by means of the Rorschach. J. Consulting Psychol. 13:196, 1949.
6. Caveness, W. F.: Emotional and psychological factors in epilepsy. Am. J. Psychiat. 112:190, 1955.
7. Fromm, E. O., and Elonen, A. S.: The use of projective techniques in the study of a case of female homosexuality. J. Proj. Tech. 15:185, 1951.
8. Haimowitz, N. R., and Haimowitz, N. L.: Personality changes in client-centered therapy, in Wolff, W. and Precker, J. A.: Success in Psychotherapy. New York, Grune & Stratton, 1952.
9. Hamlin, R. M., and Albee, G. W.: Comparison of objective test performance of subjects not under treatment with Muench's successful and less-successful groups following nondirective psychotherapy. Paper delivered at Eastern Psychological Assoc. Meeting, Philadelphia, April 1948.
10. Hamlin, R. M., Berger, B., and Cummings, S. T.: Changes in adjustment following psychotherapy as reflected in Rorschach signs, in Wolff, W., and Precker, J. A.: Success in Psychotherapy. New York, Grune & Stratton, 1952.
11. Harrower, M.: Appraising Personality. New York, W. W. Norton, 1952.
12. Harrower, M. R., and Steiner, M. E.: Large Scale Rorschach Techniques, Ed. 2. Springfield, Charles C Thomas, 1951.
13. Harrower, M., and Steiner, M. E.: Modification of the Rorschach method for use as a group test. J. Genetic Psychol. 62:119, 1943.
14. Henry, E. M., and Rotter, J. B.: Situational influences on Rorschach responses. J. Consulting Psychol. 20:457, 1956.
15. Holt, R. R., in Klopfer, B., Ainsworth, M. D., Klopfer, W. G., and Holt, R. R.: Developments in the Rorschach Technique. Yonkers-on-Hudson, World Book Company, 1954.
16. Kaplan, B., and Berger, S.: Increments and consistency of performance in four repeated Rorschach administrations. J. Proj. Tech. 20:304, 1956.
17. Klopfer, B., Ainsworth, M. D., Klopfer, W. G., and Holt, R. R.: Developments in the Rorschach Technique. Yonkers-on-Hudson, World Book Company, 1954.
18. Kubie, L. S.: The use of projective techniques in collaborative research between clinical psychologists and psychoanalysts. Paper read at American Psychiatric Association Meeting, 1957.
19. Lord, E.: Experimentally Induced Variations in Rorschach Performance. Psychological Monographs, No. 316, Vol. 64, #10, 1950.
20. Maslow, A. H.: Motivation and Personality. New York, Harper & Bros., 1954.
21. Miles, H. H. W., Barrabee, E. L., and Finesinger, J.: Evaluation of psychotherapy with a follow-up study of 62 cases of anxiety neurosis, in Podolsky, E.: The Neuroses and Their Treatment. New York, Philosophical Library, 1958.

22. Mintz, E. E., Schmeidler, G. R., and Bristol, M.: Rorschach changes during psychoanalysis. J. Proj. Tech. 20:414, 1956.
23. Muench, G. A.: An Evaluation of Non-Directive Psychotherapy. Applied Psychol. Monograph 13, 1947.
24. Piotrowski, Z., and Schreiber, M.: Rorschach perceptanalytic measurement of personality changes during and after intensive, psychoanalytically oriented psychotherapy, in Bychowski, G., and Despert, J. L.: Specialized Techniques in Psychotherapy. New York, Basic Books, 1952.
25. Roman, M.: Reaching Delinquents Through Reading. Springfield, Charles C Thomas, 1958.
26. Schafer, R.: On the psychoanalytic study of retest results. Paper delivered at Am. Psychological Assoc. Meeting, 1957.
27. Schafer, R.: Psychological test evaluation of personality change during intensive psychotherapy. Psychiatry 18:175, 1955.
28. Tompkins, S. S.: The limits of material obtainable in a single case study by daily administration of the TAT. Psychological Bulletin 39:490, 1942.
29. Watkins, J. G.: Evaluating success in psychotherapy. Am. Psychologist 4:396, 1949.
30. Wechsler, D.: The Measurement and Appraisal of Adult Intelligence, Ed. 4. Baltimore, Williams & Wilkins, 1958.